METABOLIC DISEASES – LABORATORY AND CLINICAL RESEARCH

NEUROCHEMISTRY OF METABOLIC DISEASES

LYSOSOMAL STORAGE DISEASES, PHENYLKETONURIA, AND CANAVAN DISEASE

3RD EDITION

METABOLIC DISEASES – LABORATORY AND CLINICAL RESEARCH

Additional books and e-books in this series can be found on Nova's website under the Series tab.

METABOLIC DISEASES – LABORATORY AND CLINICAL RESEARCH

NEUROCHEMISTRY OF METABOLIC DISEASES

LYSOSOMAL STORAGE DISEASES, PHENYLKETONURIA, AND CANAVAN DISEASE

3RD EDITION

SANKAR SURENDRAN
EDITOR

nova
Medicine & Health
New York

Library of Congress Cataloging-in-Publication Data

ISBN: 978-1-53618-339-9

Published by Nova Science Publishers, Inc. † New York

CONTENTS

PREFACE

The book entitled "Neurochemistry of metabolic diseases: lysosomal storage diseases, Phenylketonuria and Canavan disease" presents diseases caused by lysosomal dysfunction, abnormal levels of phenylalanine metabolism and N-acetyl aspartic acid metabolism. This book describes in-depth knowledge on potential details including cause of the disease, molecular changes, phenotype, diagnosis, pathological changes and therapeutic approaches on human patients. This book is composed for the use of experts including Physicians, Neuroscientists, Biomedical researchers, Biochemists, Molecular biologists, Basic Science Researchers and Medical Students. The first edition of this book was published in the year 2007 by Transworld Research Network/Research Signpost, India. The second edition of this book was published by NOVA Science Publishers, USA; eBook was released in the year 2011, and hardcover was released in the year 2013. The present book is third edition presents recent developments on metabolic disorders.

Metabolic disorder caused by altered levels of metabolism resulting pathophysiological abnormalities often leads to childhood death. Several new developments on metabolic diseases research have been emerging. Gaucher disease is a lysosomal storage disorder caused by glucocerebrosidase gene mutations resulting glucocerebrosidase deficiency. Current studies show that the same gene mutations also contribute to the Parkinson's disease. Tetrahydrobiopterin (BH4) has been widely used in treating patients with Phenylketonuria over a decade. Recent studies reveal that patients treated with BH4 over one-year period showed reduced levels of serum B12, folate and iron intake and therefore patients under chronic BH4 treatment needed to be advised to have additional micronutrients along with BH4. Macrocephaly was used as one of the important features to diagnose Canavan disease. However, a recent study showing a child with aspartoacylase gene mutation developed microcephaly. Hence, Canavan disease phenotype can be either macrocephaly or microcephaly. These are a few examples of recent developments on metabolic diseases research. Therefore, this third edition book is aimed to present current developments on metabolic diseases research.

Sankar Surendran MS, PhD
Texas, USA

In: Neurochemistry of Metabolic Diseases
Editor: Sankar Surendran
ISBN: 978-1-53618-339-9

Chapter 1

MUCOLIPIDOSIS DISEASE IN THE UNITED ARAB EMIRATES

Fedah E. Mohamed[1,2], Jozef Hertecant[3,4], Fatma Al-Yahyai[4], Aisha Al-Shamsi[4], Amal Al Tenaiji[5], Bassam R. Ali[1,2] and Fatma Al-Jasmi[1,3,4,*]

[1]Department of Genetics & Genomics, College of Medicine and Health Sciences, United Arab Emirates University, Al Ain, United Arab Emirates

[2]Department of Pathology, College of Medicine and Health Sciences, United Arab Emirates University, Al Ain, United Arab Emirates

[3]Department of Paediatrics, College of Medicine and Health Sciences, United Arab Emirates University, Al Ain, United Arab Emirates

[4]Department of Paediatrics, Tawam Hospital, Al Ain, United Arab Emirates

[5]Department of Paediatrics, Sheikh Khalifa Medical Centre Hospital, Abu Dhabi, United Arab Emirates

[*] Corresponding Author's Email: aljasmif@uaeu.ac.ae.

Abstract

The prevalence of autosomal recessive diseases in the United Arab Emirates (UAE) is known to be relatively high, mainly due to the increase rates of consanguineous marriages among its population. Lysosomal storage disorders are a group of more than 60 different inherited metabolic diseases that are collectively considered to be common in the UAE population. Among the Lysosomal disorders, mucolipidoses (ML) are classified into four subtypes (I – IV), characterized by the accumulation of carbohydrates and lipids in different types of cells to result abnormal function and eventually death. Symptoms in ML diseases may vary from mild musculoskeletal symptoms or learning disabilities to severe intellectual impairment and skeletal deformities. Among the four subtypes of ML, types II and III are common in the Emirati population and only one case of type IV has been reported. In contrast, ML type I has not been reported up to date. In this chapter, cases of different types of ML from the UAE are presented highlighting the main phenotype/genotype correlations.

1. Introduction

The term of " mucolipidosis" was coined in 1970, when Spranger and Wiedemann defined a group of storage diseases which had signs of both mucopolysaccharidosis and sphingolipidosis [1]. Mucolipidoses (ML) are a group of four types of disorders, classified as lysosomal storage diseases (LSDs), because they accumulate substances in the lysosomes, which are specialized sac-like components within the cells [2]. The four types of ML numbered from I – IV are classified according to the type of the mutated enzyme(s) [3]. ML II and III are caused by mutations in the same gene (*GNPTAB*), whereas ML types I and IV are caused by defects in *NEU1* and *MCOLN1* genes, respectively [4]. ML type I, also called sialidosis, results from the deficiency of the lysosomal enzyme sialidase, leading to the accumulation of its metabolites in various tissues like the brain and bone marrow [5]. The disease onset is mainly at birth or at early childhood, as affected children are recognized with coarse facial features and presented with symptoms like skeletal malformations, cherry-red macules, tremors, and seizures. Most infants with ML I have poor prognosis and die before the age of one year. ML II and III result from deficiencies in N-acetylglucosamine-1-phosphotransferase enzyme that aids the transportation process of mannose 6 phosphate dependent lysosomal enzymes [6]. ML II is a severe form of ML resembling Hurler syndrome, while ML III is a milder type of the disorder. Like ML I, ML II has an early onset, while patients affected with ML III often don't show symptoms until 3-5 years of age. Genetic defects in the *MCOLN1* results in ML IV, as most of the affected patients present with severe psychomotor delay, visual impairment, speech problems, intellectual disability, hypotonia, and spasticity [4]. It also has an early disease onset like type I and II. Therapeutic options are still unavailable for all ML types. The storage of undergraded metabolites in ML due to the quantitative and/or qualitative loss of their corresponding enzymes causes cellular and tissue dysfunction. Such metabolites may accumulate in various organs like nerve cells, liver, and muscle tissue as well as in bone marrow leading to a range of clinical presentations and phenotype based on the type of the accumulated metabolite and the affected organs [7]. Symptoms may range from mild skeletal dysfunction to severe intellectual disability and skeletal deformities [8]. The clinical diagnosis of different ML subtypes can be challenging due to the similarities in their presentations with another group of LSDs called mucopolysaccharidoses (MPS). They can be differentiated via urine analysis where patients with MPS show accumulated glycosaminoglycans molecules in their urine samples unlike ML patients.

2. United Arab Emirates and Its Population

United Arab Emirates (UAE) is one of the six gulf countries located along the eastern coast of the Arabian Peninsula [9] (Figure 1). It is a federation of seven emirates that have been united in the 1971 with Abu Dhabi as the capital of the country which compromises about 87% of the UAE's total area (Figure 1). The country officially speaks Arabic. However, most of the population speak other languages of their non-

Arabic origin speaking countries while English is mainly spoken in many institutions.

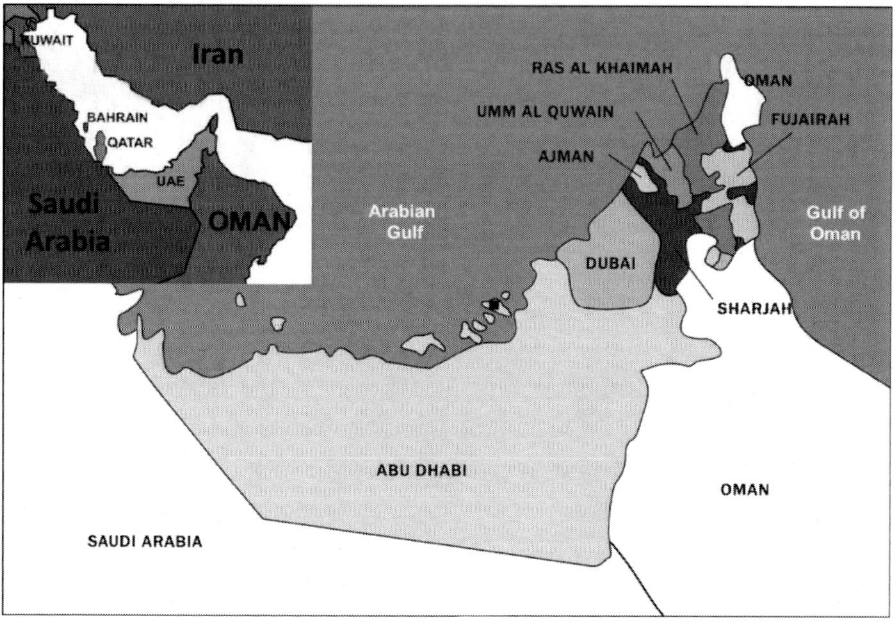

Figure 1. The Map of United Arab Emirates showing the surrounding countries (grey map) and the seven Emirates (coloured map).

The local citizen of UAE has a tribal society of which compromises more than 70 tribes of different origins. These tribes have taken place in the UAE as part of the successive waves of population movements from Yemen, Oman, and the Central and Northern Arabia. In a 2014 phylogenetic study, Garcia-Bertrand, R *et al.* have found that the Emirati population is genetically heterogenous [10].

The UAE has the seventh highest migration rate worldwide. The largest group of non-UAE nationals are South Asian (58%), followed by other Asians (17%) and Western expatriates (8.5%).

3. Genetic Diseases in UAE: Focus on Lysosomal Storage Diseases

Despite the heterogenous mix in the UAE population with the increasing numbers of immigrants from Oman, Yemen, Middle Eastern countries, North Africa, Iran, India, Pakistan, Bangladesh, Baluchistan and Europe, most of the local Bedouins are still form tribal communities which are quite isolated. Intermarriages with different nationalities are still limited [9]. The rate of consanguinity in the UAE is high and still increasing which is estimated to reach up to 50.5% among local citizens [9]. The custom of consanguinity marriages is mainly due to cultural and historical reasons not to religious aspects. Such marriages are more stable and economically beneficial through the conservation of the tribe fortune that is kept within the family structure [11]. This practice is deeply rooted in the Arabian culture and very hard to change due to the mentioned reasons. Therefore, consanguinity resulted in high prevalence of different genetic disorders, more predominantly autosomal recessive types. Diseases like, α- and β- Thalassaemia, Sickle Cell Disease, and multiple types of lysosomal storage diseases (LSDs).

Lysosomes are enclosed cytoplasmic organelles that contain a various classis of acidic hydrolases that aid the degradation of different biological components in the cell [12]. The qualitative or quantitative loss of any of these enzymes will lead to the accumulation of its corresponding substrate, hence, the occurrence of lysosomal storage disease [13]. To date, more than 60 different related LSDs have been reported [14]. In the United Arab Emirates, about 22 different LSD diseases have been reported in the population with a collective prevalence of 26.9 per 100,000 live births [15, 16] (Table 1). Based on the previously LSDs' reported cases, most of the affected individuals were mainly diagnosed with the severe infantile forms, while the milder adult forms were less common. That can be explained due to the easier recognition of such forms by their striking clinical manifestations compared to the milder forms which are easily misdiagnosed. From the Sphingolipidoses disorders group, GM1-

gangliosidosis reported the highest prevalence among all other lysosomal storage with 4.7 per 100,000 individuals [15]. Among mucopoly-saccharidoses (MPS), MPS IIIB, IVA, and VI were found the most common types with a sum birth prevalence of 5.5 per 100,000. In contrast, MPS I and II are the most prevalent worldwide [15]. On the other hand, lipid storage disorders and mucolipidoses diseases prevalence were almost like the other populations. For Mucolipidoses (ML), the most reported cases were from type II and III with a prevalence of 1.35 per 100,000 live births [15] (Table 1). Only one case of ML IV has been reported in the Emirati population while no cases of ML type I (Sialidosis) have been recognized to date.

3.1. Mucolipidosis Type II/III: Classification, Molecular Background and Diagnosis

Mucolipidosis type II and III (known as I-cell disease and pseudo-Hurler dystrophy; respectively) are autosomal recessive inherited LSDs [8]. Both disorders resulted by the malfunction of N-acetylglucosamine (GlcNAc)-1-phosphotransferase enzyme which is the main player in formation of the mannose 6-phosphate (M6P) residues that facilitates the transportation of most of the soluble lysosomal enzymes from the Golgi apparatus to lysosomes through the secretory pathway [17]. The GlcNAc-1-phosphotransferase enzyme is composed of three main subunits that are combined in a hexamer complex. The three subunits are α- and β-subunits that are expressed via the *GNPTAB* gene while the γ subunit is expressed via the *GNPTG* gene [18]. Both the α- and β-subunits are first synthesized and assembled in the endoplasmic reticulum (ER) in their inactive forms that's gets proteolytically activated in the Golgi compartment where the γ-subunit subsequently binds to the activated complex generating a fully functional enzyme for M6P formation [19]. Lysosomal enzymes are synthesized in the ER as part of the secretory pathway [20]. The nascent polypeptide chain goes through multiple folding steps through the aid of a group of ER-residing molecular chaperones and acquires a various number of glycosylation moieties on multiple asparagine residues [21]. Upon their proper folding, these enzymes will be transported to the cis Golgi network where their high mannose oligosaccharide chains will be phosphorylated generating a M6P moiety [17]. In the trans-Golgi, lysosomal enzymes carrying M6P residues will bind to the M6P receptors expressed on trans-Golgi membrane [22]. Once bound to M6P receptors, bound enzymes will be taken up via endosomes budded from the trans-Golgi to be transported to lysosomes by fusion and fission events of the two compartments [22]. In addition, a small portion of the synthesized lysosomal enzymes may get exocytosed to the extracellular milieu where they will be taken back to the cell via M6P receptors expressed on the plasma membrane via endocytosis to the lysosomes [23].

Mucolipidosis II (MIM #252500) is mainly caused by *GNPTAB* genetic modifications but it is characterized by a severe clinical manifestation. Symptoms have an early onset with fetal and early childhood occurrence and affected patients usually have short life expectancy as the disease prognosis is poor [24]. In ML II, genetic variants in *GNPTAB* are mostly deleterious resulting in almost complete loss of GlcNAc-1-phosphotransferase enzymatic activity that is comparable to the patients underlying severe clinical presentation [6]. In contrast, ML III is a milder form to ML II that is further subclassified to ML III α/β (MIM #252600) and MLIII γ (MIM #252605) caused by mutations in *GNPTAB* and *GNPTG*, respectively [6]. These forms of the disease have a late onset of symptoms and relatively better life expectancy. Usually MLIII γ patients have milder phenotype to patients affected with ML III α/β as most probably due to higher residual GlcNAc-1-phosphotransferase activity.

Mucolipidosis II can be clinically recognized due to its very early onset that can be as early as in-utero stage. Disease prognosis is poor and causes death in early childhood. Affected patients mainly present with severe musculoskeletal deformities (spinal deformity, hip dislocation and joint contractures) and progressive psychomotor retardation [25]. Most of the affected patients complain from cardiac problems, of which cardiac hypertrophy or thickening and insufficiency of the mitral and aortic valve.

Table 1. Prevalence of lysosomal storage disorders in UAE

Disorders	Total No. of patients	No. of patients	Prevalence (per 100,000)
Mucopolysaccharidoses (MPS)			
MPS I	4	1	0.25
MPS II	2	0	–
MPS IIIB	6	5	1.05
MPS IIIC	1	1	0.25
MPS IVA	4	2	1.41
MPS VI	13	2	2.51
Oligosaccharidoses			
α-Mannosidosis	6	5	1.51
β-Mannosidosis	0	0	–
Fucosidosis	3	2	2.02
α-*N*-acetyl-galactosaminidase defic.	0	0	–
Aspartylglucosaminuria	0	0	–
Sialidosis	0	0	–
Galactosialidosis	0	0	–
Sphingolipidoses			
GM1 gangliosidosis	20	14	4.66
Tay-Sachs	7	3	0.74
Sandhoff	10	4	1.21
Galactosialidosis	0	0	–
Metachromatic leukodystrophy	3	2	1.50
Niemann-Pick A	0	0	–
Niemann-Pick B	1	1	0.25
Gaucher (all types)	5	1[a]	0.25
Fabry	1	1	0.25
Krabbe	2	0	0
Farber	2	2	0.96
MSD	1	0	0
Lipid storage disorders			
Niemann-Pick C	3	1	0.25
Wolman	1	0	–
Mucolipidoses			
Mucolipidosis I	0	0	–
Mucolipidosis II/III	11	7	1.35
Mucolipidosis IV	0	0	–
Other LSD disorders			
Cystinosis	1	1	0.25
ISSD	0	0	–
Pompe disease	10	8	2.66[b]
Batten disease	2	2	3.54
Total	119	65	26.87

MPS: mucopolysaccharidoses, MSD: multiple sulfatase deficiency, ISSD: infantile sialic acid storage disease. a = Gaucher type 2, b = All cases are the infantile type.

The most common cause of death in ML II affected patients is respiratory insufficiency due to progressive narrowing of airways as result of mucosal thickening and stiffening of thoracic cage [24]. On the other hand, the two forms of ML III (ML III α/β, MLIII γ) appear with much milder range of symptoms, later onset, and slower progression. Symptoms like joint stiffness, skeletal pain, and spinal deformities [6]. The clinical presentation of ML resemble other storage disease and it should be further confirmed via biochemical analysis. Due to the reduced activity of GlcNAc-1-phosphotransferase enzyme, different lysosomal enzymes residual activities are extremely elevated (5 – 10 folds) in patients' plasma and dried blood samples compared to low activities in leucocyte or fibroblast cells. [6]. At the molecular level, targeted sequencing of *GNPTAB* and *GNPTG* genes are required to confirm the clinical diagnosis [6].

3.2. Mucolipidosis IV

Mucolipidosis IV (OMIM #252650) is a rare neurodegenerative lysosomal storage disorder inherited in an autosomal recessive manner caused by mutations in *MCOLN1* gene that encodes for the Zn^{2+} lysosomal channel mucolipin-1 [26]. Genetic defects in the gene will result in the overload of lysosomal Zn^{2+} that is thought to be the main reason for the ML IV pathology resulting in the accumulation of different lipids and proteins in cytoplasmic vacuoles derived from lysosomes [26, 27]. About 70 – 80% of reported ML IV related mutations were detected in the Ashkenazi Jews [28]. Most of ML IV patients are clinically recognized with severe cognitive impairment, eye abnormalities, increased blood gastrin levels, and iron deficiency anaemia. Unlike most LSDs, ML IV patients' usually have normal lysosomal enzymes activities and eventually normal levels of mucopolysaccharides and oligosaccharides in their urine/blood samples [29]. Neurological manifestations are common in ML IV patients who are mainly presented with spasticity, hypotonia, and inadequate mobility.

In addition to the clinical examination, ML IV is further confirmed via multiple molecular and biochemical analyses. Elevated blood gastrin levels is commonly used to confirm ML IV which is combined with MRI imaging showing a thin corpus callosum which a major feature in ML IV patients [30]. Using fibroblast cells, ML IV cells show cytoplasmic inclusions under electron microscopy. A clear cut of the diagnosis can be confirmed via targeting sequencing of the *MCOLN1* gene.

4. Clinical Cases from the UAE

In this section of the chapter, multiple ML cases from the Emirati population as well as cases from UAE residents of various nationalities are discussed.

4.1. Family 1

A 2-year-old female presented with coarse facial features, failure to thrive, developmental delay, recurrent chest infection, obstructive sleep apnea, skeletal deformities, and inguinal hernia. Genetic analysis has revealed a homozygous dinucleotide deletion *GNPTAB* gene. Together, the genetic testing, enzymatic analysis, and the patient severe progressive clinical presentation confirmed that the patient is affected with ML type II. Due to the disease progression, the child passed away at 2 years of age as a result of respiratory failure.

4.1.1. Clinical Presentation and Phenotype

The clinical presentation of the proband was consistent with the diagnosis of Mucolipidosis type II. She presented with coarse facial feature, corneal clouding, shallow orbit, gingival hypertrophy, failure to thrive, skeletal manifestations “lordosis, finger contracture”, developmental delay, at two years of age, she was able to walk in her walker, sit alone for few seconds, and speak using 6 words only.

Polysomnography study consistent with the diagnosis of severe degree of obstructive sleep apnea complicated by frequent oxygen desaturation to less than 50% with severe sleep fragmentation and disturbed sleep architecture. Status post adenoidectomy, there were no improvement in her symptoms and still suffering from the same noisy breathing and snoring with frequent sleep apnea. CPAP or tracheostomy was recommended. Parents declined tracheostomy and patient did not have access to paediatric size CPAP machine. Echo showed pulmonary hypertension and thickened mitral valve leaflets with Mild Mitral Regurgitation, thickened aortic valve leaflets, and mild TR with RVSP = 40-45 mmHg (estimated 45% of systemic). Therefore, she had severe progressive obstructive sleep apnea and secondary pulmonary hypertension which was managed with lisinopril. She had several hospitalizations because of recurrent respiratory tract infection and eventually died at 2 years of age post cardiorespiratory arrest, diabetes insipidus and severe hypoxic encephalopathy.

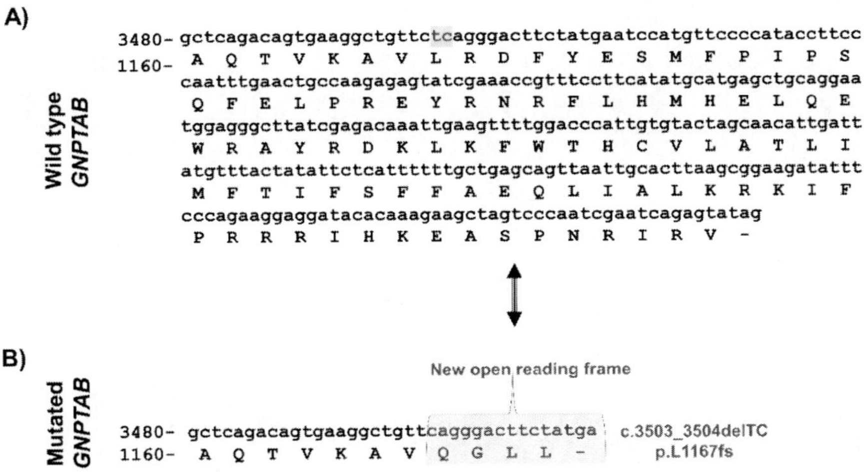

Figure 2. *In silico* analysis of c.3503_3504delTC ML II disease causing variant.

4.1.2. Biochemical and Molecular Analysis

GNPTAB gene full sequencing revealed a dinucleotide deletion in exon 19 of the gene. The detected deletion interferes with the normal reading frame resulting in a frame shift mutation that lead to the generation of a premature codon. At the protein level, the frame shift starts from 1167 amino acid for up to four amino acids before the premature stop codon that results in the loss of 86 amino acids compared to the wild type protein sequence (Figure 2). Enzymatic analysis using patient's sample confirmed ML II which was consistent with the patient clinical presentation and the diseases progression.

4.2. Family 2

A 23-month-old male Pakistani child born to a consanguineous marriage was clinically diagnosed with type II ML. He presented with coarse facial features and developmental delay. Parents are first cousin, had three miscarriages due to intrauterine death of unknown reason (Figure 3). Paternal uncle died at two years as result of high fever, suspected to have ML. The proband has a five years old female sibling who is clinically healthy but living with hearing aid.

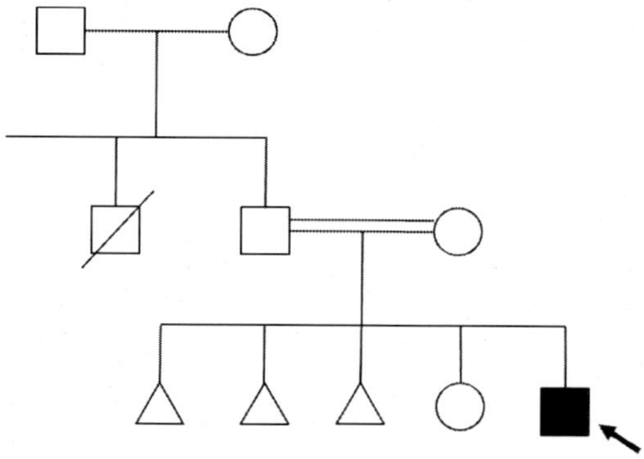

Figure 3. Family 2 pedigree.

4.2.1. Clinical Presentation and Phenotype

The proband is 23-month-old with confirmed diagnosis of ML II with initial clinical presentation to metabolic service at 18 months of age. He presented with coarse facial features and developmental delay. Prenatal history revealed decreased Fetal movement at 7 months of gestation.

abnormal bone structure of fetus was noted in the last trimester and mother informed that he may die in utero. At term, he arrived with spontaneous vaginal delivery and directly admitted to NNU for 21 days. He required phototherapy for a week due to jaundice secondary to ABO incompatibility. Developmental history; fix and follow at four months of age but no head control. At 10 months of age, started to roll over "half a turn" and sits only with support while he started to hold his hands together at the age of 12 months. He was noticed to have a pincer and palmar grasps at 14 months of age and started babbling around 17 months of age. No history of developmental regression. He presented with recurrent URTI, snoring all night and sometimes sleep apnea. On physical examination: coarse facial with thick eyebrows, no corneal clouding long eye lash, depressed nasal bridge, gum hypertrophy, high arched palate, claw hands, short neck, and contracture of multiple joints (shoulders, elbows, wrists, hips and knees). He had nail clubbing, thick pale skin with papular rash over the lower back, trunk and between scapula. Hepatosplenomegaly and heart murmur were noted on examination. He had several hospitalizations because of recurrent chest infections. There was no history of recurrent otitis media. Echo showed thickened aortic valve, causing mild aortic insufficiency.

4.2.2. Biochemical and Molecular Analysis

Clinically patient was suspected to have mucopolysaccharidosis type II but iduronate-2-sulphatase activity was within the normal range. Lysosomal enzymes activities were below the normal range indicating that the proband is affected by mucolipidosis type II/III. The full sequencing of *GNPTAB* sequencing detected a dinucleotide deletion in exon 19 of the gene which the similar variant reported in Family 1. The detected deletion interferes with the normal reading frame resulting in a frame shift mutation that lead to the generation of a premature codon. At the protein level, the frame shift starts from 1167 amino acid for up to four amino acids before the premature stop codon that results in the loss of 86 amino acids compared to the wild type protein sequence (Figure 2).

4.3. Family 3

The proband is a four-year-old Egyptian female born to non-consanguineous parents (Figure 4A). She was presented with coarse facial features, short stature, and severe skeletal deformities with joint restrictions. The clinical examination predicted ML II/III which was confirmed by *GNPTAB/GNPTG* genes sequencing and biochemical analysis of lysosomal enzymatic analysis.

4.3.1. Clinical Phenotype and Symptoms

The proband presented to our metabolic service at 28 months of age with coarse facial features, short stature, severe skeletal deformities with joint restrictions which affected her range of motion. It was noted by her parent at 15 months of age, mother also reported a change in lower back since birth with bulging deformity. Family sought medical attention and seen by several physicians in Egypt and UAE. Suspected to have MPS based on physical and radiological findings of dysostosis multiplex but Urine MPS screening was negative.

She had history recurrent URTI with adenoid hypertrophy and sleep disturbance (snoring). Developmental assessment at 28 months of age; gross motor: sitting with support at 7 months, roll over at 12 months, walking without support at 18 months, at 28 months could not walk up or downstairs, can throw and kick a ball (but weak as per parent), fine motor: good pencil grasp, scribbles but cannot draw a line or other shapes. Speech and language: cannot say a sentence of more than 2 words, follow simple command. On physical examination: coarse fascial features, no corneal clouding, macrocephaly, frontal bossing, protruding eyeballs, low set ears, long philtrum, gingival hypertrophy, wide spaced teeth, poor dentition, high arch palate, short neck, chest wall deformity. Systolic heart murmur grade II-III. hepatomegaly on abdominal examination, contracture of elbow, hands, knee and shoulders with limitation of range of movement. Clubbing of nails and toes, back deformity with gibbus. shuffling gait. Head CT: mildly dilated ventricular system, mild dilated subarchnoid CSF spaces, thinning of periventricular white matter on both sides particularly in peritrigonal region. Echo of heart showed intraventricular septum hypertrophy with mild Left Ventricular obstruction. Proband died in Egypt at 4 years of age due to respiratory illness.

4.3.2. Biochemical and Molecular Analysis

For diagnostic purposes, both *GNPTAB* and *GNPTG* genes coding regions and ~50 bases of flanking noncoding regions were sequenced and aligned to reference sequences. *GNPTG* gene sequencing was negative. In contrast, *GNPTAB* gene sequencing showed a homozygous point mutation at position 1567 (c.1567T > C) that is predicted to result in an amino acid substitution at the protein level at position 523 (p. Cys523Arg) (Figure 4B). The wild type cysteine at the stated position was found to be highly conserved among multiple eukaryotic species indicating its importance to the underlying protein function and/or structure (Figure 4C).

Table 2. Lysosomal enzymes activities in patient's fibroblast cell lysate

	Nmol/min/mg protein		
Enzyme	Activity	Normal range	Effect
Beta-glucuronidase	0.4	(2.0 – 20.0)	↓
Alpha-fucosidase	0.1	(0.8 – 6.0)	↓
Alpha-mannosidase	0.2	(0.9 – 6.0)	↓
Beta-hexosaminidase	1.7	(6.3 – 50.0)	↓
Arylsulphatase A	< 0.1	(5.0 – 25.0)	↓
Alpha-N-acetylgalactosaminidase	1.0	(0.9 – 6.0)	↓
Acid phosphatase (Normal control)	49	(14.0 – 50.0)	Normal

For further confirmation of clinical diagnosis, patient fibroblasts were subjected for lysosomal enzymatic activity analysis of a group of different hydrolases. The analysis showed that the level of enzyme activities of all the tested lysosomal enzymes in fibroblast are either at or below the bottom of the respective normal range (Table 2). In contrast, the level of the control enzyme (acid phosphatase) is clearly within the normal range. In addition, urine analysis of the proband revealed oligosaccharide pattern that is consistent with ML II/III.

A)

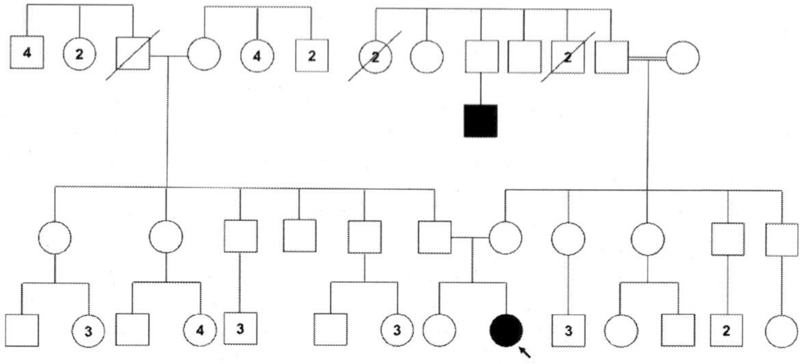

B)

Wild type	1561-	caa	gca	tgc	aat	gtc	ttg	tcc	-1581
	521-	Q	A	C	N	V	L	S	-527
Mutated	1561-	caa	gca	cgc	aat	gtc	ttg	tcc	-1581
	521-	Q	A	R	N	V	L	S	-527

C)

Wild type	SWLADKFCDQACNVLSCGFDAGDC
Mutated	SWLADKFCDQARNVLSCGFDAGD
Ptroglodytes	SWLADKFCDQACNVLSCGFDAGD
Mmulatta	SWLADKFCDQACNVLSCGFDAGD
Mmusculus	SWLADKFCDQACNVLSCGFDAGD
Ggallus	SWLADKFCDQACNVLSCGFDAGD
Trubripes	SWLADKFCDQACNILACGFDVGD
Drerio	SWLADKFCDQACNVLACGFDVGD

Figure 4. ML III family 3 characterization. A) Family 3 pedigree. Affected individuals' symbols are filled with black. Proband is marked by an arrow. B) Wild type and mutated *GNPTAB* gene and N-acetylglucosamine-1-phosphate transferase subunits alpha and beta protein sequences. Nucleotides and amino acids at the mutation positions are highlighted in yellow. C) Conservational analysis via multiple sequencing analysis performed via multiple sequencing alignment.

4.4. Family 4

The proband is a two-year-old female born to first cousin Emirati couple (Figure 5). She was presented with claw hand and restriction of joint mobility especially the hip joint. The rest of her examination was unremarkable. No corneal clouding, or organomegaly. Sanger sequencing and clinical presentation confirmed that the patient is affected with ML III. Despite the milder form of ML, the proband was found to carry the same *GNPTAB* variant detected in Family 3. Detailed family history revealed three of her paternal aunts and one uncle are affected (Figure 5).

4.4.1. Clinical Symptoms/Phenotype

Decreased range of motion of joints was noted by grandmother earlier around one to two years of age as she became more observant for the subtle features. Contractures of the hands were evident between 2 and 4 years of age. The patient with the late onset of skeletal symptoms began complaining of joint stiffness and loss of flexibility at 7 years. Regarding the developmental milestone, fine motor delay was noted in the male patient. The oldest patient had bilateral hip replacement in her late teens. The rest of clinical findings of the patients studied are presented in Table 3. The time of diagnosis for this family ranged from 2 year to 26 years.

4.4.2. Biochemical and Molecular Analysis

In addition to the clinical examination, complete sequencing of the *GNPTAB* gene in the affected individual revealed novel homozygous point mutation at position 1567 (c.1567T > C) which at the protein level results in a the substitution of the wild type cysteine to arginine at position 523 (p.Cys523Arg) (Figure 4B). The mutated amino acid at this position was found to be highly conserved among multiple eukaryotic species as indicated previously via multiple sequencing alignment (Figure 4C).

Serum lysosomal enzymatic analysis of probands serum samples were 10-30 folds higher than normal control (Table 2). While, in leukocytes enzymatic activities were in borderline low/normal.

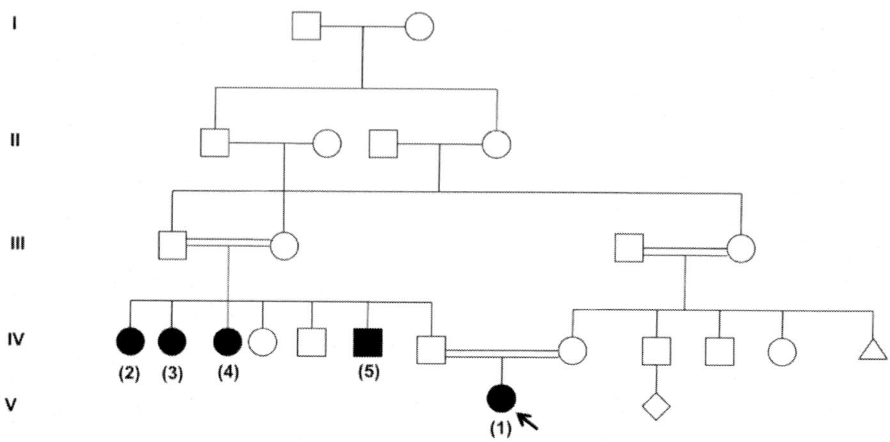

Figure 5. Family 4 pedigree. Affected individuals' symbols are filled with black. Proband is marked by an arrow.

Table 3. Clinical findings of affected individuals in Family 4

Patient #	Sex	Age	Clinical manifestations	Development	Other features
1	F	2 y	Claw hand, restriction of joint mobility of hip, shoulder	Normal	-
2	F	26 y	Bilateral hip replacement, Carpal tunnel syndrome	College graduate	Inguinal hernia, hearing loss
3	F	22 y	Bilateral femoral head necrosis, restriction of hip movement, claw hand, Scoliosis	College student	Inguinal hernia, coloboma
4	F	24 y	Right hip necrosis Restriction of elbow, hip mobility, claw hand	College graduate	Inguinal hernia, umbilical hernia mongolion spot
5	M	4y	Claw hand	Delay in fine motor skill	Extensive mongolion spot

4.5. Family 5

An 18 years old Emirati female from Al-Balushi tribe born to a consanguineous marriage has been diagnosed with ML III (Figure 6A).

The family has another four daughters of which is an eight years old female who is also affected with the same phenotype. The proband is mainly showing multiple joints contractures since early life for which she sought medical evaluation. The father has been diagnosed with Langerhans cell histiocytosis.

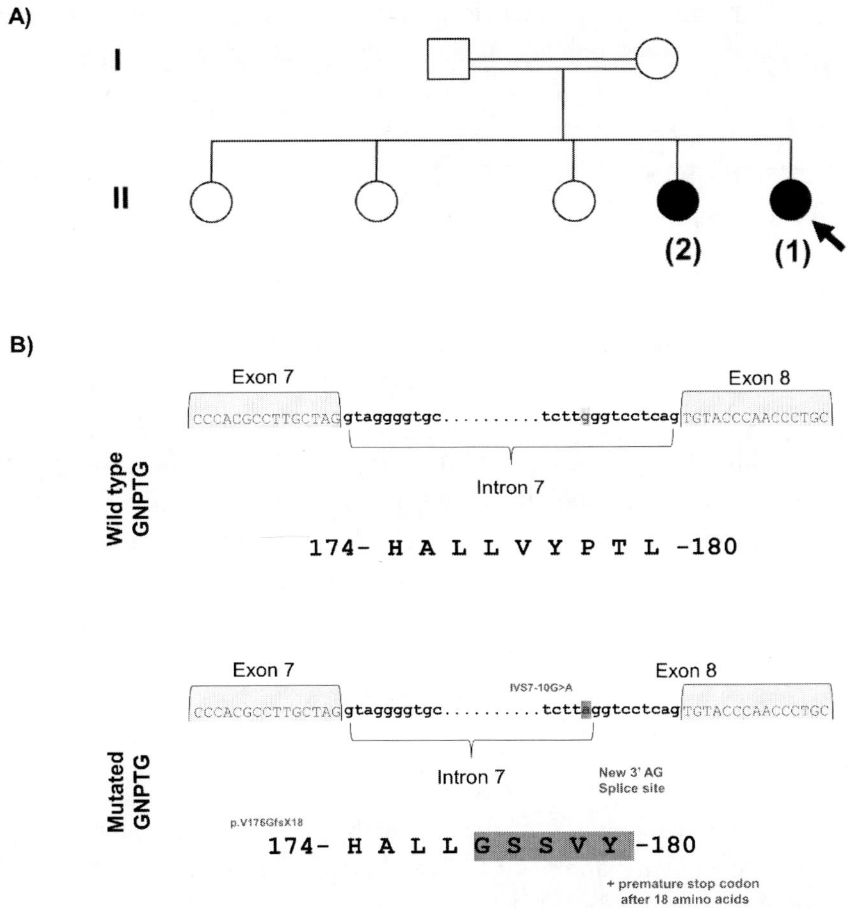

Figure 6. Family 5 ML III characterization and in silico analysis. A) Family pedigree where proband is marked by the black arrow. Filled shapes indicates affected individuals. B) in silico illustration of the detected variant in intron 7 of GNPTG gene and its effect at the protein level. Blue boxes resemble the gene exons around the detected mutation which is highlighted in green in both DNA and protein sequences. Wild type residues at the position of the detected change are highlighted in yellow.

4.5.1. Clinical Phenotype and Symptoms

The proband presented mainly with musculoskeletal manifestations with major joint pain and noticeable decreased range of motion. At the time of clinical examination, she appeared well nourished, well developed, not dysmorphic, noted to have pectus excavatum, short neck restriction shoulder movements in all directions, restriction of elbows extension. A bilateral hip internal and external movements were restricted within minimal levels. Neurological examination unremarkable.

4.5.2. Biochemical and Molecular Analysis

The full sequencing of *GNPTG* gene revealed a previously reported splice site mutation in intron 7 (IVS7-10G > A) of the gene by detecting a substitution mutation at position 11120 (g.11120G > A) [3]. This transitional mutation occurred ten nucleotides upstream from the 30-splice site of intron 7 generating a new cryptic acceptor splice site resulting in the retention of eight nucleotides in intron 7 (Figure 6B). The retention of these nucleotides leads to a change in the open reading frame and result in a frame shift mutation and a premature truncation at the protein level (Figure 6B). The corresponding translation product contains a premature stop codon after 18 amino acids (p.V176GfsX18) resulting in a predicted truncated protein of 194 amino acid which was confirmed via Pohl *et al*, through western blot analysis [3].

4.6. Family 6

The proband (patient 1 of the IV generation) is a five-year-old male born to first cousin parents of a Pakistani origin (Figure 7A). He was clinically diagnosed with ML III at the age of two years due to an insertion mutation in the *GNPTG* gene lead to a major increase in multiple serum acid hydrolases. Screening of the rest of family members for the detected variant showed that two of siblings are affected as well as first male cousin (Figure 7A).

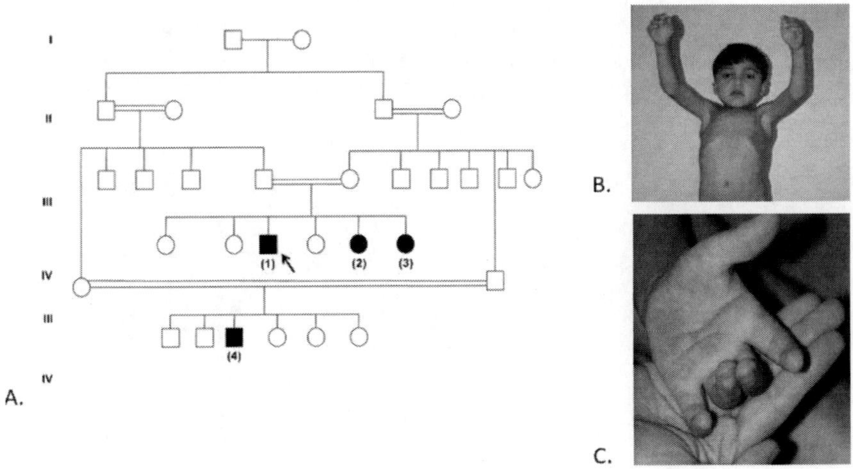

Figure 7. Family 6 MLIII characterization. A) Family pedigree where affected individuals' symbols are black filled and the proband is marked by an arrow. B) Image of affected proband at the age of five years showing the restriction of shoulder movement with no coarse facial features noted. C) Image of the proband's affected sibling (Patient 2) showing the contracture of inter- phalangeal joints.

4.6.1. Clinical Phenotype

He was first presented at two years of age with swelling and progressive stiffness in his wrists and finger joints. At five years of age no facial dysmorphism, the patient shows no signs of mental retardation. The patient's weight falls within the 10- 25th centile and his height at the 10th centile. Ophthalmological examinations did not show any corneal clouding. No organomegaly on abdominal examination. Normal cardiac echo exam. Musculoskeletal examination showed finger contracture and reduced joint mobility of elbow, shoulder, hip and knee (Figure 7B, C). The Skeletal survey showed dysostosis multiplex. Urine MPS was positive with increase in dermatan and heparan sulphate. The proband was independent in his ambulation however his affected cousin was wheelchair dependant. The youngest sibling (one month) was asymptomatic at the time of diagnosis with no skeletal manifestation. The hand x-ray showed flexion contracture of interphalangeal joints more specifically the distal IP. Carpal bones are smaller than usual. Multiplanner MRI scans of the hips showed dysplastic changes in the form of flattening of the humeral head with irregular articular surface, in addition to extensive subarticular fatty changes with no signs of acute ischemia. There are also extensive osteoarthritic changes.

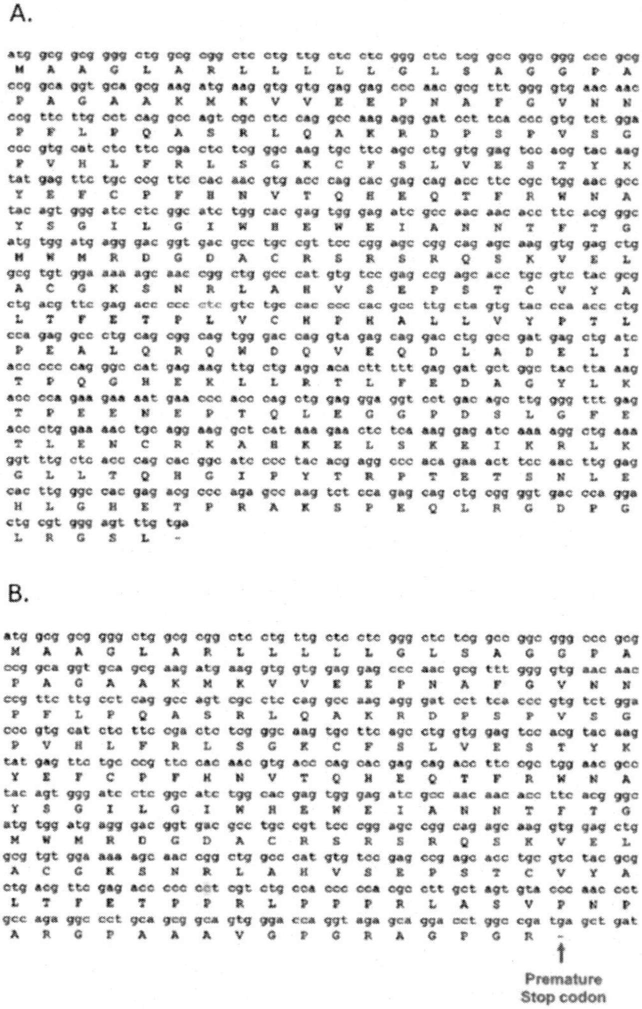

Figure 8. Family 6 MLIII characterization. A) Wild type GNPTG gene and its corresponding N- acetylglucosamine-1-phosphate transferase gamma subunit protein sequences. In red, the wild type codon at which the insertion was detected. B) Family 6 MLIII characterization. Sequences of the mutated gene and protein due to the insertion of C nucleotide at the DNA level leading to a frame shift and the generation of a premature stop codon at the protein level.

4.6.2. Biochemical and Molecular Analysis

Based on the clinical symptoms, the proband's *GNPTG* gene was fully sequenced via Sanger Sequencing which revealed a novel homozygous c.499_500insC. The detected variant was segregated from the patient's parents who were heterozygous carriers while his two female siblings were positive for variant in a homozygous state. At the protein level, the detected insertion interrupts the gene reading frame resulting in a frame shift starting from the Leucine amino acid at 167 (p.L167fs*30) that will generate a premature stop codon after 31 amino acids leading to the loss of a big chunk of the protein (108 amino acids) (Figure 8A,B). Furthermore, affected individuals had lysosomal enzymes analysis which was 10-30 folds increased in serum samples and about low/normal borderline in leukocyte cells (Table 4).

Table 4. Lysosomal enzymatic analysis in affected individuals' serum samples

Patient	Control	Family A			Family B
		Patient 1	Patient 2	Patient 3	Patient 4
Hexosaminidase (A+B)	96	2623	2841	3148	2350
β-Glucoronidase	10	105	105	105	-

4.7. Family 7

The proband is a 6-years-old female with a confirmed diagnosis of Mucolipidosis type IV. She has been clinically evaluated with global developmental delay, hypotonia, anemia, thrombocytopenia, and abnormal ophthalmological findings. Her parents are first cousins of Persian descent (Figure 9A). She has two older sisters, one of which was reported with thrombocytopenia in infancy that has resolved. She has two maternal cousins evaluated with isolated speech delay.

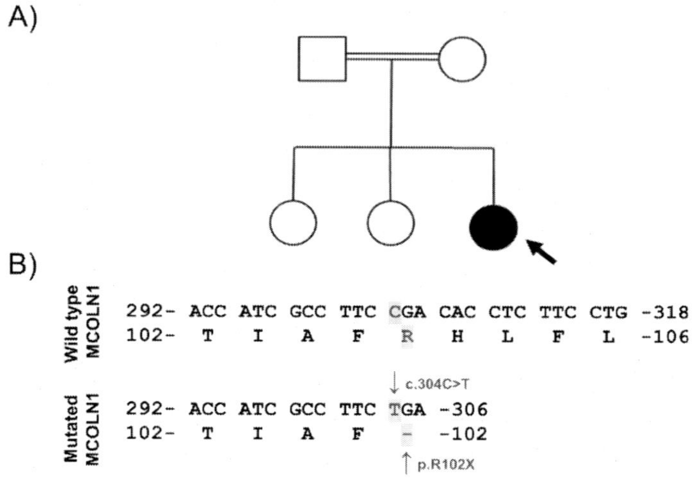

Figure 9. Characterization of an ML IV family with *MCOLN1* mutation. A) Family pedigree B) Sequences of wild type and mutated *MCOLN1* gene and mucolipin-1 protein showing the underlying detected missense mutation in exon 3 of the gene and its corresponding amino acid substitution at position 102.

4.7.1. Clinical Phenotype

The proband was born after an uneventful pregnancy and delivery at term by spontaneous vaginal delivery with a birth weight of 2.9 kilograms. There were no immediate postnatal complications and she was discharged home after her first day of life. After three days, she was readmitted to the neonatal care unit due to neonatal jaundice with indirect hyperbilirubinemia. She was also noted to have low platelets of 38 x10^9/L. She underwent phototherapy and her bilirubin levels were monitored for 5 days after which she was discharged with an acceptable platelets level of 77x10^9/L. Subsequently, she was followed in the haematology clinic for thrombocytopenia which was thought to be immune mediated. She first came to medical attention when she was presented at the age of 16 months with concerns of delayed walking. There is no clear history of motor regression. She was able to sit unsupported at the age of one year. She crawled at two years and started to stand with support and cruise at age four years. She can feed herself finger foods and drink from a cup. However, she has no pincer grasp. Currently she is unable to stand or walk independently and fully wheelchair dependent. Her parents describe slow improvement with physical therapy. In terms of speech development, there is possible regression since she was previously able to say "dada" and the names of her siblings, but she has currently lost this skill and is unable to say any words. Her mom relates this to episode of high fever at age of 1 year after which she lost speech. She has recently started to vocalize, but still communicates mainly via pointing and gestures. She is not toilet trained. There are no behavioural concerns except for occasional irritability. She has not had any major hospitalizations or chest infections. She had a hearing assessment (auditory brainstem response) which was normal. Subsequently due to hypotonia, she had a swallowing assessment which showed delayed swallow and she is currently fed a regular diet orally with no concerns. Her haematological parameters continue to show a microcytic hypochromic anaemia with a haemoglobin ranging from 72 to 101 g/L. Her serum iron levels were low; therefore, she was commenced of iron supplementation which helped to raise her iron level slightly. Platelet levels ranged from 36 - 76 $x10^{\wedge 9}$/L. Brain MRI performed at two years of age showed a thin hypo-plastic corpus callosum with normal ventricles associated with diffuse altered signal intensities in the white matter with hyper intensities on FLAIR sequences. Eye exam revealed strabismus with clear lens bilaterally. Systemic exam of the chest and abdomen was normal. There was no detected organomegaly.

4.7.2. Biomedical and Molecular Analysis

The child underwent whole exome sequencing which identified a previously reported ML IV causing point mutation (c.304C > T) in exon 3 of the *MCOLN1* gene in a homozygous pattern. At the protein level, the detected genetic variant results in the generation of premature stop codons where protein translation is terminated at position 102 (p.R102X) leading to the loss of more than two third of the total size of the protein (478/580 amino acids) (Figure 9B). The underlying variant was segregated from both parents who were heterozygous carriers for the detected change. The ML cases in UAE is summarized in Table 5.

Table 5. Summary of ML cases in UAE

Family	Proband's age of onset	ML type	Mutated gene	Detected variant		Age of Death	No. of affected cases in family	Main phenotype	Ethnicity
				DNA	Protein				
1	NA (female)	II	*GNPTAB*	c.3503_3504delTC	p.Q1167fs*4	2 years	-	- Congenital mitral insufficiency - Developmental delay - Failure to thrive - Obstructive sleep apnea	Emirati
2	Prenatal (male)	II	*GNPTAB*	c.3503_3504delTC	p.Q1167fs*4	2 years	-	-Dysmorphic features -Developmental delay	Pakistani
3	15 months female	II	*GNPTAB*	c.1567T > C	p.C523R	4 years	1	- Coarse facial features - Severe skeletal deformities with joint restrictions -Developmental delay	Egyptian
4	2-year female	III	*GNPTAB*	c.1567T > C	p.C523R	-	4	- Late onset of skeletal symptoms began complaining of joint stiffness and loss of flexibility	Emirati
5	(NA) female	III	*GNPTG*	IVS7-10G > A (g.11120G > A in intron 7)	p.V176Gfs*18	-	1	- Multiple joints contractures since early life	Emirati
6	5-year male	III	*GNPTG*	c.499_500insC	p.L167fs*30	-	3	- Progressive stiffness in joints - No facial dysmorphism - Normal development	Pakistani
7	16 months female	IV	*MCOLN1*	c.304C > T	p.R102X	-	-	- Global developmental delay - Hypotonia - Anemia and thrombocytopenia - Abnormal ophthalmological findings	Persian

Conclusion

Like most of LSDs, ML of all types are very rare disorders that are often evades diagnosis. Although the cases are increasing in this region, little clinical knowledge is known about these diseases. Further analysis is urgently needed to better understand and differentiate the subtypes of these disorders clinically as well as find a better phenotype-genotype correlation. Although multiple cases were reported with the same genotype, their clinical presentation and disease progression are totally different. As reported from families 3 and 4 mentioned in this chapter, both were reported with the point mutation (c.1567T > C) in their *GNTPAB* gene, but family 3 was diagnosed with the ML II resulting in early childhood death, while the same genetic variant resulted in the milder ML III in family 4 with several affected individuals reaching their late 20s who are university graduates.

To date, there is no approved treatment for ML diseases and patients are mainly under supportive management to ameliorate the underlying symptoms, which is mainly because of the limited knowledge available about these diseases due to its rarity. Thus, genetic counselling in families with known history of these diseases is crucial to prevent its occurrence and help the families to take correct decisions toward future marriages and pregnancies.

References

[1] Spranger, JW, Wiedemann, HR. The genetic mucolipidoses. Diagnosis and differential diagnosis. *Humangenetik*, 1970, 9, 113-139.

[2] Futerman, AH, van Meer, G. The cell biology of lysosomal storage disorders. *Nat. Rev. Mol. Cell Biol.* 2004, 5, 554-565.

[3] Pohl, S, Encarnacão, M, Castrichini, M, Müller-Loennies, S, Muschol, N, Braulke, T. Loss of N-acetylglucosamine-1-

phosphotransferase gamma subunit due to intronic mutation in GNPTG causes mucolipidosis type III gamma: Implications for molecular and cellular diagnostics. *Am. J. Med. Genet.* 2010,152A, 124-132.

[4] Bargal, R, Avidan, N, Ben-Asher, E, Olender, Z, Zeigler, M, Frumkin, A, Raas-Rothschild, A, Glusman, G, Lancet, D, Bach, G. Identification of the gene causing mucolipidosis type IV. *Nat. Genet.* 2000, 26, 118-123.

[5] d'Azzo, A, Machado, E, I. Annunziata, I. *Pathogenesis,* Emerging therapeutic targets and Treatment in Sialidosis. *Expert. Opin. Orphan Drugs.* 2015, 3, 491-504.

[6] Velho, RV, Harms, FL, Danyukova, T, Ludwig, NF, Friez, MJ, Cathey, SS, Filocamo, M, Tappino, B, Güneş, N, Tüysüz, B, Tylee, KL, Brammeier, KL, Heptinstall, L, Oussoren, E, van der Ploeg, AT, Petersen C, Alves, S, Saavedra, GD, Schwartz, IV, Muschol, N, Kutsche, K, Pohl, S. The lysosomal storage disorders mucolipidosis type II, type III alpha/beta, and type III gamma: Update on GNPTAB and GNPTG mutations. *Hum. Mutat.* 2019,40, 842-864.

[7] Ballabio, A. The awesome lysosome. *EMBO. Mol. Med.* 2016, 8, 73-76.

[8] Qian, Y, van Meel, E, Flanagan-Steet, H, Yox, A, Steet, R, Kornfeld, S. Analysis of mucolipidosis II/III GNPTAB missense mutations identifies domains of UDP-GlcNAc:lysosomal enzyme GlcNAc-1-phosphotransferase involved in catalytic function and lysosomal enzyme recognition. *J. Biol. Chem.* 2015, 290, 3045-3056.

[9] Al-Gazali, LI, Alwash, R, Abdulrazzaq, YM. United Arab Emirates: communities and community genetics. *Community Genet.* 2005, 8, 186-196.

[10] Garcia-Bertrand, R, Simms, TM, Cadenas, AM, Herrera, RJ. United Arab Emirates: phylogenetic relationships and ancestral populations. *Gene* 2014, 533, 411-419.

[11] al-Gazali, LI, Bener, A, Abdulrazzaq, YM, Micallef, R, al-Khayat, AI, Gaber, T. Consanguineous marriages in the United Arab Emirates. *J. Biosoc. Sci.* 1997, 29, 491-497.

[12] Carmona-Gutierrez, D, Hughes, AL, Madeo, F, Ruckenstuhl, C. The crucial impact of lysosomes in aging and longevity. *Ageing Res. Rev.* 2016, 32, 2-12.

[13] Ferreira, CR, Gahl, WA. Lysosomal storage diseases. *Transl. Sci. Rare Dis.* 2017, 2, 1-71.

[14] Onyenwoke, RU, Brenman, JE. Lysosomal Storage Diseases—Regulating Neurodegeneration. *J. Exp. Neurosci.* 2015, 9(Suppl 2), 81-91.

[15] Al-Jasmi, FA, Tawfig, N, Berniah, A, Ali, BR, Taleb, M, Hertecant, JL, Bastaki, F, Souid, AK. Prevalence and Novel Mutations of Lysosomal Storage Disorders in United Arab Emirates : LSD in UAE. *JIMD. Rep.* 2013, 10, 1-9.

[16] Mohamed, FE, Al Sorkhy, M, Ghattas, MA, Al-Zaabi, N, Al-Shamsi, A, Almansoori, TM, Al-Gazali, L, Al-Dirbashi, OY, Al-Jasmi, F, Ali, BR. A Novel Homozygous Missense Variant in the NAGA Gene with Extreme Intrafamilial Phenotypic Heterogeneity. *J. Mol. Neurosci.* 2020, 70, 45-55.

[17] Coutinho, MF, Prata, MJ, Alves, S. Mannose-6-phosphate pathway: a review on its role in lysosomal function and dysfunction. *Mol. Genet. Metab.* 2012,105, 542-550.

[18] Franke, M, Braulke, T, Storch, S. Transport of the GlcNAc-1-phosphotransferase alpha/beta-subunit precursor protein to the Golgi apparatus requires a combinatorial sorting motif. *J. Biol. Chem.* 2013, 288,1238-1249.

[19] Encarnacao, M, Kollmann, K, Trusch, M, Braulke, T, Pohl, S. Post-translational modifications of the gamma-subunit affect intracellular trafficking and complex assembly of GlcNAc-1-phosphotransferase. *J. Biol. Chem.* 2011, 286, 5311-5318.

[20] Walter, P, Gilmore, R, Blobel, G. Protein translocation across the endoplasmic reticulum. *Cell.* 1984, 38, 5-8.

[21] Kornfeld, S., Trafficking of lysosomal enzymes. *FASEB. J.,* 1987, 1, 462-468.

[22] Rosenfeld, MG, Kreibich, G, Popov, D, Kato, K, Sabatini, DD. Biosynthesis of lysosomal hydrolases: their synthesis in bound

polysomes and the role of co- and post-translational processing in determining their subcellular distribution. *J. Cell. Biol.* 1982, 93, 135-143.

[23] Solomon, M, Muro, S. Lysosomal Enzyme Replacement Therapies: Historical Development, Clinical Outcomes, and Future Perspectives. *Adv. Drug Deliv. Rev.* 2017, 118, 109-134.

[24] Cathey, SS, Leroy, JG, Wood, T, Eaves, K, Simensen, RJ, Kudo, M, Stevenson, RE, Friez, MJ. Phenotype and Genotype in Mucolipidoses II and III alpha/beta: A Study of 61 Probands. *J. Med. Genet.* 2010, 47, 38-48.

[25] Aggarwal, S, Coutinho, MF, Dalal, AB, Mohamed Nurul Jain, SJ, Prata, MJ, Alves, S. Prenatal skeletal dysplasia phenotype in severe MLII alpha/beta with novel GNPTAB mutation. *Gene.* 2014, 542, 266-268.

[26] Sun, M, Goldin, E, Stahl, S, Falardeau, JL, Kennedy, JC, Acierno, JS Jr, Bove, C, Kaneski, CR, Nagle, J, Bromley, MC, Colman, M, Schiffmann, R, Slaugenhaupt, SA. Mucolipidosis type IV is caused by mutations in a gene encoding a novel transient receptor potential channel. *Hum. Mol. Genet.* 2000, 9, 2471-2478.

[27] Venugopal, B, Browning, MF, Curcio-Morelli, C, Varro, A, Michaud, N, Nanthakumar, N, Walkley, SU, Pickel, J, Slaugenhaupt, SA. Neurologic, gastric, and opthalmologic pathologies in a murine model of mucolipidosis type IV. *Am. J. Hum. Genet.* 2007, 81,1070-1083.

[28] Wakabayashi, K, Gustafson, AM, Sidransky, E, Goldin, E. Mucolipidosis Type IV: an Update. *Mol. Genet. Metab.* 2011, 104, 206-213.

[29] Geer, JS, Skinner, SA, Goldin, E, Holden, KR. Mucolipidosis type IV: a subtle pediatric neurodegenerative disorder. *Pediatr. Neurol.* 2010, 42, 223-226.

[30] Frei, KP, Patronas, NJ, Crutchfield, KE, Altarescu, G, Schiffmann, R. Mucolipidosis type IV: characteristic MRI findings. *Neurology.* 1998, 51, 565-569.

In: Neurochemistry of Metabolic Diseases
Editor: Sankar Surendran
ISBN: 978-1-53618-339-9

Chapter 2

SIALIDOSIS AND GALACTOSIALIDOSIS: MOLECULAR MECHANISM AND THERAPEUTIC EFFECT

*Consolato M. Sergi**
Department of Laboratory Medicine and Pathology,
University of Alberta, Edmonton, AB, Canada and
Stollery Children's Hospital, Edmonton, AB, Canada

ABSTRACT

More than 40 years ago, two patients with clinical features reminiscent of mucopolysaccharidosis Type IH (MPS-IH), Hurler's disease, characterized by an accumulation of glycosaminoglycans or mucopolysaccharides in lysosomes, presented in pediatrics. Both patients had, however, a normal urinary excretion of acid mucopolysaccharides. The histological and ultrastructural examination of neurons, as well as

* Corresponding Author's Email: sergi@ualberta.ca.

visceral and mesenchymal tissues, exposed lysosomal storage of molecular compounds considered to be acid mucopolysaccharides and glycolipids. These patients were, subsequently, further investigated and classified as mucolipidosis I. An accumulation of sialic acid-containing compounds in cultured fibroblasts and leukocytes of such patients and massive urinary excretion of sialyl oligosaccharides pointed out to a lack the lysosomal neuraminidase or sialidase. The metabolic defect in mucolipidosis I consists of impaired catabolism of glycoprotein-derived sialyl oligosaccharides due to the genetic deficiency of neuraminidase, the gene of which was identified in 1997. In this chapter, the morphologic and biochemical aspects of sialidosis and galactosialidosis, which is a related metabolic disorder, are exposed. Current therapeutic strategies and perspectives are delineated.

1. INTRODUCTION

In 1968, two patients with clinical features reminiscent of mucopolysaccharidosis Type IH (MPS-IH), Hurler's disease, characterized by an accumulation of glycosaminoglycans or mucopolysaccharides in lysosomes, presented in pediatrics [1, 2]. Both patients had, however, a normal urinary excretion of acid mucopolysaccharides. Further histological and ultrastructural examination revealed lysosomal storage of compounds considered to be acid mucopolysaccharides and glycolipids. In 1977, these patients were classified as mucolipidosis I [3-8]. In the biochemistry of the neurons, prominently over other cellular types, the cleavage of terminal N-acetyl-neuraminic acid (sialic acid) from glycoconjugates, linked in a β-glucoside fashion is critical. The cleavage is obtained using neuraminidases and is crucial for the proper function of these cells. The intralysosomal N-α-acetyl-neuraminidase (NEU1) is unique and is different from the cytosolic form (NEU2) and the membrane-bound form (NEU3). This aspect is due to the catalytically active function. It means the NEU1 is catalytically active only when it docks to a carboxypeptidase labeled as cathepsin A (CTSA), which is also known as protective protein cathepsin A (PPCA). It forms a multi-protein complex, which contains N-acetyl-galactosamine-6-sulfate sulfatase in addition to β-galactosidase [9-11]. Genetic variations of these proteins undermine the biochemistry and function of the affected cells resulting in two lysosomal storage disorders, called sialidosis and galactosialidosis. Unlike galactosialidosis, which is due to a primary genetic defect of CTSA/PPCA causing severe disruption of the complex resulting in a combined deficiency of β-galactosidase and neuraminidase activities, sialidosis is characterized biochemically by the paucity of lysosomal NEU1 activity. The lysosomal deficiency provokes an abnormal tissue accumulation of the sialic acid-rich molecular compounds and urinary excretion of sialic acid-containing compounds. Such a collection is highly detrimental for the organism, no matter when it starts. However, the very early accumulation of compounds that cannot be cleared is characterized by an inescapable infaust prognosis for the patient [12-14]. Substantially, the severity of the lysosomal deficiency of NEU1 determines two quite different phenotypes, which are labeled sialidosis type I and sialidosis type II. Sialidosis type I, which is also called in pediatric clinical departments as non-dysmorphic type, is the mild form of the disease with late-onset, bilateral macular cherry-red spots, progressive impaired vision, and myoclonus syndrome. Sialidosis type II, which is also known as dysmorphic type in pediatric clinical departments, may present at a different age. The infantile form of sialidosis type II with onset at an early age is characterized by skeletal dysplasia, Hurler-like phenotype, dysostosis multiplex, mental retardation, and hepato-/splenomegaly. In contrast, the prenatal or perinatal form of sialidosis type II with almost exclusively prenatal onset is a severe form, which manifests itself prenatally with prominent ascites and hydrops fetalis (or *hydrops ana sarca*). Very few reports are present in the literature on sialidosis, because it is a sporadic, inherited metabolic disorder. In the literature, other names for sialidosis used are mucolipidosis type I, myoclonus cherry-red spot syndrome, and cherry-red spot myoclonus syndrome.

2. Epidemiology of Sialidosis

Although the global prevalence of sialidosis is unknown, sialidosis type I appears to be more common in individuals with Italian ancestry.

Still, it is essential to realize that this metabolic disorder has been demonstrated in a wide range of ethnicities. The ethnic analysis of the reported patients evidenced patients of Japanese, Moroccan, German, and Ashkenazi Jewish ancestry. Sialidosis affects both males and females in approximately equal rates, but the exact global incidence of sialidosis in the general population is unknown. As a matter of example, it has been suggested that the incidence in Australia is 1 in 4.2 million individuals. Still, other estimates generate incidences variables between 1 and 4 per 200,000 individuals of the overall population. The reason for this uncertainty is that sialidosis often goes misdiagnosed or, likely most often, unrecognized.

3. Genetics of Sialidosis

Sialidosis is a genetic disorder with an autosomal recessive inheritance, which is due to a deficiency of the lysosomal enzyme a-N-acetyl-neuraminidase (sialidase) or NEU1 (OMIM No. 256550). Sialidosis mutations in the *NEU1* gene cause this metabolic disorder. *NEU1* provides instructions for making an enzyme called neuraminidase 1 (NEU1), which is found explicitly in lysosomes. The intra-lysosomal NEU1 drives the break down of saccharides attached to specific proteins by removing a substance known as N-acetyl-neuraminic acid or sialic acid (Figure 1). The sialic acid family includes 43 derivatives of the nine-carbon sugar neuraminic acid, which can be usually found as components of oligosaccharide chains of mucins, glycoproteins, and, of course, glycolipids. These molecular compounds occupy precisely terminal, nonreducing positions of complex carbohydrates on both external and internal membrane areas. In these sectors, these compounds are very exposed and develop essential functions.

Drawings of two common sialic acid derivatives, Neu5Ac and Kdn. KDN is an abbreviation for 2-keto-3-deoxy-D-glycero-D-galacto-nononic acid that occurs naturally. Source: https://commons.wikimedia.org/wiki/ File: Sialic_acids.1.png. The photograph owner (Glycogorm) published this photograph in the Public Domain. The copyright holder of this work, released this work into the public domain. This applies worldwide granting anyone the right to use this work for any purpose, without any conditions, unless such conditions are required by law.

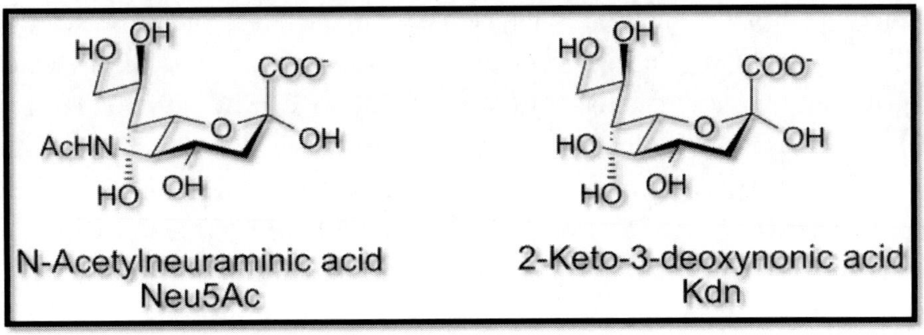

Figure 1. Chemical formula of N-acetyl-neuraminic acid or sialic acid.

Mutations in the *NEU1* gene brings to a paucity of the NEU1 enzyme. When this enzyme is lacking, sialic acid-containing compounds accumulate inside lysosomes, which are organelles that contain digestive enzymes. Lysosomes digest excess or worn-out subcellular organelles and engulfed viruses or bacteria. Individuals with sialidosis type II have alterations that severely reduce or eliminate NEU1 enzyme activity. Individuals with sialidosis type I have mutations that result in some functional NEU1 enzyme [10, 15-19]. The *NEU1* gene consists of six exons (lengths between 159 to 263 bp) and five intervening introns (lengths between 97 to 567 bp) coding for a 1.9 kb mRNA. Several genetic alterations have been reported in *NEU1* of unrelated sialidosis patients (10). Most of such mutations consist of missense mutations (17 cases), followed by two small insertions and two small deletions and one nonsense mutations [9, 20-23]. All the known mutations occurring in exons are equally distributed over the entire coding region of *NEU1*. Using 3D-modelling it was shown that only a few of the missense mutations directly affect active site residues or interfere with the correct positions of active sites within the enzyme and that most of the amino acid substitutions are localized in the putative PPCA-binding sites of NEU1 where they may be critical for the integrity of the association with PPCA [12, 24]. An intronic point mutation in *NEU1* has also been characterized in sialidosis patients [25]. An IVSE+1G > C homozygous transversion in the donor splice site of the last intron determined to skip the complete exon 5 resulting in a premature termination codon. Remarkably, *Neu1* maps to the MHC-III cluster on chromosome 6p21.3 and also has unique neighbors, of which the choline transporter-like protein 4 gene (CTL4 also called NG22) seems that it may play an essential role in degenerative diseases [9, 10, 18, 19, 26]. In neurons, choline used for the synthesis of acetylcholine is transported from extracellular spaces via a Na+-dependent, high-affinity choline transporter (CHT1). In the lack of CHT1, neurons are not able to synthesize acetylcholine [27]. Choline transport in non-neuronal cells cannot be solely dependent on CHT1 and must utilize other choline transporters, which are designated as the choline transporter-like proteins 1–5 (CTL1–5) [26]. Importantly, of the CTLs, only CTL4 appears positively linked to the synthesis of acetylcholine in two different non-neuronal cell types [28]. This aspect may broaden the relationship of sialidosis to degenerative, probably neurodegenerative diseases. It is a triggering scientific venue, which needs to be explored further.

4. PATHOGENESIS

Although the genetic etiology has been identified, the pathogenesis is still a topic of intense discussion. It is not completely clear how the intralysosomal accumulation of these compounds leads to the specific signs and symptoms of sialidosis. However, a dysregulation of the phagocytosis and mitochondrial function are strongly considered a paramount key [10]. The mouse model has been useful to explain some mechanisms of pathogenesis that occur in sialidosis [29, 30]. The *Neu1–/–* knockout (KO) mouse model clarifies some underlying molecular mechanisms of sialidosis. These rodent model mice showed NEU1 as a negative regulator of lysosomal exocytosis. In hematopoietic cells, NEU1 negatively regulates lysosomal exocytosis by processing the sialic acids on the lysosomal membrane protein 1 (LAMP1), which is plasmatic membrane protein playing a key role in the docking of lysosomes at the plasma membrane. Deficiency or impaired NEU1 activity determines defective processing of the sialic acids on LAMP1.

Table 1. Sialidosis versus Galactosialidosis

	Sialidosis Type I	Sialidosis Type II		Galactosialidosis
Synonyms	CRSM			
Age of onset	2nd decade	Perinatal	Infantile	Juvenile
Enzyme Defect	NEU1	NEU1	NEU1	CTSA
Gene locus	6p21.3	6p21.3	6p21.3	20q13.12
Phenotype (external)	-	(NI-)HF	Normal to coarse facies	Dwarfism, coarse facies
Phenotype (internal)	-	Hepato-splenomegaly	Hepato-splenomegaly, dysostosis multiplex	Heart disease, dysostosis multiplex
Neurology	MCS, TCS, PN, ataxia	-	MCS, ataxia, MR	MCS, hearing loss, MR
Ophthalmology	CRS macula, ↓ Vision	Corneal clouding	CRS macula	CRS macula, conjunctival telangiectasias, corneal clouding
Prognosis	Survival to adulthood	Death (perinatal)	Death (2nd decade)	Variable

Notes: NEU1, α-acetyl-neuraminidase; CTSA, cathepsin A; MCS, myo-clonic seizures, which are characteristically generalized affecting the limbs, triggered by voluntary movement, touch, sound, smoking, menstrual cycles, and progressive up to non-ambulatory; MR, mental retardation; (NI-)HF, non-immunologic hydrops fetalis; PN, peripheral neuropathy; TCS, tonico-clonic seizures; Dysostosis multiplex includes dolichocephaly with enlargement of the *sella turcica* and thickening of the calvarium, anterior beaking of the vertebral bodies in the lower thorax and upper lumbar regions, thickening of the medial third of the clavicle, spatulated or ear-shaped ribs, flaring of the iliac bones with evident shallow acetabulum, tapering of the terminal phalanges and widening at the distal ends with associated tapering at the proximal ends of the metacarpal bones, irregular widening of the long bones of the upper limbs with areas of cortical thinning and expansion of the medullary cavity, curving of the radius toward the ulna with the articular surfaces of the radius and the ulna facing each other, typically forming a V.

Consequently, it provokes an accumulation of LAMP1 in an over-sialylated state with a prolonged half-life. This accumulation of over-sialylated LAMP1 expands the number of LAMP1-marked lysosomes that harbor at the plasmatic membrane. It poised to engage in lysosomal exocytosis upon an influx of calcium. Experiments silencing LAMP1 in NEU1-deficient cells normalize the number of lysosomes docked at the plasmatic membrane. This event decreases the extent of lysosomal exocytosis. NEU1 loss of function eventually results in the excessive extracellular release of lysosomal luminal contents from deficient cells of several tissues and organs. Excessive lysosomal-supported exocytosis has been associated with various pathological manifestations, which are characteristic of sialidosis, including its role in neurodegeneration and links with muscle atrophy and enlarged organs (e.g., splenomegaly), but even Alzheimer disease. Further, phagocytosis in macrophages, which is regulated by NEU1, as well as NEU1-dependent regulation of insulin signaling is the additional pathways that have attracted the attention of researchers in this field [30].

5. Clinical Symptoms

Table 1 summarizes the clinical forms of sialidosis and galactosialidosis. Of particular mention is the non-immunologic hydrops fetalis (NIHF), which may remain unrecognized or misdiagnosed.

6. Diagnostics

Non-immunologic hydrops fetalis (NIHF) has a very large broad of etiologic factors and has an impressive relevance in obstetrics and fetal medicine. Lysosomal storage diseases (LSDs) should be included in the differential diagnosis of ascites in the perinatal period. The event initiating the accumulation of excessive fluid within the peritoneal cavity in infants with LSDs is controversially discussed in the literature. Several viruses have been identified in NIHF, and, probably, one of the most well-known viruses is parvovirus B19, which is quite characteristic of the 2nd trimester [31]. Congestive heart failure, liver cirrhosis, or liver dysfunction are associated with NIHF that are intriguingly linked to the perpetuation of the ascites in metabolic disease. In one of the patients identified from our biochemical and pathologic task on sialidosis includes a patient with distortion and obstruction of hepatic sinusoids and lymphatics by foam cell infiltration and swelling of the Kupffer as well as endothelial cells. Prenatal diagnosis may be achieved by analyzing of cultured amniotic fluid cells and methylamine method, which was performed for the first time, in neonatal sialidosis [32-35]. The methylamine method is a very elegant method. It is characterized by the application of methylamine, which is highly membrane-permeable and, due to its pKa of 10.6, collects mainly in the acidic lysosomal compartment. Since the lysosomal pH was not significantly altered in the patients' fibroblasts, the build-up of methylamine depends on the volume of the compartment. Thus, it represents a direct measure of its pathological enlargement. Cell lines of a patient with mucopolysaccharidosis type II and one of our patients with sialidosis These cell lines show a marked increase of the radioactivity compared with three normal controls, confirming the diagnosis of an LSD. [I4C] methylamine incorporation assay can be used as an additional tool in the diagnosis of an LSD, where excessive loading of water-soluble compounds prevails. In the last century, the successful prevention of Rhesus incompatibility in fetal medicine has been a milestone for obstetrics sciences. It has promoted a remarkable decrease in the relative incidence of non-immunologic hydrops fetalis. Among metabolic disorders that can present at birth or during pregnancy with non-immunologic hydrops fetalis, sialidosis is probably one of the rarest occurrences [10, 32, 36]. Mucopolysaccharidoses, GM1 gangliosidosis, Gaucher disease may be slightly more common likely linked to specific communities and ethnicities. Several LSDs such as mucopolysaccharidoses, GM1 gangliosidosis, Gaucher disease, and Salla disease (among others) may present at birth with NIHF. Figure 2 shows the vacuolation observed in both epithelial and mesenchymal cells of a liver with the diagnosis of prenatal sialidosis presenting with NIHF. The hepatocytes show multivacuolar changes as well as the Kupffer cells present multivacuolar changes. There is no apparent displacement of the nuclei in the hepatocytes and Kupffer cells. Kupffer cells, also known as Kupffer–Browicz cells and stellate macrophages, are specialized macrophages. Kupffer cells are located in the liver, lining the walls of the sinusoids, forming part of the mononuclear phagocyte system. The endothelial cells also show some vacuolar changes, because the change affects both epithelial and mesenchymal components. Figure 3 shows the vacuolation encountered in the placenta affecting both the Hofbauer cells and the cytotrophoblast and syncytiotrophoblast. Hofbauer cells are oval eosinophilic histiocytes with granules and vacuoles detected in the placental villous stroma. They are of mesenchymal origin and located in the mesoderm of the chorionic villus. They are particularly numerous in early pregnancy. However, the 'abnormal' multivacuolation cannot be easily identified, because they present the same features even without sialidosis. Thus, the attention needs to be brought to the cytotrophoblast and syncytiotrophoblast only.

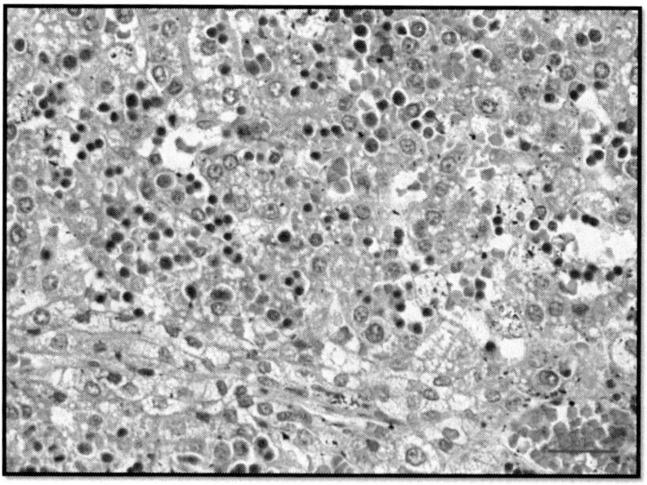

Figure 2. Liver of a patient with sialidosis presenting with NIHF.

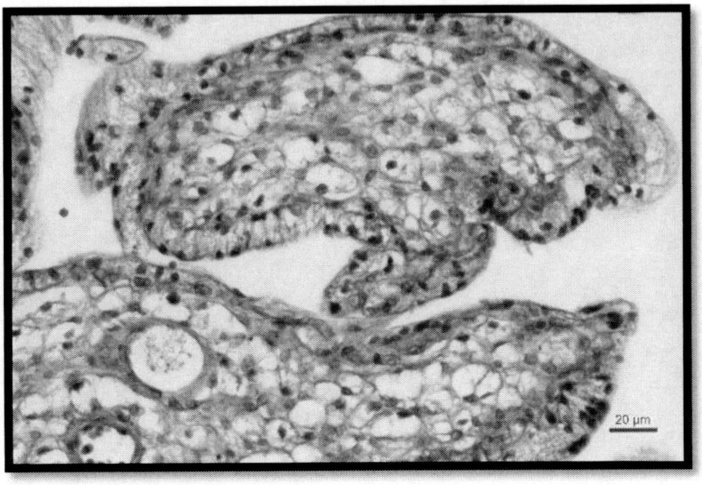

Figure 3. Placenta affected by Sialidosis.

7. Galactosialidosis

The defect underlying the disorder known as galactosialidosis relies on CTSA deficiency (Table 1). The *CTSA* (Cathepsin A) gene provides directives to build a protein called cathepsin A or CTSA, which acts as a protease. Also, CTSA can act as a protective protein, interacting explicitly with other enzymes to avert them from breaking down prematurely. Centered on this protective function, CTSA is also known as protective protein/cathepsin A or PPCA. CTSA is active in the lysosomes, which are full of enzymes able to digest and catabolize a vast number of materials [11]. CTSA interacts with the enzymes β-galactosidase (B-GAL) and neuraminidase 1 (NEU1), which play a role in the breakdown of oligosaccharides attached to glycoproteins and glycolipids. CTSA forms a unique complex with B-GAL and NEU1 directing their transport within the cell to the lysosomal compartment. CTSA is also unique because it activates the enzymes and prevents their progressive breakdown. Galactosialidosis also has other names, including deficiency of cathepsin A, Goldberg syndrome, lysosomal protective protein deficiency, neuraminidase deficiency with beta-galactosidase deficiency, and PPCA deficiency.

8. Prognosis

The outcome of patients with sialidosis is traditionally regarded as grim because patients affected with sialidosis have been often not given enough attention due to the rarity of this disease. Several discretionary actions have been suggested in improving the understanding of this disease and the evolution of the prognosis for the 21st century. This aspect cannot be stressed enough in considering the enormous contributions that have been gained in the last few years in molecular biology. Traditionally, patients affected with sialidosis type I or myoclonus have a better prognosis, while patients affected with sialidosis type II face a dismal prognosis due to the extension of the histological changes in several organs and the burden to the malfunction of the lysosomal system.

9. Therapy

It is well known that there is no specific therapy for sialidosis, but treatment is targeted toward the specific symptoms that are noticeable in each affected individual. Anti-seizure medications (anticonvulsants) may be used to treat myoclonic seizures but are not always effective, and status epilepticus and myoclonic progressive epilepsies, as well as status epilepticus, represent a frequent challenge in pediatrics. Status epilepticus is an emergency associated with significant morbidity and mortality, not only involving patients with neuraminidase deficiency. In the status epilepticus, there is a continuous seizure lasting more than 30 min. Alternatively, status epilepticus is considered when two or more seizures without full recovery of consciousness between any of them occur. Drugs used for the treatment of the status epilepticus are phenytoin, benzodiazepines, phenobarbital, and propofol, but new lines of treatment have been proposed. Propofol is useful during the acute phase but does not seem to be a good option for long-term seizure control, while phenytoin could aggravate the myoclonic seizures of some patients. Moreover, benzodiazepines are not a good option, because tonic seizures, a not uncommon type of seizure in the epileptic encephalopathies, could be iatrogenic. Some relatively more sophisticated agents, such as valproate, levetiracetam, and topiramate, may be considered a safer alternative [37]. Information on clinical trials is usually posted on the Internet at www.clinicaltrials.gov. It is a rule that all studies receiving U.S. Government funding, in addition to some supported by private companies, are posted on this government web site. New investigational therapies may include the gene-editing using CRISPR-Cas9, which is an acronym for clustered regularly interspaced short palindromic repeats (CRISPR) and CRISPR-associated protein [38, 39]. CRISPR-Cas9 is an editing tool of the genome that relies on a system identified in bacteria (prokaryotic organisms) in which bacteria use this system to defend themselves against viruses. This system snips out the virus DNA and maintains part of it behind to help the bacteria recognize it and protect against the infection next time it invades. Currently, CRISPR-Cas9 is a unique technology able to edit parts of the human genome other than prokaryotic genomes. It removes, adds, or alters sections of the DNA sequence utilizing two molecules that introduce a change into the DNA. Cas9, the first molecule, acts as a pair of "scissors" at the molecular level that can excise the two strands of DNA at an exact location in the genome with the purpose of fragments of DNA can then be added or removed according to the researcher. The second key molecule is called guide RNA, which is a small piece of the pre-designed RNA sequence of approximately 20 bases long located within a more extended RNA scaffold. The skeleton part attaches to the genomic DNA and the pre-designed sequence leads ('guides') Cas9 to the correct part of the genome. The 'guide' RNA makes sure that the Cas9 enzyme cuts at the right point in the genome, and the researcher can design the 'guide' RNA to find and bind to a specific sequence in the genomic DNA. More uniquely, the 'guide' RNA has RNA bases that are matching to those of the target DNA sequence in the human genome. This complementarity means that the 'guide' RNA will only tie exclusively to the target sequence and no other regions of the genome. CRISPR-Cas9 is not the buzz in the modern world of our century, but it has already practical consequences for humans. Different therapeutic approaches, although useful for some lysosomal storage disorders, may not be feasible in sialidosis, because of the advanced stage patients can present. Substantially, these alternative approaches include enzyme replacement therapy (ERT), substrate reduction therapy (SRT), *in vivo* gene therapy with adeno-associate viruses (AAV), allogeneic hematopoietic stem cell transplantation, *ex vivo* lentiviral modification of hematopoietic stem and progenitor cells. A clinical trial recently concluded (NCT00176917) evaluated the use of stem cell transplantation in mucolipidosis at the Masonic Cancer Center, University of Minnesota.

Conclusion

About forty years ago, Cantz et al., Durand et al., and Spranger et al., identified sialidosis, a metabolic disorder, which Pshezhetsky et al., characterized genetically cloning and mapping the human sialidase or NEU1. The importance of this disorder is now well known, and numerous mutations have been described. Moreover, the phenotype has been described in both children and adolescents, and, even in detail at the early appearance in the fetus as non-immunologic hydrops fetalis. A clinical trial using stem cell transplantation was concluded, and results seem promising. Still, the discovery of new molecular genetic techniques, such CRISPR-Cas9, may allow an impressive expansion of the venues related to the therapeutic platform in the future.

ACKNOWLEDGMENTS

This work is dedicated to Professors Cantz, Durand, and Spranger, who wisely investigated the biochemistry of challenging patients in a time where molecular biology knowledge of metabolic disorders was just initial. As a graduate from the Gaslini Children's Hospital (University of Genoa, Italy) with Prof. Durand as scientific director, and the Karls-Universität Heidelberg (Germany) with Prof. Cantz as a mentor, I consider crucial to remember these 'Fathers' of Pediatrics in 2020. I also dedicate this work to the memory of Steven Joy (1972-2019), a technician expert in ultrastructural investigations. Mr. Joy was a pillar for most of my electron microscopy studies in Alberta, Canada. Last October, he passed away prematurely. Our thoughts and prayers for him and his family at our Alberta Health Services facility of the University of Alberta Hospital.

REFERENCES

[1] Spranger, J; Wiedemann, HR; Tolksdorf, M; Graucob, E; Caesar, R. Lipomucopolysaccharidose. Eine neue Speicherkrankheit [Lipomucopolysaccharidosis, A new storage disease]. *Z. Kinderheilkd.* 1968, 103, 285-306.

[2] Berard, M; Toga, M; Bernard, R; Dubois, D; Mariani, R; Hassoun, J. Pathological findings in one case of neuronal and mesenchymal storage disease. Its relationship to lipidoses and to mucopolysaccharidoses. *Pathol. Eur.* 1968, 3, 172-183.

[3] Spranger, JW. Catabolic disorders of complex carbohydrates. *Postgrad. Med. J.* 1977, 53, 441-449.

[4] Cantz, M; Gehler, J; Spranger, J. Mucolipidosis I: increased sialic acid content and deficiency of an alpha-N-acetylneuraminidase in cultured fibroblasts. *Biochem. Biophys. Res.Commun.* 1977, 74, 732-738.

[5] Sphranger, J; Gehler, J; Cantz, M. Mucolipidosis I--a sialidosis. *Am. J. Med. Genet.* 1977, 1, 21-29.

[6] Durand, P; Gatti, R; Cavalieri, S; Borrone, C; Tondeur M; Michalski, JC; Strecker, G. Sialidosis (mucolipidosis I). *Helv. Paediatr. Acta.* 1977, 32, 391-400.

[7] Strecker, G; Peers, MC; Michalski, JC; Hondi-Assah, T; Fournet, B; Spik, G; Montreuil, J; Farriaux, JP; Maroteaux, P; Durand, P. Structure of nine sialyl-oligosaccharides accumulated in urine of eleven patients with three different types of sialidosis. Mucolipidosis II and two new types of mucolipidosis. *Eur. J. Biochem.* 1977, 75, 391- 403.

[8] Spranger, J; Cantz, M. Mucolipidosis I, the cherry red-spot--myoclonus syndrome and neuraminidase deficiency. *Birth Defects Orig. Artic. Ser.* 1978, 14, 105-112.

[9] Pshezhetsky, AV; Richard, C; Michaud, L; Igdoura, S; Wang, S; Elsliger, MA; Qu, J; Leclerc, D; Gravel, R; Dallaire, L; Potier, M. Cloning, expression and chromosomal mapping of human lysosomal sialidase and characterization of mutations in sialidosis. *Nat. Genet.* 1997,15, 316-320.

[10] Khan, A; Sergi, C. Sialidosis: A Review of Morphology and Molecular Biology of a Rare Pediatric Disorder. *Diagnostics (Basel).* 2018, 8, pii: E29.

[11] Bonten, EJ; Annunziata, I; d'Azzo, A. Lysosomal multienzyme complex: pros and cons of working together. *Cell Mol. Life Sci.* 2014, 71, 2017-2032.

[12] Lukong, KE; Seyrantepe, V; Landry, K; Trudel, S; Ahmad, A; Gahl, WA; Lefrancois, S; Morales, CR; Pshezhetsky, AV. Intracellular distribution of lysosomal sialidase is controlled by the internalization signal in its cytoplasmic tail. *J. Biol. Chem.* 2001, 276, 46172-46181.

[13] Pshezhetsky, AV; Ashmarina, M. Lysosomal multienzyme complex: biochemistry, genetics, and molecular pathophysiology. *Prog. Nucleic Acid Res. Mol. Biol.* 2001, 69, 81- 114.

[14] Achyuthan, KE; Achyuthan AM. Comparative enzymology, biochemistry and pathophysiology of human exo-alpha-sialidases

(neuraminidases). *Comp. Biochem. Physiol B. Biochem. Mol. Biol.* 2001, 129, 29-64.

[15] Pshezhetsky AV, Ashmarina M. Keeping it trim: roles of neuraminidases in CNS function. *Glycoconj. J.* 2018, 35, 375-386.

[16] Pan, X; De Aragao, CBP; Velasco-Martin, JP; Priestman, DA; Wu, HY; Takahashi, K; Yamaguchi, K; Sturiale, L; Garozzo, D; Platt, FM; Lamarche-Vane, N;Morales, CR; Miyagi, T; Pshezhetsky, AV. Neuraminidases 3 and 4 regulate neuronal function by catabolizing brain gangliosides. *FASEB. J.* 2017, 31, 3467-3183.

[17] Martins, C; Hulkova, H; Dridi, L; Dormoy-Raclet, V; Grigoryeva, L; Choi, Y; Langford- Smith, A; Wilkinson, FL; Ohmi, K; DiCristo, G; Hamel, E; Ausseil, J; Cheillan, D; Moreau, A; Svobodová, E; Hájková, Z; Tesařová, M; Hansíková, H; Bigger, BW; Hrebícek, M; Pshezhetsky, AV. Neuroinflammation, mitochondrial defects and neurodegeneration in mucopolysaccharidosis III type C mouse model. *Brain.* 2015, 138, 336-355.

[18] Seyrantepe, V; Iannello, A; Liang, F; Kanshin, E; Jayanth, P; Samarani, S; Szewczuk, MR; Ahmad, A; Pshezhetsky, AV. Regulation of phagocytosis in macrophages by neuraminidase 1. *J. Biol. Chem.* 2010, 285, 206-215.

[19] Liang, F; Seyrantepe, V; Landry, K; Ahmad, R; Ahmad, A; Stamatos, NM; Pshezhetsky, AV. Monocyte differentiation up-regulates the expression of the lysosomal sialidase, Neu1, and triggers its targeting to the plasma membrane via major histocompatibility complex class II-positive compartments. *J. Biol. Chem.* 2006, 281, 27526-27538.

[20] Bonten, E; van der Spoel, A; Fornerod, M; Grosveld, G; d'Azzo, A. Characterization of human lysosomal neuraminidase defines the molecular basis of the metabolic storage disorder sialidosis. *Genes Dev.* 1996, 10, 3156-3169.

[21] Lukong, KE; Elsliger, MA; Chang, Y; Richard, C; Thomas, G; Carey W; Tylki- Szymanska, A; Czartoryska, B; Buchholz, T; Criado, GR; Palmeri, S; Pshezhetsky, AV. Characterization of the sialidase molecular defects in sialidosis patients suggests the structural

organization of the lysosomal multienzyme complex. *Hum. Mol. Genet.* 2000, 9, 1075-1085.

[22] Bonten, EJ; Arts, WF; Beck, M; Covanis, A; Donati, MA; Parini, R; Zammarchi E; d'Azzo A. Novel mutations in lysosomal neuraminidase identify functional domains and determine clinical severity in sialidosis. *Hum. Mol. Genet.* 2000, 9, 2715-2725.

[23] Naganawa, Y; Itoh, K; Shimmoto, M; Takiguchi, K; Doi, H; Nishizawa, Y; Kobayashi, T; Kamei, S; Lukong, KE; Pshezhetsky, AV; Sakuraba, H. Molecular and structural studies of Japanese patients with sialidosis type 1. *J. Hum. Genet.* 2000, 45, 241-249.

[24] Lukong, KE; Landry, K; Elsliger, MA; Chang, Y; Lefrancois, S; Morales, CR; Pshezhetsky, AV. Mutations in sialidosis impair sialidase binding to the lysosomal multienzyme complex. *J. Biol. Chem.* 2001, 276, 17286-17290.

[25] Penzel, R; Uhl, J; Kopitz, J; Beck, M; Otto, HF; Cantz, M. Splice donor site mutation in the lysosomal neuraminidase gene causing exon skipping and complete loss of enzyme activity in a sialidosis patient. *FEBS. Lett.* 2001,501, 135-138.

[26] O'Regan, S; Traiffort, E; Ruat, M; Cha, N; Compaore, D; Meunier, FM. An electric lobe suppressor for a yeast choline transport mutation belongs to a new family of transporter- like proteins. *Proc. Natl. Acad. Sci. USA.* 2000, 97, 1835-1840.

[27] Ferguson, SM; Blakely, RD. The choline transporter resurfaces: new roles for synaptic vesicles? *Mol. Interv.* 2004, 4, 22-37.

[28] Song, P; Rekow, SS; Singleton, CA; Sekhon, HS; Dissen, GA; Zhou, M; Campling, B; Lindstrom, J; Spindel, ER. Choline transporter-like protein 4 (CTL4) links to non-neuronal acetylcholine synthesis. *J. Neurochem.* 2013, 126, 451-461.

[29] Yogalingam, G; Bonten, EJ; van de Vlekkert, D; Hu, H; Moshiach, S; Connell, SA; d'Azzo, A. Neuraminidase 1 is a negative regulator of lysosomal exocytosis. *Dev. Cell.* 2008, 15, 74-86.

[30] Dridi, L; Seyrantepe, V; Fougerat, A; Pan, X; Bonneil, E; Thibault, P; Moreau, A; Mitchell, GA; Heveker, N; Cairo, CW; Issad, T;

Hinek, A; Pshezhetsky, AV. Positive regulation of insulin signaling by neuraminidase 1. *Diabetes.* 2013, 62, 2338-2346.

[31] Schiesser, M; Sergi, C; Enders, M; Maul, H; Schnitzler, P. Discordant outcomes in a case of parvovirus b19 transmission into both dichorionic twins. *Twin. Res. Hum. Genet.* 2009, 12, 175-179.

[32] Sergi, C; Penzel, R; Uhl, J; Zoubaa, S; Dietrich, H; Decker, N; Rieger, P; Kopitz, J; Otto, HF; Kiessling, M; Cantz, M. Prenatal diagnosis and fetal pathology in a Turkish family harboring a novel nonsense mutation in the lysosomal alpha-N-acetyl-neuraminidase (sialidase) gene. *Hum. Genet.* 2001,109, 421-428.

[33] Paton, BC; Schneider-Jakob, HR; Kopitz, J; Harzer, K; Poulos, A; Cantz, M. Further evidence that human lysosomal sialidase is not derived from prosaposin. Prosaposin biosynthesis and ganglioside sialidase studies in prosaposin- and sialidase-deficient fibroblast lines. *Biol. Chem. Hoppe. Seyler.* 1994,375, 25-29.

[34] Schneider-Jakob, HR; Cantz, M. Lysosomal and plasma membrane ganglioside GM3 sialidases of cultured human fibroblasts. Differentiation by detergents and inhibitors. *Biol. Chem. Hoppe. Seyler.* 1991, 372, 443-450.

[35] Lieser, M; Harms, E; Kern, H; Bach, G; Cantz, M. Ganglioside GM3 sialidase activity in fibroblasts of normal individuals and of patients with sialidosis and mucolipidosis IV. Subcellular distribution and and some properties. *Biochem. J.* 1989, 260, 69-74.

[36] Sergi, C; Beedgen, B; Kopitz, J; Zilow, E; Zoubaa, S; Otto, HF; Cantz, M; Linderkamp, O. Refractory congenital ascites as a manifestation of neonatal sialidosis: clinical, biochemical and morphological studies in a newborn Syrian male infant. *Am. J. Perinatol.* 1999, 16, 133-141.

[37] Bragatti, JA; Torres, CM; Netto, CB; Vedolin, L; Garzon, E; Rieder, CR; Schwartz, IV; Bianchin, MM. Topiramate is effective for status epilepticus and seizure control in neuraminidase deficiency. *Arq. Neuropsiquiatr.* 2011, 69, 565-566.

[38] Zhang, Z; Ursin, R; Mahapatra, S; Gallicano, GI. CRISPR/CAS9 ablation of individual miRNAs from a miRNA family reveals their

individual efficacies for regulating cardiac differentiation. *Mech. Dev.* 2018, 150, 10-20.

[39] Tomberg, K; Westrick, RJ; Kotnik, EN; Cleuren, AC; Siemieniak, DR; Zhu, G; Saunders, TL; Ginsburg, D. Whole exome sequencing of ENU-induced thrombosis modifier mutations in the mouse. *PLoS Genet.* 2018, 14, e1007658.

In: Neurochemistry of Metabolic Diseases ISBN: 978-1-53618-339-9
Editor: Sankar Surendran

Chapter 3

MUCOPOLYSACCHARIDOSIS TYPE III (SANFILIPPO DISEASE) SUBTYPES A, B, C, D: MOLECULAR MECHANISM AND THERAPEUTIC EFFECT

Karolina Pierzynowska, Estera Rintz, Lidia Gaffke, Zuzanna Cyske, Magdalena Podlacha, Joanna Brokowska and Grzegorz Wegrzyn*

Department of Molecular Biology, University of Gdansk, Gdansk, Poland

ABSTRACT

Sanfilippo disease is also known as mucopolysaccharidosis type III (MPS III). This metabolic disorder belongs to the group of lysosomal storage disorders (LSD). The primary stored glycosaminoglycan (GAG) in MPS III is heparan sulfate (HS), though secondary storage of dermatan

* Corresponding Author's Email: grzegorz.wegrzyn@biol.ug.edu.pl.

sulfate (DS) has also been reported. There are four different genetic and biochemical conditions which are commonly called Sanfilippo syndrome due to very similar clinical symptoms and accumulation of HS as a primary storage material. These conditions, called subtypes A, B, C, and D of MPS III, are caused by mutations in *SGSH, NAGLU, HGSNAT,* and *GNS* resulting is deficiency of activity of heparan N-sulfatase, α-N-acetylglucosaminidase, acetyl-CoA: α-glucosaminide acetyltransferase, and N-acetylglucosamine-6-sulfatase, respectively. MPS III patients are asymptomatic, and the diagnosis is made usually at the age of about 4 years. Neurodegeneration is the major clinical problem in MPS III, and progressive cognitive deficiency and behavioral changes are characteristic symptoms in this disease. Currently, there is no cure for Sanfilippo disease. However, there are intensive studies devoted to develop effective therapeutic options for MPS III.

1. Introduction

Mutations in four different genes (*SGSH, NAGLU, HGSNAT,* and *GNS*), coding for four enzymes involved in degradation of heparan sulfate (HS), one of glycosaminoglycans (GAGs) (heparan N-sulfatase, α-N-acetylglucosaminidase, acetyl-CoA:α-glucosaminide acetyltransferase, and N-acetylglucosamine-6-sulfatase, respectively), cause the disease called Sanfilippo syndrome or mucopolysaccharidosis type III. Depending on the kind of genetic defect and deficiency of particular enzyme, four subtypes of MPS III are distinguished and called A, B, C, and D, respectively (Table 1). Clinically, all subtypes of MPS III are similar, with only some differences in the course of the disease which, however, need to be confirmed if they are specific to the subtype or particular mutations.

In 1963, Sylvester Sanfilippo et al. described clinical symptoms of mental retardation which were correlated with accumulation of HS [1]. The newly described disease has been, therefore, identified as the third type of mucopolysaccharidosis, and it is now known as MPS III or Sanfilippo syndrome, after the surname of the discoverer. Most probably, the disease of the patient described in the article by Sanfilippo et al. [1] should be classified as MPS IIIA. Nevertheless, it is possible that another patient, described in the literature two years before publication of the report by

Sanfilippo et al., suffered from MPS III rather than MPS I, as suggested by the authors [2]. Subsequent studies led to discovery of patients with HS storage in which symptoms were similar to those described by Sanfilippo et al. [1], but different enzymatic defects could be identified. Therefore, various genetically and biochemically identified diseases in which HS accumulates and is accompanied with severe mental and behavioral disorders have been classified as subtypes of MPS III, called MPS IIIB [3], MPS IIIC [4, 5], and MPS IIID [6].

Table 1. Subtypes of Sanfilippo disease (MPS III)

Disease	OMIM no.	Mutated gene	Deficient enzyme	Stored GAG
MPS IIIA	252900	*SGSH*	heparan N-sulfatase	HS (secondary DS storage)
MPS IIIB	252920	*NAGLU*	α-N-acetylglucosaminidase	HS (secondary DS storage)
MPS IIIC	252930	*HGSNAT*	acetylCoA:α-glucosaminide acetyltransferase	HS (secondary DS storage)
MPS IIID	252940	*GNS*	N-acetylglucosamine-6-sulfatase	HS (secondary DS storage)

2. Diagnostics

Despite resulting from four different genetic defects, all subtypes (A, B, C and D) of Sanfilippo disease are characterized with accumulation of HS in lysosomes and with similar clinical symptoms [7, 8, 9]. Therefore, symptoms and diagnostics of MPS III will be described together for all the disease subtypes.

2.1. Clinical Symptoms

The major clinical problems of patients suffering from Sanfilippo disease arose from gradual neurodegeneration which results in cognitive decline and other neurological dysfunctions. The most commonly occurring MPS III symptoms include cognitive decline, lack of speech/speech delay, developmental delay, seizures, hyperactivity, aggression-like behavior, and sleep disturbances. Each symptom can, however, be pronounced differentially in individual patients, ranging from mild to severe. Although somatic symptoms of MPS III are generally milder than in other MPS types, they can still be serious dysfunctions, significantly affecting functions of the organism. They include facial dysmorphology, hepatomegaly, frequent ear and respiratory system infections, scoliosis, kyphosis, lumbar lordosis, hip dysplasia, carpal tunnel syndrome, hirsutism, and low hair line. Changes in hair morphology are characteristic and easily visible under electron microscope. This feature has been suggested as a diagnostic marker [10, 11]. Two patients with Sanfilippo disease is shown in Figure 1.

The clinical course of Sanfilippo disease is specific. Patients are usually born asymptomatic [12, 13, 14, 15], and symptoms do not develop for several months or a few years [16]. Delayed cognitive development and speech deficiency are often the first clinical signals of the disease. Then, behavioral disorders become evident, initially without any deficits in physical performance. Progressive cognitive deterioration follows these symptoms and hyperactivity is more and more pronounced in time. Sleeping deficits become evident then. Aggressive-like behavior and reduced fear are very often pronounced [17]. The behavior of patients at this stage of the disease is similar to that of autistic children, and in fact, MPS III is sometimes misdiagnosed as autism spectrum disorder. The late phase of the disease consists of a decline in motor functions, dementia, spasticity and problems with swallowing. The average life span is between 2 and 3 decades.

It is worth noting that variability of MPS III symptoms is huge between patients. Apart from severe deterioration, reported for most of patients, considerably milder course of the disease has been described in the literature [18, 19]. As mentioned above, clinical symptoms of MPS III patients might be untypical which can lead to misdiagnosis, with autism and idiopathic developmental delay, attention deficit/hyperactivity disorder (ADHD) being incorrectly suspected [8, 20, 21, 22, 23, 24]. However, since symptoms of Sanfilippo syndrome are progressive, they become more specific at later stages of the disease [25].

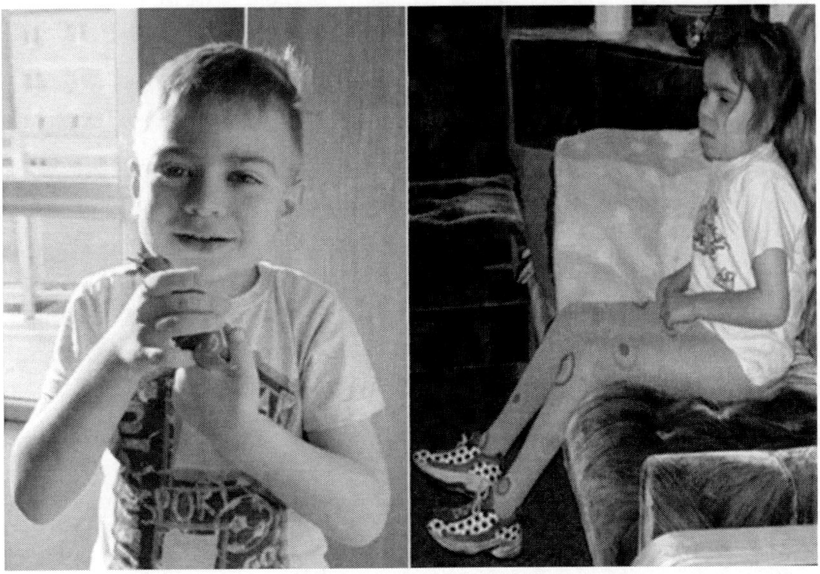

Figure 1. Patients with characteristic features of Sanfilippo disease.

2.2. Genetics

Four subtypes of MPS III (A, B, C, and D) are caused by mutations in following genes: *SGSH, NAGLU*, *HGSNAT* and *GNS*, respectively. These genes code for enzymes involved in HS degradation, heparan N-sulfatase, α-N-acetylglucosaminidase, acetyl-CoA:α-glucosaminide acetyltransferase, and N-acetylglucosamine-6-sulfatase, respectively (Table 1). Thus, detection of mutations in one of these genes is the simplest way for genetic diagnosis of Sanfilippo disease. Numbers of mutations reported for various subtypes of MPS III are different ranging from about 20 in subtype D, through about 70 I in subtype C, to over 150 in subtypes A and B [26]. Recent studies indicated that apart from specific mutations in *SGSH, NAGLU*, *HGSNAT* or *GNS*, expression of a large group of genes coding for proteins involved in various cellular processes is considerably changed in each MPS III subtype [27, 28, 29]. Therefore, it appears that impaired regulation of a battery of genes might contribute to development of secondary or tertiary changes in cellular processes, affecting physiology of cells and organs in Sanfilippo disease patients. Such dysregulations can significantly modulate the course of the disease due to disturbance of crucial cellular functions [30].

2.3. Stored Compounds

The primary biochemical defect in Sanfilippo disease is impaired degradation of HS [7, 8, 9]. This defect has been demonstrated in both animal models of MPS III and human patients [31, 32]. As the primary storage material, HS is considered to be the main biomarker for this disease. Nevertheless, secondary storage of dermatan sulfate (DS) [33] and globotriaosylsphingosine (LysoGb3) [34] has been reported. Although accumulation of DS and LysoGb3 may be important to understand details of MPS III pathomechanism, the use of these compounds as biomarkers is questionable.

For a quick diagnostic tests, semi-quantitative chromatographic methods are used for rough determination of HS levels in urine, or rarely in plasma. For more detailed studies, some more advanced methods can be used, like liquid chromatography/tandem mass spectrometry [35] other biochemical and biophysical approaches [36, 37, 38, 39, 40, 41, 42, 43, 44, 45]. In all subtypes of Sanfilippo disease the HS levels are similar, and any differences are perhaps related to severity of particular mutations [45]. When making diagnostic test, it is necessary to use age-related reference values, as it was shown that plasma and urinary HS levels decrease in age [36]. Interestingly, correlations between levels of HS in biological material (urine and plasma) and severity of the disease could be detected [18, 46]. Additional biomarkers of MPS III have been suggested which might facilitate to assess severity of the disease. They include changes in hair morphology, specific proteins, disability level, behavioral disturbances, and cognitive skills [11, 47, 48].

2.4. Biochemistry

To distinguish between particular MPS III subtypes, measurement of activities of four enzymes, heparan N-sulfatase, α-N-acetyl-glucosaminidase, acetyl-CoA:α-glucosaminide acetyltransferase, and N-acetylglucosamine-6-sulfatase, is used as the primary biochemical assay. As a standard, determination of these activities in extracts from leukocytes or cultured fibroblasts is used [49].

More advanced biochemical analyses of enyzmes may be crucial to understand genotype-phenotype correlations. For example, determination of the heparan N-sulfatase crystal structure facilitated prediction of severity of MPS IIIA [50]. Recommendations on laboratory diagnostics of MPS III include determination of HS levels in urine and/or plasma, then measurement the enzyme activity, followed by identification of mutations [51]. In addition, a computational algorithm also be useful in predicting effects of mutations at the protein level [52].

2.5. Radiology

In MPS III patients, neurological symptoms predominate while somatic changes are relatively mild relative to other MPS types. Nevertheless, radiological examination of patients may facilitate monitoring of the disease course and predicting severity. In fact, radiological studies indicated various abnormalities in structures of different organs in patients suffering from Sanfilippo syndrome. The most important ones are listed below.

Changes in teeth of MPS III patients consist of obliterated pulp chambers and root canals [53]. Osteonecrosis accompanied with femoral head and hip dysplasia may occur [54]. Tachypnea was demonstrated in some patients [55], as was precocious puberty in boys [56]. Changes in the brain include diffuse hypomyelination with thinning of the corpus callosum [57], which can suggest a possible mechanism of sleeping problems [58], compromised blood-brain-barrier integrity [59], and stunted growth [60].

3. Crucial Role of Heparan Sulfate in MPS III Pathogenesis

Because mutations causing Sanfilippo syndrome occur in genes coding for enzymes involved in degradation of HS (Table 1), lysosomal storage of this GAG is the primary cellular defect in this disease. Single catabolic pathway of HS degradation. However, the storage itself (and resultant dysfunction of lysosomes) is only partially responsible for appearance of MPS III symptoms. Recent studies demonstrated that non-degraded extracellular HS, as well as secondary effects of the storage, may contribute significantly to development of various dysfunction.

When normal neural cells were exposed to exogenous soluble HS fragments, activation of integrin-based focal adhesions could be observed which modulated the attachment of cells to the extracellular matrix [61]. Abnormal cell polarization and improperly oriented migration were also observed in these cells [61]. Moreover, accumulation of HS was suggested to be responsible for enhanced oxidative stress, microglial activation, and neurodegeneration [62].

It is also worth mentioning that the primary HS storage leads to a network of pathological cellular processed which result in secondary storage various compounds, including DS (another GAG), gangliosides, ceramides, galactosylceramides and sphingomyelin [63, 33, 34]. It is likely that these secondary effects induce cellular stress responses, leading to global changes in gene expression regulation which cause further disturbances in different cellular processes [27, 28, 29, 30], and subsequent neuroinflammation and neurodegeneration [64].

4. Animal Models

As in many genetic diseases, the most commonly used animal models in studies on Sanfilippo disease are mice. In the MPS IIIA mouse model, symptoms resembling MPS III patients are evident, including hyperactivity, rapid exploratory behavior, and reduced fear [65]. It was suggested that neuronopathy of these animals might be related to the observed impaired exocytosis [66]. Unexpectedly, significant differences were noted between male and female MPS IIIA mice [65], contrary to patients suffering from Sanfilippo syndrome A.

In the MPS IIIB mouse model, neuropathology was detected in both central and peripheral systems [67]. Symptoms resembles those occurring in human patients, including hyperactivity, progressive impairment in sensory functions and reduced response to pain stimulation [67, 68].

In the MPS IIIC mouse model, neuroinflammation and neuro degeneration have been described [69]. Moreover, dysmorphology of mitochondria was evident, and impaired energy metabolism was measured in cells [69].

Apart from mice, emu is employed as another animal model for MPS IIIB [70]. Symptoms observed in the birds well resemble those in humans and mice, indicating that the emu mode can also be useful in studies on this subtype of Sanfilippo disease [70].

5. Potential Therapeutic Approaches

Currently, no therapy is available for Sanfilippo disease [71]. However, there are various therapeutic approaches which were proposed and which are being tested. Various therapies are at different stages of research and tests, from *in vitro* studies, through experiments on animal models, to clinical trials. Below, they are summarized briefly, with a few most promising options discussed in somewhat more detail.

5.1. Enzyme Replacement Therapy (ERT)

Enzyme replacement therapy (ERT) consists of administration of human recombinant enzyme to patients lacking such protein due to mutations in corresponding gene. Since the most commonly used method of enzyme administration is intravenous injection, efficacy of ERT is generally restricted to somatic tissues and organs due to inefficient crossing the blood-brain-barrier by proteins. Therefore, serious problems were met in applying ERT as a therapy for MPS III in which neurodegeneration is the major problem [9].

There are various attempts to overcome this drawback of ERT. First, intrathecal or intra-spinal enzyme injection is possible. Experiments on animals suggested that this method of drug administration can be relatively safe [72] and allows for effective penetration of the enzyme to the brain [73, 74]. However, positive therapeutic effects could be observed mostly if ERT was started early, as efficacy in animals at advanced disease stages was low [75]. Fusion of the enzyme with a molecule that can naturally cross the blood-brain-barrier is another approach. For example, heparan N-sulfatase has been attached to a part of apolipoprotein B [76], α-N-acetylglucosaminidase was fused to the receptor-binding motif of insulin-like growth factor 2 [77, 78], and sulfamidase was bound to the insulin receptor antibody [79]. Below, recent reports on potential ERT for MPS III are summarized in somewhat more detail.

An approach involving the administration of an enzyme, sulfamidase, by injection into the cerebrospinal fluid (CSF) has been tested [74]. According to the authors of that report, the key parameter is the site of enzyme administration. Studies conducted on the MPS IIIA mouse model involving the administration of recombinant human sulfamidase (rhSGSH) by three different pathways (intrathecal lumbar, cisternal and ventricular) indicated that despite the highest invasiveness, the ventricular administration of the enzyme leads to the largest statistically significant decreases in substrate levels and reducing microglial activation. Single lumbar enzyme administration did not lead to reduction in substrate levels and gave poor effects on the improvement of morphology and physiology of nerve tissue [74]. Not only the exact site of administration but also the dose of the enzyme may be key to the effects of the treatment. That is why different doses of rhSGSH infused into CSF via the cisterna magna in MPS IIIA Huntaway dogs were tested [80]. The authors determined a dose- and frequency-dependent reduction in HS in the CSF and deeper layers of the cerebral cortex, improved lysosomal functionality as well as reduced activation of microglia and other inflammatory markers. The same team conducted a study on the effectiveness of sustained release of enzyme (delivered by an osmotic pump) in MPS IIIA mice [81]. During these studies, almost normalization of primary stored HS in both hemispheres of the brain and cervical spinal cord was observed, as was a reduction in the amount of secondary stored GM3 ganglioside markers and inflammatory markers [81]. This approach seemed to be important because of the limitation of frequent infusions in medical facilities in patients with MPS IIIA. Positive research results prompted the authors to test this approach using a SynchroMed II® pump attached to a spinal infusion cannula on the MPS IIIA canine model [82]. These studies have shown that the use of a slow infusion as well as the use a recombinant enzyme without pump, led to a significant reduction in HS levels, but it was less efficient in reducing secondary effects of the disease (activation of microglia or storage of GM3 ganglioside) [82]. One of the newest approaches is the use of chemically modified recombinant human sulfamidase (CM-rhSulfamidase) with disrupted glycans [83]. This enzyme exhibits reduced glycan receptor-mediated endocytosis which may indicate non-receptor mediated uptake by cells. CM-rhSulfamidase showed prolonged exposure in plasma and distribution to the brain, and was present in both vascular profiles and the brain parenchyma after intravenous administration. Studies on the mouse model of MPS IIIA indicated that weekly intravenous administration of this enzyme led to a decrease in HS concentration in CNS and improved the cognitive, motor and social activities of animals. The conducted research became the basis for the clinical trial initiated using this modified enzyme [83].

Recombinant human heparan N-sulfatase (rhHNS) bioavailability and efficiency experiments were also performed on the cynomolgus monkey

MPS IIIA model. Biodistribution of the enzyme by intrathecal and intravenous administration was determined in that study. Experimental trials indicated that the enzyme persisted in the tissues of the central nervous system after intrathecal administration, but not intravenous [84]. Another enzyme used in therapy for MPS IIIA was fused to monoclonal IgG antibody against mouse transferrin receptor (TfR), by which SGSH is transported to the brain. Intraperitoneal injections of cTfRMAb-SGSH for a period of 6 weeks led to a decrease in HS levels in the brain and liver and to increase in latency in the rotarod test of motor activity in male mice [85].

Two clinical trials with patients suffering from Sanfilippo type A have been stared or continued recently. One of them was an open-label, phase 1/2 dose-escalation, safety trial of intrathecal recombinant human heparan-N-sulfatase (rhHNS), administered via intrathecal drug delivery device (IDDD) (NCT01155778) [86]. Patients (n = 12) received different rhHNS concentrations (10, 45 or 90 mg) every month for half a year. All patients experienced adverse effects (10 patients reported strong adverse effects). None of these effects has been assessed as being related to the experimental therapy used. The results of this phase indicated general safety and good tolerance of rhHNS administered via IDDD. The treatment led to a statistically significant decrease in HS levels in CSF. However, the authors suggested caution in interpreting the results of the study due to the small size of the group subjected to the clinical trial [86]. Continuation of this study in the phase IIb randomized open-label trial (21 patients, 45 mg of rhHNS, administered every 2 weeks, every 4 week or no administration (control)) indicated a reduced level of HS in CSF and urine [87]. However, the assumed improvement in cognitive abilities was not achieved. Reported adverse effects that occurred during the clinical trial were mostly mild [87].

One of the newest enzyme replacement therapy for Sanfilippo type B is intracerebroventricular injection of BMN-250 which is a recombinant NAGLU enzyme consisting of human NAGLU fused with insulin-like growth factor 2 (IGF2). Studies on the efficiency of BMN-250 uptake carried out on lines of fibroblast, neurons, astrocytes and microglia showed a significant improvement in recombinant-enzyme uptake efficiency, relative to non-recombinant enzyme, in neurons and astrocytes [88]. Test performed on the *NAGLU*$^{-/-}$ mice indicated greater enzyme uptake and decreased levels of HS in the brain. Experimental dose-dependent biodistribution of NAGLU-IGF2 research show that 4-times administration of 100 ug BMN 250 (during the 2 weeks) led to uptake of enzyme in all cell types, broad biodistribution and above-normal NAGLU activity in neurons, leading to the removal of HS from cells and secondary effects associated with lysosome functions. This effect lasted about 28 days [89]. Subsequent studies, also conducted on the mouse model of MPS IIIB, aimed at comparing intracerebroventricular and intravenous supply of the enzyme showed limited benefits of intravenous administration compared to simultaneous intravenous and intracerebroventricular administration. This effect was probably due to the limited distribution of the enzyme to the vascular endothelial cells of the brain after intravenous administration without reaching the nerve cells [90]. Another approach for the treatment of MPS IIIB was tested in the experimental study in a mouse model *NAGLU*$^{-/-}$ in which mouse embryonic fibroblasts have been reprogrammed into iPSC cells and corrected *ex vivo* using a lentiviral vector to drive human *NAGLU* overexpression [91]. Enzyme activity was detected in almost all animals undergoing modified cell implantation. In the area of the transplanted brain, the authors observed a significant decrease in HS storage, no microglia activation, and reduced astrocyte activation [91].

The 1/2 phase of the clinical trial with SBC-103 (a recombinant human alpha-N-acetylglucosaminidase (rhNAGLU)), administered by intravenous infusion, ended in 2018. Safety and dose of the enzyme were evaluated on 11 patients. Serious adverse effects occurred in 3 patients, and 8 of them reported mild infusion-associated reactions what indicated a generally good tolerability of the drug. No clinical effects depending on the applied enzyme dose were observed. The decrease in HS in CSF in patients who received the enzyme was small [92].

5.2. Hematopoietic Stem Cell Therapy (HSCT)

Although hematopoietic stem cell therapy (HSCT) was found relatively effective in other MPS types, the use of this method in Sanfilippo disease is controversial. Despite some encouraging results were obtained with the MPS IIIB mouse model [93], no therapeutic effects could be observed in MPS III patients [94]. Namely, 2 cases of early (before onset of clinical neurological symptoms) bone marrow-derived hematopoietic stem cell transplantation (HSCT) in combination with the use of umbilical cord blood-derived hematopoietic stem cells (UCBT) in patients with MPS IIIA and IIIB have been described. Although the transplantation was successful, both patients showed significant deterioration of neurological function and behavior, without lowering HS levels in CSF [94]. Allogeneic hematopoietic cell transplantation (HCT) tests for MPS have been carried out in accordance with the new international HCT guidelines. 62 patients participated in that study, 2 of whom suffered from Sanfilippo disease. The results of these tests indicated that matched unrelated cord blood donors should be preferred donors for HCT compared to matched unrelated donors or noncarrier matched sibling donors. The authors also point out the need for newborn screening because younger age of the transplant procedure is associated with reduction of HCT-related toxicity [95]. However, a proof of efficacy of HCT in MPS III remains lacking. Thus, one can conclude that this therapeutic approach (HSCT or HCT) appears ineffective in Sanfilippo disease while the reason of such a poor response to the treatment, relative to other MPS types, remains unclear.

5.3. Gene Therapy

Gene therapy was called a hope for patients suffering from various inherited diseases [96]. Regarding Sanfilippo disease, positive effects of gene therapy have been demonstrated first in studies on MPS IIIA mice [97]. Then, improved behavior of mice was reported after administration of a viral vector carrying a modified *SGSH* gene [76]. In MPS IIIB mouse model, combination of different viral vectors carrying a recombinant *NAGLU* gene resulted in significant improvement of symptoms, including longer life span [98]. The next step was positive verification of safety of gene therapy with experiments on nonhuman primates after administration of a viral vector with the human *NAGLU* gene [99].

The first clinical trial on gene therapy for MPS III was performed with an adeno-associated viral vector bearing the *SGSH* gene [100]. Four MPS IIIA patients were treated. The administration procedure was relatively well tolerated, but improvement in symptoms was negligible [100]. Since recent years were quite rich in studies on gene therapy in Sanfilippo disease, and the results are promising, this topic will be discussed in some more details below.

Among vectors used to deliver therapeutic DNA to cells, retroviruses, lentiviruses, adenoviruses, and adeno-associated viruses (AAV) are commonly used. However, AAV-based ones appear to be the most promising. Typical AAV-based therapeutic tool is a non-enveloped virus lacking any viral genes and containing DNA sequences of interest. Several serotypes of AAV vectors have been developed which differ from each other in levels of transduction and cellular tropism [101]. The use of AAV vectors has been proven to be one of the safest and most effective strategies for gene therapies [102]. One of the most promising approach is the use of recombinant AAV serotype 9 vector (AAV9) encoding a missing enzyme that is delivered directly to the cerebrospinal fluid (CSF) of mice. Experiments on MPS IIIB [103] as well as MPS IIID mice [104] resulted in normalization of GAG content, gaining NAGLU or GNS enzyme activity, and reduction of lysosomal pathology, including cessation of neuroinflammation. The treatment restored the pattern of gene expression in the brain like in healthy animals, behavioral changes diminished, and extending lifespan of affected animals was evident. Moreover, after single intra-CSF administration of NAGLU-coding AAV9 vector into MPS IIIB canine model, levels of enzymatic activity in CSF were similar in dogs with and without preexisting immunity. The presence of circulating antibodies did not impact NAGLU transgene articulation in

CSF, which is a strong advantage over other methodologies dependent on systemic delivery of vectors [Ribera et al. 2015]. A clinical trial phase-I/II, with dose escalation study of ABO-101 (AAV9-NAGLU), has been approved. Moreover, orphan drug designation has been acknowledged to this therapeutic approach [105].

There is also intravenous AAV9 vector delivery approach, based on the ability of the vector to cross blood-brain-barrier, which provided widespread of enzyme in CNS. Safe profile in non-human primates at the designed minimal efficacious clinical dose, $2x10^{13}$ vg/kg systemically injected, has been reported [106]. However, a dose-dependent, sex-associated and genotype-specific acute severe liver toxicity was observed at a high dose (2×10^{14}vg/kg) in mice, probably because of transgene overexpression in liver. Two doses (1×10^{14}vg/kg and 2×10^{14}vg/kg) of rAAV9-CMV-hNAGLU vector in MPSIIIB mice were tested in GLP-compliant toxicology/biodistribution study [106]. After 6 months of administration, neither adverse signs nor toxicity were observed, in spite of the fact that one mouse had liver pallor after underwent necropsy, 5 days post injection. Even though antibodies against AAV9 and NAGLU were detected, they did not affect enzyme activity. In order to test how intravenous injection, affect pre-symptomatic MPS IIIB mice, 5×10^{12} vg/kg rAAV9-CMV-hNAGLU vector virions were administrated at the age of 1 month [107]. Major metabolite abnormalities were corrected, while some of them were even 'over-corrected' [107].

In order to address a limitation of preexisting Ab, or repeat administration of vector, an alternate vector was constructed, using self-complementary (sc) AAVrh74-hSGSH vector with ability to cross the blood-brain-barrier. This vector, containing human sulfoglucosamine sulfohydrolase (SGSH) gene, was administrated to MPSIIIA mice by an intravenous injection. Results indicated restoration of SGSH activity and reduction in GAG storage with improved behavioral performance, and extended survival. Moreover, it has been shown that AAVrh74-hSGSH vector administration led to correction of majority of the transcriptional abnormalities in the brain and blood [108]. Previously, in studies with MPSIIIA mice, conventional single-stranded rAAV9 vector with stronger promoter was used with similar therapeutic effect at the dose ~10-fold higher [97]. This indicated that using self-complementary AAVrh74-hSGSH vector system can have higher transduction efficiency at lower doses [108]. Another approach using self-complementary adeno-associated virus serotype 9 (scAAV9) was employed in MPS IIIA mice, where authors tested 10 days treatment at different stages of disease at the age of 1, 2, 3, 6 and 9 months [109]. In every group, GAG storage in CNS was improved, while lifespan was normalized only among animals that received treatment at the age of 1, 2 and 3 months. These mice showed improved behavior, reduced lysosomal GAG storage and neuroinflammatation. At later stages of the disease, therapy was not as effective as when administrated at early stages of Sanfilippo IIIA disease [109]. As intravenous vector delivery seems to be one of the less invasive way, there is ongoing clinical trial phase I/II with one injection of self-complementary adeno-associated virus serotype 9 (scAAV9) carrying the human *SGSH* gene, for MPS IIIA with three different doses in order to check safety and efficiency [NCT02716246, www.clinicaltrials. Gov; date last accessed March 23 2020].

Interestingly, comparing transduction of different serotypes of recombinant adeno-associated viruses (rAAV) in MPS IIIB, it has been shown that although all serotypes performed comparably, some differences were observed in certain focal areas. When administered bilaterally into the thalamus, rAAV serotypes 8 and 9 proved to be superior to AAV5 and rh10, both in biodistribution and transduction efficiency profiles. Particularly, authors infer that AAV8, and to a lesser extent AAV9, represented best candidates for early gene therapy treatment of MPS [110]. Then, AVV serotypes 5, 8, 9 and rh10 were injected intra-parenchymally into MPSIIIB mice brain. It has been noticed that AAV8 was more efficient than others for gene delivery to most brain structures such as cerebral cortex, hippocampus and thalamus. Moreover, AAV8 had demonstrated improved transduction of *NAGLU* compering to healthy littermates [111]. To enhance neurotropism of recombinant adeno-associated viruses (AVVs), alternative capsid engineering has been developed [112]. Generated AAV-TT vector displayed strong neurotropism and showed more efficient transduction of photoreceptors compared to AAV2 vector in rodents. It was the only vector that administrated at low doses was able to correct neurological phenotype and lysosomal storage in the MPS IIIC mouse model [112].

On the contrary, there was intraparenchymal administration of a gene vector (AAVrh10-SGSH-IRES-SUMF1) into pre-symptomatic MPSIIIA mice (5-week old) [113]. After this administration, catabolism of HS has been improved, and reduced neuroinflammatory activation of microglia was observed, as was decreased secondary subtracted storage accumulation. Since those improvements were observed only close to the injection site, multi-site injection would be necessary in order to achieve therapeutically meaningful CNS transduction of a vector. In fact, uncontrolled clinical trial phase 1/2 was performed for intracerebral gene therapy of MPS IIIB with multi-site injection of rAAV2/5 vector bearing the *NAGLU* gene. The vector was endured and sustained enzyme production in the brain, with best results in younger patients [114].

Another approach was to modify AAVrh10 vector in a way to improve SGSH enzyme activity in MPS IIIA mice. First, the murine phosphoglycerate kinase (PGK) promoter was replaced with promoter of a chicken beta actin/CMV composite (CAG) promotor (SAF302). Second, sulfatase modifying factor 1 (SUMF1) was removed. Then, three different vectors were injected intracranially to MPS IIIA mice. Removal of SUMF1 have not make significant difference while promotor exchange has increased the amount of SGSH expressed in the brain. However, single injection of the vector led to distribution of the enzyme only in the brain area of the injection [115].

An alternative method for the treatment of MPS IIIB was experimental therapy with a mouse model *NAGLU*$^{-/-}$ in which mouse embryonic fibroblasts have been reprogrammed into iPSC cells and corrected *ex vivo* using a lentiviral vector driving human *NAGLU* overexpression [116]. Enzyme activity was detected in almost all animals undergoing modified cell implantation. In the area of the transplanted brain, a significant decrease in HS storage, no microglia activation, and reduced astrocyte activation was observed [116]. Using lentiviral vector and the myeloid-specific CD11b promoter, driving the expression of *NAGLU* an *ex vivo* haematopoietic stem cell gene therapy was developed in mouse model of MPS IIIB [117]. The treatment led to behavioral correction, normalization of HS levels, reduction of inflammatory cytokine expression, and correction of neuroinflammation [117].

5.4. Substrate Reduction Therapy (SRT)

Substrate reduction therapy (SRT) in MPS is based on inhibition of GAG synthesis, thus, a balance between production and degradation of these compound can be restored [118]. Small RNA molecules were used to inhibit expression of genes coding for enzymes involved in GAG synthesis. Specific siRNA or shRNA molecules which impaired expression of such genes were used to reduce GAG levels effectively in MPS IIIA and IIIB cells [119, 120]. More recent studies tested the use of siRNA to silence the genes encoding the enzymes involved in the GAG synthesis, EXTL2 and EXTL3, in MPS IIIC. The results indicated inhibition of GAG synthesis after 3 days of the treatment and a reduction in the level of HS after 2 weeks [121]. Despite positive effects in experiments on cellular models of MPS III, the major problem in the therapeutic use of small RNAs is effective delivery of these molecules into patients' cells.

Two small molecules which can cross the blood-brain-barrier, rhodamine B ((9-(2-carboxyphenyl)-6-diethylamino-3-xanthenylidene)-dimethyl ammonium chloride) and genistein (5, 7-dihydroxy-3- (4-hydroxyphenyl)-4*H*-1-benzopyran-4-one), were proposed to be used for SRT in MPS III. Rhodamine B caused impaired HS synthesis in MPS IIIA cells *in vitro* [122]. Experiments on MPS IIIA mice revealed a rhodamine B-mediated decrease in HS storage and improved animal behavior [123]. This treatment appeared to be safe for mice [124]. It was proposed that this compound can act through down-regulation of expression of GAG synthesis-related genes [125].

Genistein was found to be a GAG synthesis inhibitor [126]. This isoflavone blocks epidermal growth factor receptor, causing a decreased efficiency of signal transduction which is necessary for activation of expression of genes coding enzymes involved in GAG production [127]. Importantly, genistein crosses the blood-brain-barrier [128].

Various groups have demonstrated impaired GAG synthesis in genistein-tretaed MPS (types I, II, IIIA, IIIB, VII) and mucolipidosis type II cells [126, 127, 129, 130, 131, 132], while contradictory results were also published [133]. On the other hand, flavonoid-rich extracts from *Medicago sativa* has been reported to reduce GAG levels in MPS III cells [134], corroborating results of the former reports. Surprisingly, genistein has also been found as a factor stimulating expression of genes coding for lysosomal enzymes through activation of transcription factor EB [135]. Recently, a study on the effect of cyclodextrin encapsulation on the efficiency of genistein and daidzein on reducing the efficiency of GAG synthesis was conducted. Both pure isoflavones and their co-ground cyclodextrin complexes reduced GAG levels without any observed cytotoxicity effects [136].

Experiments with the mouse model of Sanfilippo syndrome B indicated reduction of GAG storage in somatic organs and the brain [137, 138]. Behavior of animals was completely corrected [138]. Intriguingly, decreased GAG storage was reported also in genistein-treated MPS II mice [139] but not in MPS I mice [140].

Preliminary clinical studies with the use of genistein demonstrated a decreasd GAG storage in MPS II, IIIA and IIIB patients, and improved cognitive abilities, behavior, and sleeping [141, 142, 143, 144], while another study reported a lack of positive effects [145]. On the other hand, statistically significant decrease in plasma and urinary GAG levels was shown in genistein-treated MPS III patients during a randomized, crossover, placebo-controlled trial [146]. Genistein was shown to be safe in in a long-term treatment [147].

Table 2. Therapeutic strategies for MPS III – Summary of recent studies

Therapeutic strategy	Drug/compound	Sanfilippo disease subtype	Used model	Results	Reference
Enzyme replacement therapy	rhSGSH	A	cynomolgus monkeys	relatively safe	[72]
	rhSGSH	A	dog	effective penetration of the enzyme to the brain	[73]
	rhSGSH	A	mouse	effective penetration of the enzyme to the brain	[74]
	rhSGSH	A	mouse	efficacy in animals at advanced disease stages was low efficacy	[75]
	rhNAGLU-ApoB	B	mouse	improvement of brain pathology, recovery of a normal behavioral phenotype	[76]
	rhNAGLU-IGF-II	B	patients' cell lines	GAG storage was reduced	[77]
	rhNAGLU-IGF-II	B	mouse	reduction in HS levels in brain, reduced secondary accumulation	[78]
	rhSGSH-IGF-II	A	mouse	reduction in HS levels in CSF and microglial activation (after ventricular administration)	[79]
	rhSGSH	A	Huntaway dogs	reduction in HS levels in CSF and cerebral cortex and reduction in activation of microglia, improvement of lysosomal functions (CSF infusion)	[80]
	rhSGSH (osmotic pump)	A	mouse	reduction in HS levels in SCF and cortex as well as GM3 ganglioside levels and inflammatory markers	[81]
	rhSGSH (SynchroMed II® pump)	A	Huntaway dogs	reduction in HS in CSF and small efficient in reducing GM3 ganglioside levels and microglia activation	[82]

Table 2. (Continued)

Therapeutic strategy	Drug/compound	Sanfilippo disease subtype	Used model	Results	Reference
Enzyme replacement therapy	CM-rhSulfamidase	A	mouse	reduction in HS levels in CNS and improvement of the cognitive, motor and social activity (after intravenous administration)	[83]
	rhHNS	A	Cynomolgus monkeys	biodistribution of the enzyme for CNF cells is more effective after intrathecal compare to intravenous administration	[84]
	cTfRMAb-SGSH	A	mouse	reduction in HS levels in the brain and liver, increase of latency in rotarod test of motor activity (after intraperitoneal injections)	[85]
	rhHNS (delivered by IDDD)	A	patients	well-toleration rhHNS administered via IDDD, reduction on HS levels in CSF	[86]
	rhHNS (delivered by IDDD)	A	patients	reduction in HS levels in CSF and urine, lack of improvement in cognitive abilities	[87]
	BMN 250	B	patients' cell lines	improvement in enzyme uptake efficiency in neurons and astrocytes	[88]
	BMN 250	B	mouse	high efficiency enzyme uptake, reduction in HS levels, improvement of lysosome functions (after intracerebroventricular administration)	[89]
	BMN 250	B	mouse	limited benefits of intravenous administration compared to simultaneous intravenous and intracerebroventricular administration	[90]
	SBC 103	B	patients	well-toleration therapy for patients, insignificant reduction of HS in CSF	[92]

Therapeutic strategy	Drug/compound	Sanfilippo disease subtype	Used model	Results	Reference
Hematopoietic stem cell therapy	HCT	B	mouse	improved disease outcomes	[93]
	combination of HSCT and UCBT (early therapy)	A and B (case reports)	patients	lack of reduction of HS levels in CSF, lack of improvement of neurological function and behavior	[94]
	HCT	unknown	patients	preferred donor for HCT is matched unrelated cord blood donor, reduction of HCT-related toxicity in young age patients	[95]
Gene Therapy	Intra-CSF administration				
	rAAV9-NAGLU	B	mouse	reduction in HS levels, NAGLU or GNS enzyme activity and lysosomal pathology, also neuroinflammation was normalized	[103]
	rAAV9-NAGLU	B	dogs with/without preexisting immunity	levels of enzymatic activity in CSF were similar in dogs with/without preexisting immunity	[103]
	rAAV9-NAGLU	D	mouse	reduction in HS levels, GNS enzyme activity and lysosomal pathology, also neuroinflammation was normalized	[104]
	Intravenous injection				
	AAV2/8- SGSH	A	mouse	improved behavior of mice	[76]
	AAV9- SGSH	A	mouse	reduction in GAG levels in CNS and peripheral tissues	[97]
	rAAV9-hNAGLU	B	nonhuman primates	safety of gene therapy	[99]
	rAAV9-CMV-hNAGLU	B	mouse	no adverse signs were observed nor toxicity	[106]

Table 2. (Continued)

Therapeutic strategy	Drug/compound	Sanfilippo disease subtype	Used model	Results	Reference
Gene therapy	rAAV9-CMV-hNAGLU	B	mouse	metabolite abnormalities were corrected	[107]
	scAAVrh74-hSGSH	A	mouse	restoration of SGSH activity and GAG storage, improved behavioral performance, extended survival	[108]
	scAAV9	A	mouse	improved GAG storage in CNS, normalized lifespan	[109]
	lentiviral vector and the myeloid-specific CD11b promoter with NAGLU expression	B	mouse	behavioral correction, normalization of HS level, reduced inflammatory cytokine expression, reduced neuroinflammatory and lysosomal compartment size	[117]
	scAAV9	A	clinical trial phase I/II	Trial is ongoing, no results available yet	NCT02716246, www.clinicaltrials. Gov
	Intra-brain injection				
	combined neonatal intracranial AAV and systemic lentiviral gene therapy	B	mouse	significant improvement of symptoms, including longer life span	[98]
	AAVrh-SGSH	A	clinical trial phase I/II	well tolerated, but improvement in symptoms was negligible	[100]

Therapeutic strategy	Drug/compound	Sanfilippo disease subtype	Used model	Results	Reference
Gene therapy	Intra-brain injection				
	rAAV serotypes, -5, -8, -9 and -rh10, administered bilaterally into the thalamus	B	mouse	AAV8 and -9 superior in biodistribution and transduction efficiency profiles	[110]
	AVV serotypes -5, -8, -9 and -rh10 intraparenchymal injected	B	mouse	AAV8 more efficient than others for gene delivery to most brain structures and improved transduction in NAGLU	[111]
	AAVrh10-SGSH-IRES-SUMF1, Intracerebral injections	A	mouse	improved catabolism of HS, reduced neuroinflammatory activation of microglia and secondary subtracted storage accumulation	[113]
	lentiviral vector with NAGLU overexpression	B	mouse embryonic fibroblasts have been reprogrammed into iPSC cells	reduction in HS levels, no microglia activation, reduced astrocyte activation	[116]
	AAV-TT, Intracranial injections	C	mouse	administrated at low doses is able to correct neurological phenotype and lysosomal storage	[112]
	Three modified AAVrh10 vectors intracranial injection	A	mouse	promotor exchange has increased the amount of SGSH expressed in the brain	[115]

Table 2. (Continued)

Therapeutic strategy	Drug/compound	Sanfilippo disease subtype	Used model	Results	Reference
Substrate reduction therapy	siRNA for EXTL2 and EXTL3	C	patients' cell lines	inhibition of GAG synthesis, reduction in the level of HS storage	[121]
	rhodamine B	A	patients' cell lines	impaired HS synthesis	[122]
	rhodamine B	A	mouse	decrease in HS storage and improved animal behavior	[123]
	rhodamine B	A	mouse	safe treatment	[124]
	rhodamine B	-	chondrocyte monolayer cell culture	down-regulation of expression of GAG synthesis-related genes	[125]
	genistein	A, B	patients' cell lines	GAG synthesis inhibition	[126]
	genistein	A, B	patients' cell lines	blocking epidermal growth factor receptor	[127]
	genistein	A, B	patients' cell lines	impaired GAG synthesis	[129, 130]
	genistein	-	Cell lines	stimulating expression of genes coding for lysosomal enzymes through activation of transcription factor EB	[135]
	cyclodextrin encapsulation of genistein and daidzein	unknown	patients' cell lines	reduction of GAG levels by both pure isoflavones and their co-ground cyclodextrin complexes	[136]
	genistein	B	mouse	reduction of GAG storage in somatic organs and the brain	[137, 138]

Therapeutic strategy	Drug/compound	Sanfilippo disease subtype	Used model	Results	Reference
Substrate reduction therapy	genistein	B	mouse	behavior of animals was completely corrected	[138]
	genistein	A, B	preliminary clinical studies	decreasd GAG storage	[143, 144]
	genistein	all	patients	lack of positive effects with low dose	[145]
	genistein	all	randomized controlled crossover trial	decrease in GAG levels in urine and plasma, no effects on total behavior scores	[146]
	genistein	all	patients	high dose is safe in a long-term treatment	[147]
Other therapies	miglustat	A	mouse	improved learning and some biochemical parameters	[150]
	miglustat	A	patients	no improvement	[151]
	Coenzyme Q_{10}	A, B	cell lines	Reduced GAG levels and enhanced exocytosis is some cell lines	[152]
	U1 snRNAs		cell lines	increased activity of the deficient enzyme	[153]
	five non-aminoglycoside compounds	B, C	patients' cell lines	some compounds causing an increase in the deficient enzyme activities	[154]
	trehalose	B	mouse	prolonged life span, reduced hyperactivity and anxiety, reduction of neuroinflammation in the brain and retina	[156]

5.5. Other Therapies

There were also other therapeutic approaches tested for Sanfilippo syndrome. An inhibitor of glycosphingolipid synthesis, miglustat (*N*-1-butyl-2-(hydroxymethyl) piperidine-3,4,5-triol or N-butyldeoxynojiri-mycin), which is a drug registered for therapy of Gaucher disease and Niemann-Pick disease type C [148, 149], was assessed. MPS IIIA mice treated with this compound revealed improved learning and some biochemical parameters [150], but no improvement was observed in MPS III patients [151].

Coenzyme Q_{10} (CoQ_{10}) was tested in experiments with MPS IIIA and MPS IIIB fibroblasts, and some positive effects were reported, though the results were different for different cell lines [152]. This research line needs further studies to assess CoQ10 supplementation as a putative treatment option in Sanfilippo disease.

Since in patients suffering from MPS IIIC, many mutations have been mapped to conserved donor or acceptor splice sites, it was suggested that medication of the splicing process might have therapeutic effects [153]. Therefore, modified U1 snRNAs which can recognize mutated donor sites have been designed and tested in cellular models to assess their potential to re-establish normal splicing. In fact, correctly spliced molecules could be detected in this system, suggesting that modified U1 snRNAs might have a therapeutic potential [153]. In the case of a mutation in the acceptor splice site, a molecular chaperone – glucosamine – has been used, and increased activity of the deficient enzyme could be detected relative to non-treated cells [153]. These approaches indicate that the use of modified U1 snRNAs and molecular chaperones might be considered in further works on developing drugs for MPS III where splice site mutations occur.

If non-sense mutation is responsible for a disease, one of potential therapeutic options is the use of compounds which are able to cause stop codon read through. Different kinds of such molecules, including gentamycin, geneticin and five non-aminoglycoside compounds, were tested in experiments of cells derived from patients suffering from Sanfilippo disease types B and C [154]. The obtained results were different from different compounds, some causing an increase in the deficient enzyme activities by 1.5-2-fold, while some showing no significant effects [154]. Thus, this type of therapy has some potential in treatment of MPS III, but improvement of efficiency is necessary before it can be considered for clinical use.

Finally, it was suggested recently that stimulation of autophagy, a cellular process devoted to degradation of damaged or unwanted macromolecules and organelles, might be a potential therapeutic approach for MPS [155]. Indeed, one of autophagy inducers, trehalose, has been tested in MPS IIIB mice, and the results were encouraging. Namely, life span of animals was prolonged, hyperactivity was reduced, as was anxiety, and reduction of neuroinflammation in the brain and retina was evident [156]. This work indicated a novel opportunity is searching for effective therapy of Sanfilippo disease.

CONCLUSION

Sanfilippo syndrome (or MPS III) is a severe disease caused be HS storage resulting from mutations in one of genes (SGSH, NAGLU, HGSNAT or GNS) coding enzymes involved in degradation of this GAG. Diagnostics of MPS III is based on assessment of clinical phenotypes, determination of GAG levels in urine and/or plasma, measurement of the activities of relevant enzymes, and identification of mutations in corresponding genes. No therapy is currently available for this disease, but there are various approaches to find effective treatment. The therapeutic strategies for MPS III, and results of recent studies, are summarized in Table 2.

ACKNOWLEDGMENTS

This work was supported by Fundacja Sanfilippo (Poland) and National Science Center (Poland) (grants no 2017/25/B/NZ2/00414 and 2018/29/N/NZ2/00802).

CONFLICT OF INTEREST

The authors declare no conflict of interest.

REFERENCES

[1] Sanfilippo, SJ; Podosin, R; Langer, L; Good, RA. Mental retardation associated with acid mucopolysacchariduria (heparitin sulfate type). *J. Pediatr.* 1963, 63, 837-838.

[2] Harris, RC. Mucopolysaccharide disorder: a possible new genotype of Hurler's syndrome. *Am. J. Dis. Child.* 1961, 102, 741.

[3] O'Brien, JS. Sanfilippo syndrome: profound deficiency of alpha-acetylglucosaminidase activity in organs and skin fibroblasts from type-B patients. *Proc. Nat. Acad. Sci. USA.* 1972, 69, 1720-1722.

[4] Kresse, H; von Figura, K; Bartsocas, C. Clinical and biochemical findings in a family with Sanfilippo disease, type C. (Abstract) *Clin. Gene.* 1976, 10, 364.

[5] Klein, U; Kresse H; von Figura, K. Sanfilippo syndrome type C: deficiency of acetyl-CoA: alpha-glucosaminide N-acetyltransferase in skin fibroblasts. *Proc. Nat. Acad. Sci. USA.* 1978, 75, 5185-5189.

[6] Kresse, H; Paschke, E; von Figura, K; Gilberg W; Fuchs W. Sanfilippo disease type D: deficiency of N-acetylglucosamine-6-sulfate sulfatase required for heparan sulfate degradation. *Proc. Nat. Acad. Sci. USA.* 1980, 77, 6822-6826.

[7] Valstar, MJ; Ruijter GJ; van Diggelen OP; Poorthuis BJ; Wijburg FA. Sanfilippo syndrome: a mini-review. *J. Inherit. Metab. Dis.* 2008, 31, 240-252.

[8] Wijburg, FA; Wegrzyn G; Burton BK; Tylki-Szymanska A. Mucopolysaccharidosis type III (Sanfilippo syndrome) and misdiagnosis of idiopathic developmental delay, attention deficit/hyperactivity disorder or autism spectrum disorder. *Acta Paediatr.* 2013, 102, 462-470.

[9] Gilkes, JA; Heldermon CD. Mucopolysaccharidosis III (Sanfilippo Syndrome)- disease presentation and experimental therapies. *Pediatr. Endocrinol. Rev.* Suppl 1, 2014, 1, 133-140.

[10] Malinowska, M; Jakobkiewicz-Banecka, J; Kloska, A; Tylki-Szymanska, A; Czartoryska, B; Piotrowska, E; Wegrzyn, A; Wegrzyn, G. Abnormalities in the hair morphology of patients with some but not all types of mucopolysaccharidoses. *Eur. J. Pediatr.* 2008, 167, 203-209.

[11] Narajczyk, M.; Tylki-Szymanska, A; Wegrzyn, G. Changes in hair morphology as a biomarker in gene expression-targeted isoflavone therapy for Sanfilippo disease. *Gene.* 2012, 504, 292-295.

[12] Valstar, MJ; Neijs, S; Bruggenwirth, HT; Olmer, R; Ruijter, G; Wevers, RA; van Diggelen, OP; Poorthuis, BJ; Halley DJ; Wijburg, FA. Mucopolysaccharidosis type IIIA: clinical spectrum and genotype-phenotype correlations. *Ann. Neurol.* 2010, 68, 876-887.

[13] Valstar, MJ; Bruggenwirth, HT; Olmer, R; Wevers, RA; Verheijen, FW; Poorthuis, BJ; Halley DJ; Wijburg, FA. Mucopolysaccharidosis type IIIB may predominantly present with an attenuated clinical phenotype. *J. Inherit. Metab. Dis.* 2010, 33, 759-767.

[14] Ruijter, GJ; Valstar, MJ; van de Kamp, JM; van der Helm, RM; Durand, S; van Diggelen, OP; Wevers, RA; Poorthuis, BJ; Pshezhetsky, AV; Wijburg, FA. Clinical and genetic spectrum of Sanfilippo type C (MPS IIIC) disease in The Netherlands. *Mol. Genet. Metab.* 2008, 93, 104-111.

[15] Malm, G; Mansson, JE. Mucopolysaccharidosis type III (Sanfilippo disease) in Sweden: clinical presentation of 22 children diagnosed during a 30-year period. *Acta. Paediatr.* 2010, 99, 1253-1257.

[16] Andrade, F; Aldamiz-Echevarria, L; Llarena M; Couce ML. Sanfilippo syndrome: Overall review. *Pediatr. Int.* 2015, 57, 331-338.

[17] Grant, S; Cross, E; Wraith, JE; Jones, S; Mahon, L; Lomax, M; Bigger B; Hare, D. Parental social support, coping strategies, resilience factors, stress, anxiety and depression levels in parents of children with MPS III (Sanfilippo syndrome) or children with intellectual disabilities (ID). *J. Inherit. Metab. Dis.* 2013, 36, 281-291.

[18] Coppa, GV; Galeotti, F; Zampini, L; Galeazzi, T; Padella, L; Santoro, L; Maccari, F; Gabrielli O; Volpi, N. Mild mental retardation and low levels of urinary heparan sulfate in a patient with the attenuated phenotype of mucopolysaccharidosis type IIIA. *Clin. Biochem.* 2013, 46, 688-690.

[19] Verhoeven, WM; Csepan, R; Marcelis, CL; Lefeber, DJ; Egger JI; Tuinier, S. Sanfilippo B in an elderly female psychiatric patient: a rare but relevant diagnosis in presenile dementia. *Acta Psychiatr. Scand.* 2010, 122, 162-165.

[20] Brady, J; Trehan, A; Landis, D; Toro, C. Mucopolysaccharidosis type IIIB (MPS IIIB) masquerading as a behavioural disorder. *BMJ Case Rep.* 8, 2013.

[21] Saini, AG; Singhi, A; Sahu, JK; Ganesan, SL; Vyas, S; Rao, S; Sachdeva, MU. Hyperactivity, unexplained speech delay, and coarse facies--is it Sanfilippo syndrome? *J. Child Neurol.* 2014, 29, NP9-12.

[22] Buhrman, D; Thakkar, K; Poe, M; Escolar, ML. Natural history of Sanfilippo syndrome type *J. Inherit. Metab. Dis.* 2014, 37, 431-437.

[23] Delgadillo, V; del M. O'Callaghan M; Gort, L; Coll, MJ; Pineda, M. Natural history of Sanfilippo syndrome in Spain. *Orphanet J. Rare Dis.* 2013, 8, 189.

[24] Rumsey, RK; Rudser, K; Delaney, K; Potegal, M; Whitley, CB; Shapiro E. Acquired autistic behaviors in children with mucopolysaccharidosis type IIIA. *J. Pediatr.* 2014, 164, 1147-1151.

[25] Cross, EM; Grant, S; Jones, S; Bigger, SW; Wraith, JW; Mahon, LV; Lomax, M; Hare, DJ. An investigation of the middle and late behavioural phenotypes of mucopolysaccharidosis type-III. *J. Neurodev. Disord.* 2014, 6, 46.

[26] Stenson, PD; Mort, M; Ball, EV; Shaw, K; Phillips, A; Cooper, DN. The Human Gene Mutation Database: building a comprehensive mutation repository for clinical and molecular genetics, diagnostic testing and personalized genomic medicine. *Hum. Genet.* 2014, 133, 1-9.

[27] Pierzynowska, K; Gaffke, L; Podlacha, M; Węgrzyn, G. Genetic base of behavioral disorders in mucopolysaccharidoses: transcriptomic studies. *Int. J. Mol. Sci.* 2020, 21, E1156.

[28] Gaffke, L; Pierzynowska, K; Podlacha, M; Hoinkis, D; Rintz, E; Brokowska, J; Cyske, Z; Wegrzyn, G. Underestimated aspect of mucopolysaccharidosis pathogenesis: Global changes in cellular processes revealed by transcriptomic studies. *Int. J. Mol. Sci.* 2020, 21, E1204.

[29] Brokowska, J; Pierzynowska, K; Gaffke, L; Rintz, E; Węgrzyn, G. Expression of genes involved in apoptosis is dysregulated in mucopolysaccharidoses as revealed by pilot transcriptomic analyses. *Cell. Biol. Int.* 2020. doi: 10.1002/cbin.11332.

[30] Gaffke, L; Pierzynowska, K; Podlacha, M; Brokowska, J; Węgrzyn, G. Changes in cellular processes occurring in mucopolysaccharidoses as underestimated pathomechanisms of these diseases. *Cell. Biol. Int.* 2019. doi: 10.1002/cbin.11275.

[31] Mohammed, EE; Snella, EM; Rutz-Mendicino, MM; Echevarria, FD; Awedikian, R; Whitley, EM; Ellinwood, NM. Accelerated clinical disease and pathology in mucopolysaccharidosis type IIIB and GalNAc transferase double knockout mice. *Mol. Genet. Metab.* 2012, 107, 129-135.

[32] de Ruijter, J; de Ru, MH; Wagemans, T; Ijlst, L; Lund, AM; Orchard, PJ; Schaefer, GB; Wijburg, FA; van Vlies; N. Heparan sulfate and dermatan sulfate derived disaccharides are sensitive markers for newborn screening for mucopolysaccharidoses types I, II and III. *Mol. Genet. Metab.* 2012, 107, 705-710.

[33] Lamanna, WC; Lawrence, R; Sarrazin, S; Esko, JD. Secondary Storage of Dermatan Sulfate in Sanfilippo Disease. *J. Biol. Chem.* 2010, 286, 6955–6962.

[34] Baydakova, G; Ilyushkina, A; Gaffke, L; Pierzynowska, K; Bychkov, I; Ługowska, A; Wegrzyn, G; Zakharova, E. Elevated LysoGb3 Concentration in the Neuronopathic Forms of Mucopolysaccharidoses. *Diagnostics.* 2020, 10, 155.

[35] Chuang, CK; Lin, HY; Wang, TJ; Tsai, CC; Liu, HL; Lin, SP. A modified liquid chromatography/tandem mass spectrometry method for predominant disaccharide units of urinary glycosaminoglycans in patients with mucopolysaccharidoses. *Orphanet. J. Rare Dis.* 2014, 9, 135.

[36] Tomatsu, S; Gutierrez, MA; Ishimaru, T; Pena, OM; Montano, AM; Maeda, H; Velez-Castrillon, S; Nishioka, T; Fachel, AA; Cooper, A; Thornley, M; Wraith, E; Barrera, LA; Laybauer, LS; Giugliani, R; Schwartz, IV; Frenking, GS; Beck, M; Kircher, SG; Paschke, E; Yamaguchi, S; Ullrich, K; Isogai, K; Suzuki, Y; Orii T; Noguchi, A. Heparan sulfate levels in mucopolysaccharidoses and mucolipidoses. *J. Inherit. Metab. Dis.* 2005, 28, 743-757.

[37] Oguma, T; Tomatsu, S; Montano, AM; Okazaki, O. Analytical method for the determination of disaccharides derived from keratan, heparan, and dermatan sulfates in human serum and plasma by high-performance liquid chromatography/turbo ionspray ionization tandem mass spectrometry. *Anal. Biochem.* 2007, 368, 79-86.

[38] Tomatsu, S; Montano, AM; Oguma, T; Dung, VC; Oikawa, H; Gutierrez, ML; Yamaguchi, S; Suzuki, Y; Fukushi, M; Barrera, LA; Kida, K; Kubota, M; Orii, T. Validation of disaccharide compositions derived from dermatan sulfate and heparan sulfate in

mucopolysaccharidoses and mucolipidoses II and III by tandem mass spectrometry. *Mol. Genet. Metab.* 2010, 99, 124-131.

[39] Tomatsu, S; Montano, AM; Oguma, T; Dung, VC; Oikawa, H; de Carvalho, TG; Gutierrez, ML; Yamaguchi, S; Suzuki, Y; Fukushi, M; Sakura, N; Barrera, L; Kida, K; Kubota, M; Orii, T. Dermatan sulfate and heparan sulfate as a biomarker for mucopolysaccharidosis I. *J. Inherit. Metab. Dis.* 2010, 33, 141-150.

[40] Rowan, DJ; Tomatsu, S; Grubb, AJH; Montano, AM; Sly, WS. Assessment of bone dysplasia by micro-CT and glycosaminoglycan levels in mouse models for mucopolysaccharidosis type I, IIIA, IVA, and VII. *J. Inherit. Metab. Dis.* 2013, 36, 235-246.

[41] Tomatsu, S; Fujii, T; Fukushi, M; Oguma, T; Shimada, T; Maeda, M; Kida, K; Shibata, Y; Futatsumori, H; Montano, AM; Mason RW; Yamaguchi, S; Suzuki, Y; Orii, T. Newborn screening and diagnosis of mucopolysaccharidoses. *Mol. Genet. Metab.* 2013, 110, 42-53.

[42] Tomatsu, S; Shimada, T; Mason, RW; Kelly, J; LaMarr, WA; Yasuda, E; Shibata, Y; Futatsumori, H; Montano, AM; Yamaguchi, S; Suzuki, Y; Orii, T. Assay for glycosaminoglycans by tandem mass spectrometry and its applications. *J. Anal. Bioanal. Tech.* 2014, (Suppl 2), 006.

[43] Tomatsu, S; Shimada, T; Mason, RW; Montano, AM; Kelly, J; LaMarr, WA; Kubaski, F; Giugliani, R; Guha, R; Yasuda, E; Mackenzie, W; Yamaguchi, S; Suzuki, Y; Orii, T. Establishment of glycosaminoglycan assays for mucopolysaccharidoses. *Metabolites.* 2014, 4, 655-679.

[44] Tomatsu, S; Kubaski, F; Sawamoto, K; Mason, RW; Yasuda, E; Shimada, T; Montano, AM; Yamaguchi, S; Suzuki, Y; Orii, T. Newborn screening and diagnosis of mucopolysaccharidoses: application of tandem mass spectrometry. *Nihon Masu Sukuriningu Gakkai Shi.* 2014, 24, 19-37.

[45] Shimada, T; Kelly, J; LaMarr, WA; van Vlies, N; Yasuda, E; Mason, RW; Mackenzie, W; Kubaski, F; Giugliani, R; Chinen, Y; Yamaguchi, S; Suzuki, Y; Orii, KE; Fukao, T; Orii, T; Tomatsu, S. Novel heparan sulfate assay by using automated high-throughput

mass spectrometry: Application to monitoring and screening for mucopolysaccharidoses. *Mol. Genet. Metab.* 2014, 113, 92-99.

[46] de Ruijter, J; Ijlst, L; Kulik, W; van Lenthe, H; Wagemans, T; van Vlies, N; Wijburg, FA. Heparan sulfate derived disaccharides in plasma and total urinary excretion of glycosaminoglycans correlate with disease severity in Sanfilippo disease. *J. Inherit. Metab. Dis.* 2013, 36, 271-279.

[47] Delaney, KA; Rudser, R; Yund, BD; Whitley, CB; Haslett, PA; Shapiro, EG. Methods of neurodevelopmental assessment in children with neurodegenerative disease: Sanfilippo syndrome. *JIMD Rep.* 2014, 13, 129-137.

[48] Shapiro, EG; Nestrasil, I; Ahmed, A; Wey, A; Rudser, KR; Delaney, KA; Rumsey, RK; Haslett, PA; Whitley, CB; Potegal, M. Quantifying behaviors of children with Sanfilippo syndrome: the Sanfilippo behavior rating scale. *Mol. Genet. Metab.* 2015, 114, 594-598.

[49] Piotrowska, E; Jakóbkiewicz-Banecka, J; Tylki-Szymańska, A; Czartoryska, B; Węgrzyn, A; Węgrzyn G. Correlation between severity of mucopolysaccharidoses and combination of the residual enzyme activity and efficiency of glycosaminoglycan synthesis. *Acta. Paediatr.* 2009, 98, 743-749.

[50] Sidhu, NS; Schreiber, K; Propper, K; Becker, S; Uson, I; Sheldrick, GM; Gartner, J; Kratzner, R; Steinfeld, R. Structure of sulfamidase provides insight into the molecular pathology of mucopolysaccharidosis IIIA. *Acta Crystallogr. D. Biol. Crystallogr.* 2014, 70, 1321-1335.

[51] Bodamer, OA; Giugliani, R; Wood, T. The laboratory diagnosis of mucopolysaccharidosis III (Sanfilippo syndrome): A changing landscape. *Mol. Genet. Metab.* 2014, 113, 34-41.

[52] Ugrinov, KG; Freed, SD; Thomas, CL; Lee, SW. A multiparametric computational algorithm for comprehensive assessment of genetic mutations in mucopolysaccharidosis type IIIA (Sanfilippo syndrome). *PLoS One.* 2015, 10, e0121511.

[53] Mellara T de, S; Azevedo, DT; Faria, G; Nelson Filho, P; Queiroz, AM; Brentegani, LG. Dental findings and management in a mucopolysaccharidosis type IIIB patient. *J. Dent. Child. (Chic).* 2012, 79, 176-180.

[54] de Ruijter, J; Maas, M; Janssen, A; Wijburg, FA. High prevalence of femoral head necrosis in mucopolysaccharidosis type III (Sanfilippo disease): a national, observational, cross-sectional study. *Mol. Genet. Metab.* 2013, 109, 49-53.

[55] Chiang, J; Raiman, J; Cutz, E; Solomon, M; Dell, S. Tachypnea of infancy as the first sign of Sanfilippo syndrome. *Pediatrics.* 2014, 134, e884-888.

[56] Jurecka, A; Tylki-Szymanska, A. Gynecomastia in MPS IIIA boys: related to treatment or precocious puberty? *Mol. Genet. Metab.* 2014, 111, 61-62.

[57] Sharkia, R; Mahajnah, M; Zalan, A; Sourlis, C; Bauer, P; Schols, L. Sanfilippo type A: new clinical manifestations and neuro-imaging findings in patients from the same family in Israel: a case report. *J. Med. Case Rep.* 2014, 8, 78.

[58] Mahon, LV; Lomax, M; Grant, S; Cross, E; Hare, DJ; Wraith, JE; Jones, S; Bigger, B; Langford-Smith, K; Canal, M. Assessment of sleep in children with mucopolysaccharidosis type III. *PLoS One.* 2014, 9, e84128.

[59] Garbuzova-Davis, S; Mirtyl, S; Sallot, SA; Hernandez-Ontiveros, DG; Haller, E; Sanberg, PR. Blood-brain barrier impairment in MPS III patients. *BMC. Neurol.* 2013, 13, 174.

[60] de Ruijter, J; Broere, L; Mulder, M; van der Ploeg, AT; Rubio-Gozalbo, ME; Wortmann, SB; Visser, G; Wijburg, FA. Growth in patients with mucopolysaccharidosis type III (Sanfilippo disease). *J. Inherit. Metab. Dis.* 2014, 37, 447-454.

[61] Bruyere, J; Roy, E; Ausseil, J; Lemonnier, T; Teyre, G; Bohl, D; Etienne-Manneville, S; Lortat-Jacob, H; Heard, JM; Vitry, S. Heparan sulfate saccharides modify focal adhesions: implication in mucopolysaccharidosis neuropathophysiology. *J. Mol. Biol.* 2015, 427, 775-791.

[62] Trudel, S; Trecherel, E; Gomila, C; Peltier, M; Aubignat, M; Gubler, B; Morliere, P, Heard, Ausseil, J. Oxidative stress is independent of inflammation in the neurodegenerative Sanfilippo syndrome type B. *J. Neurosci. Res.* 2015, 93, 424-432.

[63] Dawson, G; Fuller, M; Helmsley, KM; Hopwood, JJ. Abnormal gangliosides are localized in lipid rafts in Sanfilippo (MPS3a) mouse brain. *Neurochem. Res.* 2012, 37, 1372-1380.

[64] Wilkinson, FL; Holley, RJ; Langford-Smith, KJ; Badrinath, S; Liao, A; Langford-Smith, A; Cooper, JD; Jones, SA; Wraith, JE; Wynn, RF; Merry, CL; Bigger, BW. Neuropathology in mouse models of mucopolysaccharidosis type I, IIIA and IIIB. *PLoS One.* 2012, 7, e35787.

[65] Langford-Smith, A; Langford-Smith, KJ; Jones, SA; Wynn, RF; Wraith, JE; Wilkinson, FL; Bigger, BW. Female mucopolysaccharidosis IIIA mice exhibit hyperactivity and a reduced sense of danger in the open field test. *PLoS. One.* 2011, 6, e25717.

[66] Keating, DJ; Winter, MA; Hemsley, KM; Mackenzie, KD; Teo, EH; Hopwood, JJ; Brooks, DA; Parkinson-Lawrence, EJ. Exocytosis is impaired in mucopolysaccharidosis IIIA mouse chromaffin cells. *Neuroscience.* 2012, 227, 110-8.

[67] Fu, H; Bartz, JD; Jr. Stephens, RL; McCarty, DM. Peripheral nervous system neuropathology and progressive sensory impairments in a mouse model of Mucopolysaccharidosis IIIB. *PLoS. One*. 2012, 7, e45992.

[68] Langford-Smith, A; Malinowska, M; Langford-Smith, KJ; Wegrzyn, G; Jones, S; Wynn, R; Wraith, JE; Wilkinson, FL; Bigger, BW. Hyperactive behaviour in the mouse model of mucopolysaccharidosis IIIB in the open field and home cage environments. *Genes. Brain.* Behav. 2011, 10, 673-82.

[69] Martins, C; Hulkova, H; Dridi, L; Dormoy-Raclet, V; Grigoryeva, L; Choi, Y; Langford-Smith, A; Wilkinson, FL; Ohmi, K; DiCristo, G; Hamel, E; Ausseil, J; Cheillan, D; Moreau, A; Svobodova, E; Hajkova, Z; Tesarova, M; Hansikova, H; Bigger, BW; Hrebicek, M;

Pshezhetsky, AV. Neuroinflammation, mitochondrial defects and neurodegeneration in mucopolysaccharidosis III type C mouse model. *Brain.* 2015, 138, 336-355.

[70] Palmieri, C; Giger, U; Wang, P; Pizarro, M; Shivaprasad, HL. Pathological and biochemical studies of mucopolysaccharidosis type IIIB (Sanfilippo syndrome type B) in juvenile emus (Dromaius novaehollandiae). *Vet. Pathol.* 2015, 52, 160-169.

[71] Gaffke, L; Pierzynowska, K; Piotrowska, E; Węgrzyn, G. How close are we to therapies for Sanfilippo disease? *Metab. Brain. Dis.* 2017, 33, 1–10.

[72] Pfeifer, RW; Felice, BR; Boyd, RB; Butt, MT; Ruiz, JA; Heartlein, MV; Calias, P. Safety evaluation of chronic intrathecal administration of heparan N-sulfatase in juvenile cynomolgus monkeys. *Drug. Deliv. Transl. Res.* 2012, 2, 187-200.

[73] Marshall, NR; Hassiotis, S; King, B; Rozaklis, T; Trim, PJ; Duplock, SK; Winner, LK; Beard, H; Snel, MW; Jolly, RD; Hopwood, JJ; Hemsley, KM. Delivery of therapeutic protein for prevention of neurodegenerative changes: comparison of different CSF-delivery methods. *Exp. Neurol.* 2015, 263, 79-90.

[74] Beard, H; Luck, AJ; Hassiotis, S; King, B; Trim, PJ; Snel, MF; Hopwood, JJ; Hemsley, KM. Determination of the role of injection site on the efficacy of intra-CSF enzyme replacement therapy in MPS IIIA mice. *Mol. Genet. Metab.* 2015, 115, 33-40.

[75] Hassiotis, S; Beard, H; Luck, A; Trim, PJ; King, B; Snel, MF; Hopwood, JJ; Hemsley, KM. Disease stage determines the efficacy of treatment of a paediatric neurodegenerative disease. *Eur. J. Neurosci.* 2014, 39, 2139-2150.

[76] Sorrentino, NC; D'Orsi, L; Sambri, I, Nusco, E; Monaco, C; Spampanato, C; Polishchuk, E; Saccone, P; De Leonibus, E; Ballabio, A; Fraldi, A. A highly secreted sulphamidase engineered to cross the blood-brain barrier corrects brain lesions of mice with mucopolysaccharidoses type IIIA. *EMBO. Mol. Med.* 2013, 5, 675-690.

[77] Kan, SH; Troitskaya, LA; Sinow, CS; Haitz, K; Todd, AK; Di Stefano, A; Q. Le, A; Dickson, PI; Tippin, BL; Insulin-like growth factor II peptide fusion enables uptake and lysosomal delivery of alpha-N-acetylglucosaminidase to mucopolysaccharidosis type IIIB fibroblasts. *Biochem. J.* 2014, 458, 281-289.

[78] Kan, SH; Aoyagi-Scharber, M; Q. Le, S; Vincelette, J; Ohmi, K; Bullens, S; Wendt, DJ; Christianson, TM; Tiger, PM; Brown, JR; Lawrence, BR; Yip, R; Holtzinger, J; Bagri, A; Crippen-Harmon, D; Vondrak, KN; Chen, Z; Hague, CM; Woloszynek, JC; Cheung, DS; Webster, KA; Adintori, EG; Lo, MJ; Wong, W; Fitzpatrick, PA; LeBowitz, JH; Crawford, BE; Bunting, S; Dickson, PI; Neufeld, EF. Delivery of an enzyme-IGFII fusion protein to the mouse brain is therapeutic for mucopolysaccharidosis type IIIB. *Proc. Natl. Acad. Sci. USA.* 2014, 111, 14870-14875.

[79] Boado, RJ; Lu, JZ; Hui, EK; Lin, H; Pardridge, WM. Insulin receptor antibody-sulfamidase fusion protein penetrates the primate blood-brain barrier and reduces glycosoaminoglycans in Sanfilippo type A cells. *Mol. Pharm.* 2014, 11, 2928-2934.

[80] King, B; Marshall, N; Beard, H; Hassiotis, S; Trim, PJ; Snel, MF; Rozaklis, T; Jolly, RD; Hopwood, JJ; Hemsley, KM. Evaluation of enzyme dose and dose-frequency in ameliorating substrate accumulation in MPS IIIA Huntaway dog brain. *J. Inherit. Metab. Dis.* 2015, 38, 341–350.

[81] King, B; Hassiotis, S; Rozaklis, T; Beard, H; Trim, P. J; Snel, MF; Hopwood, JJ; Hemsley, KM. Low-dose, continuous enzyme replacement therapy ameliorates brain pathology in the neurodegenerative lysosomal disorder mucopolysaccharidosis type IIIA. *J. Neurochem.* 2016, 137, 409–422.

[82] King, B; Marshall, NR; Hassiotis, S; Trim, PJ; Tucker, J; Hattersley, K; Hopwood, JJ; Hemsley, K. M. Slow, continuous enzyme replacement via spinal CSF in dogs with the paediatric-onset neurodegenerative disease, MPS IIIA. *J. Inherit. Metab. Dis.* 2017, 40, 443–453.

[83] Gustavsson, S; Ohlin Sjöström, E; Tjernberg, A; Janson, J; Westermark, U; Andersson, T; Makower, Å; Arnelöf, E; Andersson, G; Svartengren, J; Ekholm, C; Svensson, Gelius, S. Intravenous delivery of a chemically modified sulfamidase efficiently reduces heparan sulfate storage and brain pathology in mucopolysaccharidosis IIIA mice. *Mol. Genet. Metab. Rep.* 2019, 21, 100510.

[84] Chung, JK; Pan, L; Palmieri, K; Youssef, AS; McCauley, TG. Whole Body and CNS Biodistribution of rhHNS in Cynomolgus Monkeys after Intrathecal Lumbar Administration: Treatment Implications for Patients with MPS IIIA. *Int. J. Mol. Sci*. 2017, 18(12), 2594.

[85] Boado, RJ; Lu, JZ; Hui, EK; Pardridge, WM. Reduction in Brain Heparan Sulfate with Systemic Administration of an IgG Trojan Horse-Sulfamidase Fusion Protein in the Mucopolysaccharidosis Type IIIA Mouse. *Mol. Pharm.* 2018, 15, 602-608.

[86] Jones, SA; Breen, C; Heap, F; Rust, S; de Ruijter, J; Tump, E; Marchal, J. P; Pan, L; Qiu, Y; Chung, JK; Nair, N; Haslett, PA, Barbier, AJ; Wijburg, FA. A phase 1/2 study of intrathecal heparan-N-sulfatase in patients with mucopolysaccharidosis IIIA. *Mol. Genet. Metab.* 2016, 118, 198-205.

[87] Wijburg, FA; Whitley, CB; Muenzer, J; Gasperini, S; Del Toro, M; Muschol, N; Cleary, M; Sevin, C; Shapiro, E; Bhargava, P; Kerr, D; Alexanderian, D. Intrathecal heparan-N-sulfatase in patients with Sanfilippo syndrome type A: A phase IIb randomized trial. *Mol. Genet. Metab.* 2019, 126, 121-130.

[88] Yogalingam, G; Luu, AR; Prill, H; Lo, M. J; Yip, B; Holtzinger, J; Christianson, T; Aoyagi-Scharber, M; Lawrence, R; Crawford, BE; LeBowitz, JH. BMN 250, a fusion of lysosomal alpha-N-acetylglucosaminidase with IGF2, exhibits different patterns of cellular uptake into critical cell types of Sanfilippo syndrome B disease pathogenesis. *PLoS. One.* 2019, 14, e0207836.

[89] Aoyagi-Scharber, M; Crippen-Harmon, D; Lawrence, R; Vincelette, J; Yogalingam, G; Prill, H; Yip, BK; Baridon, B; Vitelli, C; Lee, A; Gorostiza, O; Adintori, EG; Minto, WC; Van Vleet, JL; Yates, B;

Rigney, S; Christianson, TM; Tiger, PMN; Lo, MJ; Holtzinger, J; Fitzpatrick, PA; LeBowitz, JH; Bullens, S; Crawford, BE; Bunting, S. Clearance of Heparan Sulfate and Attenuation of CNS Pathology by Intracerebroventricular BMN 250 in Sanfilippo Type B Mice. *Mol. Ther. Methods. Clin. Dev.* 2017, 6, 43–53.

[90] Grover, A; Crippen-Harmon, D; Nave, L; Vincelette, J; Wait, JCM; Melton, AC; Lawrence, R; Brown, JR; Webster, KA; Yip, BK; Baridon, B; Vitelli, C; Rigney, S; Christianson, TM; Tiger, PMN; Lo, MJ; Holtzinger, J; Shaywitz, AJ; Crawford, BE; Fitzpatrick, PA; LeBowitz, JH; BullensS; Aoyagi-Scharber, M; Bunting, S; O'Neill, CA, Pinkstaff J, Bagri, A. Translational studies of intravenous and intracerebroventricular routes of administration for CNS cellular biodistribution for BMN 250, an enzyme replacement therapy for the treatment of Sanfilippo type B. *Drug Deliv. Transl. Res.* 2020, 10, 425-439.

[91] Clarke, D; Pearse, Y; Kan, S; Le, S. Q; Sanghez, V; Cooper, JD; Dickson, PI; Iacovino, M. Genetically Corrected iPSC-Derived Neural Stem Cell Grafts Deliver Enzyme Replacement to Affect CNS Disease in Sanfilippo B Mice. *Mol. Ther. Methods Clin. Dev.* 2018, 10, 113–127.

[92] Whitley, CB; Vijay, S; Yao, B; Pineda, M; Parker, GJM; Rojas-Caro, S; Zhang, X; Dai, Y; Cinar, A; Bubb, G; Patki, KC; Escolar, ML. Final results of the phase 1/2, open-label clinical study of intravenous recombinant human N-acetyl-α-d-glucosaminidase (SBC-103) in children with mucopolysaccharidosis IIIB. *Mol. Genet. Metab.* 2019, 126, 131-138.

[93] Willing, AE; Garbuzova-Davis, SN; Zayko, O; Derasari, HM; Rawls, AW; James, CR; Mervis, RF; Sanberg, CD; Kuzmin-Nichols, N; Sanberg, PR. Repeated administrations of human umbilical cord blood cells improve disease outcomes in a mouse model of Sanfilippo syndrome type III B. *Cell. Transplant.* 2014, 23, 1613-1630.

[94] Welling, L; Marchal, JP; van Hasselt, P; van der Ploeg, AT; Wijburg, FA; Boelens, JJ. Early umbilical cord blood-derived stem

cell transplantation does not prevent neurological deterioration in mucopolysaccharidosis type III. *JIMD. Rep.* 2015, 18, 63-68.

[95] Aldenhoven, M; Jones, SA; Bonney, D; Borrill, RE; Coussons, M; Mercer, J; Bierings, MB; Versluys, B; van Hasselt, PM; Wijburg, FA; van der Ploeg, AT; Wynn, RF; Boelens, JJ. Hematopoietic Cell Transplantation for Mucopolysaccharidosis Patients Is Safe and Effective: Results after Implementation of International Guidelines. *Biol. Blood Marrow. Transplant.* 2015, 21, 1106–1109.

[96] Rastall, DP; Amalfitano, A. Recent advances in gene therapy for lysosomal storage disorders. *Appl. Clin. Genet.* 2015, 8, 157–169.

[97] Ruzo, A; Marco, S; Garcia, M; Villacampa, P; Ribera, A; Ayuso, E; Maggioni, L; Mingozzi, F; Haurigot, V; Bosch, F. Correction of pathological accumulation of glycosaminoglycans in central nervous system and peripheral tissues of MPSIIIA mice through systemic AAV9 gene transfer. *Hum. Gene Ther.* 2012, 23, 1237-1246.

[98] Heldermon, CD; Qin, EY; Ohlemiller, KK; Herzog, ED; Brown, JR; Vogler, C; Hou, W; Orrock, JL; Crawford, BE; Sands, MS. Disease correction by combined neonatal intracranial AAV and systemic lentiviral gene therapy in Sanfilippo syndrome type B mice. *Gene Ther*. 2013, 20, 913-921.

[99] Murrey, DA; Naughton, BJ; Duncan, FJ; Meadows, AS; Ware, TA; Campbel, K; Bremer, WG; Walker, C; Goodchild, L; Bolon, B; La Perle, K; Flanigan, K; McBride, KL; McCarty, DM; Fu, H. Feasibility and safety of systemic rAAV9-hNAGLU delivery for treating MPS IIIB: Toxicology, bio-distribution and immunological assessments in primates. *Hum. Gene Ther. Clin. Dev*. 2014, 25, 72-84.

[100] Tardieu, M; Zerah, M; Husson, B; de Bournonville, S; Deiva, K; Adamsbaum, C; Vincent, F; Hocquemiller, M; Broissand, C; Furlan, V; Ballabio, A; Fraldi, A; Crystal, RG; Baugnon, T; Roujeau T; Heard O Danos, JM. Intracerebral administration of adeno-associated viral vector serotype rh.10 carrying human SGSH and SUMF1 cDNAs in children with mucopolysaccharidosis type IIIA

disease: results of a phase I/II trial. *Hum. Gene Ther.* 2014, 25, 506-16.

[101] Srivastava, A. *In vivo* tissue-tropism of adeno-associated viral vectors. *Curr. Opin. Virol.* 2016, 21, 75–80.

[102] Naso, MF; Tomkowicz, B; Perry, WL; Strohl, WR. Adeno-Associated Virus (AAV) as a Vector for Gene Therapy. *Bio Drugs.* 2017, 31, 317–334.

[103] Ribera, A; Haurigot, V; Garcia, M; Marcó, S; Motas, S; Villacampa, P; Maggioni, L; León, X; Molas, M; Sánchez, V; Muñoz, S; Leborgne, C; Moll, X; Pumarola, M; Mingozzi, F; Ruberte, J; Añor, S; Bosch, F. Biochemical, histological and functional correction of mucopolysaccharidosis Type IIIB by intra-cerebrospinal fluid gene therapy. *Hum. Mol. Genet.* 2015, 24, 2078–2095.

[104] Roca, C; Motas, S; Marcó, S; Ribera, A; Sánchez, V; Sánchez, X; Bosch, F. 17). Disease correction by AAV-mediated gene therapy in a new mouse model of mucopolysaccharidosis type IIID. *Hum. Mol. Genet.* 2017, 26, 1535–1551.

[105] Lau, AA; Hemsley, KM. Adeno-associated viral gene therapy for mucopolysaccharidoses exhibiting neurodegeneration. *J. Mol. Med.* 2017, 95, 1043–1052.

[106] Meadows, AS; Duncan, FJ; Camboni, M; Waligura, K; Montgomery, CL; Zaraspe, K; Zaraspe, K; Naughton, BJ; Bremer, WG; Shilling, C; Walker, CM; Bolon, B; Flanigan, KM; McBride, KL; McCarty, DM; Fu, H. A GLP-compliant toxicology and biodistribution study: systemic delivery of a rAAV9 vector for the treatment of mucopolysaccharidosis IIIB. *Hum. Gene Ther. Clin. Dev.* 2015, 26, 228-242.

[107] Fu, H; Meadows, AS; Ware, T; Mohney, RP; McCarty, DM. Near-Complete Correction of Profound Metabolomic Impairments Corresponding to Functional Benefit in MPS IIIB Mice after IV rAAV9-hNAGLU Gene Delivery. *Mol. Ther.* 2017, 25, 792–802.

[108] Duncan, FJ; Naughton, BJ; Zaraspe, K; Murrey, DA; Meadows, AS; Clark, KR; Newsom, DE; White, P; Fu, H; McCarty, DM. Broad Functional Correction of Molecular Impairments by Systemic

Delivery of scAAVrh74-hSGSH Gene Delivery in MPS IIIA Mice. *Mol. Ther.* 2015, 23, 638–647.

[109] Fu, H; Cataldi, MP; Ware, TA; Zaraspe, K; Meadows, AS; Murrey, DA; McCarty, DM. Functional correction of neurological and somatic disorders at later stages of disease in MPS IIIA mice by systemic scAAV9-hSGSH gene delivery. *Hum. Gene Ther. Clin. Dev.* 2016, 3, 16036.

[110] Gilkes, JA; Bloom, MD; Heldermon, CD. Preferred transduction with AAV8 and AAV9 via thalamic administration in the MPS IIIB model: A comparison of four rAAV serotypes. *Mol. Genet. Metab. Rep.* 2015, 6, 48–54.

[111] Gilkes, JA; Bloom, MD; Heldermon, CD. Mucopolysaccharidosis IIIB confers enhanced neonatal intracranial transduction by AAV8 but not by 5, 9 or rh10. *Gene Ther.* 2016, 23(3), 263–271.

[112] Tordo, J; O'Leary, C; Antunes, ASLM; Palomar, N; Aldrin-Kirk, P; Basche, M; Bennett, A; D'Souza, Z; Gleitz, H; Godwin, A; Holley, RJ; Parker, H; Liao, AY; Rouse, P; Youshani, AS; Dridi, L; Martins, C; Levade, T; Stacey, KB; Davis, DM; Dyer, A; Clément, N; Björklund, T; Ali, RR; Agbandje-McKenna, M; Rahim, AA; Pshezhetsky, A; Waddington, SN; Linden, RM; Bigger, BW; Henckaerts, E. A novel adeno-associated virus capsid with enhanced neurotropism corrects a lysosomal transmembrane enzyme deficiency. *Brain.* 2018, 141, 2014–2031.

[113] Winner, LK; Beard, H; Hassiotis, S; Lau, AA; Luck, A. J; Hopwood, JJ; Hemsley, KM. A Preclinical Study Evaluating AAVrh10-Based Gene Therapy for Sanfilippo Syndrome. *Hum. Gene Ther.* 2016, 27, 363–375.

[114] Tardieu, M; Zérah, M; Gougeon, ML; Ausseil, J; de Bournonville, S; Husson, B; Zafeiriou, D; Parenti, G; Bourget, P; Poirier, B; Furlan, V; Artaud, C; Baugnon, T; Roujeau, T; Crystal, RG; Meyer, C; Deiva, K; Heard, JM. Intracerebral gene therapy in children with mucopolysaccharidosis type IIIB syndrome: an uncontrolled phase 1/2 clinical trial. *Lancet Neurol.* 2017, 16, 712–720.

[115] Gray, AL; O'Leary, C; Liao, A; Agundez, L; Youshani, A. S; Gleitz, HF; Parker, H; Taylor, JT; Danos, O; Hocquemiller, M; Palomar, N; Linden, RM; Henckaerts, E; Holley, RJ; Bigger, B. An improved AAV vector for neurological correction of the mouse model of Mucopolysaccharidosis IIIA. *Hum. Gene Ther.* 2019, 30, 1052-1066.

[116] Clarke, D; Pearse, Y; Kan, S; Le, SQ; Sanghez, V; Cooper, JD; Dickson, PI; Iacovino, M. Genetically Corrected iPSC-Derived Neural Stem Cell Grafts Deliver Enzyme Replacement to Affect CNS Disease in Sanfilippo B Mice. *Mol. Ther. Methods Clin. Dev.* 2018, 10, 113–127.

[117] Holley RJ; Ellison, SM; Fil D, O'Leary, C; McDermott, J; Senthivel, N; Langford-Smith, AWW; Wilkinson, FL; D'Souza, Z; Parker, H; Liao, A; Rowlston, S; Gleitz, HFE; Kan, SH; Dickson, PI; Bigger, BW. Macrophage enzyme and reduced inflammation drive brain correction of mucopolysaccharidosis IIIB by stem cell gene therapy. *Brain.* 2018, 141, 99-116.

[118] Jakobkiewicz-Banecka, J; Piotrowska, E; Gabig-Ciminska, M; Borysiewicz, E; Slominska-Wojewodzka, M; Narajczyk, M; Wegrzyn, A; Wegrzyn, G. Substrate reduction therapies for mucopolysaccharidoses. *Curr. Pharm. Biotechnol.* 2011, 12, 1860-1865.

[119] Kaidonis, X; Liaw, WC; Roberts, AD; Ly, M; Anson, D; Byers, S. Gene silencing of EXTL2 and EXTL3 as a substrate deprivation therapy for heparan sulphate storing mucopolysaccharidoses. *Eur. J. Hum. Genet.* 2010, 18, 194-199.

[120] Dziedzic, D; Wegrzyn, G; Jakobkiewicz-Banecka, J. Impairment of glycosaminoglycan synthesis in mucopolysaccharidosis type IIIA cells by using siRNA: a potential therapeutic approach for Sanfilippo disease. *Eur. J. Hum. Genet.* 2010, 18, 200-205.

[121] Canals, I; Benetó, N; Cozar, M; Vilageliu, L; Grinberg, D. EXTL2 and EXTL3 inhibition with siRNAs as a promising substrate reduction therapy for Sanfilippo C syndrome. *Sci. Rep.* 2015, 8, 5, 13654.

[122] Robert, AL; Thomas, BJ; Wilkinson, AS; Fletcher, JM; Byers, S. Inhibition of glycosaminoglycan synthesis using rhodamine B in a mouse model of mucopolysaccharidosis type IIIA. *Pediatr. Res.* 2006, 60, 309-314.

[123] Roberts, AL; Rees, MH; Klebe, S; Fletcher, JM; Byers, S. Improvement in behaviour after substrate deprivation therapy with rhodamine B in a mouse model of MPS IIIA. *Mol. Genet. Metab.* 2007, 92, 115-121.

[124] Roberts, AL; Fletcher, JM; Moore, L; Byers, S. Trans-generational exposure to low levels of rhodamine B does not adversely affect litter size or liver function in murine mucopolysaccharidosis type IIIA. *Mol. Genet. Metab.* 2010, 101, 208-213.

[125] Derrick-Roberts, AL; Marais, W; Byers, S. Rhodamine B and 2-acetamido-1;3;6-tri-O-acetyl-4-deoxy-4-fluoro-D-glucopyranose (F-GlcNAc) inhibit chondroitin/dermatan and keratan sulphate synthesis by different mechanisms in bovine chondrocytes. *Mol. Genet. Metab.* 2012, 106, 214-220.

[126] Piotrowska, E; Jakobkiewicz-Banecka, J; Baranska, S; Tylki-Szymanska, A; Czartoryska, B; Wegrzyn, A; Wegrzyn, G. Genistein-mediated inhibition of glycosaminoglycan synthesis as a basis for gene expression-targeted isoflavone therapy for mucopolysaccharidoses. *Eur. J. Hum. Genet.* 2006, 14, 846-852.

[127] Jakobkiewicz-Banecka, J; Piotrowska, E; Narajczyk, M; Baranska, S; Wegrzyn, G. Genistein-mediated inhibition of glycosaminoglycan synthesis; which corrects storage in cells of patients suffering from mucopolysaccharidoses; acts by influencing an epidermal growth factor-dependent pathway. *J. Biomed. Sci.* 2009, 16; 26.

[128] Wegrzyn, A. Gene expression-targeted isoflavone therapy. *IUBMB. Life.* 2012, 64, 307-315.

[129] Arfi, A; Richard, M; Gandolphe, C; Scherman, D. Storage correction in cells of patients suffering from mucopolysaccharidoses types IIIA and VII after treatment with genistein and other isoflavones. *J. Inherit. Metab. Dis.* 2010, 33, 61-67.

[130] Kloska, A; Jakobkiewicz-Banecka, J; Narajczyk, M; Banecka-Majkutewicz, Z; Wegrzyn, G. Effects of flavonoids on glycosaminoglycan synthesis: implications for substrate reduction therapy in Sanfilippo disease and other mucopolysaccharidoses. *Metab. Brain Dis.* 2011, 26, 1-8.

[131] Otomo, T; Hossain, MA; Ozono, K; Sakai, N. Genistein reduces heparan sulfate accumulation in human mucolipidosis II skin fibroblasts. *Mol. Genet. Metab.* 2012, 105, 266-269.

[132] Moskot, M; Jakobkiewicz-Banecka, J; Kloska, A; Smolinska, E; Mozolewski, P; Malinowska, M; Rychlowski, M; Banecki, B; Wegrzyn, G; Gabig-Ciminska, M. Modulation of expression of genes involved in glycosaminoglycan metabolism and lysosome biogenesis by flavonoids. *Sci. Rep.* 2015, 5, 9378.

[133] Kingma, SD; Wagemans, T; IJlst, L; Wijburg, FA; van Vlies, N. Genistein increases glycosaminoglycan levels in mucopolysaccharidosis type I cell models. *J. Inherit. Metab. Dis.* 2014, 37, 813-821.

[134] Fumić, B; Končić, MZ; Jug, M. Therapeutic Potential of Hydroxypropyl-β-Cyclodextrin-Based Extract of Medicago sativa in the Treatment of Mucopolysaccharidoses. *Planta Med.* 2017, 83, 40-50.

[135] Moskot, M; Montefusco, S; Jakobkiewicz-Banecka, J; Mozolewski, P; Wegrzyn, A; Di Bernardo, D; Wegrzyn, G; Medina, DL; Ballabio, A; Gabig-Ciminska, M. The phytoestrogen genistein modulates lysosomal metabolism and transcription factor EB (TFEB) activation. *J. Biol. Chem.* 2014, 289, 17054-17069.

[136] Fumić, B; Jablan, J; Cinčić, D; Zovko, Končić M; Jug, M. Cyclodextrin encapsulation of daidzein and genistein by grinding: implication on the glycosaminoglycan accumulation in mucopolysaccharidosis type II and III fibroblasts. *J. Microencapsul.* 2018, 35, 1-12.

[137] Malinowska, M; Wilkinson, FL; Bennett, W; Langford-Smith, KJ; O'Leary, HA; Jakobkiewicz-Banecka, J; Wynn, R; Wraith, JE; Wegrzyn, G; Bigger, BW. Genistein reduces lysosomal storage in

peripheral tissues of mucopolysaccharide IIIB mice. *Mol. Genet. Metab.* 2009, 98, 235-242.

[138] Malinowska, M; Wilkinson, FL; Langford-Smith, KJ; Langford-Smith, A; Brown, JR; Crawford, BE; Vanier, MT; Grynkiewicz, G; Wynn, RF; Wraith, JE; Wegrzyn, G; Bigger, BW. Genistein improves neuropathology and corrects behaviour in a mouse model of neurodegenerative metabolic disease. *PLoS. One.* 2010, 5, e14192.

[139] Friso, A; Tomanin, R; Salvalaio, M; Scarpa, M. Genistein reduces glycosaminoglycan levels in a mouse model of mucopolysaccharidosis type II. *Br. J. Pharmacol.* 2010, 159, 1082-91.

[140] Kingma, SD; Wagemans, T; IJlst, L; Seppen, J; Gijbels, MJ; Wijburg, FA; van Vlies, N. Adverse effects of genistein in a mucopolysaccharidosis type I mouse model. *JIMD. Rep.* 2015, 23, 77-83.

[141] Piotrowska, E; Jakobkiewicz-Banecka, J; Tylki-Szymanska, A; Liberek, A; Maryniak, A; Malinowska, M; Czartoryska, B; Puk, E; Kloska, A; Liberek, T; Baranska, S; Wegrzyn, A; Wegrzyn, G. Genistin-rich soy isoflavone extract in substrate reduction therapy for Sanfilippo syndrome: An open-label; pilot study in 10 pediatric patients. *Curr. Ther. Res. Clin. Exp.* 2008, 69, 166-179.

[142] Piotrowska, E; Jakobkiewicz-Banecka, J; Maryniak, A; Tylki-Szymanska, A; Puk, E; Liberek, A; Wegrzyn, A; Czartoryska, B; Slominska-Wojewodzka, M; Wegrzyn, G. Two-year follow-up of Sanfilippo Disease patients treated with a genistein-rich isoflavone extract: assessment of effects on cognitive functions and general status of patients. *Med. Sci. Monit.* 2011, 17, CR196-202.

[143] Marucha, J; Tylki-Szymanska, A; Jakobkiewicz-Banecka, J; Piotrowska, E; Kloska, A; Czartoryska, B; Wegrzyn, G. Improvement in the range of joint motion in seven patients with mucopolysaccharidosis type II during experimental gene expression-targeted isoflavone therapy (GET IT). *Am. J. Med. Genet. A.* 2011, 155A,2257-2262.

[144] MalinovA, V; Wegrzyn, G; Narajczyk, M. The use of elevated doses of genistein-rich soy extract in the gene expression-targeted isoflavone therapy for Sanfilippo disease patients. *JIMD. Rep.* 2012, 5; 21-25.

[145] Delgadillo, V; O'Callaghan, M; Mdel, M; Artuch, R; Montero, R; Pineda, M. Genistein supplementation in patients affected by Sanfilippo disease. *J. Inherit. Metab. Dis.* 2011, 34, 1039-1044.

[146] de Ruijter, J; Valstar, MJ; Narajczyk, M; Wegrzyn, G; Kulik, W; Ijlst, L; Wagemans, T; van der Wal, MV; Wijburg, FA. Genistein in Sanfilippo disease: a randomized controlled crossover trial. *Ann. Neurol.* 2012, 71, 110-120.

[147] Kim, KH; Dodsworth, C; Paras, A; Burton, BK. High dose genistein aglycone therapy is safe in patients with mucopolysaccharidoses involving the central nervous system. *Mol. Genet. Metab.* 2013, 109, 382-385.

[148] Cox, TM; Aerts, JM; Andria, G; Beck, M; Belmatoug, N; Bembi, B; Chertkoff, R; Vom Dahl, S; Elstein, D; Erikson, A; Giralt, M; Heitner, R; Hollak, C; Hrebicek, M; Lewis, S; Mehta, A; Pastores, GM; Rolfs, A; Miranda, MC; Zimran, A. The role of the iminosugar N-butyldeoxynojirimycin (miglustat) in the management of type I (non-neuronopathic) Gaucher disease: a position statement. *J. Inherit. Metab. Dis.* 2003, 26, 513-526.

[149] Lyseng-Williamson, KA. Miglustat: a review of its use in Niemann-Pick disease type C. *Drugs.* 2014, 74, 61-74.

[150] Kaidonis, X; Byers, S; Ranieri, E; Sharp, P; Fletcher, J; Derrick-Roberts, A. N-butyldeoxynojirimycin treatment restores the innate fear response and improves learning in mucopolysaccharidosis IIIA mice. *Mol. Genet. Metab.* 2016, 118, 100-110.

[151] Guffon, N; Bin-Dorel, S; Decullier, E; Paillet, C; Guitton, J; Fouilhoux, A. Evaluation of miglustat treatment in patients with type III mucopolysaccharidosis: a randomized; double-blind; placebo-controlled study. *J. Pediatr.* 2011, 159, 838-844.

[152] Matalonga, L; Arias, A; Coll, MJ; Garcia-Villoria, J; Gort, L; Ribes, A. Treatment effect of coenzyme Q (10) and an antioxidant cocktail

in fibroblasts of patients with Sanfilippo disease. *J. Inherit. Metab. Dis.* 2014, 37, 439-446.

[153] Matos, L; Canals, I; Dridi, L; Choi, Y; Prata, MJ; Jordan, P; Desviat, LR; Pérez, B; Pshezhetsky, AV; Grinberg, D; Alves, S; Vilageliu, L. Therapeutic strategies based on modified U1 snRNAs and chaperones for Sanfilippo C splicing mutations. *Orphanet J. Rare Dis.* 2014, 9, 180.

[154] Gómez-Grau, M; Garrido, E; Cozar, M; Rodriguez-Sureda, V; Domínguez, C; Arenas, C; Gatti, RA; Cormand, B; Grinberg, D; Vilageliu, L. Evaluation of Aminoglycoside and Non-Aminoglycoside Compounds for Stop-Codon Readthrough Therapy in Four Lysosomal Storage Diseases. *PLoS One.* 2015, 10, e0135873.

[155] Pierzynowska, K; Gaffke, L; Podlacha, M; Brokowska, J; Węgrzyn, G. Mucopolysaccharidosis and autophagy: controversies on the contribution of the process to the pathogenesis and possible therapeutic applications. *Neuromolecular. Med.* 2020, 22, 25-30.

[156] Lotfi, P; Tse, DY; Di Ronza, A; Seymour, ML; Martano, G; Cooper, JD; Pereira, FA; Passafaro, M; Wu, SM; Sardiello, M. Trehalose reduces retinal degeneration; neuroinflammation and storage burden caused by a lysosomal hydrolase deficiency. *Autophagy.* 2018, 14, 1419-1434.

In: Neurochemistry of Metabolic Diseases ISBN: 978-1-53618-339-9
Editor: Sankar Surendran

Chapter 4

MUCOPOLYSACCHARIDOSIS TYPE VII/SLY DISEASE: MOLECULAR MECHANISM AND THERAPEUTIC EFFECT

Adriana M. Montano*
Department of Pediatrics,
Department of Biochemistry and Molecular Biology,
School of Medicine, Saint Louis University,
St. Louis, MO, US

ABSTRACT

Mucopolysaccharidosis VII (MPS VII) also known as Sly disease, is an ultra-rare lysosomal disorder, characterized by hepatosplenomegaly, skeletal abnormalities and mental retardation. The most severe cases of MPS VII are characterized by hydrops fetalis, a condition in which excess fluid builds up in the body before birth. This disorder is caused by deficiency of the lysosomal enzyme β-glucuronidase (GUSB), causing the accumulation of heparan, dermatan and chondroitin-4 and -6 sulfate

* Corresponding Author's Email: adriana.montano@health.slu.edu.

in the lysosomes. To date, 63 distinct mutations in the GUSB gene causing the disorder have been reported. The disease has three distinct clinical presentations: (*i*) non-immune neonatal *hydrops fetalis* (NIHF); (*ii*) Infantile or adolescent form with history of *hydrops fetalis*; and (*iii*) Infantile or adolescent form without known *hydrops fetalis*. NIHF is the most severe form of MPS VII disease and history of NIHF has been reported in 48% of patients with MPS VII. The infantile form of MPS VII with severe phenotype is characterized by short stature, generalized skeletal dysplasia, coarse facial features, hepatosplenomegaly, umbilical and/or inguinal hernia, heart and lung disease, and cognitive impairment. There is no cure for this disorder, but two treatments have emerged as gold standard since the disease was first reported in 1973. Several MPS VII patients have undergone hematopoietic stem cell transplantation but with high mortality and morbidity. Recently, first clinical trial of enzyme replacement therapy (ERT) was conducted in 2018. Long-term administration of ERT for at least 144 weeks in 12 patients revealed several clinical benefits. Patients showed dramatic decrease in urinary glycosaminoglycans (GAGs), and improvement in the multi-domain responder index which measured motor function, mobility, pulmonary function and visual acuity. Currently, experimental treatments are being developed to tackle the limitations of the current therapies. Unmet needs include neurologic and skeletal manifestations and, management of secondary effects of GAG accumulation including inflammation.

1. INTRODUCTION

Mucopolysaccharidosis VII (MPS VII, Sly Disease, MIM 611499) is an ultra-rare autosomal recessive disorder caused by the deficiency of the lysosomal enzyme β-glucuronidase (GUS, EC 3.2.1.31) [1]. Absence of GUS enzyme results in the systemic accumulation of glycosaminoglycans (GAGs), heparan sulfate (HS), dermatan sulfate (DS), chondroitin-4-sulfate (C4S) and chondroitin-6-sulfate (C6S), causing cellular and organ dysfunction [2].

MPS VII was first described in 1973 in an African American boy who presented with unusual facial features at seven months of age. This patient also suffered from frequent upper respiratory infections, developmental delay by 30 months of age, hepatomegaly, and short stature [2]. MPS VII patients exhibit a heterogeneous phenotype ranging from lethal *hydrops fetalis* to a milder phenotype [3, 4]. Most patients with the severe phenotype have skeletal abnormalities, short stature, cardiac manifestations, pulmonary involvement, hepatosplenomegaly, and cognitive decline [3]. MPS VII remains an ultra-rare disease with an estimated frequency of 1 in 300,000 to 2,000,000 live births. A total of 148 patients have been reported in several countries around the world [2, 5]. This low frequency may be partially explained by the large number of misdiagnosed or non-diagnosed individuals due to the heterogeneity of the disease. Recently, it was reported that almost half of the patients with MPS VII have had a history of *hydrops fetalis*. The high rate of fetal demise due to *hydrops fetalis* then suggests that a large portion of patients with MPS VII may go undiagnosed [4]. Increased suspicion of MPS VII when a patient present with *hydrops fetalis* will aid to provide early treatment and improve outcomes.

Current diagnosis of MPS VII patients is delayed from months to years unless the proband has a relative with the disorder. If there is no presence of *hydrops fetalis,* MPS VII patients will exhibit signs and symptoms around six months of age due to the presence of hepatosplenomegaly, inguinal or umbilical hernias, skeletal abnormalities and/or abnormal frequent respiratory infections. Therefore, implementation of newborn screening is advisable for early detection, management and treatment of this patient population.

Palliative treatments have been implemented for many years for MPS VII patients to manage their symptoms. Currently there are two treatments that ameliorate the progression of the disease: Hematopoietic Stem Cell Transplantation (HSCT) and Enzyme replacement therapy (ERT). Two decades ago experimental approaches of HSCT in mice showed that this treatment was more successful in neonates rather than in adult mice, however there were side effects caused by the radiation exposure in neonates [6]. MPS VII patients that had HSCT have shown improvements in motor function and decrease of upper respiratory and ear infections. Unfortunately, cognitive impairment has been refractory to this treatment and there is increased mortality and morbidity. ERT for MPS VII patients has recently been approved by the FDA and EMA. ERT has shown some improvement in fatigue, motor function, pulmonary function and GAG reduction in 12 patients [7]. Further study is needed to understand whether ERT will delay progression of MPS VII disease, and improve cardiovascular, neurological and skeletal disorder seen in the disease. This chapter presents recent advances in understanding the MPS VII clinical phenotype, highlight challenges of treatments, and discusses new therapeutic approaches.

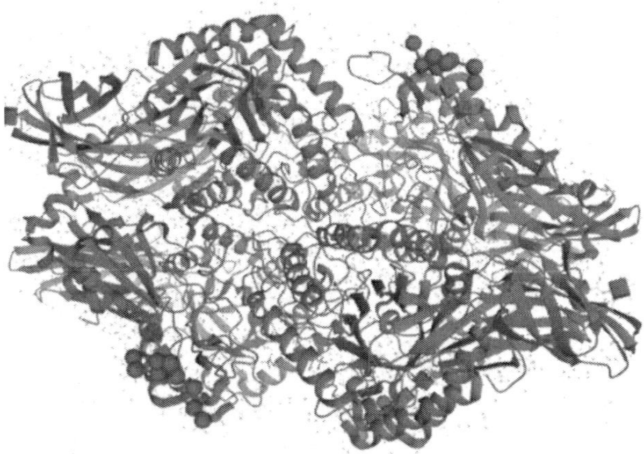

Figure 1. Tridimensional structure of human β-glucuronidase. PDB ID 3HN3. Image reconstructed from the RCSB Protein Data Bank. Klei, Ghosh, and Anumula. Human beta-glucuronidase at 1.7 A resolution. 10.2210/pdb3HN3/pdb.

2. Gene Defect Causing the Disease

Sly disease is caused by mutations in the GUSB gene, which is located on chromosome 7q11.21-7q11.22, and contains 12 exons and 11 introns spanning 21 kb [8, 9]. The mature enzyme, GUSB is a tetramer; each monomer contains four potential N-linked glycosylation sites at Asn173, Asn272, Asn402 and Asn631 [10]. Its four chains are held together by non-covalent interactions [11]. Each monomer is made up of three domains, a jelly roll-like domain containing the lysosomal targeting residues, a triosephosphate isomerase (TIM) barrel domain (active site), and an immunoglobulin region constant domain [11-13]. The loop comprising residues 189 to 199 forms a β-hairpin motif which is exposed on the surface and enables recognition of lysosomal enzymes by a phosphotransferase [11]. The structure of human β-glucuronidase is shown in Figure 1.

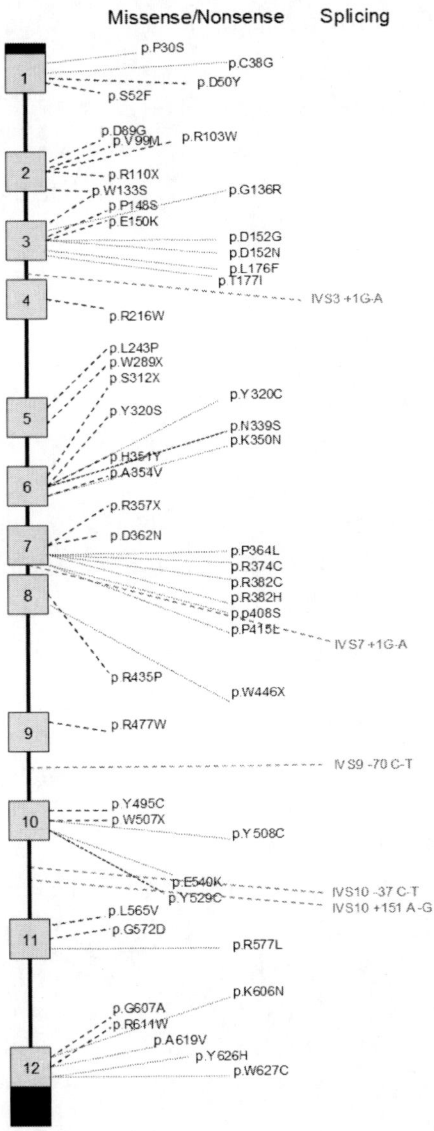

Figure 2. Location of missense, nonsense and splicing mutations in the GUSB gene.

To date, 63 GUSB mutations have been reported by The Human Gene Mutation Database (HGMD®) [14], of which 52 (82.5%) are missense/nonsense, five (7.9%) are splice site-related, four (6.3%) are small deletions, one is a large deletion, and one mutation reduces GUSB promoter activity [15]. The most prevalent mutation found in different populations is p. Leu176Phe (p.L176F) [3, 16-18]. Mutations in the GUSB gene are shown in Figure 2.

3. Biochemical Diagnosis

3.1. GAG Determination

The first step to confirm the clinical suspicion of MPS VII is the quantitation of GAGs (CS, HS and DS) in urine. Over the years, methods to quantify GAGs in biological fluids have evolved considerably. For many years, the quantitative analysis of total urinary GAG has been performed by spectrophotometric analysis using dimethyl methylene blue (DMB) [19]. Although this methodology has been helpful as a diagnostic tool, it has encountered several limitations including poor sensitivity and the potential of providing false negative results. In a study evaluating sensitivity and specificity of the DMB method, researchers found false negative results in 15% of all MPS patients analyzed, and false positive results in 2.9% of controls samples illustrating its limitations as a first-line screening method [20].

To improve sensitivity and specificity of GAG analyses, tandem-mass spectrometry has recently been introduced in lysosomal research and diagnostics. From LC-MS/MS analyzing disaccharides specific for each type of GAG (KS, HS-NS, HS-0S, HS-6S, DS, CS) [21-23] to detecting specific nonreducing ends of GAGs (HS) [24]. Each of these techniques has shown much better reliability and sensitivity and is used currently in several diagnostic laboratories. In patients with MPS VII, CS levels in urine tends to be higher than HS and DS, which amounts could vary [25].

It is important to note that GAG levels change with age and the results should be interpreted accordingly. GAG levels are high in newborns up to five years of age and decrease afterwards reaching a plateau around 18 years of age with levels close to healthy controls [20, 26, 27].

3.2. Enzyme Activity and Molecular Studies

The gold standard to reach a definitive diagnosis of MPS VII is by demonstrated reduced GUSB enzyme activity in fibroblasts or lymphocytes. Patients with MPS VII will have reduced levels of GUSB enzyme to below-10% of normal values. Although precise phenotype/genotype correlation has not been achieved by looking at mutations in such a heterogenous patient population, patients with GUSB enzyme activity close to zero tend to exhibit a more severe phenotype than patients with a residual activity closer to the 10% threshold [3, 28].

3.3. Prenatal Diagnosis

Prenatal screening of MPS VII usually follows an abnormal ultrasound, suspicion due to non-immune *hydrops fetalis* (NIHF) or a history of a sibling affected by the disease. GUSB enzyme activity can be measured in cultured chorionic villus cells by 11-14 weeks of pregnancy or in amniotic fluid after 15 weeks of gestation [29, 30]. There have been reports of diagnosis of MPS VII as early as twelve weeks of gestation based on a previous pregnancy and presence of NIHF with a confirmatory enzymatic diagnosis [31, 32].

4. Pathology

Glycosaminoglycans (GAGs) are repeating disaccharide units covalently attached to the core proteins forming proteoglycans (PGs) [33].

PGs are ubiquitously distributed in extracellular matrix and on the cell surface. There are two types of GAGs: non-sulfated GAGs like hyaluronic acid (HA) and sulfated GAGs including heparan sulfate (HS), dermatan sulfate (DS), keratan sulfate (KS), and chondroitin sulfate (CS) [34]. The GAG chains are modified differentially by sulfation generating high structural diversity, which is an important characteristic linked to their specific function in cells and tissues. Most of the enzymes involved in the synthesis of GAGs have been identified. In MPS VII, the GAGs that accumulate in the lysosomes of the cells are HS, C4S, C6S, and DS; and the enzyme β-glucuronidase is responsible for removing glucuronic acid residues present in each of these GAGs [1]. Dermatan, heparan and chondroitin sulfate catabolism is shown in Figure 3.

Post-mortem histological studies have revealed several brain abnormalities present in patients with MPS VII. GAG accumulation has been observed in gray matter and neurons. Most neuronal lysosomal distention was observed in substantia nigra and hippocampus, followed by cerebral neocortex, glia and cerebellar purkinje cells [35].

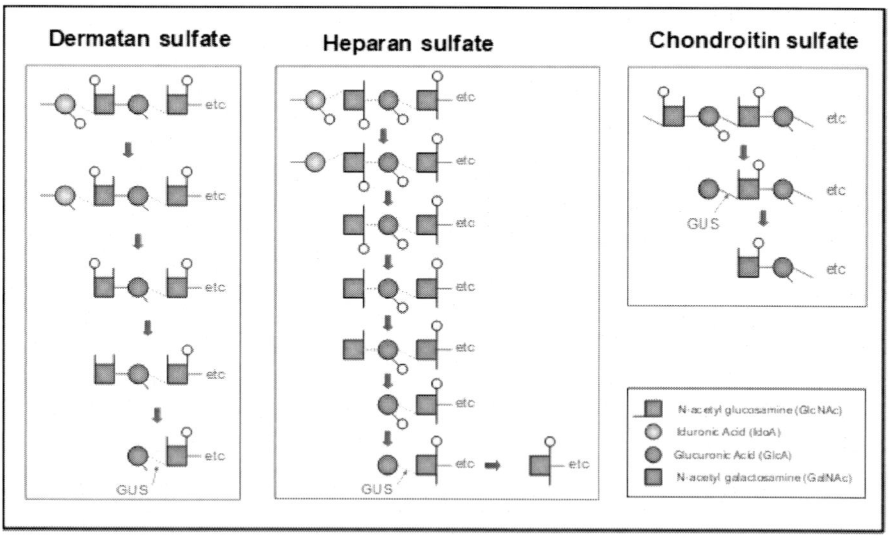

Figure 3. Removal of glucuronic acid by action of β-glucuronidase (GUS/GUSB) in dermatan, heparan and chondroitin sulfate catabolism.

One of the main causes of mortality in MPS VII patients is cardiovascular disease. *Post-mortem* studies have shown enlarged hearts, fibrosis, thickened heart valves and calcified mitral and aortic valves along with hypertrophic cardiomyopathy and disrupted elastin laminae [35-37]. Mitral valve disease occurs at early in life in MPS VII patients causing mitral regurgitation [35]. An autopsy of a 19-year-old patient also revealed abnormal collagen structure in the mitral valves with neovascularization and GAG accumulation in fibroblasts [38].

5. CLINICAL PHENOTYPE AND MANIFESTATIONS

Since MPS VII is a highly heterogeneous, and ultra-rare disorder, precise epidemiological data are hard to obtain. Recently, information on 56 patients from 11 different countries was collected to attempt to understand the disease severity, its rate of progression and the distribution of symptoms [3]. In that study, patients with MPS VII were classified based on their phenotype into three different groups: (*i*) non-immune neonatal *hydrops fetalis* (NIHF), (*ii*) Infantile or adolescent form with history of *hydrops fetalis*, and (*iii*) Infantile or adolescent form without known *hydrops fetalis* [3].

Presence of NIHF is characteristic of the most severe form of MPS VII disease. NIHF has been reported multiple times in fetuses of different ethnical backgrounds with MPS VII who had marked ascites, hepatosplenomegaly, and liver and heart disease, among other findings [39, 40]. NIHF has been reported as early as 10 weeks of gestation with foamy macrophages in several organs [31]. Recently it was found that about half of the patients reported with MPS VII phenotype have had NIHF *in utero* or at delivery [32]. In addition, it was found that about 20% of the patients with NIHF had consanguineous parents [32]. The high incidence of NIHF in patients with MPS VII suggests the importance of adding this lysosomal disease into the differential diagnosis of NIHF.

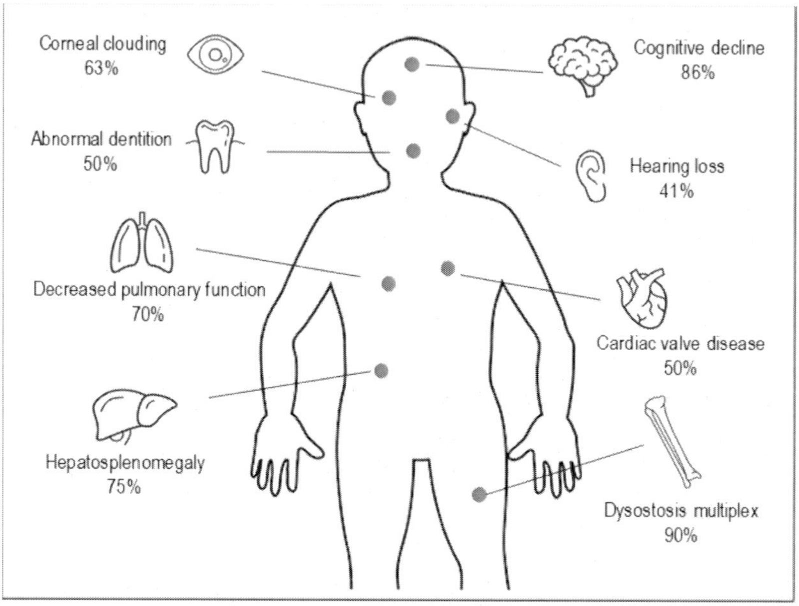

Figure 4. Most common clinical manifestations in patients with MPS VII.

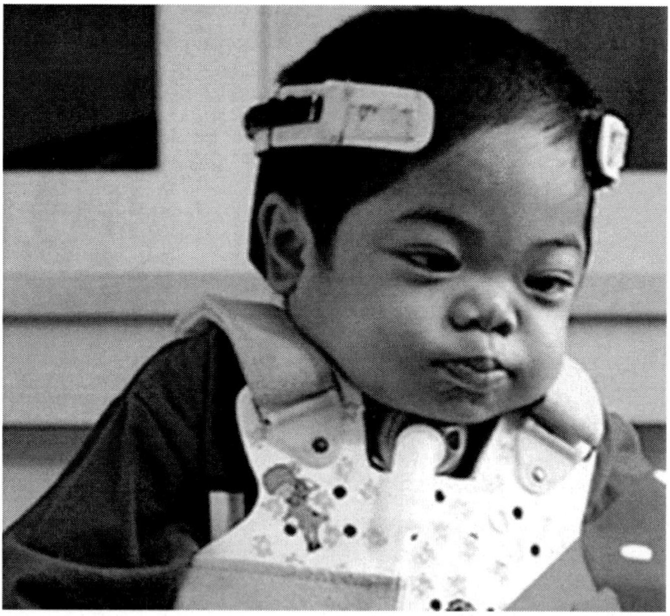

Figure 5. Patient with the severe form of MPS VII disease.

Infantile or adolescent form of MPS VII disease is also characterized by heart disease, corneal clouding, coarse facial features, and upper respiratory infections [2, 3]. Infantile form of MPS VII with severe phenotype is characterized by a short stature, generalized skeletal dysplasia, coarse facial features, hepatosplenomegaly, umbilical and/or inguinal hernia, heart and lung disease, and cognitive impairment [3]. The clinical symptoms observed in patients with MPS VII are shown in Figure 4. A child with Sly disease, showing short neck, coarse facial features and prominent forehead, is shown in Figure 5.

6. Therapeutic Approaches

For years, only palliative and symptomatic-care treatments were available to manage and improve the quality of life of patients with MPS VII [41]. These treatments include acetaminophen and non-steroidal anti-inflammatory drugs (NSAIDs) for pain management, surgeries to correct the bone deformities, antibiotic treatment for recurrent infections, and physical therapy, among others [3, 42]. There are two treatments that are currently the gold standard approaches: hematopoietic stem cell transplantation (HSCT) and enzyme replacement therapy (ERT).

6.1. Hematopoietic Stem Cell Transplantation

Several patients with lysosomal storage disorders have been treated with HSCT by transplanting donor cells of normal individuals providing a continuous source of enzyme [43, 44]. This approach can provide a life-long source of enzyme decreasing GAG accumulation thus slowing down the progression of the disease. If done early in life (before 18 months of age), HSCT can largely prevent the steady cognitive decline seen in untreated patients with MPS I. The obstacles associated with HSCT include: (*i*) difficulty finding a compatible donor, (*ii*) high morbidity, (*iii*) high mortality, (*iv*) infection, (*v*) organ failure, (*vi*) graft-versus-host disease, and (*vii*) growth disturbance [45].

The first report of HSCT in MPS VII was published in 1998 describing a Japanese patient of 12 years of age who had an HLA-identical unrelated female donor. After HSCT the patient had positive outcomes including a dramatic decrease of upper respiratory and ear infections, decreased snoring and improved motor function [46]. However, there was no improvement in the cognitive function of the patient.

In 2016, the outcomes of HSCT in five patients with MPS VII were published. Three of them survived to the procedure [3]. Of the three patients that survived, the first patient underwent HSCT at two years of age following engraftment failure. At four years of age this patient required another HSCT. The outcome of the second HSCT was not reported in this patient. The second patient underwent HSCT at three years of age, with initial signs and symptoms typical of a severe phenotype including difficulty breathing, hepatosplenomegaly, inguinal hernia, coarse facial features, prominent forehead, mental retardation, developmental delay, and short neck. At 15 years of age the patient exhibited moderate symptoms of the disease indicating significant improvement after HSCT. The third patient underwent HSCT at seven months of age with some symptoms of the disease present, including *hydrops fetalis* and tachycardia. At 15 months, the patient did not have hepatosplenomegaly, reached normal milestones however, he exhibited some cardiomyopathy [3].

Due to the rarity, the heterogeneity of the MPS VII disease and the limited reports on HSCT in this patient population, it is challenging to reach a conclusion on the efficacy of this approach.

6.2. Enzyme Replacement Therapy

ERT takes advantage of the endosomal/lysosomal pathway by using the mannose-6 phosphate ligand and the mannose-6 phosphate receptor (M6PR) to target the enzyme to the lysosomes [47]. The challenges found in ERT include: (*i*) the lack of efficacy in treating neurological manifestations, (*ii*) reduced efficacy addressing cardiovascular disease, (*iii*) limited delivery of enzyme to chondrocytes to tackle skeletal manifestations, (*iv*) immune response to the administered enzyme, and (*v*) high costs [3, 48].

The first use of experimental ERT was described in a 12 year old MPS VII patient who had no other clinically viable option [47]. Once ERT started, urinary GAG levels decreased more than a half and hepatosplenomegaly was reversed to normal by 24 weeks after treatment initiation. ERT was very well tolerated without any serious adverse events [49]. A phase III clinical trial was conducted by Ultragenyx Pharmaceuticals and vestronidase alfa (the commercial name for GUSB enzyme) was approved by the FDA in 2017 and by EMA in 2018 for treatment of the non-neurological manifestations [48]. Optimal dose that provided the best reduction of urinary GAGs was 4 mg/kg administered intravenously every other week [50, 51].

Long-term safety and efficacy studies were conducted in 12 subjects for up to 144 weeks after termination of Phase III clinical trial. Results showed sustained decrease in urinary GAG excretion, fatigue, and improvement in the multi-domain responder index (MDRI) score which includes six measurements of motor function, range of motion, mobility, pulmonary function, and visual acuity [7]. It was noticed that patients missing a dose or discontinuing treatment, had elevated levels of urinary GAGs like those before treatment. Although ERT does not address the neurological symptoms of the disease, it has shown clinical improvement in MPS VII patients and appeared to have a favorable effect on the course of the disease.

7. Treatment Challenges

Current challenges of ERT include the limited vascularization in some tissues including cartilage and cardiac valves which impede recombinant enzyme reaching therapeutic levels in these sites. In MPS VII cardiac and skeletal manifestations are progressive, detrimental for patients, and remain unmet needs.

7.1. Cardiovascular Disease

Understanding the pathophysiology of the cardiac manifestations is still a work in progress. To address cardiovascular disease in MPS VII there has been some exciting progress in canine models of MPS VII. In one of the studies, intravenous administration in neonate dogs with a gamma retroviral vector expressing GUSB, showed a reduction in cardiovascular disease by normalization of (*i*) the aortic diameter, (*ii*) the thickening of the tricuspid, aortic, and pulmonary valves, and (*iii*) aortic valve insufficiency [52]. In a long-term study, it was found that neonatal injection with the same gamma retroviral vector in dogs could improve the function of the mitral valve for at least seven years and aortic valve for 11 years [53]. Although GUSB activity in aorta was low [54], a possible explanation for this overall improvement in heart pathology could be the sustained high levels of GUSB achieved in the blood (9.5-fold the level found in normal dogs). Some dogs with higher GUSB level in serum had better outcome than others (5 years vs. 8-10 years). Using the same strategy with gamma retroviral vector in newborn MPS VII mice it was observed that after 10 months of age aortic disease still developed and progressed, showing lack of effectiveness in addressing aortic abnormalities [55]. Possibly higher levels of expression would have been required to match the canine results. Neonatal administration of lentiviral-mediated gene therapy in two models of MPS VII mice resulted in sustained expression of GUSB for up to one year with GAG reduction in the heart [56].

7.2. Central Nervous System Manifestations

Correction of central nervous system pathology has been a long pursuit in the MPS field. The blood–brain barrier (BBB) provides a shield that regulates the brain's microenvironment needed for appropriate neuronal function [57]. Epithelial cells in the BBB are organized together by tight junctions creating a blockade to serum molecules and ions. This unique characteristic of the BBB becomes an obstacle in the delivery of drugs to the brain including ERT. It has been shown in mice that access to M6PR located on the brain capillaries is limited to the first two weeks of life [58, 59]. This indicates that after this period little of the administered recombinant enzyme will be taken up by the M6PR, thus explaining the limited delivery and efficacy observed in the brain after the newborn period.

Adeno associated virus, lentivirus and retroviruses have been used in small and large animal models of MPS VII showing improvement by reversing brain lesions [60-63]. Recent studies in MPS VII dogs have shown that intrathecal injection via the cisterna magna with AAV9 or AAVrh10 vectors carrying the canine GUSB cDNA, resulted in over 100% normal GUSB activity in brain tissue homogenates and reduced GAGs compared with untreated dogs [64]. Implantation in MPS VII mice of GUSB-secreting fibroblasts enclosed in alginate microcapsules fibroblasts into the lateral brain ventricles resulted in improvement of CNS pathology [65].

7.3. Skeletal Manifestations

Since most of the recombinant enzyme is delivered to major visceral organs, only a small fraction is distributed to bone marrow and to the bone making limited correction in bone a great limitation to ERT. Researchers in the field have conducted studies in small and large animals seeking understanding of the pathophysiology of cartilage and bone disease in MPS VII. Studies in MPS VII dogs have shown that there is (*i*) increased water content in the epiphyses of the bones due to high GAG content, (*ii*) impaired hypertrophic differentiation of epiphyseal chondrocytes during development, (*iii*) evidence of spinal deformity due to reduced stiffness, and (*iv*) impeded ability of bone formation and remodeling by overall GAG accumulation in chondrocytes, osteoblasts and osteocytes [66, 67]. Gene therapy has been attempted in MPS VII dogs to evaluate its efficacy on skeletal lesions. It has been shown that, if gene therapy is administered in neonates, some abnormalities are ameliorated; however some abnormalities that are clinically relevant were not reversed [68].

7.4. Future Treatments for MPS VII

Include prenatal, early postnatal administration of ERT to improve efficacy outcomes, management of secondary effects of GAG accumulation, improved administration of enzyme to manage neurologic and skeletal manifestations, and clinical development of gene therapy, among others. Approach for diagnosis and treatment of MPS VII patients is given in Figure 6.

Early administration of enzyme in other MPS diseases has been found to slow the progression of the disease and treated patients exhibit milder phenotype than untreated siblings at the same age [69]. To make sure that early ERT administration becomes a reality, we must first make sure that we have national implementation of newborn screening for this disorder.

Novel experimental studies in MPS VII mice treating animals in utero with ERT or HSCT to improve survival have been explored to minimize the effects of GAG accumulation in tissues, especially brain and bone [70]. The results obtained are the first step towards a very exciting field that can be applicable to all the MPS disorders.

GAG accumulation in the MPS causes secondary effects including the activation of signal transduction pathways, particularly of inflammation. Tackling inflammation may result in clinical benefit for MPS VII patients mainly by addressing the skeletal manifestations seen in severe phenotypes. A phase II clinical study with pentosan polysulfate in four MPS I patients revealed that it was well tolerated in patients, and patients had reduction in urinary GAGs and improvement in joint mobility when administered concomitant to ERT [71, 72]. Additional exploration of this approach is needed to understand its efficacy.

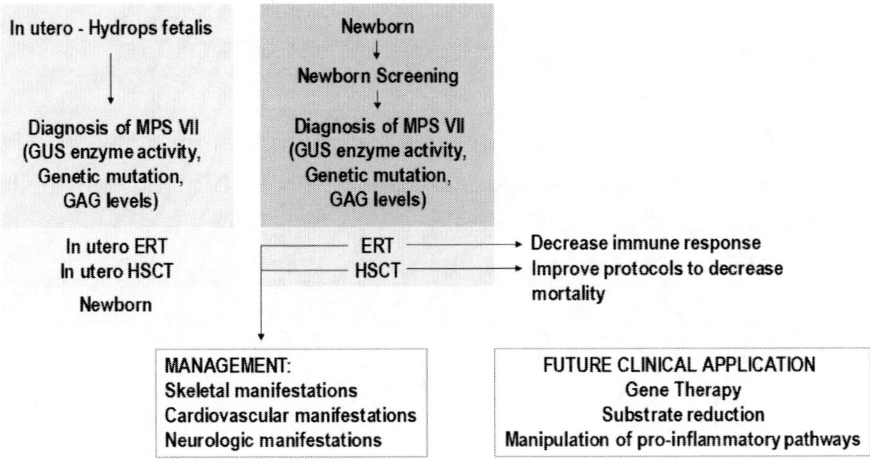

Figure 6. Diagram with the ideal approach for diagnosis and treatment of MPS VII patients. Development of early treatments that tackle skeletal, cardiovascular and neurologic manifestations will provide better quality of life to patients. Improvement of existing treatments and advancements in new therapeutic strategies are pivotal to address current unmet medical needs.

Immune response to ERT, especially in patients with null mutations, represents a big obstacle in the treatment not only by reducing efficacy of the treatment but also by causing harmful side effects in patients who must take immunosuppressants. Approaches like oral tolerance, which is natural and safe, may minimize immune response to ERT in MPS patients, and are currently being developed in animal models. The use an immunodominant peptide or the enzyme used for ERT to orally induce tolerance prior to ERT resulted in several improvements to ERT in MPS IVA mice including (*i*) decreased splenocyte proliferation, (ii) modulation of the cytokine secretion profile, (*iii*) decrease in enzyme-specific IgG or IgE in plasma, and (*iv*) decreased GAG storage in liver and plasma [73].

CONCLUSION

MPS VII is a heterogenous and progressive disease that affects the patients systemically. Therefore, management of patients in a clinical setting remains one of the most important challenges that need to be addressed. Starting with an appropriate diagnosis, followed by early treatment under the care of a multidisciplinary team is a requirement that needs to be established. Although this disease and its animal models have been extensively studied, the long-term outcomes of ERT are still under investigation. The emergence of new and additive treatments hopefully will alleviate the most challenging limitations of the current ones.

REFERENCES

[1] Sukegawa, K; Tomatsu, S; Kondo, N; Orii, T. Mucopolysaccharidosis Type VII (Sly Disease). *Ryoikibetsu. Shokogun. Shirizu.* 1998, 449-452.

[2] Sly, WS; Quinton, BA.; McAlister, WH; Rimoin, DL. Beta glucuronidase deficiency: report of clinical, radiologic, and biochemical features of a new mucopolysaccharidosis. *J. Pediatr.* 1973, 82, 249-257.

[3] Montaño, AM; Lock-Hock, N; Steiner, RD; Graham, BH; Szlago, M; Greenstein, R; Pineda, M; Gonzalez-Meneses, A; Coker, M; Bartholomew, D; Sands, MS; Wang, R; Giugliani, R; Macaya, A; Pastores, G; Ketko, AK; Ezgu, F; Tanaka, A; Arash, L; Beck, M; Falk, RE; Bhattacharya, K; Franco, J; White, KK; Mitchell, GA; Cimbalistiene, L; Holtz, M; Sly, WS. Clinical course of Sly syndrome (Mucopolysaccharidosis type VII). *J. Med. Genet.* 2016, 53, 403-418.

[4] Holtz, M; Montano, AM; Sly, WS. Association between mucopolysaccharidosis Type VII and hydrops fetalis. *Ultrasound Obstet. Gynecol.* 2020, 55, 416-417.

[5] Muenzer, J. Overview of the mucopolysaccharidoses. *Rheumatology (Oxford). 2011,* 50, v4-12.

[6] Sands, MS; Barker, JE; Vogler, C; Levy, B; Gwynn, B; Galvin, N; Sly, WS; Birkenmeier, E. Treatment of murine mucopoly-

saccharidosis type VII by syngeneic bone marrow transplantation in neonates. *Lab. Invest.* 1993, 68, 676-686.

[7] Wang, RY; da Silva Franco, JF; Lopez-Valdez, J; Martins, E; Sutton, VR; Whitley, CB; Zhang, L; Cimms, T; Marsden, D; Jurecka, A; Harmatz, P. The long-term safety and efficacy of vestronidase alfa, rhGUS enzyme replacement therapy, in subjects with mucopolysaccharidosis VII. *Mol. Genet. Metab.* 2020, 129, 219-227.

[8] Speleman, F;Vervoort, R;van Roy, N; Liebaers, I; Sly, WS; Lissens, W. Localization by fluorescence in situ hybridization of the human functional beta-glucuronidase gene (GUSB) to 7q11.21 --> q11.22 and two pseudogenes to 5p13 and 5q13. *Cytogenet. Cell Genet.* 1996, 72, 53-55.

[9] Miller, RD; Hoffmann, JW; Powell, PP; Kyle, JW; Shipley, JM; Bachinsky, DR; Sly, WS. Cloning and characterization of the human beta-glucuronidase gene. *Genomics* 1990, 7, 280-283.

[10] Shipley, JM;Grubb, JH, Sly, WS. The role of glycosylation and phosphorylation in the expression of active human beta-glucuronidase. *J. Biol. Chem.* 1993, 268, 12193-12198.

[11] Hassan, MI; Waheed, A; Grubb, JH; Klei, HE; Korolev, S; Sly, WS. High resolution crystal structure of human beta-glucuronidase reveals structural basis of lysosome targeting. *PLoS One.* 2013, 8, e79687.

[12] Khan, FI; Shahbaaz, M; Bisetty, K; Waheed, A; Sly, WS; Ahmad, F, Hassan, MI. Large scale analysis of the mutational landscape in beta-glucuronidase: A major player of mucopolysaccharidosis type VII. *Gene* 2016, 576, 36-44.

[13] Jain, S; Drendel, WB; Chen, ZW; Mathews, FS; Sly, WS; Grubb, JH. Structure of human beta-glucuronidase reveals candidate lysosomal targeting and active-site motifs. *Nat. Struct. Biol.* 1996, 3, 375-381.

[14] Stenson, PD; Ball, EV; Mort, M; Phillips, AD; Shiel, JA; Thomas, NS; Abeysinghe, S; Krawczak, M; Cooper, DN. Human Gene Mutation Database (HGMD): 2003 update. *Hum. Mutat.* 2003, 21, 577-581.

[15] Gratz, M; Kunert-Keil, C; John, U; Cascorbi, I; Kroemer, HK. Identification and functional analysis of genetic variants of the

human beta-glucuronidase in a German population sample. *Pharmacogenet. Genomics* 2005, 15, 875-881.

[16] Vervoort, R; Buist, NR; Kleijer, WJ; Wevers, R; Fryns, JP; Liebaers, I; Lissens, W. Molecular analysis of the beta-glucuronidase gene: novel mutations in mucopolysaccharidosis type VII and heterogeneity of the polyadenylation region. *Hum. Genet.* 1997, 99, 462-468.

[17] Tomatsu, S; Montano, AM; Dung, VC; Grubb, JH; Sly, WS. Mutations and polymorphisms in GUSB gene in mucopolysaccharidosis VII (Sly Syndrome) *Hum. Mutat.* 2009, 30, 511-519.

[18] Shamseldin, HE; Tulbah, M; Kurdi, W; Nemer, M; Alsahan, N; Al Mardawi, E; Khalifa, O; Hashem, A; Kurdi, A; Babay, Z; Bubshait, DK; Ibrahim, N; Abdulwahab, F; Rahbeeni, Z; Hashem, M; Alkuraya, FS. Identification of embryonic lethal genes in humans by autozygosity mapping and exome sequencing in consanguineous families. *Genome Biol.* 2015, 16, 116.

[19] Whitley, CB; Ridnour, MD; Draper, KA; Dutton, CM; Neglia, JP. Diagnostic test for mucopolysaccharidosis. I. Direct method for quantifying excessive urinary glycosaminoglycan excretion. *Clin. Chem.* 1989, 35, 374-379.

[20] Gray, G; Claridge, P; Jenkinson, L; Green, A. Quantitation of urinary glycosaminoglycans using dimethylene blue as a screening technique for the diagnosis of mucopolysaccharidoses: an evaluation. *Ann. Clin. Biochem.* 2007, 44, 360-363.

[21] Tomatsu, S; Shimada, T; Mason, RW; Kelly, J; LaMarr, WA; Yasuda, E; Shibata, Y; Futatsumori, H; Montano, AM; Yamaguchi, S; Suzuki, Y; Orii, T. Assay for Glycosaminoglycans by Tandem Mass Spectrometry and its Applications. *J. Anal. Bioanal. Tech.* 2014, 2014, 006.

[22] Tomatsu, S; Shimada, T; Mason, RW; Montano, AM; Kelly, J; LaMarr, WA; Kubaski, F; Giugliani, R; Guha, A; Yasuda, E; Mackenzie, W; Yamaguchi, S; Suzuki, Y; Orii, T. Establishment of

glycosaminoglycan assays for mucopolysaccharidoses. *Metabolites.* 2014, 4, 655-679.

[23] Chuang, CK; Lin, HY; Wang, TJ; Tsai, CC; Liu, HL; Lin, SP. A modified liquid chromatography/tandem mass spectrometry method for predominant disaccharide units of urinary glycosaminoglycans in patients with mucopolysaccharidoses. Orphanet. *J. Rare Dis.* 2014, 9, 135.

[24] Lawrence, R; Brown, JR; Al-Mafraji, K; Lamanna, WC; Beitel, JR; Boons, GJ; Esko, JD; Crawford, BE. Disease-specific non-reducing end carbohydrate biomarkers for mucopolysaccharidoses. *Nat. Chem. Biol.* 2012, 8, 197-204.

[25] Zaia, J. On-line separations combined with MS for analysis of glycosaminoglycans. *Mass. Spectrom. Rev.* 2009, 28, 254-272.

[26] Hintze, JP; Tomatsu, S; Fujii, T; Montano, AM; Yamaguchi, S; Suzuki, Y; Fukushi, M; Ishimaru, T; Orii, T. Comparison of liquid chromatography-tandem mass spectrometry and sandwich ELISA for determination of keratan sulfate in plasma and urine. *Biomark. Insights.* 2011, 6, 69-78.

[27] Langereis, EJ; Wagemans, T; Kulik, W; Lefeber, DJ; van Lenthe, H; Oussoren, E; van der Ploeg, AT; Ruijter, GJ; Wevers, RA; Wijburg, FA; van Vlies, N. A Multiplex Assay for the Diagnosis of Mucopolysaccharidoses and Mucolipidoses. *PLoS One.* 2015, 10, e0138622.

[28] Storch, S; Wittenstein, B; Islam, R; Ullrich, K; Sly, WS; Braulke, T. Mutational analysis in longest known survivor of mucopolysaccharidosis type VII. *Hum. Genet.* 2003, 112, 190-194.

[29] Akella, RR; Kadali, S. Amniotic fluid glycosaminoglycans in the prenatal diagnosis of mucopolysaccharidoses - A useful biomarker. *Clin. Chim. Acta.* 2016, 460, 63-66.

[30] Jelin, AC; Sagaser, KG; Wilkins-Haug, L. Prenatal Genetic Testing Options. *Pediatr. Clin. North Am.* 2019, 66, 281-293.

[31] Van Dorpe, J; Moerman, P; Pecceu, A; Van den Steen, P; Fryns, JP. Non-immune hydrops fetalis caused by beta-glucuronidase

deficiency (mucopolysaccharidosis VII). Study of a family with 3 affected siblings. *Genetic Couns.* 1996, 7, 105-112.
[32] Holtz, M; Montano, AM; Sly, WS. Association between mucopolysaccharidosis Type VII and hydrops fetalis. *Ultrasound Obstet. Gynecol.* 2020, 55, 416-417.
[33] Mizumoto, S;Yamada, S; Sugahara, K. Human genetic disorders and knockout mice deficient in glycosaminoglycan. *Biomed. Res. Int.* 2014, 2014, 495764.
[34] Gandhi, NS; Mancera, RL. The structure of glycosaminoglycans and their interactions with proteins. *Chem. Biol. Drug Des.* 2008, 72, 455-482.
[35] Vogler, C; Levy, B; Kyle, JW; Sly, WS; Williamson, J; Whyte, MP. Mucopolysaccharidosis VII: postmortem biochemical and pathological findings in a young adult with beta-glucuronidase deficiency. *Mod. Pathol.* 1994, 7, 132-137.
[36] Gniadek, TJ; Singer, N; Barker, NJ; Spevak, PJ; Crain, BJ; Valle, D; Halushka, MK. Cardiovascular pathologies in mucopolysaccharidosis type VII (Sly Syndrome). *Cardiovasc. Pathol.* 2015, 24, 322-326.
[37] Lew, V; Pena, L; Edwards, R; Wang, RY. Cardiovascular Histopathology of a 11-Year Old with Mucopolysaccharidosis VII Demonstrates Fibrosis, Macrophage Infiltration, and Arterial Luminal Stenosis. *JIMD. Rep.* 2018, 39, 31-37.
[38] Bigg, PW; Baldo, G; Sleeper, MM; O'Donnell, PA; Bai, H; Rokkam, VR; Liu, Y; Wu, S; Giugliani, R; Casal, ML; Haskins, ME., Ponder, KP. Pathogenesis of mitral valve disease in mucopolysaccharidosis VII dogs. *Mol. Genet. Metab.* 2013,110, 319-328.
[39] Kooper, AJA; Janssens, PMW; de Groot, ANJA; Liebrand-van Sambeek, MLF; van den Berg, CJMG; Tan-Sindhunata, GB; van den Berg, PP; Bijlsma, EK; Smits, APT, Wevers, RA. Lysosomal storage diseases in non-immune hydrops fetalis pregnancies. *Clin. Chim. Acta.* 2006, 371, 176-182.
[40] Lissens, W; Dedobbeleer, G; Foulon, W; De Catte, L; Charels, K; Goossens, A; Liebaers, Beta-glucuronidase deficiency as a cause of

prenatally diagnosed non-immune hydrops fetalis. *Prenat. Diagn.* 1991, 11, 405-410.

[41] Valayannopoulos, V; Wijburg, FA. Therapy for the mucopolysaccharidoses. *Rheumatol.* 2011, 50, Suppl 5, v49-59.

[42] Congedi, S;Orzalesi, M;Di Pede, C; Benini, F. Pain in Mucopolysaccharidoses: Analysis of the Problem and Possible Treatments. *Int. J. Mol. Sci.* 2018, 19, 3063.

[43] Hoogerbrugge, PM; Brouwer, OF; Bordigoni, P; Ringden, O; Kapaun, P; Ortega, JJ; O'Meara, A; Cornu, G; Souillet, G; Frappaz, D; Blanche, S; Fischer, A. Allogeneic bone marrow transplantation for lysosomal storage diseases. *Lancet* 1995, 345, 1398-1402.

[44] Kohn, AF; Grigull, L; du Moulin, M; Kabisch, S; Ammer, L; Rudolph, C; Muschol, NM. Hematopoietic stem cell transplantation in mucopolysaccharidosis type IIIA: A case description and comparison with a genotype-matched control group. *Mol. Genet. Metab. Rep.* 2020, 23, 100578.

[45] Wynn, RF; Wraith, JE;Mercer, J; O'Meara, A; Tylee, K; Thornley, M; Church, HJ; Bigger, BW. Improved metabolic correction in patients with lysosomal storage disease treated with hematopoietic stem cell transplant compared with enzyme replacement therapy. *J. Pediatr.* 2009, 154, 609-611.

[46] Yamada, Y; Kato, K; Sukegawa, K; Tomatsu, S; Fukuda, S; Emura, S; Kojima, S; Matsuyama, T; Sly, WS; Kondo, N; Orii, T. Treatment of MPS VII (Sly disease) by allogeneic BMT in a female with homozygous A619V mutation. *Bone Marrow Transplant.* 1998, 21, 629-634.

[47] Grubb, JH; Vogler, C; Sly, WS. New strategies for enzyme replacement therapy for lysosomal storage diseases. *Rejuvenation Res.* 2010, 13, 229-236.

[48] Vartanyan, A; Montaño, AM. Causal Therapies in Mucopoly saccharidoses: Enzyme Replacement Therapy. *J. Child Sci.* 2018, 8, e156–e162.

[49] Fox, JE; Volpe, L; Bullaro, J; Kakkis, ED; Sly, WS. First human treatment with investigational rhGUS enzyme replacement therapy in

an advanced stage MPS VII patient *Mol. Genet. Metab.* 2015, 114, 203-208.

[50] Cadaoas, J; Boyle, G; Jungles, S; Cullen, S; Vellard, M; Grubb, JH; Jurecka, A; Sly, W; Kakkis, E. Vestronidase alfa: Recombinant human beta-glucuronidase as an enzyme replacement therapy for MPS VII. *Mol. Genet. Metab.* 2020, 130, 65-76.

[51] Harmatz, P; Whitley, CB; Wang, RY; Bauer, M; Song, W; Haller, C; Kakkis, E. A novel Blind Start study design to investigate vestronidase alfa for mucopolysaccharidosis VII, an ultra-rare genetic disease. *Mol. Genet. Metab.* 2018, 123, 488-494.

[52] Ponder, KP; Melniczek, JR; Xu, L; Weil, MA; O'Malley, TM; O'Donnell, PA; Knox, VW; Aguirre, GD; Mazrier, H; Ellinwood, NM; Sleeper, M; Maguire, AM; Volk, SW; Mango, RL; Zweigle, J; Wolfe, JH; Haskins, ME. Therapeutic neonatal hepatic gene therapy in mucopolysaccharidosis VII dogs. *Proc. Natl. Acad. Sci.* USA. 2002, 99, 13102-13107.

[53] Bigg, PW; Sleeper, MM; O'Donnell, PA; Liu, Y; Wu, S; Casal, ML; Haskins, ME. Ponder, KP. The effect of neonatal gene therapy with a gamma retroviral vector on cardiac valve disease in mucopolysaccharidosis VII dogs after a decade. *Mol. Genet. Metab.* 2013, 110, 311-318.

[54] Metcalf, JA; Linders, B; Wu, S; Bigg, P; O'Donnell, P; Sleeper, MM; Whyte, MP; Haskins, M; Ponder, KP. Upregulation of elastase activity in aorta in mucopolysaccharidosis I and VII dogs may be due to increased cytokine expression. *Mol. Genet. Metab.* 2010, 99, 396-407.

[55] Baldo, G; Wu, S; Howe, RA; Ramamoothy, M; Knutsen, RH; Fang, J; Mecham, RP; Liu, Y; Wu, X; Atkinson, JP; Ponder, KP. Pathogenesis of aortic dilatation in mucopolysaccharidosis VII mice may involve complement activation. *Mol. Genet. Metab.* 2011, 104, 608-619.

[56] Derrick-Roberts, AL; Pyragius, CE; Kaidonis, XM; Jackson, MR; Anson, DS; Byers, S. Lentiviral-mediated gene therapy results in sustained expression of beta-glucuronidase for up to 12 months in the

gus(mps/mps) and up to 18 months in the gus(tm(L175F)Sly) mouse models of mucopolysaccharidosis type VII. *Hum. Gene Ther.* 2014, 25, 798-810.

[57] Daneman, R; Prat, A. The blood-brain barrier. *Cold Spring Harb Perspect Biol.* 2015, 7, a020412.

[58] Urayama, A; Grubb, JH; Sly, WS; Banks, WA. Mannose 6-phosphate receptor-mediated transport of sulfamidase across the blood-brain barrier in the newborn mouse. *Mol. Ther.* 2008, 16, 1261-1266.

[59] Sly, WS; Vogler, C. The final frontier -- crossing the blood-brain barrier. *EMBO. Mol. Med.* 2013, 5, 655-657.

[60] Bosch, A; Perret, E; Desmaris, N; Heard, JM. Long-term and significant correction of brain lesions in adult mucopolysaccharidosis type VII mice using recombinant AAV vectors. *Mol. Ther.* 2000, 1, 63-70.

[61] Bosch, A; Perret, E; Desmaris, N; Trono, D; Heard, JM. Reversal of pathology in the entire brain of mucopolysaccharidosis type VII mice after lentivirus-mediated gene transfer. *Hum. Gene Ther.* 2000, 11, 1139-1150.

[62] Cubizolle, A; Serratrice, N; Skander, N; Colle, MA; Ibanes, S; Gennetier, A; Bayo-Puxan, N; Mazouni, K; Mennechet, F; Joussemet, B; Cherel, Y; Lajat, Y; Vite, C; Bernex, F; Kalatzis, V; Haskins, ME; Kremer, EJ. Corrective GUSB transfer to the canine mucopolysaccharidosis VII brain. *Mol. Ther.* 2014, 22, 762-773.

[63] Ariza, L; Gimenez-Llort, L; Cubizolle, A; Pages, G; Garcia-Lareu, B; Serratrice, N; Cots, D; Thwaite, R; Chillon, M; Kremer, EJ; Bosch, A. Central nervous system delivery of helper-dependent canine adenovirus corrects neuropathology and behavior in mucopolysaccharidosis type VII mice. *Hum. Gene Ther.* 2014, 25, 199-211.

[64] Gurda, BL; De Guilhem De Lataillade, A; Bell, P; Zhu, Y; Yu, H; Wang, P; Bagel, J; Vite, CH; Sikora, T; Hinderer, C; Calcedo, R; Yox, AD; Steet, RA; Ruane, T; O'Donnell, P; Gao, G; Wilson, JM; Casal, M; Ponder, KP; Haskins, ME. Evaluation of AAV-mediated Gene Therapy for Central Nervous System Disease in Canine Mucopolysaccharidosis VII. *Mol. Ther.* 2016, 24, 206-216.

[65] Ross, CJ; Bastedo, L; Maier, SA; Sands, MS; Chang, PL. Treatment of a lysosomal storage disease, mucopolysaccharidosis VII, with microencapsulated recombinant cells. *Hum. Gene Ther.* 2000, 11, 2117-2127.

[66] Smith, LJ; Martin, JT; Szczesny, SE; Ponder, KP; Haskins, ME; Elliott, DM. Altered lumbar spine structure, biochemistry, and biomechanical properties in a canine model of mucopolysaccharidosis type VII. *J. Orthop. Res.* 2010, 28, 616-622.

[67] Peck, SH; O'Donnell, PJ; Kang, JL; Malhotra, NR; Dodge, GR; Pacifici, M; Shore, EM; Haskins, ME; Smith, LJ. Delayed hypertrophic differentiation of epiphyseal chondrocytes contributes to failed secondary ossification in mucopolysaccharidosis VII dogs. *Mol. Genet. Metab.* 2015, 116, 195-203.

[68] Xing, EM; Knox, VW; O'Donnell, PA; Sikura, T; Liu, Y; Wu, S; Casal, ML; Haskins, ME; Ponder, KP. The effect of neonatal gene therapy on skeletal manifestations in mucopolysaccharidosis VII dogs after a decade. *Mol. Genet. Metab.* 2013, 109, 183-193.

[69] Furujo, M; Kosuga, M; Okuyama, T. Enzyme replacement therapy attenuates disease progression in two Japanese siblings with mucopolysaccharidosis type VI: 10-Year follow up. *Mol. Genet. Metab. Rep.* 2017, 13, 69-75.

[70] Nguyen, QH; Witt, RG; Wang, B; Eikani, C; Shea, J; Smith, LK; Boyle, G; Cadaoas, J; Sper, R; MacKenzie, JD; Villeda, S; MacKenzie, TC. Tolerance induction and microglial engraftment after fetal therapy without conditioning in mice with Mucopolysaccharidosis type VII. *Sci. Transl. Med.* 2020, 12, eaay8980.

[71] Hennermann, JB; Gokce, S; Solyom, A; Mengel, E; Schuchman, EH., Simonaro, CM. Treatment with pentosan polysulphate in patients with MPS I: results from an open label, randomized, monocentric phase II study. *J. Inherit. Metab. Dis.* 2016, 39, 831-837.

[72] Fecarotta, S; Gasperini, S; Parenti, G. New treatments for the mucopolysaccharidoses: from pathophysiology to therapy. *Ital. J. Pediatr.* 2018, 44, 124.

[73] Sosa, AC; Kariuki, B; Gan, Q; Knutsen, AP; Bellone, CJ; Guzman, MA; Barrera, LA; Tomatsu, S; Chauhan, AK; Armbrecht, E; Montano, AM. Oral immunotherapy tolerizes mice to enzyme replacement therapy for Morquio A syndrome. *J. Clin. Invest.* 2020, 130, 1288-1300.

In: Neurochemistry of Metabolic Diseases
Editor: Sankar Surendran
ISBN: 978-1-53618-339-9

Chapter 5

GM2 GANGLIOSIDOSIS /TAY SACHS DISEASE: MOLECULAR MECHANISM AND THERAPEUTIC EFFECT

Jayesh Sheth* and Aadhira Nair
Foundation for Research in Genetics and Endocrinology (FRIGE),
Institute of Human Genetics, Ahmedabad, Gujarat, India

ABSTRACT

GM2 gangliosidoses are a group of autosomal recessive disorders caused by mutations in anyone of these three genes: *HEXA*, *HEXB*, and *GM2A*. The proteins encoded by these genes are essential for the catabolism of GM2 ganglioside. Deficiency of these enzymes leads to an accumulation of the substrate inside neuronal lysosomes and nerve cell death. Tay-Sachs disease, Sandhoff disease and GM2 activator protein deficiency are included under GM2 gangliosidoses. The incidence and prevalence of Tay-Sachs disease is found to be higher in certain populations particularly the Ashkenazi Jews, which suggests a founder

---

* Corresponding Author's Email: jayesh.sheth@frige.co.in.

effect involvement in case of these disorders. Considering this data, carrier screening and prenatal diagnosis holds promise for proper management and prevention of the disease. The current diagnostics strategy includes enzyme assay and molecular diagnosis. Establishing a genotype-phenotype relationship will also be essential from the point of view of patient prognosis and evaluating success of various therapies. The different treatment strategies explored include enzyme replacement therapy, substrate reduction therapy as well as gene therapy. With advancements in technology, the primary aim will be to provide timely and adequate diagnosis, its prevention through prenatal study followed by efficient therapy that aids in successful survival of the patients.

1. INTRODUCTION

Gangliosides are glycosphingolipids with presence of one or more sialic acid groups. The accumulation of GM2 gangliosides (monosialoganglioside2) in the central nervous system results in development of a severe neurological condition known as GM2 gangliosidosis. This includes a group of inherited metabolic disorders due to deficient β-hexosaminidase activity or absence of GM2 activator protein [1, 2]. Tay-Sachs disease (TSD) and Sandhoff disease (SD) included under GM2 gangliosidoses, are caused due to mutations present in *HEXA* and *HEXB* gene that encode α and β subunits of β-hexosaminidase-A respectively [3, 4], whereas mutations in *GM2A* gene results in another GM2 gangliosidoses- GM2 activator protein deficiency [1]. Tay-Sachs disease is the most common of the three forms presented with an incidence of 1/100,000 live births [5]. This frequency is higher in Ashkenazi Jewish population with 1/4000 [2]. Also, among the Lysosomal storage disorders in India, Tay-Sachs disease is one of the common lipid storage disorders [6, 7]. The mode of inheritance of these disorders is autosomal recessive emphasizing the need for the correct diagnosis in an index case and ensuring its prevention in subsequent pregnancies. The severity of the condition and its age of onset are highly determined by the residual enzyme activity. Accordingly, the condition is categorized as infantile acute, juvenile sub-acute and adult chronic forms based on the age when the first symptoms are noticed. The commonly observed symptoms vary from infantile form presented with seizures, neuro-regression, muscle weakness, hyperacusis and cherry red spot on fundus to an adult form with progressive dementia and gait disturbances [7, 8]. There are reports of over 199 disease causing mutations in *HEXA* gene as per the Human Gene Mutation Database (HGMD) as assessed on 23rd April 2020 (http://www.hgmd.cf.ac.uk/). Certain mutations are present in specific ethnicities like c.1421+1G > C, c.1274_1277dupTATC and c.805G > A are the most commonly prevalent in 98% of Ashkenazi Jews and 35% non-Ashkenazi Jews population [9–11] and c.1385A > T (E462V) and c.964G > T (D322Y) mutation in the India Gujarati ethnic population [3, 6, 12]. However, such studies have not been carried out for all the different ethnicities. The presence of particular mutations in certain communities denote the effect of founder mutation and this knowledge will be beneficial from the point of view of carrying out carrier screening in those populations followed by precise genetic counseling and prenatal diagnosis for prevention of the disease. At present, the therapeutic approach for GM2 gangliosidosis is not providing a permanent cure but is based on reducing symptom effects or delaying the progression in case of adult forms.

2. Brief History

Tay-Sachs disease was first identified by a British ophthalmologist-Warren Tay in 1881 in an infant with severe neurological dysfunction, aged 1 year. The distinct clinical feature observed was the presence of symmetrical changes in the yellow spot in each eye- now known as the cherry-red spot. However, the original patient died at 18 months and later, Tay found another family member of the patient affected with the same condition denoting its heritable nature. He gave a detailed clinical report of the same in 1884. Independently, an American neurologist, Bernard Sachs recorded a similar finding in a child with arrested cerebral development and was the first to publish a brain cortical pathology of the disease in 1887 and hence the combined terminology is given to the condition- Tay-

Sachs disease. Later, Ernst Klenk in 1942 discovered the accumulation of an unknown glycosphingolipid in the brains of these patients and coined the term- ganglioside as they were abundantly found in ganglion cells. However, it took two decades for identification of the main storage material in the brains of TSD patients- GM2 ganglioside by Svennerholm. Further studies by Makita and Yamakawa in 1969 helped in elucidating its structure [2].

Robinson and Sterling in 1968 had separated the two forms Hex-A and Hex-B from the total β-N-acetyl-hexosaminidase (hex). It was only in 1969, when the deficiency of β-hexosaminidase activity particularly the Hex-A form in TSD patients was discovered [13] and this is also referred as the B variant. In 1968, while isolating the storage material from brains of TSD patients, Konrad Sandhoff discovered additional accumulation of globoside in visceral tissues in one of the TSD cases. This was designated as the O variant and some of these were later called as Sandhoff disease [14]. He attributed deficiency of both Hex-A and Hex-B in this condition. In some of the O variant cases, there were normal levels of Hex-A and Hex-B but absence of total Hex activity against the natural substrate. These were then referred to as the AB variants and later in 1978 Ernst Conzelmann discovered the deficiency of GM2-activator protein to be the cause of this condition [2].

3. Nature and Function of the Gangliosides

Ganglioside was the term given by Klenk to neuraminic acid-containing Glycosphingolipids (GSLs) that are abundant in ganglion cells. Gangliosides are highly heterogeneous molecules showing a great structural and functional diversity. Their structure consists of a ceramide attached to a glycan chain via glycosidic bond at 1-hydroxyl position [15] and also contains 1-4 sialic acid (N-acetylneuraminic acid, NANA) residues [16]. The human brain has 12 different types of gangliosides, all having basic tetra-saccharide chains to which sialic acid residues are attached except GM2 and GM3 in which there is a tri-saccharide chain. The structure of GM2 ganglioside is depicted in Figure 1.

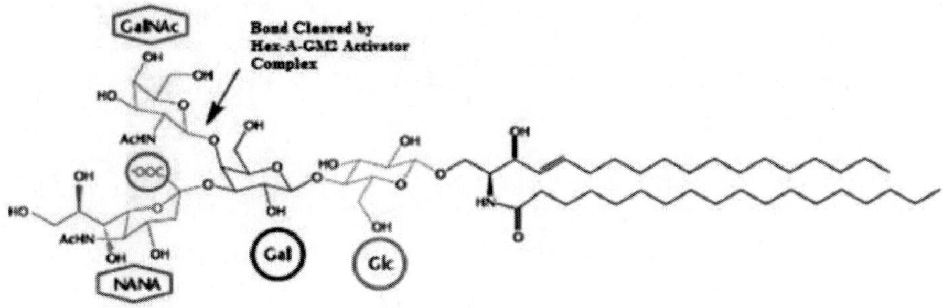

Figure 1. Structure of GM2 ganglioside.

The primary site where gangliosides are found is in the plasma membrane of animal cells. The hydrophobic ceramide moiety helps in their attachment to the membrane. The cerebral gray matter has the highest concentration of ganglioside particularly in the region of nerve endings and dendrites. The brain ganglioside is distributed across neurons, glial cells and other cell types [17, 18].

Gangliosides are responsible in a number of cellular processes like cell differentiation and cell adhesion [19–21]. The quantitative and qualitative patterns of expression of glycosphingolipids indicate their participation in dynamic neurodevelopmental processes [22]. Gangliosides also aid in adjusting intracellular and intranuclear calcium homeostasis [23]. One study suggests that axonal membrane ganglioside acts as ligand for MAG (myelin associated glycoprotein)- a oligodendrocyte protein that favors axon-glia interactions [24]. Subsequently, a study on mice performed by Allende and Proia in 2014 provides experimental evidence in support of this theory. In conclusion, all the collaborative studies point out the essential status of gangliosides for myelin function and stability [25].

4. Structure, Biosynthesis and Uptake of B-Hexosaminidase

Robinson and Sterling were the first to distinguish two forms of β-hexosaminidase as acidic form A and basic form B with differences in their sialic acid content. However, using immunohistochemical techniques, Srivastava and Buetler gave further insights suggesting the two forms to share a common subunit. They showed Hex-A to be a heteropolymer (αβ) and Hex-B to be a homopolymer (ββ). The presence of another isoform Hex-S (αα) was also predicted [26] (Figure 2).

In the year 1996, the first predicted 3D structure of the catalytic domain of human Hex was derived using bacterial chitobiase by Tews et al., [27]. The subunits are composed of two domains with the catalytic domain present in domain II. The importance of dimerization of α and β for activity in each subunit is suggested by structural studies [28]. However, there is no evidence until now of the independent monomeric subunits possessing enzymatic activity. Further, the availability of crystallographic structure of Hex-A, Hex-B and GM2 activator protein has provided fine details about the effects of pathogenic mutations on the protein structure and mechanism of catalysis [29–31]. These discoveries with respect to structure determination of the protein has helped in its better understanding and establishing a correlation between changes at DNA level and that on the protein. In a study by Sheth et al., 2014, structural protein analysis was performed using crystallographic structure of HEXA as template for two novel missense variants found. The study demonstrated that the missense variants disrupted the β-sheet, changing the enzyme configuration and simultaneously destabilizing the structure [12]. Considering this, establishing a genotype-phenotype correlation is critical to be addressed from the point of view of patient's prognosis as well in planning effective treatments for GM2 gangliosidosis. In this view, a study by Ou and colleagues developed a method for establishing a genotype-phenotype correlation for gangliosidosis mutations using in silico tools. They also conducted 3D structural analysis to determine the mechanism from which a particular mutation causes GM2 gangliosidosis. The study also proposed a model for predicting the disease subtypes of autosomal recessive disorders based on the presence of mutant alleles [32].

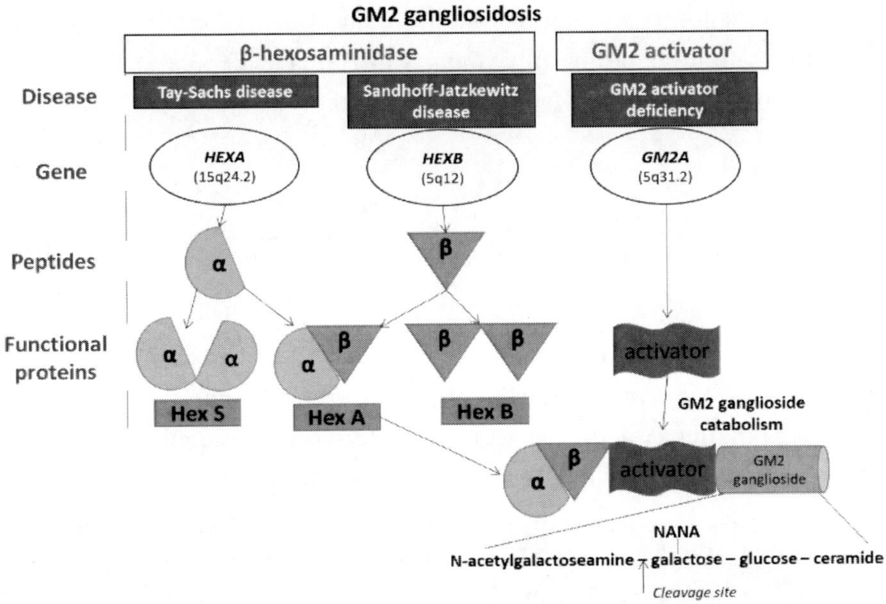

Figure 2. Catabolism of the GM2 ganglioside by the β-hexosaminidase system.

The biosynthesis and uptake of β-hexosaminidase has been elucidated efficiently by the experimental studies of William Sly, Stuart Kornfeld and Elizabeth Neufeld. The major discovery was identification of mannose-6-phosphate as recognition tags for the correct targeting of nascent proteins to the lysosomes [33]. The principal process steps of protein modification in its pathway to the lysosome involve following steps: 1) β-hexosaminidase isozymes first appear in a precursor form; 2) Mannose 6-phosphate (M6P) motifs are attached to these precursors, and 3) after traversing the Golgi and on reaching the lysosome, the precursors are converted into mature forms of smaller molecular mass [26]. In case of the complex Hex-A, the two subunit chains α and β are synthesized independently in the endoplasmic reticulum (ER). This is followed by modifications involving acquisition of N-linked oligosaccharides and intrachain disulphide bonds, attachment of M6P moieties and loss of signal peptide. The precursor enzyme with the help of M6P receptors is transported to Golgi and subsequently to the lysosomes. Inside the lysosomes, they are proteolytically processed to their mature forms [33]. A noteworthy demonstration by the studies of D'Azzo is that the association of β-chain with α-chain not only imparts the latter with a catalytic activity but also helps in its transportation to the lysosomes [34].

5. GENE DEFECT CAUSING THE DISEASE

The enzymatic hydrolysis of GM2 ganglioside inside the lysosomes by β-hexosaminidase requires the association of GM2 with a substrate specific cofactor- GM2 activator protein encoded by *GM2A* gene. It is a small glycolipid binding protein that forms a water-soluble complex with GM2 ganglioside. There are two isoenzymes for β-hexosaminidase namely Hex-A and Hex-B. Hex-A is a heterodimer consisting of α and β subunits encoded by *HEXA* and *HEXB* respectively. A number of studies and considerable effort was involved in cloning and characterization of all three genes. In, 1984 Myerowitz and Proia were the first to isolate cDNA clones of α-subunit of Hex-A [35]. The human *HEXA* gene is located on chromosome 15q23-q24 with 14 exons and 13 introns, spanning a region of approximately 35 kb. The coding sequence consists of 528 amino acids including a 22 amino acid signal sequence peptide at the N-terminus [36]. The fact that human *HEXB* gene also encompasses 14 exons and the intron/exon boundaries are conserved between the two genes in 12/13 introns is noteworthy [37]. It is localized to chromosome 5q12 spanning a region of 40 kb.

The comparison of the α-subunit of French-Canadian population with the available cDNA probes at DNA level revealed presence of a large 5' deletion in the α-chain gene. This deletion spans a region of 7.6 kb encompassing part of intron-1, all of exon-1 and extends 2 kb upstream that has the putative promoter region. This 7.6 kb deletion is seen in almost 70% infantile TSD cases in French Canadian population. In case of

Ashkenazi Jewish population, a 4 bp insertion (c.1278insTATC) within exon-11 and a G > A transversion at the 5'splice site of intron 12 accounts for 95% of infantile TSD alleles [28] and also commonly seen in 20.58% of the Indian infantile TSD patients mainly Muslims [6]. The 4 bp insertion leads to an early termination codon resulting in deficiency of α-subunit mRNA [9]. The p. Gly269Ser mutation results in adult-onset disease [38]. The resultant mutant Hex-A enzyme due to sequence alteration at a particular position will have change in its properties like inefficient biochemical activity or impairment of substrate binding at catalytic site. The structure of the enzyme and its ability to interact with its substrate and /or activator is influenced by the conformational changes due to missense mutations [28, 39].

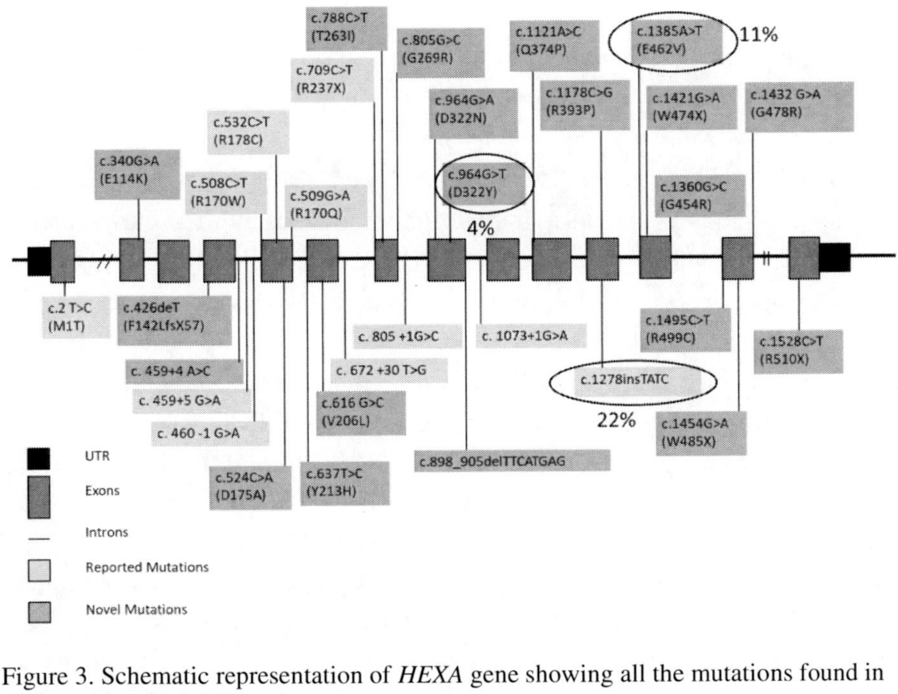

Figure 3. Schematic representation of *HEXA* gene showing all the mutations found in TSD patients from India.

A study on 34 Indian families affected with TSD detected 25 variants, out of which 15 were novel [6]. The variants p. D322Y, p. E462V and c.1278insTATC were the most commonly seen with 5.88%, 14.7% and

20.58% respectively. All the patients were presented with infantile form of the disease. Table 1 depicts an overall picture of the Tay-Sachs patients highlighting the key clinical and molecular details as observed in India. The different mutations found in *HEXA* gene in case of Indian TSD patients has been schematically represented in Figure 3. There have been cases where no variant was identified in two patients and only a single variant was identified in three patients after sequencing the coding region of *HEXA*. Multiplex ligation-dependent probe amplification (MLPA) was carried out which indicated presence of homozygous deletion of exon-2 and exon-3 in two patients, compound heterozygous deletion of exon-1 in two patients and duplication of exon-1 in one patient [40]. The clinical, biochemical and molecular profile of all the 5 patients is shown in Table 2. Thus, we find all types of mutations including missense, nonsense, small deletions, small insertions, indels, large deletions as well as duplication in *HEXA* gene to be associated with infantile form of TSD.

One report from India (1) describes a case of GM2 gangliosidosis AB variant due to a novel homozygous nonsense mutation (c.472G > T) in exon-4 of *GM2A* gene. The GM2A gene is localized to human chromosome 5q31.2 spread across a 16kb sequence with 4 exons and 3 introns and it was successfully cloned by Schröder and colleagues [41]. In total, there are reports of only thirteen molecularly proven cases of GM2 activator deficiency from different parts of the world, indicating its rare diagnosis. Another case of GM2 activator deficiency from India showed presence of a homozygous mutation c.243–2A > T in intron 3 of *GM2A* gene [42]. The molecular details of all the cases along with their effect on the protein and the ethnicity in which they were reported are systematically depicted in Table 3. These include missense, nonsense and frame-shift mutations. The mutational profile in Indian patients with Sandhoff disease was studied by Tamhankar, Sheth and colleagues. Their report suggests c.850C > T (p. R248X) mutation as the most common mutation (21%) (Figure 4) observed in children with Sandhoff disease in India. Also, they observed a significant difference in the molecular profile in SD cases versus TSD cases. A major proportion of indels were reported in SD cases as compared to missense mutations predominantly seen in TSD cases [4].

Table 1. Biochemical and molecular analysis in patients with Tay-Sachs disease

Patient ID	Hex-A activity (MUGS) (nmol/hr/mg) = (x)	Total Hex activity (MUG) = (y)	Hex A % =(x/y) X 100	Genotypes	Zygosity	Reference
T1	6.1	2451	0.25	Ex12:c.1385A > T (p.E462V)	Homozygous	Mistri et al., 2011 Sheth et al., 2014 Sheth et al., 2018
T2	4.7	2049.7	0.23	Ex12:c.1385A > T (p.E462V)	Homozygous	
T3	1.39	ND	-	Ex12:c.1385A > T (p.E462V)	Homozygous	
T26	1.95	-	-	Ex12:c.1385A > T (p.E462V)	Homozygous	
T29	1.46		-	Ex12:c.1385A > T (p.E462V) Ex11:c.1278insTATC (p.Y427IfsX5)	Compound Heterozygous	Mistri et al., 2011 Myerowitz and Costigan, 1988
T4	2.5	862	0.29	Ex11:c.1278insTATC (p.Y427IfsX5)	Homozygous	Myerowitz and Costigan, 1988
T19	0.59*	NA	-	Ex11:c.1278insTATC (p.Y427IfsX5)	Homozygous	
T21	1.3*	NA	-	Ex11:c.1278insTATC (p.Y427IfsX5)	Homozygous	
T34	1.47	-		Ex11:c.1278insTATC (p.Y427IfsX5)	Homozygous	
T25	1.0	-		NA Mother- Ex11:c.1278insTATC (p.Y427IfsX5) Father- Ex11:c.1278insTATC (p.Y427IfsX5)	NA Father: Heterozygous Mother: Heterozygous	
T23	1.43	432.0		Ex11:c.1278insTATC (p.Y427IfsX5) Ex2:c.271G > T (p.E91X)	Compound Heterozygous	Myerowitz and Costigan, 1988 Mistri et al., 2019
T31	0.4	709.2	-	Ex11:c.1259G > A (p.W420X)	Homozygous	Mistri et al., 2019
T18	1.7	424	0.4	Ex11:c.1259G > A (p.W420X)	Homozygous	
T5	6.7	1525	0.44	Ex8:c.964G > T (p.D322N)	Homozygous	Mistri et al., 2011 Sheth et al., 2014

Table 1. (Continued)

Patient ID	Hex-A activity (MUGS) (nmol/hr/mg) = (x)	Total Hex activity (MUG) = (y)	Hex A % =(x/y) X 100	Genotypes	Zygosity	Reference
T6	8.1	1301.5	0.62	In4:c.459+4A > C	Homozygous	Sheth et al., 2014
T7	9.0	1807	0.50	In4:c.460-1G > A	Homozygous	Mistri et al., 2019
T8	12.5	2499.9	0.50	In9:c.1073+1G > A Ex2:c.316C > T (p.Q106X)	Compound Heterozygous	Akli et al., 1991 Akerman et al, 1997
T9	5.2	1000	0.52	Ex13:c.1495C > T (p. R499C)	Homozygous	Mules et al., 1992
T10	9.6	1682.2	0.57	Ex6:c.616G > C (p. V206L)	Homozygous	Mistri et al., 2019
T11	7.5	1958.8	0.38	Ex6:c.637T > C (p.Y213H)	Homozygous	Mistri et al., 2019
T12	5.6	1280.1	0.44	Ex1:c.2T. > C (p. M1T)	Homozygous	Harmon et al., 1993
T13	1.2 Hex-A% Mother: 59% Father: 62%	-	-	NA Mother - Ex5:c.509G > A (p. R170Q) Father - Ex5:c.509G > A (p. R170Q)	NA Father: Heterozygous Mother: Heterozygous	Nakona et al., 1990
T14	1.5	1502	0.10	Ex12:c.1360G > C (p. G454R)	Homozygous	Mistri et al., 2019
T15	2.3	-	-	In2:c.347-1G > A	Homozygous	Mistri et al., 2019
T16	24.0*	1481.0	1.6	NA Mother – Ex12:c.1349delC (p. A450VfsX3) Father – Ex12:c.1349delC (p. A450VfsX3)	NA Father: Heterozygous Mother: Heterozygous	Mistri et al., 2019
T17	3.5	801.3	0.43	Ex8:c.964G > T (p. D322Y) Ex11:c.1259G > A (p. W420X)	Compound Heterozygous	Mistri et al., 2011 Mistri et al., 2019
T20	1.53	NA	-	Ex13:c.1424C > G (p. P475R)	Homozygous	Mistri et al., 2019
T22	2.5	752.4	0.33	Ex8:c.982T > G (p. C328G)	Homozygous	Mistri et al., 2019

Patient ID	Hex-A activity (MUGS) (nmol/hr/mg) = (x)	Total Hex activity (MUG) = (y)	Hex A % =(x/y) X 100	Genotypes	Zygosity	Reference
T24	2.6	-	-	Ex7:c.770T > C (p. F257S)	Homozygous	Mistri et al., 2019
T27	0.5*	-	-	Ex13 :c.1444G > T (p. E482X)	Homozygous	Mistri et al., 2019
T28	2.0	466		Ex7:c.754C > T (p. R252C)	Homozygous	Mistri et al., 2019
T30	1.0*	-	-	Ex1:c.53delG (p. G18DfsX82)	Homozygous	Mistri et al., 2019
T32	0.74*			Ex8:c.964G > T (p. D322Y)	Homozygous	Mistri et al., 2011
T33	3.8	394.0		Ex1:c.26C > A (p.S9X)	Homozygous	Mistri et al., 2019
T34	6.2	2585.3	0.24	Ex11:c.1278insTATC (p. Y427IfsX5)	Homozygous	Myerowitz and Costigan, 1988
T35	0.00	833.2	0.00	Ex11:c.1278insTATC (p. Y427IfsX5)	Homozygous	
T36	9.3	2250.3	0.4	Ex11:c.1278insTATC (p. Y427IfsX5)	Homozygous	
T37	2.5	1890.0	0.13	Ex11:c.1278insTATC (p. Y427IfsX5) Ex8:c.964 G > A (p. D322N)	Compound Heterozygous	Myerowitz and Costigan, 1988 Mistri et al., 2011 Sheth et al., 2014
T38	14.5	1999.9	0.35	Ex8:c.964 G > T (p. D322Y)	Homozygous	Mistri et al., 2011
T39	8.9	2254.3	0.39	Ex8:c.964 G > T (p. D322Y)	Homozygous	Mistri et al., 2011
T40	8.3	1612.9	0.5	Ex8:c.964 G > T (p. D322Y)	Homozygous	Mistri et al., 2011
T41	HLC Mother: 60.7% Father: 63.9%	-	-	Mother – Ex13:c.1454 G > A/ - (p. W485X/ -) Father – Ex13:c.1454 G > A/ -(p. W485X/ -)	Father: Heterozygous Mother: Heterozygous	Sheth et al., 2014
T42	10.7 HLC Mother: 58% Father: 57%	1785.0	-	Mother – Ex13:c.1454 G > A/ - (p. W485X/ -) Father – Ex13:c.1454 G > A/ -(p. W485X/ -)	Father: Heterozygous Mother: Heterozygous	Sheth et al., 2014

Table 1. (Continued)

Patient ID	Hex-A activity (MUGS) (nmol/hr/mg) = (x)	Total Hex activity (MUG) = (y)	Hex A % =(x/y) X 100	Genotypes	Zygosity	Reference
T43	12.4	2129.0	0.58	Ex10:c.1121 A > C (p. Q374P)	Homozygous	Sheth et al., 2014
T44	10.8	1273.2	0.84	Ex14:c.1528 C > T (p. R510X)	Homozygous	Sheth et al., 2014
T45	6.2	1721.0	0.36	Ex7:c.788 C > T (p. T263I)	Homozygous	Sheth et al., 2014
T46	7.0	2602.7	0.27	Ex5:c.524A > C (p. D175A) Ex7:c.805G > C (p. G269R)	Compound Heterozygous	Sheth et al., 2014
T47	9.6	1589.0	0.6	In7:c.805+1 G > C	Homozygous	Mistri et al., 2012
T48	0.00	1781.0	0.0	In4:c.459+5 G > A	Homozygous	Sheth et al., 2014
T49	12.8	2050.0	0.6	Ex8:c.898_905delTTCATGAG (p. F300HfsX21)	Homozygous	Sheth et al., 2014
T50	7.9	2185.7	0.36	Ex12:c.1385 A > T/ ? (p. E462V/ ?)	-	Mistri et al., 2011 Sheth et al., 2014 Sheth et al., 2018
T51#	HLC Mother: 53.8% Father: 58.8%	-	-	Mother – Ex5: c.532 C > T/ - (p. R178C/-) Father – [?/ -] (?/ -)	-	Sheth et al., 2014
T52	10.5	1978.3	0.53	NF	-	-
T53	8.3	1859.0	0.44	NF	-	-

*Enzyme study carried out at other centers; #DNA of index case is not available.

Normal range for Hex-A - 80 to 410 nmol/hr./mg and for total-Hex-723 to 2700 nmol/hr./mg.

HLC-heat labile activity in carrier parents.

Table 2. Clinical, biochemical and molecular details of the Indian patients with Tay–Sachs disease

Patient ID	Age at diagnosis (Months/Sex)	Native State	Cosanguinity	Hex-A activity (MUGS) (nmol/hr/mg) = (x)	Total Hex activity (MUG) = (y)	ψ Hex A % = (x/y) X 100	Genotypes		Phenotypes
							Nucleotide level (Allele from Father/ Allele from Mother)	Protein level (Allele from Father/ Allele from Mother)	
1	18/M	Gujarat	No	0.9	1292.1	0.07	Exon-2-3del/ Exon-2-3del	Not identified/ Not identified	Regression of milestone, cherry red spot, abnormal muscle tone, hyperacusis, seizures, abnormal MRI
2	14/M	Gujarat	No	1.05	Not done	-	Exon-2-3del/ Exon-2-3del	Not identified/ Not identified	Regression of milestone, cherry red spot, poor vision, abnormal muscle tone, hyperacusis, seizures, abnormal MRI, abnormal EEG
3	12/F	Gujarat	No	3.8	2185.7	0.17	c.1385A > T/Exon-1 deletion	p.E462V/ Not identified	Regression of milestone, cherry red spot, abnormal muscle tone, seizures, hyperacusis, hearing impairment
4	13/F	Gujarat	No	2.5	1635	0.15	c.1385A > T/Exon-1 deletion	p.E462V/ Not identified	Regression of milestone, hypotonia, hyperacusis, cherry red spot, abnormal MRI
5	13/M	Karnataka	Yes	1.78	2198.2	0.08	c.1527-2 A > T/Exon-1 duplication	Not identified/ Not identified	Regression of milestone, cherry red spot, hypotonia

Normal total-hexosaminidase values using MUG substrate in our controls –723 to 2700 nmol/hr/mg protein and normal Hex-A activity using MUGS substrate- 80 to 410 nmol/hr/mg. ψ The MUG/MUGS ratio for Hex A is 3.7:1 [11].

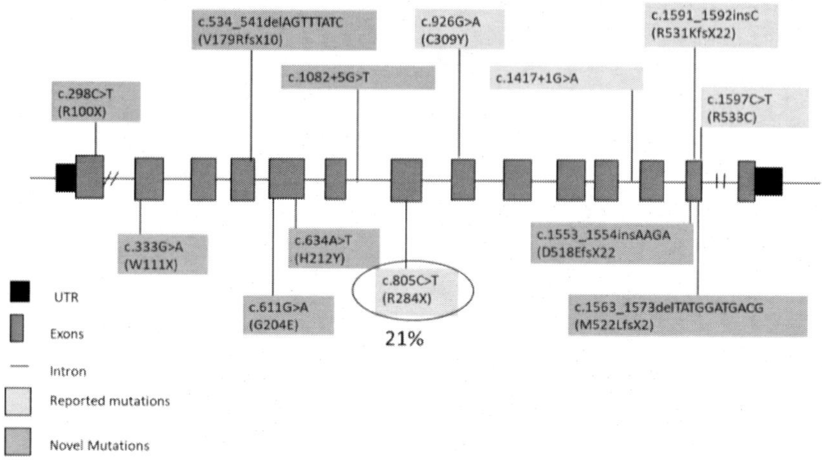

Figure 4. Schematic representation of *HEXB* gene showing all the mutations found in SD patients from India.

6. Biochemical Diagnosis

The determination of β-hexosaminidase deficiency in the serum and leukocytes is the basis for the biochemical diagnosis of GM2 gangliosidosis. Serum, white blood cells, cultured somatic tissues including amniocytes and even dried blood spots on filter paper can be used for testing hexosaminidase levels. This employs the use of a fluorogenic substrate the-GlcNAc derivative of 4-methylumbelliferone (4MUG). Both the isoforms-Hex-A and Hex-B can utilize this substrate and convert it to a fluorescent product 4-methylumbelliferone. Differences in the thermal, pH or electrochemical properties distinguishes the two isoforms. Hex-A is heat labile at 50°C whereas Hex-B is heat stable. Hence, the primary assay calculates the total hexosaminidase activity using MUG substrate. This is followed by subjecting a second serum aliquot to heat, thereby inactivating Hex-A and reflecting only Hex-B activity. Thus, the residual Hex-A activity is then calculated by subtracting Hex-B activity from total hexosaminidase activity. To achieve more specificity, another substrate 4-methylumbelliferyl-GlcNAc-6-sulfate (4MUGS) is used in addition to 4MUG, wherein only Hex-A can act on this substrate. It is important to run assay of control enzyme activity simultaneously using healthy subjects to determine a normal range. The above assay has few

Table 3. Review of molecularly proven cases of GM2 Gangliosidosis-AB variant

Case	Mutation	Location	Effect	Ethnicity	Reference
1	c.412T > C (p.C107R) [#] (Homozygous)	Exon 3	Reduced interaction with Hex A	US Black	Schroder et al., 1991
2	c.412T > C (p.C138R) [#] (Homozygous)	Exon 3	Reduced interaction with Hex A	US Black	Xie et al., 1992
3	c.506G > C (p.R169P) (Homozygous)	Exon 4	Pre-matured protein degradation	Indian	Schroder et al., 1993
4	c.262_264delAAG(p.88Kdel) (Homozygous)	Exon 3	Absence of mature CRM	Saudi Arabia	Schepers et al., 1996
5	c.410delA (p.H137PfsX34) (Homozygous)	Exon 3	Absence of mature CRM	Spanish	Schepers et al., 1996
6	c.160G > T (p.E54X) (Homozygous)	Exon 2	Absence of mRNA or CRM	Laotian, Hmong	Chen et al., 1999
7	c.522T > G (p.L174R) (Homozygous)	Exon 4	Pre-matured protein degradation	Indian	Kolodny et al., 2008
8	c. 160G > T (p.E54X) (Homozygous)	Exon 2	Absence of mRNA or CRM	Hmong	Renaud et al., 2015
9	c.164C > T (p.P55L) (Homozygous)	Exon 2	Reduced interaction with Hex A	Saudi Arabia	Salih et al., 2015
10	c.472G > T (p.E158X) (Homozygous)	Exon 4	Absence of mRNA or CRM	Indian	Sheth et al., 2015
11	c.369_371delinsATTAA (p.P124Lfs*48) (Homozygous)	Exon 3	Non-sense mediated mRNA decay	Turkey	Brackmann et al., 2016
12	c.259G > T (p.E87X) c.164C > T (p.P55L) (Compound heterozygous)	Exon 3 Exon 2	Non-sense mediated mRNA decay Reduced interaction with Hex A	Canada	Martins et al., 2017
13	c.243-2A > T (Homozygous)	Intron 3	Splicing affected	Indian	Kochumon et al., 2017

[#] The mutations identified by Schroder et al., (1991) (CYS107ARG) and Xie et al., (1992) (CYS138ARG) are the same but derived from different amino acid numbering systems.

limitations such as in case of pregnant women or those taking oral contraceptives pills (OCPs) a circulating heat-stable hexosaminidase P is synthesized. This can falsely decrease the calculated serum activity of hexosaminidase A relative to that of total hexosaminidase. This is why carrier status in pregnant women or those taking OCPs should be assessed in leukocytes, as opposed to serum. Another limitation is due to the effect of some mutations imparting thermal stability to Hex-A. As a result, using the heat inactivation assay will give false positive results.

The testing for the AB variant TSD with activator deficiency involves using a labeled GM2 ganglioside rather than a chromogenic substrate. It has been demonstrated that presence of two alleles-R247W and R249W do not lead to disease conditions in tested individuals as they can process normal GM2 ganglioside substrate. But, when tested with 4MUGS substrate, they show reduced activity. Hence these alleles are termed as pseudo deficiency alleles.

7. Carrier Screening for TSD

Though lysosomal enzymes show overlapping activity in leucocytes hence carrier identification cannot be confirmed by enzymes study. Nonetheless, for TSD, serum or plasma level can be used as a marker for carrier screening.

TSD carrier screening in certain populations like Ashkenazi Jewish, French Canadian, or Cajun descents (ACOG, 2005) has been recommended by The American Congress of Obstetrics and Gynecologists. However, due to multiethnic and endogamous marriages, carrier screening using enzyme study has become challenging. In our center we have a limited experience of carrier screening by enzymes study from plasma or serum, while study by Lazarin et al., (2013) have shown that, nearly 40% of carriers of diseases/mutations most prevalent in the Ashkenazi Jewish population for TSD, did not report Jewish ancestry [43]. Recent study by Strom et al., (2013) suggests that performance by enzymatic assays may not be optimal in the general population [44]. Therefore, in the era of NGS, identification of the risk allele in the ethnicity or population remains the gold standard for carrier screening of Gm2 gangliosidosis.

8. Prenatal Diagnosis of GM2 Gangliosidosis

With the limited availability of therapeutic option; prenatal diagnosis (PD) remains the only preventable measure for storage disorders. In our study of one hundred forty pregnancies having confirmed diagnosis of LSDs in index case, prenatal diagnosis was carried out by enzymes study during antenatal period from uncultured and/or cultured chorionic villus (CV/CCV) and cultured amniotic fluid (CAF) cells. In seven pregnancies, molecular analysis was additionally carried out where mutation was known in an index case. Table 4 depicts the biochemical and molecular diagnosis of the above-mentioned prenatal samples of our study. Of 140 pregnancies, 60 (42.9%) were diagnosed as affected, 13 (9.3%) had an intermediate enzyme activity and 67 (47.8%) had normal enzyme activity. Results were confirmed in 83 cases whereas 57 cases were lost from the follow-up. In one case, enzyme b-galactose-6 sulphate sulphatase specific for Morquio-A disorder [mucopolysaccharidosis-IVA (MPS-IVA)] had shown 30% reduced activity in CV cells and the case was diagnosed as carrier for MPS-IVA while it delivered an affected child. Further molecular analysis in seven cases that included six with Tay-Sachs and one with Gaucher disease, confirmed the results obtained by enzymatic study during PD. PD of LSDs can be carried out by enzymes study from CV/CCV and CAF with an accuracy of molecular method. However, in cases of MPS and mucolipidosis, Amniotic fluid (AF) is preferred over CV/CCV. In addition, special care is needed while interpreting enzyme results encompassing carrier status and they need to be further evaluated by molecular studies [7, 45].

Table 4. Prenatal Diagnosis of Tay-Sach's disease (TSD): Biochemical and Molecular based Diagnosis

Sr. No	Types of Specimen	Hex-A activity (nmol/h/mg protein	Diagnosis	Mutation present in Index case	Mutation analysis in Prenatal sample.
1.	CT cells	21.7 nmol	TSD	c.1277_1278insTATC/ c.1277_1278insTATC	c.1277_1278insTATC/ c.1277_1278insTATC
2.	CT cells	359.2	TSD	D322N/ D322N	Absent
3.	CT cells	403.5	TSD	D322N/ c.1277_1278insTATC	Absent
4.	AF cells	23.4 nmol	TSD	E114K/E114K	E114K/E114K
5.	AF cells	247.2 nmol (50% of control mean)	TSD	D322N/ D322N	D322N/ Normal allele (Heterozygous mutation)
6.	AF cells	650.2	TSD	W485X/ W485X	Absent

Normal Range of Hex-A: [(CT: 271–1621 nmol/h/mg protein); (AF:271-2213.2 nmol/h/mg protein)].

9. Clinical Symptoms/Phenotype

9.1. Infantile Acute Form

The infantile TSD also known as the B variant is the most severe form causing multiple anomalies in the affected individual followed by early death. These patients generally lack Hex-A or have only 0.1% of the normal Hex-A enzyme activity resulting in complete discrepancy in GM2-ganglioside breakdown. These children are born normal at birth, showing clinical manifestations in 2-3 months of age. The first distinctive signs include exaggerated startle response, generalized hypotonia, and failure to follow objects visually. The gross accumulation of GM2 gangliosides in the neuronal cells is the main reason for the neurodegeneration as well as muscle weakness which may cause paralysis in some cases. The lipid deposition in the bipolar ganglion cells of the retina causes the appearance of a cherry-red spot on the macula which can be observed by fundoscopic examination. Hyperacusis-a distinct feature can aid in an early diagnosis of the condition. There is rapid deterioration of the nervous system leading to difficulty in swallowing, uncontrolled seizures, spasticity, blindness and dementia due to progression of the condition. The patients generally die by the age of 2 to 4 years [46]. Figure 5 depicts the distinct clinical phenotype in the infantile form of TSD.

A study by Bley and colleagues on TSD and SD infantile forms stated that the most initial symptoms were developmental arrest (83%), abnormal startle response (65%), and reduced muscle tone (60%) [46]. Macrocephaly generally begins by the age of 18 months. The most common neuroimaging findings are signal changes like hyperintensity or hypointensity in the basal ganglia and cerebral white matter on T2-weighted sequences on magnetic resonance imaging (MRI) studies [3]. A population-based review of GM2 gangliosidosis patients in UK was carried out by Smith and colleagues. They reported death in 40 of the 41 infantile patients within the range of 18 months-6 year 9 months. In 53% cases, pneumonia and/or respiratory failure was the cause of death and for the remaining it was unspecified [47]. A study by Er et al., 2018 reported similar findings thus, indicating pneumonia and/or respiratory failure to be a major cause of death [48].

The infantile form of Sandhoff disease shows a similar clinical manifestation like that of TSD, however, liver and spleen enlargement are a key feature in SD. Presence of hypointense thalami is another significant feature of infantile form of SD. This is due to calcium accumulation, loss of axon and myelin in the central cortical neurons, and gliosis [49].

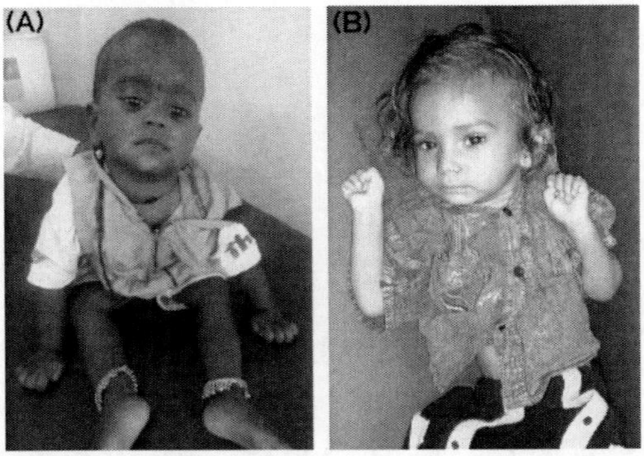

Figure 5. Clinical symptoms in patients with Tay-Sachs disease. A) A child showing global developmental delay and poor social responses and the infantile form TSD patient. B) A child with global developmental delay, hypotonia, microcephaly, hyperacusis and cherry red spot at macula.

It should be noted that there exists clinical variation which can be attributed to the presence of different underlying mutations. The observed abnormalities may vary from mild ataxia of limbs and trunk to dystonia and dysarthria. In some, seizures may be absent while others may show increased levels of creatine phosphokinase levels.

A late infantile form alternatively known as the B1 variant is also observed which is more or less similar to the infantile form in clinical features. These individuals show normal Hex-A activity with 4MUG substrate but reduced activity when natural or 4MUGS substrate is employed. A specific mutation R178H in the α-subunit of Hex-A has been reported from Portugal and Mediterranean region to be associated with this variant [50, 51].

9.2. Juvenile Subacute Form

These patients show 0.5% of the normal Hex-A activity. The deterioration of gait and posture is seen in early stages which progresses with age. The involvement of the brain may or may not be present with dementia and chronic organic mental syndrome seen in some. It is observed that 50% of the affected individuals show cerebellar atrophy. The vision status may be normal but optic atrophy and retinitis pigmentosum can be seen later with disease progression. These patients generally die by the age of 15 years [52]. Smith et al., (2012) reported 2/6 children to have visual deterioration in his study. Also, hypertonia and increased myotatic reflexes were reported in 50% and 80% of the early-juvenile TSD cases respectively. Increased myotatic reflex was also a major finding in juvenile SD cases (75%) in their study. A review study on juvenile SD cases by Hendriksz et al., (2004) demonstrated that maximum patients were presented with a mixture of cerebellar and pyramidal signs-ataxia combined with hyperreflexia, particularly of the lower limbs with progression of disease. Also, bowel and bladder problems were encountered by patients, sometimes with diarrhea followed by constipation and with urinary incontinence indicating autonomic dysfunction rather than a simple cognitive decline [53].

9.3. Late-Adult Onset Form

The clinical features in these patients are recorded in later years particularly early adolescence, generally after 10 years of age. These patients show less than 10% of the normal enzyme activity usually in the range of 2-4%. There is slow progression in neurologic defects leading to lack of coordination, hand tremors, progressive dystonia, dysarthria, dyskinesia, ataxia, lower motor neuron disease (LMD) with proximal muscle wasting, cramping and weakness. It is found that almost one third of the patients present with psychosis. The psychiatric abnormalities include a range of conditions from acute hebephrenic schizophrenia, agitation, delusions to hallucinations, paranoia and recurrent depression but, dementia being uncommon. There is evidence indicating GM2 gangliosidosis adult patients presented with heterogeneous phenotype [54]. There are also reports of GM2 gangliosidosis adult patients mimicking symptoms suggesting spinal muscular atrophy [55, 56].

The review study on GM2 gangliosidosis adult patients by Masingue et al., 2020 has effectively differentiated the clinical features into 4 categories: 1) initial LMD-cause of proximal lower limb weakness and progressing to upper limbs; 2) cerebellar ataxia; 3) psychiatric disorder or psychosis (only in TSD patients); 4) a complex clinical picture combining all the above 3 phenotypes. Another highlight of the study is the determination of key parameters in order to differentiate adult TSD and SD cases, although they have majority similarities. A noteworthy finding was observation of sensory neuropathy in 69% of SD cases as compared to only 10% TSD cases. Generally, at the molecular level, these patients show presence of compound heterozygous status for the alleles, common mutations being Arg505Glu for SD and Gly269Ser for TSD cases [57]. We have also identified adult onset TSD in a male child of 12 yrs. of age with a novel compound heterozygous mutation (c.1496G > A/c.902T > G) in

HEXA gene with a less than 10% of HEX-A enzyme activity in leukocytes. This child was normal till 5 year of age, thereafter developed gait ataxia, slurred speech, tremors in hand, absent cherry red spot with an MRI showing mild cortical atrophic changes. It is highly likely that many cases of adult onset TSD might have been missed due to heterogeneous phenotype.

10. Pathology

The widespread accumulation of GM2 gangliosides inside the lysosomes of neuronal cells give rise to structures known as membranous cytoplasmic bodies (MCBs). These can be detected immunohisto-chemically using antibodies. However, the path from ganglioside accumulation to progressive neurodegeneration and death is yet to be defined. Initial studies on brains of affected individuals have shown neuronal depletion in cerebral cortex and demyelination in cerebral white matter. The disease progression is suggested to be a result of a primary consequence followed by a secondary one. There are ongoing studies to understand and simplify this pathway. The studies till date support the accumulation of ganglioside in the neurons as a primary cause of neuronal damage leading to subsequent demyelination and inflammation.

10.1. Accumulation of GM2 Ganglioside and Other Glycolipids and Its Implicated Effects

Studies have shown the presence of the unacylated metabolite lyso-GM2 (sialylgangliotriaosylsphingosine) in the brain and plasma of patients and animal models of GM2 gangliosidosis to have toxic effects. Also, there is evidence regarding disruption of the endosomal transport and sorting inside the lysosomes due to sphingolipid accumulation. Another manifestation due to accumulation of storage material is the impairment in normal fusion of autophagosome and lysosomes. This results in the formation of inclusion bodies containing aggregates of polyubiquitinated proteins [26]. Suzuki and colleagues demonstrated presence of α-synuclein- a naturally expressed protein in neurons and glia in human lipidoses [58] and SD mice brains [59]. The protein is reported in young SD animal models and the amount is shown to increase with age and disease severity [60]. Also, recent study shows truncation of α-synuclein by the inflammasome protein caspase-I causing its accumulation and subsequently, neurotoxicity [61].

10.2. Demyelination and Neuroinflammation

A histological evidence of severe and extensive demyelination along with a 50-80% biochemical decrease in cerebrosides was obtained from the white matter studies on GM2 gangliosidosis by Haberland and colleagues. The studies also proposed a link between failure in myelination and reduced cerebroside synthesis [62]. Another study aimed to determine the expression of oligodendrocyte-specific genes in SD mice found their downregulation in all regions of the brain at an early age. The mRNA expression of a key enzyme Uridine diphosphate (UDP) galactose-ceramide transferase, involved in galacto-cerebroside biosynthesis was observed to be reduced at all ages (5-19 weeks), and even before the development of other disease signs [60].

The innate inflammatory response is chronically stimulated in case of neurodegenerative disorders causing overexpression of cytokines and proapoptotic molecules resulting in severe neuronal damage. The studies using expression analysis of cerebral cortex from GM2 gangliosidosis patients showed inflammation to be a cause of neuronal cell death [63]. The inflammatory response being a dynamic process involves several molecules, many of them having overlapping functions. A study by Hayase et al., 2010 showed a significantly increased level of tumour necrosis factor-α (TNF-α) in the cerebrospinal fluid of TSD patients, thereby inducing inflammatory response, which may contribute to disease progression [64]. In order to study the effect of inflammation in GM2 gangliosidosis, several investigators targeted the elements like Macrophage inflammatory protein 1α (MIP-1α) [65], TNF-α [66]. Utz et al., 2015 demonstrated the association of increased levels of five possible inflammatory biomarkers- ENA-78, MCP-1, MIP-1α, MIP-1β and TNFR2 with infantile gangliosidosis. The observations from these manipulation studies denote a modest improvement in lifespan with better understanding of the disease features in SD mouse [67].

10.3. Neuronal Death and Degeneration

The neuronal death in GM2 gangliosidosis was investigated by Huang et al., 1997 and Wada et al., 2000, wherein they identified TUNEL positive cells in human and murine brains, which is considered a signature of apoptotic demise [68, 69]. However, no such observation was made by Sargeant and colleagues in SD mouse brains. A decrease in neuronal numbers with age in Ventroposterior Medial and Ventroposterior Lateral (VPM/VPL) nuclei of the thalamus was observed along with increase in activated microglia. The lateral vestibular nucleus of the brain stem showed abundant cell loss and a significant low number of cells in the ventral spinal cord [70]. It is noteworthy that neuronal dysfunction is widespread and demonstrable from a young age even before disease signs are visible as compared to neuronal loss; however, this is not universal in SD mouse [60]. All the investigations indicate neuronal dysfunction to be potential in disease manifestations characterizing GM2 gangliosidosis.

10.4. Imaging Studies

Magnetic resonance imaging (MRI) studies have been carried out in GM2 gangliosidosis patients. However, they do not clearly distinguish between the different forms of the condition. Generally, extensive T2-wieghted hyperintensities in the cerebral white matter, basal ganglia, thalamus, pyramidal tract and cerebellum are seen in MRI of the patients with infantile form (26). The changes in intensity/density likely suggest accumulation of calcium or GM2 ganglioside in the cerebral white matter. Also, the cerebral white matter shows an increased abundance of creatine and energy rich phosphocreatine at an increased abundance than that present in basal ganglia [71].

The late onset form is characterized by cerebellar atrophy and often hypo density of the thalamus. A study including late onset patients demonstrated diffused cerebellar atrophy in all cases along with reduced levels of N-acetylaspartate in cerebellum as shown by magnetic resonance spectroscopy [72]. Figure 6 shows the MRI scan of the brain revealing hyper intensity and hypo intensity in T2/T1 weighted images (A) & (B) which is usually seen in GM2 gangliosidosis patients due to GM2 activator protein deficiency. Another study carried out to quantify brain MRI volume during the disease progression in gangliosidosis, revealed that the intracranial volume both, brain tissue volume and ventricular volume increased consistently with time. The study concludes quantitative MRI to be a robust non-invasive method for monitoring CNS changes in the clinical course of gangliosidosis [52].

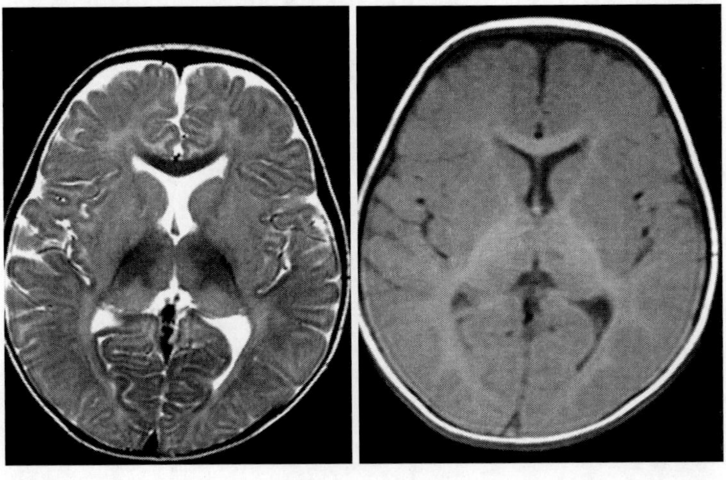

Figure 6. MRI scan of the brain showing putaminal hyperintensity and thalamic hypointensity with some unmyelinated white matter in T2/T1 weighted images (A)-(B), seen in a child with Gm2 activator protein deficiency.

11. Effect and Side Effect of Therapy

A number of therapies have been proposed with a view to improve the lives of GM2 gangliosidosis patients. These include substrate reduction [73], bone marrow transplantation [74], hematopoietic [75] or neural stem cell transplantation [76], use of anti-inflammatory drugs [64], administration of purified enzyme [77] and gene therapy helping in restoration of dysfunctional protein expression [78].

11.1. Substrate Reduction Therapy

The main aim of this approach is to reduce the rate of glycolipid synthesis by partially inhibiting the respective enzymes using small molecules [79]. This idea was first proposed by Norman Radin for the treatment of Gaucher disease [80]. Miglustat- (N-butyldeoxynojirimycin, NB-DNJ) a small iminosugar is a competitive inhibitor of gylcosylceramide synthase. As, glycosylceramide is the first step in the biosynthesis of glycosphingolipids, use of these inhibitors could be a potential target for therapy. Prior studies have shown prevention of GM2 ganglioside accumulation in TSD murine models by using miglustat [73, 81]. A study was carried out to assay the clinical efficacy of NB-DNJ in two TSD infantile patients. They showed a significant concentration of NB-DNJ in their cerebrospinal fluid; however, this did not stop the neurologic dysfunction in patients [73]. Also, there are studies reporting the inefficiency of the drug in meeting its endpoint target in a clinical trial of late-onset TSD patients [82, 83]. The studies also show that the major drug related events because of miglustat in infantile GM2 patients were abdominal discomfort and flatulence while in the juvenile group; they were diarrhea and weight loss [84].

11.2. Enzyme Replacement Therapy

This approach has been very effective in treatment of lysosomal storage disorders; however, the intravenous administration restricts the enzyme to cross the blood-brain barrier. As a result, this therapy is not promising for prevention of CNS neurodegeneration [85, 86]. Nevertheless, there are continuous efforts for developing strategies to synthesize and deliver enzyme efficiently. The production of recombinant HexA enzyme using methylotrophic yeast Ogataea minuta (Om) culture, to simultaneously express both *HEXA* and *HEXB* genes is one of the possibilities. In order to expose mannose-6-phosphate (M6P) residues on the N-glycans, the purified HexA was treated with α-mannosidase [77, 87]. On testing the therapeutic efficacy of the recombinant HexA in SD mice, the noteworthy outcomes were improvement of motor function, increase of survival rate and inhibition of the induction of MIP-1α [77]. Also, in a study by Tropak et al., 2016, a hybrid μ subunit having the critical characteristics of α and β subunits was created. HEK239 cells with CRISPR deleted *HEXA* and *HEXB* genes, stably expressing the μ subunit were used to purify the HexM μ-homodimer. The combination of HexM with GM2A allowed the hydrolysis of a derivative of GM2 ganglioside both *in cellulo* and *in vitro* [88]. A chimeric HexB was created by modifying the nucleotide sequence of the human *HEXB* gene. Intracerebroventricular administration of this protein to SD model mice effectively reduced the GM2 ganglioside accumulation in parenchyma and also restored Hexosaminidase activity in the brain [89].

11.3. Gene Therapy

This is based on the principle of manipulating a targeted region in the genome to rectify the gene defect. This area has been exploited, particularly for providing solutions to neurodegenerative disorders which are generally caused by single gene defects. In the mid-1990s, several experiments were carried out in this view and Akli et al., 1996 was the first to produce TSD patient skin-derived fibroblasts expressing *HEXA* gene by adenovirus transduction [90]. There were supporting studies that suggested the intravenous co-administration of adenoviral vectors expression of both *HEXA* and *HEXB*, preferentially transduced the liver cells in HEXA knockout mice [91]. However, there were limitations in the successful use of adenoviral vectors, the major reason being its inability to cross the blood-brain barrier [92]. Secondly, there is a high risk of development of hepatocellular carcinoma due to accumulation of the vector and overexpression of the transgene in the liver [93]. The major challenges to overcome the blood-brain barrier and ensure minimal side effects are the choice of vector and delivery method of therapeutic genes [94].

Recently, adeno-associated virus (AAV) has shown a great potential in developing approaches for GM2 gangliosidosis gene therapy [95]. These are small 20-25nm in diameter, non-enveloped single-stranded DNA viruses of the Parvoviridae family. Recombinant AAV (rAAV) serotypes 2/1 or 2/2 encoding the *HEXA* and *HEXB* gene cDNA when intracranially administered to SD model mice, resulted in efficient spread of HexA and increase in mouse survival rate without any apparent cytotoxicity due to rAAV use [78, 96]. The inability of the AAVs to carry the cDNA of both *HEXA* and *HEXB* genes due to their less capacity (from 2.1-4.5 kb), adds an undesirable complexity and expense limiting its use as a treatment option in clinic [26]. The expression of both subunits α and β is required for the effective recovery of the secretion of the absent heterodimeric HexA isoenzyme [89]. In this view, a self-complementary AAV9.47 (scAAV9.47-HEXM) encoding a hybrid μ subunit was designed by Tropak et al., 2016 and its intracranial administration in the brain of TSD model mice was found to decrease GM2 ganglioside amount. Further studies provide evidence for long term decrease in GM2 ganglioside accumulation in the CNS of newborn TSD model mice following intravenous administration of scAAV9.47-HEXM with a decreased distribution of this vector as compared to other serotypes namely AAV9, AAVrh10 or AAVrh8 [97]. Recently, the modified human Hex μ subunit (HEXM) was used by Ou and colleagues to treat neonatal Sandhoff mice. The plasma MUGS and MUG analysis 4 months after the i.v. of AAV vectors, showed up to 144- and 17-fold of wild-type levels ($n = 10$, $p < 0.0001$), respectively. The highlight of the study was that the MUGS and MUG activities in the brain also increased significantly compared with untreated Sandhoff mice ($p < 0.001$). Further, the reduced level of GM2 gangliosides in multiple tissues, except the brain, of treated mice was confirmed by HPLC-MS/MS analysis [98]. Subsequently, the therapeutic efficacy of AAVrh8-based gene therapy on the Jacob sheep TSD model was also demonstrated through an experimental study. They observed that following intracranial injection of AAV, the sheep showed delay in the appearance of symptoms and/or decrease in the acquired symptoms of the disease. The distribution of HexA was excellent in the sheep brain when there was a co-injection of AAVrh8-HEXA and AAVrh8-HEXB as compared to injection with only AAVrh8-HEXA. On analyzing the sheep spinal cord, it was observed that the HexA distribution was low in addition to decreased activation and proliferation of microglia in the sheep brain following gene therapy [95].

Another important criterion to be considered is the safety check on the use of virus-based vectors as there are a number of side-effects associated with it. Several studies have been carried out in this regard, wherein one study shows that intracranial injection of AAVrh8-cmHexα/β led to development of dyskinesia, ataxia and loss of dexterity in most of the monkeys [99]. The authors also observed a sharp increase in Hex activity in the thalamus, suggesting a probable association of severe neurotoxicity with Hex overexpression.

11.4. Bone Marrow Transplantation

This approach has been exploited in a few experimental studies with no considerable benefit to human patients [100] as compared to SD mouse in which survival was improved and decrease in the rate of disease progression was observed [101]. A study by Jacobs et al., 2005 demonstrated the application of bone marrow transplantation with the following substrate reduction therapy (miglustat). There was increase in

HexA activity in leukocytes and plasma 23 months after transplantation but there was no change in the course of neurological dysfunction [74].

Conclusion

GM2 gangliosidoses (TSD, SD and GM2A) are the rare forms of lipid storage disorder. The most common type is known as infantile Tay–Sachs disease. The main clinical phenotype is regression of learned skill, presence of cherry red spot, hyperacusis, seizure and accumulation of gangliosides in the brain. Enzyme analysis is the gold standard for the diagnosis followed by mutation study of *HEXA* and *HEXB* genes. Prenatal diagnosis can be carried out using direct enzyme study from chorionic villi or cultured fibroblasts with an accuracy of molecular testing. In few of the cases large deletion or duplication can be observed, this necessitates MLPA study where NGS or Sanger sequencing has failed to identify the mutation in enzymatically confirmed cases. Therapeutic options are very limited until now with a future hope of gene therapy.

References

[1] Sheth, J, Datar, C, Mistri, M, Bhavsar, R, Sheth, F, Shah, K. GM2 gangliosidosis AB variant: novel mutation from India -a case report with a review. *BMC. Pediatr.* 2016, 16, 88.

[2] Ferreira, CR, Gahl, WA. Lysosomal storage diseases. *Transl. Sci. rare Dis.* 2017, 2, 1–71.

[3] Mistri, M, Tamhankar, PM, Sheth, F, Sanghavi, D, Kondurkar, P, Patil, S, Idicula-Thomas, S, Gupta, S, Sheth, J. Identification of novel mutations in HEXA gene in children affected with Tay Sachs disease from India. *PLoS. One.* 2012, 7, e39122.

[4] Tamhankar, PM, Mistri, M, Kondurkar, P, Sanghavi, D, Sheth, J. Clinical, biochemical and mutation profile in Indian patients with Sandhoff disease. *J. Hum. Genet.* 2016, 61, 163–166.

[5] Lew, RM, Burnett, L, Proos, AL, Delatycki, MB. Tay-Sachs disease: current perspectives from Australia. *Appl. Clin. Genet.* 2015, 8, 19–25.

[6] Mistri, M, Mehta, S, Solanki, D, Kamate, M, Gupta, N, Kabra, M, Puri, R, Girisha, K, Hariharan, S, Nampoothiri, S, Sheth, F, Sheth, J. Identification of novel variants in a large cohort of children with Tay-Sachs disease: An initiative of a multicentric task force on lysosomal storage disorders by Government of India. *J. Hum. Genet.* 2019, 64, 985–994.

[7] Sheth, J, Mistri, M, Sheth, F, Shah, R, Bavdekar, A, Godbole, K, Nanavaty, N, Datar, C, Kamate, M, Oza, N, Ankleshwaria, C, Mehta, S, Jackson, M. Burden of lysosomal storage disorders in India: experience of 387 affected children from a single diagnostic facility. *JIMD. Rep.* 2014, 12, 51–63.

[8] Mittal, P, Gupta, R, Garg, P, Mittal, A, Kaur, H, Gupta, S. CT and MRI findings in a case of infantile form of GM2 gangliosidosis: Tay-Sachs disease. *Neurol. India.* 2016, 64, 1372-1373.

[9] Myerowitz, R, Costigan, FC. The major defect in Ashkenazi Jews with Tay-Sachs disease is an insertion in the gene for the alpha-chain of beta-hexosaminidase. *J. Biol. Chem.* 1988, 263, 18587–18589.

[10] Kaback, M, Lim-Steele, J, Dabholkar, D, Brown, D, Levy, N, Zeiger, K. Tay-Sachs Disease— Carrier Screening, Prenatal Diagnosis, and the Molecular Era: An International Perspective, 1970 to 1993. *JAMA.* 1993, 270, 2307–2315.

[11] Zampieri, S, Montalvo, A, Blanco, M, Zanin, I, Amartino, H, Vlahovicek, K, Szlago, M, Schenone, A, Pittis, G, Bembi, B, Dardis, A. Molecular analysis of HEXA gene in Argentinean patients affected with Tay–Sachs disease: Possible common origin of the prevalent c.459+5A > G mutation. *Gene* 2012, 499, 262– 265.

[12] Sheth, J, Mistri, M, Datar, C, Kalane, U, Patil, S, Kamate, M, Shah, H, Nampoothiri, S, Gupta, S, Sheth, F. Expanding the spectrum of HEXA mutations in Indian patients with Tay-Sachs disease. *Mol. Genet. Metab. Rep.* 2014, 1, 425–430.

[13] Okada, S, O'Brien, JS. Tay-Sachs Disease: Generalized Absence of a Beta-D-N-Acetylhexosaminidase Component. *Science* 1969, 165, 698-700.

[14] Sandhoff, K, Andreae, U, Jatzkewitz, H. Deficient hexosaminidase activity in an exceptional case of Tay-Sachs disease with additional storage of kidney globoside in visceral organs. *Pathol. Eur.* 1968, 3, 278-285.

[15] Kolter, T. Ganglioside biochemistry. *ISRN. Biochem.* 2012, 2012, 506160.

[16] Schnaar, RL, Gerardy-Schahn, R, Hildebrandt, H. Sialic acids in the brain: gangliosides and polysialic acid in nervous system development, stability, disease, and regeneration. *Physiol. Rev.* 2014, 94, 461–518.

[17] Tropak, MB, Bukovac, SW, Rigat, BA, Yonekawa, S, Wakarchuk, W, Mahuran, DJ. A sensitive fluorescence-based assay for monitoring GM2 ganglioside hydrolysis in live patient cells and their lysates. *Glycobiology.* 2010, 20, 356– 365.

[18] Suzuki, K. The pattern of mammalian brain gangliosides. II. Evaluation of the extraction procedures, postmortem changes and the effect of formalin preservation. *J. Neurochem.* 1965, 12, 629–638.

[19] Roseman, S. Studies on Specific Intercellular Adhesion1. *J. Biochem.* 1985, 97, 709–718.

[20] Varki, A, Hooshmand, F, Diaz, S, Varki, NM, Hedrick, SM. Developmental abnormalities in transgenic mice expressing a sialic acid-specific 9-O-acetylesterase. *Cell.* 1991, 65, 65–74.

[21] Nelson, J, Crowhurst, J, Carey, B, Greed, L. Incidence of the mucopolysaccharidoses in Western Australia. *Am. J. Med. Genet.* 2003, 123A, 310–313.

[22] Yu, RK, Nakatani, Y, Yanagisawa, M. The role of glycosphingolipid metabolism in the developing brain. *J. Lipid Res.* 2009, 50, S440–445.

[23] Ledeen, RW, Wu, G. Nuclear sphingolipids: metabolism and signaling. *J. Lipid Res.* 2008, 49, 1176–1186.

[24] Yin, X, Crawford, TO, Griffin, JW, Tu, PH, Lee, VM, Li, C, Roder, J, Trapp, BD. Myelin-associated glycoprotein is a myelin signal that modulates the caliber of myelinated axons. *J. Neurosci.* 1998, 18, 1953–1962.

[25] Yu, RK, Tsai, Y-T, Ariga, T. Functional roles of gangliosides in neurodevelopment: an overview of recent advances. *Neurochem. Res.* 2012, 37, 1230–1244.

[26] Cachon-Gonzalez, MB, Zaccariotto, E, Cox, TM. Genetics and Therapies for GM2 Gangliosidosis. *Curr. Gene Ther.* 2018, 18, 68–89.

[27] Tews, I, Perrakis, A, Oppenheim, A, Dauter, Z, Wilson, KS, Vorgias, CE. Bacterial chitobiase structure provides insight into catalytic mechanism and the basis of Tay–Sachs disease. *Nat. Struct. Biol.* 1996, 3, 638–648.

[28] Mahuran, DJ. Biochemical consequences of mutations causing the GM2 gangliosidoses. *Biochim. Biophys. Acta. – Mol. Basis Dis.* 1999, 1455, 105–138.

[29] Lemieux, MJ, Mark, BL, Cherney, MM, Withers, SG, Mahuran, DJ, James, MNG. Crystallographic structure of human beta-hexosaminidase A: interpretation of Tay-Sachs mutations and loss of GM2 ganglioside hydrolysis. *J. Mol. Biol.* 2006, 359, 913–929.

[30] Mark, BL, Mahuran, DJ, Cherney, MM, Zhao, D, Knapp, S, James, MNG. Crystal structure of human beta-hexosaminidase B: understanding the molecular basis of Sandhoff and Tay-Sachs disease. *J. Mol. Biol.* 2003, 327, 1093–1109.

[31] Wright, CS, Li, S-C, Rastinejad, F. Crystal structure of human GM2-activator protein with a novel β-cup topology1 1Edited by D. Rees. *J. Mol. Biol.* 2000, 304, 411–422.

[32] Ou, L, Kim, S, Whitley, CB, Jarnes-Utz, JR. Genotype-phenotype correlation of gangliosidosis mutations using in silico tools and homology modeling. *Mol. Genet. Metab. Rep.* 2019, 20, 100495.

[33] Hasilik, A, Neufeld, EF. Biosynthesis of lysosomal enzymes in fibroblasts. Phosphorylation of mannose residues. *J. Biol. Chem.* 1980, 255, 4946–4950.

[34] Proia, RL, d'Azzo, A, Neufeld, EF. Association of alpha-and beta-subunits during the biosynthesis of beta-hexosaminidase in cultured human fibroblasts. *J. Biol. Chem.* 1984, 259, 3350–3354.

[35] Myerowitz, R, Proia, RL. cDNA clone for the alpha-chain of human beta-hexosaminidase: deficiency of alpha-chain mRNA in Ashkenazi Tay-Sachs fibroblasts. *Proc. Natl. Acad. Sci. USA*. 1984, 81, 5394–5398.

[36] Proia, RL, Soravia, E. Organization of the gene encoding the human beta-hexosaminidase alpha-chain. *J. Biol. Chem.* 1987, 262, 5677–5681.

[37] Triggs-Raine, BL, Akerman, BR, Clarke, JT, Gravel, RA. Sequence of DNA flanking the exons of the HEXA gene, and identification of mutations in Tay-Sachs disease. *Am. J. Hum. Genet.* 1991, 49, 1041–1054.

[38] Jeyakumar, M, Butters, TD, Dwek, RA, Platt, FM. Glycosphingolipid lysosomal storage diseases: therapy and pathogenesis. *Neuropathol. Appl. Neurobiol.* 2002, 28, 343-357.

[39] Tropak, MB, Mahuran, D. Lending a helping hand, screening chemical libraries for compounds that enhance beta-hexosaminidase A activity in GM2 gangliosidosis cells. *FEBS. J.* 2007, 274, 4951–4961.

[40] Sheth, J, Mistri, M, Mahadevan, L, Mehta, S, Solanki, D, Kamate, M, Sheth, F. Identification of deletion-duplication in HEXA gene in five children with Tay-Sachs disease from India. *BMC. Med. Genet.* 2018, 19, 109.

[41] Schröder, M, Klima, H, Nakano, T, Kwon, H, Quintern, LE, Gärtner, S, Suzuki, K, Sandhoff, K. Isolation of a cDNA encoding the human GM2 activator protein. *FEBS. Lett.* 1989, 251, 197–200.

[42] Kochumon, SP, Yesodharan, D, Vinayan, KP, Radhakrishnan, N, Sheth, JJ, Nampoothiri S. GM2 activator protein deficiency, mimic of Tay-Sachs disease. *Int. J. Epilepsy.* 2017, 4, 184–187.

[43] Lazarin, GA, Haque, IS, Nazareth, S, Iori, K, Patterson, AS, Jacobson, JL, Marshall, JR, Seltzer, WK, Patrizio, P, Evans, EA, Srinivasan, BS. An empirical estimate of carrier frequencies for 400+ causal Mendelian variants results from an ethnically diverse clinical sample of 23,453 individuals. *Genet. Med.* 2013, 15, 178–186.

[44] Strom, C, Park, N, Morgan, C, Lobo, R, Crossley, B, Sharma, R, Bonilla-Guerrero, R, Salazar, D. Tay-Sachs carrier screening in the genomics age: Gene sequencing versus enzyme analysis in non-Jewish individuals. *Open. J. Genet.* 2013, 3, 61–66.

[45] Lazarin, GA, Haque, IS, Nazareth, S, Iori, K, Patterson, AS, Jacobson, JL, Marshall, JR, Seltzer, WK, Patrizio, P, Evans, EA, Srinivasan, BS. An empirical estimate of carrier frequencies for 400+ causal Mendelian variants: results from an ethnically diverse clinical sample of 23,453 individuals. *Genet. Med.* 2013, 15, 178-186.

[46] Bley, AE, Giannikopoulos, OA, Hayden, D, Kubilus, K, Tifft, CJ, Eichler, FS. Natural history of infantile GM2 gangliosidosis. *Pediatrics*. 2011,128, 1233– 1241.

[47] Smith, NJ, Winstone, AM, Stellitano, L, Cox, TM, Verity, CM. GM2 gangliosidosis in a UK study of children with progressive neurodegeneration: 73 cases reviewed. *Dev. Med. Child. Neurol.* 2012, 54, 176–182.

[48] Er, E, Canda, E, Yazici, H, Eraslan, C, Sozmen, E, Ucar, SK, et al., An Evalution of the Demographic and Clinical Characterictics of Patients with GM2 Gangliosidosis. *J. Pediatr. Res.* 2018, 5, 12-16.

[49] Sass, K, Lemire, E. Infantile sandhoff's disease. *South African J. Radiol*. 2009, 13, 66-70.

[50] Brown, CA, Neote, K, Leung, A, Gravel, RA, Mahuran, DJ. Introduction of the alpha subunit mutation associated with the B1 variant of Tay-Sachs disease into the beta subunit produces a beta-

hexosaminidase B without catalytic activity. *J. Biol. Chem.* 1989, 264, 21705–21710.

[51] dos Santos, MR, Tanaka, A, sá Miranda, MC, Ribeiro, MG, Maia, M, Suzuki, K. GM2-gangliosidosis B1 variant: analysis of beta-hexosaminidase alpha gene mutations in 11 patients from a defined region in Portugal. *Am. J. Hum. Genet.* 1991, 49, 886–890.

[52] Nestrasil, I, Ahmed, A, Utz, JM, Rudser, K, Whitley, CB, Jarnes-Utz, JR. Distinct progression patterns of brain disease in infantile and juvenile gangliosidoses: Volumetric quantitative MRI study. *Mol. Genet. Metab*. 2018, 123, 97–104.

[53] Hendriksz, CJ, Corry, PC, Wraith, JE, Besley, GTN, Cooper, A, Ferrie, CD. Juvenile Sandhoff disease-Nine new cases and a review of the literature. *J Inherit Metab Dis*. 2004, 27, 241–249.

[54] Barritt, AW, Anderson, SJ, Leigh, PN, Ridha, BH. Late-onset Tay–Sachs disease. *Pract Neurol*. 2017, 17, 396-399.

[55] Jamrozik, Z, Ługowska, A, Gołębiowski, M, Królicki, L, Mączewska, J, Kuźma-Kozakiewicz, M. Late onset GM2 gangliosidosis mimicking spinal muscular atrophy. *Gene*. 2013, 527, 679–682.

[56] Deik, A, Saunders-Pullman, R. Atypical presentation of late-onset Tay-Sachs disease. *Muscle Nerve.* 2014, 49, 768–771.

[57] Masingue, M, Dufour, L, Lenglet, T, Saleille, L, Goizet, C, Ayrignac, X, et al., Natural History of Adult Patients with GM2 Gangliosidosis. *Ann. Neurol*. 2020, 87, 609-617.

[58] Suzuki, K, Iseki, E, Togo, T, Yamaguchi, A, Katsuse, O, Katsuyama, K, Kanzaki, S, Shiozaki, K, Kawanishi, C, Yamashita, S, Tanaka, Y, Yamanaka, S, Hirayasu, Y. Neuronal and glial accumulation of α-and β-synucleins in human lipidoses. *Acta. Neuropathol*. 2007, 114, 481-489.

[59] Suzuki, K, Iseki, E, Katsuse, O, Yamaguchi, A, Katsuyama, K, Aoki, I, Yamanaka, S, Kosaka, K. Neuronal accumulation of α-and β-synucleins in the brain of a GM2 gangliosidosis mouse model. *Neuroreport*. 2003, 14, 551-554.

[60] Cachón-González, M-B, Wang, SZ, Ziegler, R, Cheng, SH, Cox, TM. Reversibility of neuropathology in Tay-Sachs-related diseases. *Hum. Mol. Genet*. 2014, 23, 730-748.

[61] Wang, W, Nguyen, LTT, Burlak, C, Chegini, F, Guo, F, Chataway, T, Ju S, Fisher OS, Miller DW, Datta D, Wu F, Wu CX, Landeru A, Wells JA, Cookson MR, Boxer MB, Thomas CJ, Gai WP, Ringe D, Petsko GA, Hoang QQ. Caspase-1 causes truncation and aggregation of the Parkinson's disease-associated protein α-synuclein. *Proc. Natl. Acad. Sci. USA*. 2016, 113, 9587-9592.

[62] Haberland, C, Brunngraber, E, Witting, L, Brown, B. The white matter in GM2 gangliosidosis. A comparative histopathological and biochemical study. *Acta. Neuropathol*. 1973, 24, 43-55.

[63] Myerowitz, R, Lawson, D, Mizukami, H, Mi, Y, Tifft, CJ, Proia, RL. Molecular pathophysiology in Tay–Sachs and Sandhoff diseases as revealed by gene expression profiling. *Hum. Mol. Genet*. 2002, 11, 1343-1351.

[64] Hayase, T, Shimizu, J, Goto, T, Nozaki, Y, Mori, M, Takahashi, N, Namba, E, Yamagata, T, Momoi, MY. Unilaterally and rapidly progressing white matter lesion and elevated cytokines in a patient with Tay-Sachs disease. *Brain Dev*. 2010, 32, 244-247.

[65] Wu, YP, Proia, RL. Deletion of macrophage-inflammatory protein 1 alpha retards neurodegeneration in Sandhoff disease mice. *Proc. Natl. Acad. Sci. USA*. 2004, 101, 8425-8430.

[66] Abo-ouf, H, Hooper, AWM, White, EJ, Janse van Rensburg, HJ, Trigatti, BL, Igdoura, SA. Deletion of tumor necrosis factor-α ameliorates neurodegeneration in Sandhoff disease mice. *Hum. Mol. Genet*. 2013, 22, 3960-3975.

[67] Utz, JRJ, Crutcher, T, Schneider, J, Sorgen, P, Whitley, CB. Biomarkers of central nervous system inflammation in infantile and juvenile gangliosidoses. *Mol. Genet. Metab*. 2015, 114, 274–280.

[68] Huang, JQ, Trasler, JM, Igdoura, S, Michaud, J, Hanai, N, Gravel, RA. Apoptotic Cell Death in Mouse Models of GM2 Gangliosidosis and Observations on Human Tay-Sachs and Sandhoff Diseases. *Hum. Mol. Genet*. 1997, 6, 1879-1885.

[69] Wada, R, Tifft, CJ, Proia, RL. Microglial activation precedes acute neurodegeneration in Sandhoff disease and is suppressed by bone marrow transplantation. *Proc. Natl. Acad. Sci. USA*. 2000, 97, 10954-10959.

[70] Sargeant, TJ, Wang, S, Bradley, J, Smith, NJC, Raha, AA, McNair, R, Ziegler, RJ, Cheng, SH, Cox, TM, Cachón-González, MB. Adeno-associated virus-mediated expression of β-hexosaminidase prevents neuronal loss in the Sandhoff mouse brain. *Hum. Mol. Genet*. 2011, 20, 4371-4380.

[71] Aydin, K, Bakir, B, Tatli, B, Terzibasioglu, E, Ozmen, M. Proton MR spectroscopy in three children with Tay-Sachs disease. *Pediatr Radiol*. 2005, 35(11), 1081–1085.

[72] Assadi, M, Baseman, S, Janson, C, Wang, DJ, Bilaniuk, L, Leone, P. Serial 1H-MRS in GM2 gangliosidoses. *Eur. J. Pediatr*. 2008, 167, 347–352.

[73] Bembi, B, Marchetti, F, Guerci, VI, Ciana, G, Addobbati, R, Grasso, D, Barone, R, Cariati, R, Fernandez-Guillen, L, Butters, T, Pittis, MG. Substrate reduction therapy in the infantile form of Tay-Sachs disease. *Neurology*. 2006, 66, 278-280.

[74] Jacobs, JFM, Willemsen, MAAP, Groot-Loonen, JJ, Wevers, RA, Hoogerbrugge PM. Allogeneic BMT followed by substrate reduction therapy in a child with subacute Tay-Sachs disease. *Bone Marrow Transplant*. 2005, 36, 925-926.

[75] Stepien, KM, Lum, SH, Wraith, JE, Hendriksz, CJ, Church, HJ, Priestman, D, Platt, FM, Jones, S, Jovanovic, A, Wynn R. Haematopoietic stem cell transplantation arrests the progression of neurodegenerative disease in late-onset Tay-Sachs disease. *JIMD. Rep*. 2018, 41, 17–23.

[76] Gonzalez, R, Hamblin, MH, Lee, JP. Neural Stem Cell Transplantation and CNS Diseases. *CNS. Neurol. Disord. Drug Targets*. 2016, 15, 881-886.

[77] Tsuji, D, Akeboshi, H, Matsuoka, K, Yasuoka, H, Miyasaki, E, Kasahara, Y, Kawashima, I, Chiba, Y, Jigami, Y, Taki, T, Sakuraba,

H, Itoh, K. Highly phosphomannosylated enzyme replacement therapy for GM2 gangliosidosis. *Ann. Neurol.* 2011, 69, 691–701.

[78] Cachón-González, MB, Wang, SZ, McNair, R, Bradley, J, Lunn, D, Ziegler, R, Cheng, SH, Cox, TM. Gene transfer corrects acute GM2 gangliosidosis-potential therapeutic contribution of perivascular enzyme flow. *Mol. Ther.* 2012, 20, 1489-1500.

[79] Platt, FM, Jeyakumar, M, Andersson, U, Heare, T, Dwek, RA, Butters, TD. Substrate reduction therapy in mouse models of the glycosphingolipidoses. *Philos. Trans. R. Soc. Lond. B. Biol. Sci.* 2003, 358, 947–954.

[80] Radin, NS. "Treatment of Gaucher disease with an enzyme inhibitor." *Glycoconj J*. 1996, 13, 153-157.

[81] Platt, FM, Neises, GR, Reinkensmeier, G, Townsend, MJ, Perry, VH, Proia, RL, Winchester, B, Dwek, RA, Butters, TD. Prevention of lysosomal storage in Tay-Sachs mice treated with N-butyldeoxynojirimycin. *Science*. 1997, 276, 428-431.

[82] Shapiro, BE, Pastores, GM, Gianutsos, J, Luzy, C, Kolodny, EH. Miglustat in late-onset Tay-Sachs disease: a 12-month, randomized, controlled clinical study with 24 months of extended treatment. *Genet. Med*. 2009, 11, 425-433.

[83] Maegawa, GHB, Banwell, BL, Blaser, S, Sorge, G, Toplak, M, Ackerley, C, Hawkins, C, Hayes, J, Clarke, JT. Substrate reduction therapy in juvenile GM2 gangliosidosis. *Mol. Genet. Metab*. 2009, 98, 215-224.

[84] Maegawa, GHB, van Giersbergen, PLM, Yang, S, Banwell, B, Morgan, CP, Dingemanse, J, Tifft, CJ, Clarke, JT. Pharmacokinetics, safety and tolerability of miglustat in the treatment of pediatric patients with GM2 gangliosidosis. *Mol. Genet. Metab*. 2009, 97, 284-291.

[85] Jakóbkiewicz-Banecka, J, Węgrzyn, A, Węgrzyn, G. Substrate deprivation therapy: a new hope for patients suffering from neuronopathic forms of inherited lysosomal storage diseases. *J. Appl. Genet*. 2007, 48, 383-388.

[86] Sorrentino, NC, D'Orsi, L, Sambri, I, Nusco, E, Monaco, C, Spampanato, C, Polishchuk, E, Saccone, P, De Leonibus, E, Ballabio, A, Fraldi, A. A highly secreted sulphamidase engineered to cross the blood-brain barrier corrects brain lesions of mice with mucopolysaccharidoses type IIIA. *EMBO. Mol. Med.* 2013, 5, 675-690.

[87] Akeboshi, H, Chiba, Y, Kasahara, Y, Takashiba, M, Takaoka, Y, Ohsawa, M, Tajima, Y, Kawashima, I, Tsuji, D, Itoh, K, Sakuraba, H, Jigami, Y. Production of recombinant beta-hexosaminidase A, a potential enzyme for replacement therapy for Tay-Sachs and Sandhoff diseases, in the methylotrophic yeast Ogataea minuta. *Appl. Environ. Microbiol.* 2007, 73, 4805-4812.

[88] Tropak, MB, Yonekawa, S, Karumuthil-Melethil, S, Thompson, P, Wakarchuk, W, Gray, SJ, Walia, JS, Mark, BL, Mahuran, D. Construction of a hybrid β-hexosaminidase subunit capable of forming stable homodimers that hydrolyze GM2 ganglioside in vivo. *Mol. Ther. Methods Clin. Dev.* 2016, 3, 15057.

[89] Matsuoka, K, Tamura, T, Tsuji, D, Dohzono, Y, Kitakaze, K, Ohno, K, Saito, S, Sakuraba, H, Itoh, K. Therapeutic potential of intracerebroventricular replacement of modified human β-hexosaminidase B for GM2 gangliosidosis. *Mol. Ther.* 2011, 19, 1017-1024.

[90] Akli, S, Guidotti, JE, Vigne, E, Perricaudet, M, Sandhoff, K, Kahn, A, Poenaru, L. Restoration of hexosaminidase A activity in human Tay-Sachs fibroblasts via adenoviral vector-mediated gene transfer. *Gene Ther.* 1996, 3, 769-774.

[91] Guidotti, JE, Mignon, A, Haase, G, Caillaud, C, McDonell, N, Kahn, A, Poenaru, L. Adenoviral Gene Therapy of the Tay-Sachs Disease in Hexosaminidase A-Deficient Knock-Out Mice. *Hum. Mol. Genet.* 1999, 8, 831-838.

[92] Gray, SJ, Woodard, KT, Samulski, RJ. Viral vectors and delivery strategies for CNS gene therapy. *Ther. Deliv.* 2010, 1, 517-534.

[93] Nakamura, T, Sato, K, Hamada, H. Reduction of natural adenovirus tropism to the liver by both ablation of fiber-coxsackievirus and

adenovirus receptor interaction and use of replaceable short fiber. *J. Virol*. 2003, 77, 2512-2521.

[94] Kyrkanides, S, Miller, JH, Brouxhon, SM, Olschowka, JA, Federoff, HJ. β-hexosaminidase lentiviral vectors: transfer into the CNS via systemic administration. *Mol. Brain. Res*. 2005, 133, 286-298.

[95] Gray-Edwards, HL, Randle, AN, Maitland, SA, Benatti, HR, Hubbard, SM, Canning, PF, Vogel, MB, Brunson, BL, Hwang, M, Ellis, LE, Bradbury, AM, Gentry, AS, Taylor, AR, Wooldridge, AA, Wilhite, DR, Winter, RL, Whitlock, BK, Johnson, JA, Holland, M, Salibi, N, Beyers, RJ, Sartin, JL, Denney, TS, Cox, NR, Sena-Esteves, M, Martin, DR. Adeno-Associated Virus Gene Therapy in a Sheep Model of Tay–Sachs Disease. *Hum. Gene Ther*. 2017, 29, 312-326.

[96] Cachón-González, MB, Wang, SZ, Lynch, A, Ziegler, R, Cheng, SH, Cox, TM. Effective gene therapy in an authentic model of Tay-Sachs-related diseases. *Proc. Natl. Acad. Sci. USA*. 2006, 103, 10373-10378.

[97] Karumuthil-Melethil, S, Nagabhushan Kalburgi, S, Thompson, P, Tropak, M, Kaytor, MD, Keimel, JG, et al., Novel Vector Design and Hexosaminidase Variant Enabling Self-Complementary Adeno-Associated Virus for the Treatment of Tay-Sachs Disease. *Hum. Gene Ther*. 2016, 27, 509-521.

[98] Ou, L, Przybilla, MJ, Tăbăran, AF, Overn, P, O'Sullivan, MG, Jiang, X, Sidhu, R, Kell, PJ, Ory, DS, Whitley, CB. A novel gene editing system to treat both Tay–Sachs and Sandhoff diseases. *Gene Ther*. 2020. doi: 10.1038/s41434-019-0120-5.

[99] Golebiowski, D, van der Bom, IMJ, Kwon, CS, Miller, AD, Petrosky, K, Bradbury, AM, Maitland, S, Kühn, AL, Bishop, N, Curran, E, Silva, N, GuhaSarkar, D, Westmoreland, SV, Martin, DR, Gounis, MJ, Asaad, WF, Sena-Esteves M. Direct Intracranial injection of AAVrh8 encoding monkey β-N-acetylhexosaminidase causes neurotoxicity in the primate brain. *Hum. Gene Ther*. 2017, 28, 510-522.

[100] Hoogerbrugge, PM, Brouwer, OF, Bordigoni, P, Ringden, O, Kapaun, P, Ortega, JJ, O'Meara, A, Cornu, G, Souillet, G, Frappaz, D, Blanche, S, Fischer, A. Allogeneic bone marrow transplantation for lysosomal storage diseases. The European group for Bone marrow transplantation. *Lancet*. 1995, 345, 1398-1402.

[101] Norflus, F, Tifft, CJ, McDonald, MP, Goldstein, G, Crawley, JN, Hoffmann, A, Sandhoff, K, Suzuki, K, Proia, RL. Bone marrow transplantation prolongs life span and ameliorates neurologic manifestations in Sandhoff disease mice. *J. Clin. Invest*. 1998, 101, 1881-1888.

In: Neurochemistry of Metabolic Diseases ISBN: 978-1-53618-339-9
Editor: Sankar Surendran

Chapter 6

GM2 GANGLIOSIDOSES TYPE II/SANDHOFF DISEASE (SD): DIAGNOSIS AND THERAPEUTIC EFFECT

Ali R. Tavasoli[1,*], Parastoo Rostami[2], Ali Hosseini[3], Masoud Garshasbi[4], Morteza Heidari[1] and Mahmoud R. Ashrafi[1]

[1]Myelin Disorders Clinic, Pediatric Neurology Division, Children's Medical Center, Pediatrics Center of Excellence, Tehran University of Medical Sciences, Tehran, Iran
[2]Growth and Development Research Center, Division of Endocrinology and Metabolism, Children's Medical Center, Tehran University of Medical Sciences, Tehran, Iran
[3]Prenatal Diagnosis and Genetic Research Center, Dastgheib Hospital, Shiraz University of Medical Sciences, Shiraz, Iran
[4]Department of Medical Genetics, Faculty of Medical Sciences, Tarbiat Modares University, Tehran, Iran

---

[*] Corresponding Author's Email: a_tavasoli@sina.tums.ac.ir.

ABSTRACT

Sandhoff disease (SD) or GM2-gangliosidosis type II is an inborn error of metabolism of lysosomal storage disorders due to β-Hexosaminidase A and B enzymes deficiency. Mutations in the *HEXB* gene which encodes β-Hexosaminidase A and B are inherited as an autosomal respective pattern and results in the repletion of GM2-ganglioside mainly in the neurons. Therefore, prominent clinical features in patients with SD are progressive neurologic deterioration include; seizures, ataxia, hypotonia, movement disorder, etc. SD based on age at onset classified into three groups; infantile, juvenile and adult form. Clinical, physical (such as hepatosplenomegaly and cherry red spot) and para clinic (laboratory and radiologic) findings are nonspecific in patients with SD, so SD should be considered in any children with unexplained neurologic symptoms especially neurologic egression. The diagnosis of SD is confirmed by enzyme activity assay and molecular study. To date, no curative treatment is available; although, novel approaches such as gene and stem cell therapy are under investigation.

1. INTRODUCTION

The lysosome is an organelle in the cytoplasm containing hydrolytic enzymes. The size of lysosomes varies and the inside is acidic (PH 4.5-5) compared to basic cytosol (PH 7-7.2), because these hydrolyzes enzymes need an acidic environment to function. The membrane of the lysosome defends the cytosol against degradative enzymes [1]. Lysosomal storage disorders (LSDs) are inherited defects of lysosomal hydrolysis which is needed to breakdown lipids, carbohydrates, nucleic acids and proteins in the cells. These disorders lead to a variety of symptoms based on the type of substrate and the place of accumulation [2]. Therefore, the nature of these diseases is progressive, but the speed of progression is variable [3-5]. More than 70 lysosomal storage diseases are identified with the incidence of about 1 in 7000–8000 live births [6, 7]. Sphingolipidoses are a subgroup of the LSDs which consist of some disorders include; Niemann-Pick, Gaucher disease, GM1-gangliosidosis, GM2-gangliosidosis, Krabbe disease, Fabry disease, etc. GM2-gangliosidosis are a subgroup of sphingolipidoses in which, GM2-ganglioside accumulates especially, in the neuron and some visceral organs as a consequence of an inherited defect in hydrolysis or activator proteins which are responsible for their degradative reactions [8]. GM2-gangliosidoses, in turn, are classified into three major subgroups: Sandhoff disease (0 variant, OMIM # 268800), Tay-Sachs disease (B variant, # 272800), and GM2 activator protein deficiency (AB variant, OMIM # 272750). GM2 activator protein is required for the activity of β-Hexosaminidase A in the lysosome [9]. Sandhoff disease is a rare autosomal recessive inborn error of metabolism that constitute 7% of cases of GM2 gangliosidosis [10, 11]. Because of the pattern of inheritance (as autosomal recessive), the prevalence of this disorder is high among populations with a high rate of consanguineous marriages. The incidence of Sandhoff disease has been reported as 1 in 384000 live births. SD is caused by the deficiency of two enzymes β-Hexosaminidase A (β subunit) and B (subunit β/β) which they hydrolyze the GM2 ganglioside in the lysosome [12].

2. Gene Defect Causing Defect

HEXB gene, mapped to the 15q13.3 chromosome, encodes the β-Hexosaminidase A and B. About 116 pathogenic variants in *HEXB* gene include; missense/nonsense, splicing, regulatory, small deletions, small insertions, small indels, gross deletions/insertions are listed within the Human Gene Mutation Database (HGMD pro, http://www.hgmd.cf.ac.uk/ac/index.php), which they can destroy the activity of enzymes and leading to the accumulation of GM2 ganglioside and other toxic molecules, especially in the neurons and spinal cord. Progressive accumulation of GM2 ganglioside destroys the neurons that cause most of the manifestations of Sandhoff disease [13, 14].

3. Biochemical and Pathologic Findings

GM2-ganglioside which is located in the cell membrane is degraded by two enzymes include; β-Hexosaminidase A [heterodimer (α/β)], β-hexosaminidase B [homodyne (β/β)], and a GM2 activator protein in the lysosome [15] (Figure 1). Besides, as mentioned before, GM2 activator protein is also required for the activity of β-Hexosaminidase A in the lysosome (Figure 2).

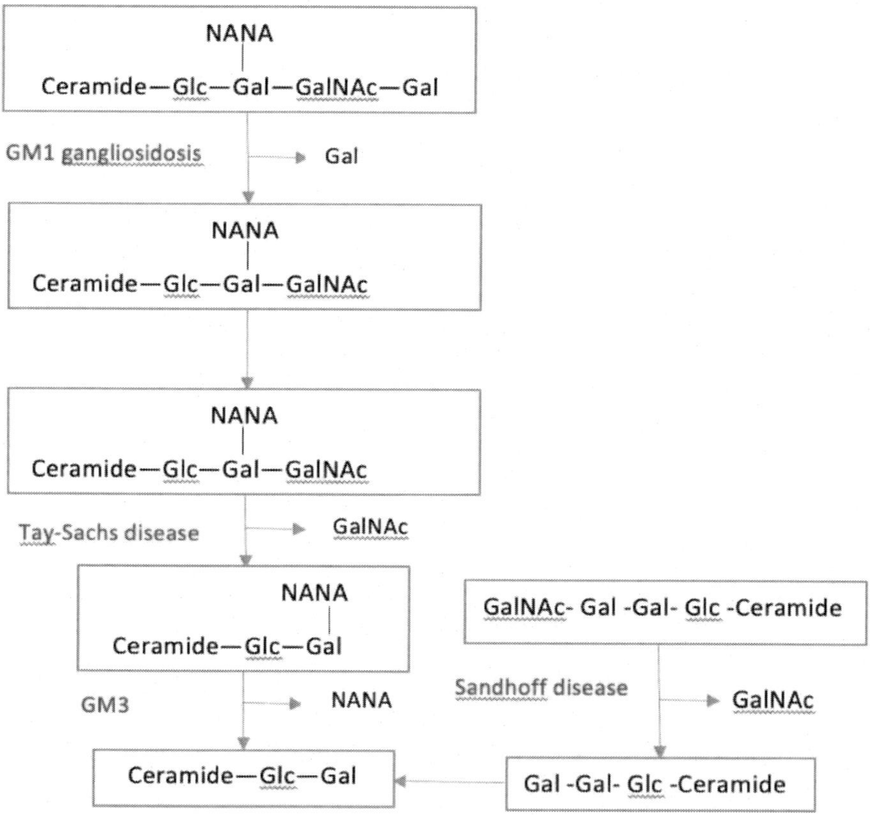

Figure 1. The pathway of sphingolipid in the cell and related Sphingolipidosis. (Glc: Glucosylcerebroside; Gal: Galactocerebroside; NAN: N-acetylneuraminic acid.).

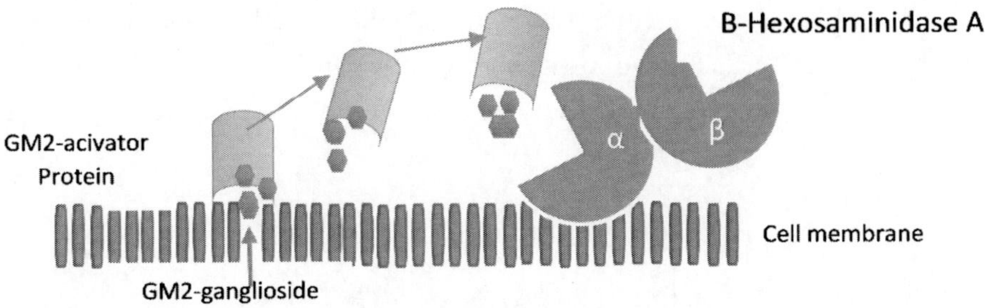

Figure 2. Hydrolysis pathway of the GM2-ganglioside in the lysosome.

In LSDs, the storage of sphingolipids in the lysosomes disrupting other structures in the cytoplasm. In the brain, expansion intracellular organelles lead to axonal swelling and abnormal dendritogenesis. These effects together with biochemical damage caused by sphingolipids that are toxic to the cell and unusual calcium regulation may be responsible for the pathogenesis of sphingolipidosis [16]. Improper increased innate immune system activity has been postulated to be responsible in neuroinflammation and then starting of the neurodegeneration process. Neuropathological investigations have showed that microglia and astrocytes are among the most affected cells in central nervous system [17]. The significance increased level of TNFα and IL-1β and also relationship between the storage of sphingolipids and the degree of brain inflammation has been shown in animal model studies [18]. Significant dysfunction in any other organ except for the brain is not expected in SD [19]. Recently, inductive effect of extra gangliosides on alpha-synuclein proteins aggregation in brain has been documented but the exact pathomechanisms has been remained to be clarified [20, 21]. This phenomenon could result in parkinsonism as an expected clinical manifestation. Detection of vacuolated lymphocytes in the peripheral blood smear may be helpful for diagnosis. Oligosaccharides assay in the urine may also be another useful diagnostic tool [22, 23]. Proton magnetic resonance spectroscopy (MRS) of the brain metabolites allows more information on the pathophysiology of the SD in the children. In this disorder, the level of N-acetylaspartylglutamate (as a marker for normal neuroaxonal tissue) decreases but the level of inositol (presents in the astrocytes) increases on

MRS that indicate neuroaxonal damage and gliosis [24-26]. Wilken et al. have shown the storage of oligosaccharides contain N-acetylhexosamine in both the gray and white matter that correlate to the pathophysiology of the SD [27].

4. Clinical Manifestations

Sandhoff disease was first described by Warren Tay in 1881 [28, 29]. Because of deficiency of β-Hexosaminidase A and B activity, the signs and symptoms of Tay-Sachs disease and SD are the same and based on the residual enzyme activity and age at onset classified into three subgroups: infantile, juvenile and adult or late-onset [30]. According to the pathophysiology of the disease progressive neurological involvement is expected to be prominent manifestations of these diseases [31, 32]. The infantile form of SD presents at about 4-6 months of age with symptoms include; axial hypotonia, muscle weakness, seizure, loss of acquired developmental milestones, developmental regression, startle response to sounds (but less common than Tay-Sachs), poor fix and follow, abnormal eye movement and cardiac involvement [33, 34]. The most commonly seen types of seizures in SD are myoclonic and tonic-clonic that usually present after the first year old [35]. The frequency of seizures increases with age [34]. Some clues on physical examination include; hepatosplenomegaly (but less common than Tay-Sachs), diffuse dermal melanocytosis [28, 36], coarse/Doll face and brisk deep tendon reflexes (Figure 3) [34, 37]. On ophthalmologic examination, the cherry red spot may be detected [38, 39]. The cherry-red spot is a sign in the macula due to storage of lipid substances within the cells of the retina, but as the macula is free of neuronal ganglion cells, these materials could not be stored and permit the examinee to look at the patient's eye through the macula and see a red spot (choroid layer) on a white background of the retina. Brown and black red spot have also been reported instead of cherry red spot depending on the race and retinal pigments variation, therefore, the perifoveal white patch has been recommended as a more accurate terminology for this pathologic condition [40, 41]. Generally speaking, a combination of neurologic regression which starts at six months of age, hyperacusis and cherry red spot in eye examination are good clinical points to consider GM2-Gangliosidosis including SD as an important clinical differential diagnosis. Detection of diffuse dermal melanocytosis, organomegaly, and coarse facies supports the diagnosis of SD. The clinical manifestations of juvenile or late infantile forms begin between 2 and 10 years old with seizures, mental deterioration, ataxia, dysarthria, myoclonus, bone disorders, and insomnia/hypersomnolence but without cherry red spot and organomegaly [42]. They develop macrocephaly after 2 years of age. The most common clinical presentation of the adult-onset form of SD is similar to juvenile form but more slowly progressive include; upper and lower motor neuron involvement, spinocerebellar ataxia, psychosis, sleep disorder, anxiety, fatigue, mood fluctuations, Parkinson's disease, impaired concentration and muscles weakness [23, 43, 44].

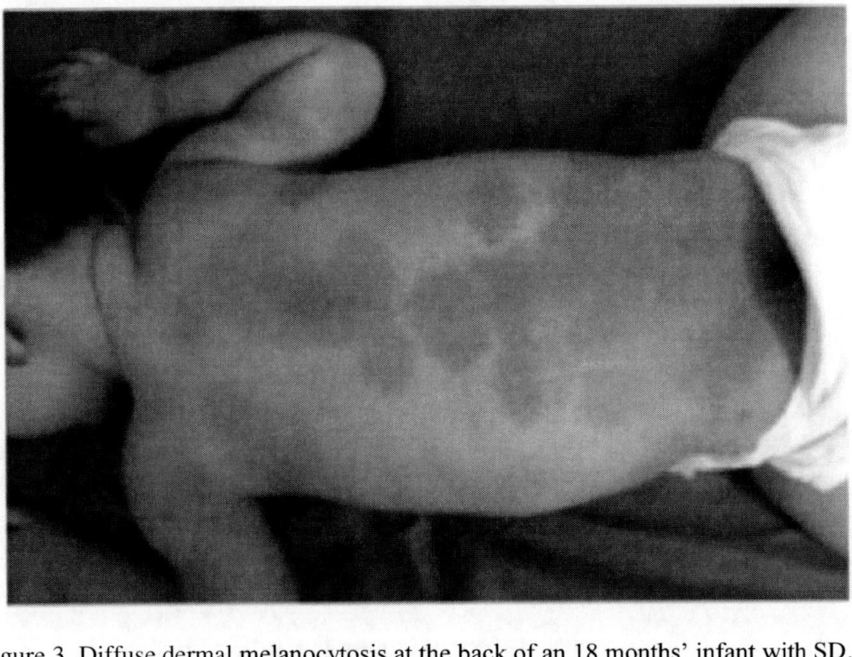

Figure 3. Diffuse dermal melanocytosis at the back of an 18 months' infant with SD.

5. Magnetic Resonance Imaging Findings

Regards to Global Leukodystrophy Initiative (GLIA) consensus, heritable white matter disorders of the central system with/without peripheral nervous system are classified in two main groups: genetic leukoencephalopathy (GLE) in which cerebral white matter is affected secondary to a background metabolic or systemic disorder and classic leukodystrophy (CL) in which cerebral white matter is primarily affected due to a genetic disorder and alters myelin and its' hemostasis [45, 46]. SD is considered as a genetic leukoencephalopathy in which the hypomyelination pattern of cerebral white matter is prominently evident in brain magnetic resonance imaging (MRI). In hypomyelination pattern involvement, abnormal white matter signal changes are seen as mild hyperintense lesions in T2-W MRI images but homologous involved areas in T2-W sequences appear normal in T1-W sequences or mild hypointense [47, 48] (Figure 4. A, D). Another principle pattern of white matter involvement in inherited brain white matter disorders is a demyelination pattern in which abnormal white matter signal changes are significantly high in T2-W MRI images and their homologous involved area shows clearly hypointense signals in T1-W sequences [49]. Other primary diagnostic findings that have been observed in brain MRI of patients with Sandhoff disease are bilateral thalamic hyperdensity on computed tomography (CT), bilateral thalamic hyperintensity in T1-W images and hypointensity in T2-W images, high signal abnormalities in the caudate nucleus, putamen and globus pallidus, brain atrophy and delayed myelination [50]. (Figure 4. A, B, C, and E). Intracellular calcium bonding with the collection of GM2 ganglioside is proposed as the mechanism of thalamic signal changes in brain MRI and CT-Scan that causes disruption of myelin and axon in the neurons (Figure 4. A, B, and C). Finally, these changes are induced by the significant aspects of Sandhoff disease [51]. However, the severity of neurologic signs has shown no relation to the extent of central nervous system involvement [24].

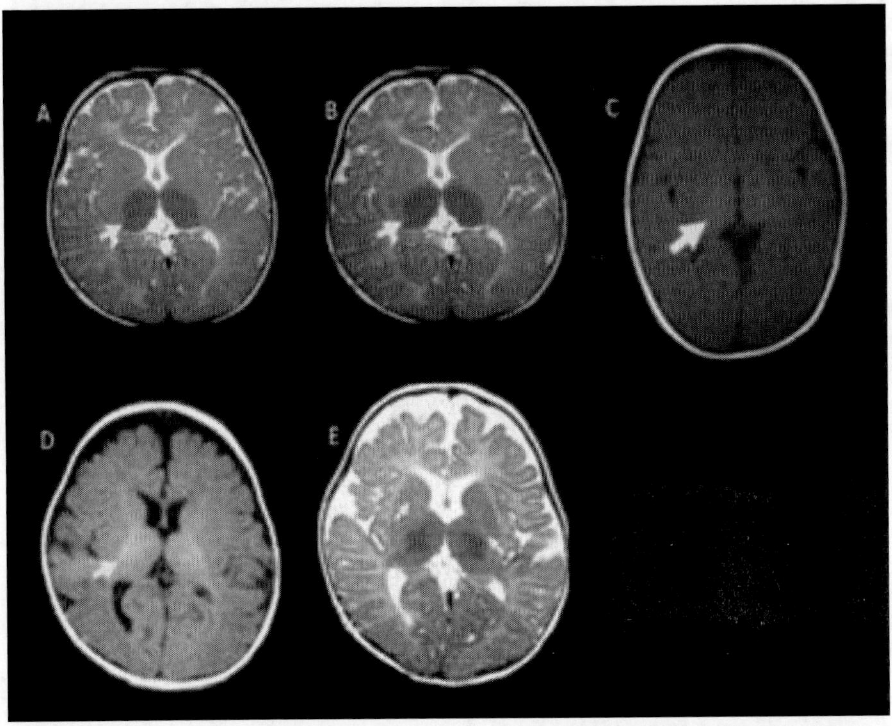

Figure 4. A, B; T2-W sequences of brain MRI of two patients with SD at ages of 4 y and 10 m. respectively revealing a diffuse hypomyelination pattern of cerebral white matter in addition to bilateral symmetric thalamus hypo intensity (thick yellow arrows). C, D; T1-W sequences of brain MRI of another two patients at ages 2 and 5 years old, respectively with diagnosis of SD shows moderate bilateral symmetric thalamus hyperintensity (thick yellow arrows). E; T2-W sequence of brain MRI of an 8 months' female patient with SD consists of brain atrophy especially in anterior parts in addition to abnormal basal ganglia signals (short yellow arrows).

6. Diagnosis

Sandhoff disease should be considered in any child with unexplained neurological regression. Since the inheritance of the disease is autosomal recessive, the history of consanguineous marriage and any other involved sibling in the family may be helpful. The presence of cherry red spot on ophthalmologic examination and hepatosplenomegaly are important clues for the diagnosis but the absence of these signs could not rule out the disorder. SD can be readily confirmed by enzyme activity testing on leukocytes or cultured fibroblasts, in which β-Hexosaminidases A and B activity has been decreased or absent. Gene analysis assay to recognize the precise molecular defect in enzymatically confirmed patients should be carried out to allow identification of carriers in the family and permit prenatal diagnosis (Figure 5). Newborn screening by enzyme activity testing in dried blood spots (DBS) is possible [52].

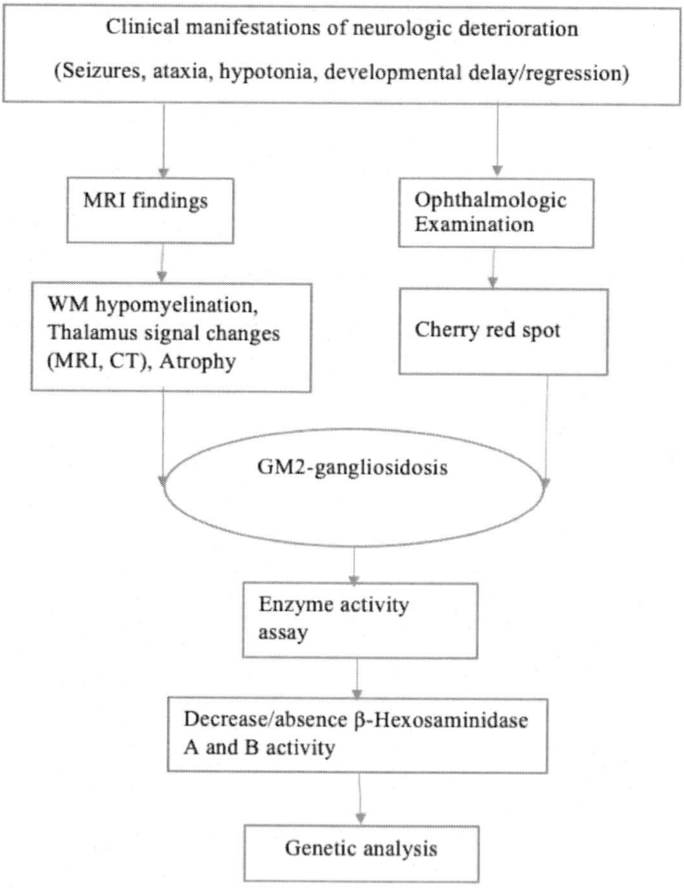

Figure 5. Diagnosis approach to a child suspected to GM2-gangliosidosis.

In case of finding no mutation by direct sequencing of *HEXB* gene, deletion & duplication analysis using Multiplex Ligation-dependent Probe Amplification (MLPA) or Comparative Genomic Hybridization (CGH) array would be applied. In the situation that the analysis of the *HEXB* gene revealed no pathogenic variant, a targeted Next Generation Sequencing (NGS) panel and/or Whole Exome Sequencing (WES) would be applicable to consider the related genes and conditions [53-55]. Indications for *HEXB* gene testing are patients with the prevalent symptoms of the Sandhoff disease (SD), individuals with the positive family history of the SD and individuals with a suspected family history of the SD or related conditions [54, 56].

7. Therapeutical Approaches

Unfortunately, there is no curative treatment available for SD. Seizures are usually managed by anticonvulsant drugs. Chaperone therapy with pyrimethamine has been shown to be inefficient but Ketogenic diet has improved cardiac function and reduced the frequency of seizures in some patients with Sandhoff [57]. Regards to the role of neuroinflammation hypothesis in LSDs, anti-inflammatory drugs have been postulated to be effective in halting neurodegeneration process and life span expansion [23]. Miglustat is a substrate reduction therapy is under investigation to see whether it can impact on the quality of life in affected patients with SD [58]. Intrathecal stem cell and gene therapy are tested in the animal model studies [59].

7.1. Gene and Stem Cell Therapy for Sandhoff Disease

Like the majority of the genetic conditions, SD is currently incurable and conventional treatments are unable to amend the patients' condition. The advent of the gene and cell therapy has opened a new horizon in the therapy of the neurogenetic conditions; although, the progress is slow and there are still several barriers to reach the final goal.

Gene therapy is mainly divided in into two approaches: 1) *In-Vivo* gene therapy, in which the targeted DNA/RNA sequence inserted into the viral vectors (adenoviruses, retroviruses and etc.) or non-viral delivery systems (nanoparticles, plasmids and etc.) and then injected into the patient's cells. 2) The *Ex-Vivo* gene therapy, in which cells recovered from the patient, genetically modified *In-Vitro* (in the laboratory) and then injected back into the patient's body [60].

The first trials to fix the mutated *HEXA* and *HEXB* commence in the 1990s and gene therapy with different vectors such as adenovirus, adeno-associated virus and non-viral vectors were used to transfer the wild-type DNA or complementary DNA (cDNA) into the SD patient's cells. Intracranial injection of recombinant AAV (rAAV) containing HEXA & HEXB cDNA in mice model of SD led to stable expression of the enzyme in the nerve cells and increased the survival rate of the studied mice; however, due to the complexity of the gene therapy and some ethical and safety concerns this interesting approach is still far from the clinic [59, 61].

There are different types of stem cells that potentially can be used in the mice model of SD. Among them, neural stem cells (NSCs) and induced Pluripotent stem cells (iPS) are two suitable stem cells that regularly used in the mice models [62, 63]. In some studies, has been shown that NSC intracranial injection into the SD mice model can lead to the restoring of the β-hexosaminidase enzyme activity, improvement of the neurologic and behavioral condition, increase the lifespan, and slow down the progression of the disease. The iPS derives from the mature and differentiated cells and is pluripotent and capable of differentiating to the neural cells. There are several studies utilizing the iPS in neurologic conditions like SD and resulted in significant findings. The comparison of the Sandhoff model mice untreated and treated with iPS revealed that treated mice have a longer lifespan, better motor control, less storage of GM2 gangliosides in the brain, and less inflammation [64-66].

8. Natural History of Sandhoff Disease

The prognosis of infantile SD is poor and death is usually occurring by 3 years of age due to frequent seizures and aspiration pneumonia. The Kaplan-Meyer survival curve in a case series of 25 patients with infantile SD showed that 50% of patients had died at age of 22 months [34] (Figure 6). According to the largest cohort study of infantile GM2-Gangliosidosis to date, SD is a ruinous disorder; the survival rate of affected patients by the age of 5 years was twenty five percent and about fifty percent of the patients had died by the age of 3 years [67]. The natural history of the juvenile and adult forms of the SD may differ from the infantile type. The available data on the natural history of 155 Juvenile patients and or subacute GM2-Gangliosidosis cases revealed a heterogeneous clinical course; about fifty percent of the GM2- Gangliosidosis patients had died in the first decade and the survival rate of them by the age of 20 years was twenty five percent [68].

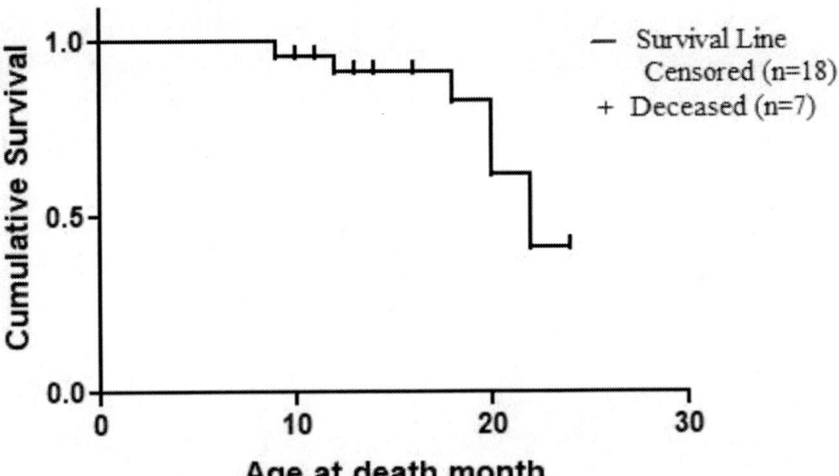

Figure 6. Survival rate in juvenile GM2-Gangliosidosis.

9. Genetic Counseling

As an autosomal recessive lipid storage disorder, Sandhoff disease progressively affects the neural cells. Infantile type is the most common and severe of the SD. Mainly, families with a positive history of the SD are seeking genetic counseling and the best pregnancy options. During the process of the genetic counseling for SD and other lysosomal storage disorders, the nature of the condition explains to the parents and the family planning options as well as complications will be discussed. After the family received all the needed information regarding the SD, genetic carrier screening may be offered to the relatives of the affected index. Parents who are the carrier of the *HEXB* mutation can benefit from the prenatal diagnosis (PND) or preimplantation genetic diagnosis (PGD) after receiving the potential uses and limitations of each approaches. In some religions or nations, PND is forbidden or limited to a specific time so it is important to provide the information to the families at the right time preferably before pregnancy [54, 69].

The genotype-phenotype correlation using in-silico pathogenicity prediction and clinical findings has shown the nonsense variants, splicing variants, stop codon variants and missense variants in the conserved domains of *HEXB* correlate with the severe and infantile type of SD (13, 70)

Conclusion

Sandhoff disease is a rare lysosomal storage disorder that should be considered in children with progressive neurologic deterioration. Due to a lack of specific clinical features for early diagnosis, in suspect patients, enzyme activity assay or molecular testing is necessary. Early diagnosis and management of the juvenile and adult forms of SD may reduce the severity of the disability and result in the increased quality of life in the patients. Prenatal diagnosis (PND) or Pre-implantation Genetic Diagnosis

(PGD) in families with affected members allow us to prevent them from giving birth to additional patients.

REFERENCES

[1] Ishida, Y; Nayak, S; Mindell, JA; Grabe, M. A model of lysosomal pH regulation. *J. Gen. Physiol.*, 2013, 141, 705-720.

[2] Vanier, MT; Caillaud, C; Levade, T. Disorders of Sphingolipid Synthesis, Sphingolipidoses, and Niemann-Pick Disease Type C and Neuronal Ceroid Lipofuscinoses. In: Saudubray, JM; Baumgartner, MR; EdsInborn, JW. Metabolic Diseases: *Diagnosis and Treatment*. 16th ed. Berlin: Springer, 2016, 551-575.

[3] Bellettato, CM; Scarpa, M. Pathophysiology of neuropathic lysosomal storage disorders. *J Inherit Metab Di.*, 2010, 33, 347-362.

[4] Sun, A. Lysosomal storage disease overview. *Ann Transl Med.*, 2018, 6, 476.

[5] Vitner, EB; Farfel-Becker, T; Ferreira, NS, Leshkowitz, D; Sharma, P; Lang, KS; Futerman, AH. Induction of the type I interferon response in neurological forms of Gaucher disease. *Neuroinflammation.*, 2016, 13, 104.

[6] Platt, FM; d'Azzo, A; Davidson, BL; Neufeld, EF; Tifft, CJ. Lysosomal storage diseases. *Nat. Rev. Dis. Primers.*, 2018, 4, 1-25.

[7] Winchester, B; Vellodi, A; Young, E. The molecular basis of lysosomal storage diseases and their treatment. *Biochem. Soc. Trans.*, 2000, 28, 150-154.

[8] Schulze, H; Sandhoff, K. Sphingolipids and Lysosomal Pathologies. *Biochim. Biophys. Acta.*, 2014, 1841, 799-810.

[9] Lloyd-Evans, E; Haslett, LJ. The lysosomal storage disease continuum with ageing-related neurodegenerative disease. *Ageing Res. Rev.*, 2016, 32, 104-121.

[10] Taghizadeh, H; taghizadeh, e. A case report of Sandhoff disease in Gachsaran. *Razi. J. Med. Sci.*, 2017, 24, 37-40.

[11] Zhan, L; Dongfang, L; Pinggan, L; Liang, L; Luo, X; Huang, K. Infantile Sandhoff disease: a case report and literature review. *J. Clin. Ped.*, 2017, 35, 694-7.

[12] Sakpichaisakul, K; Taeranawich, P; Nitiapinyasakul, A; Sirisopikun, T. Identification of Sandhoff disease in a Thai family: clinical and biochemical characterization. *J Med Assoc Thai.*, 2010, 93, 1088-1092.

[13] Mahdieh, N; Mikaeeli, S; Tavasoli, AR; Rezaei, Z; Maleki, M; Rabbani, B. Genotype, phenotype and in silico pathogenicity analysis of HEXB mutations: Panel based sequencing for differential diagnosis of gangliosidosis. *Clin Neuro Neurosurg.*, 2018, 167, 43-53.

[14] Cooper, D; Ball, E; Stenson, P. HGMD–The Human Gene Mutation Database at the Institute of Medical Genetics in Cardiff. *Zugriff im Juli.*, 2017.

[15] Tropak, MB; Yonekawa, S; Karumuthil-Melethil, S; Thompson, P; Wakarchuk, W; Gray, SJ; Walia, JS; Mark, BL; Mahuran, D. Construction of a hybrid β-hexosaminidase subunit capable of forming stable homodimers that hydrolyze GM2 ganglioside *in vivo. Mol. Ther. Methods Clin. Dev.*, 2016, 3, 15057.

[16] Cox, TM; Cachón-González, MB. The cellular pathology of lysosomal diseases. *J. Pathol.*, 2012, 226, 241-254.

[17] Vitner, EB; Futerman, AH; Platt, N. Innate immune responses in the brain of sphingolipid lysosomal storage diseases. *Biol Chem.*, 2015, 396, 659-667.

[18] Jeyakumar, M; Smith, DA; Williams, IM; Borja, MC; Neville, DC; Butters, TD; Dwek, RA, Platt, FM. NSAIDs increase survival in the Sandhoff disease mouse: synergy with N-butyldeoxynojirimycin. *Ann Neurol.*, 2004, 56, 642-649.

[19] Tutor, J. Biochemical characterization of the GM2 gangliosidosis B1 variant. *Braz J Med Biol Res.*, 2004, 37, 777-83.

[20] Paciotti, S; Albi, E; Parnetti, L; Beccari, T. Lysosomal Ceramide Metabolism Disorders: Implications in Parkinson's Disease. *J. Clin. Med.*, 2020, 9, 594.

[21] Ysselstein, D; Shulman, JM; Krainc, D. Emerging links between pediatric lysosomal storage diseases and adult parkinsonism. *Mov. Disord.*, 2019, 34, 614-624.

[22] Liu, M; Huang, D; Wang, H; Zhao, L; Wang, Q; Chen, X. Clinical and Molecular Characteristics of Two Chinese Children with Infantile Sandhoff Disease and Review of the Literature. *J. Mol. Neurosci.*, 2020, 70, 481-487.

[23] Robak, LA; Jansen, IE; Van Rooij, J; Uitterlinden, AG; Kraaij, R; Jankovic, J. International Parkinson's Disease Genomics Consortium (IPDGC); Heutink, P; Shulman, JM. Excessive burden of lysosomal storage disorder gene variants in Parkinson's disease. *Brain.*, 2017, 140, 3191-3203.

[24] Bjartmar, C; Battistuta, J; Terada, N; Dupree, E; Trapp, BD. N-acetylaspartate is an axon-specific marker of mature white matter *in vivo*: a biochemical and immunohistochemical study on the rat optic nerve. *Ann Neurol.*, 2002, 51, 51-58.

[25] Brand, A; Richter-Landsberg, C; Leibfritz, D. Multinuclear NMR studies on the energy metabolism of glial and neuronal cells. *Dev. Neurosci.*, 1993, 289-298.

[26] Michaelis, T, Helms, G; Merboldt, KD; Hänicke, W; Bruhn, H; Frahm, J. Identification of scyllo-inositol in proton NMR spectra of human brain *in vivo*. *NMR. Biomed.*, 1993, 6, 105-109.

[27] Wilken, B; Dechent, P; Hanefeld, F; Frahm, J. Proton MRS of a child with Sandhoff disease reveals elevated brain hexosamine. *Eur. J. Paediatr. Neurol.*, 2008, 12, 56-60.

[28] Gomez-Lira, M; Mottes, M; Perusi, C; Pignatti, P; Rizzuto, N; Gatti, R; Salviati, A. A novel 4-bp deletion creates a premature stop codon and dramatically decreases HEXB mRNA levels in a severe case of Sandhoff disease. *Mol. Cell Probes.*, 2001, 15, 75-79.

[29] Muldoon, LL; Neuwelt, EA; Pagel, MA; Weiss, DL. Characterization of the molecular defect in a feline model for type II GM2-gangliosidosis (Sandhoff disease). *Am. J. Pathol.*, 1994, 144, 1109-1118.

[30] Scarpelli, M, Tomelleri, G, Bertolasi, L; Salviati, A. Natural history of motor neuron disease in adult onset GM2-gangliosidosis: a case report with 25 years of follow-up. *Mol Genet Metab Rep.*, 2014, 269-272.

[31] Loth, MK; Choi, J; McGlothan, JL; Pletnikov, MV; Pomper, MG; Guilarte, TR. TSPO in a murine model of Sandhoff disease: presymptomatic marker of neurodegeneration and disease pathophysiology. *Neurobiol. Dis.*, 2016, 85, 174-186.

[32] Myerowitz, R; Lawson, D; Mizukami, H; Mi, Y; Tifft, CJ; Proia, RL. Molecular pathophysiology in Tay–Sachs and Sandhoff diseases as revealed by gene expression profiling. *Hum. Mol. Genet.*, 2002, 11, 1343-1350.

[33] Blieden, LC; Desnick, RJ; Carter, JB; Krivit, W; Moller, JH; Sharp, HL. Cardiac involvement in Sandhoff's disease: Inborn error of glycosphingolipid metabolism. *Am. J. Cardiol.*, 1974, 34, 83-8.

[34] Tavasoli, AR; Parvaneh, N; Ashrafi, MR; Rezaei, Z; Zschocke, J; Rostami, P. Clinical presentation and outcome in infantile Sandhoff disease: a case series of 25 patients from Iranian neurometabolic bioregistry with five novel mutations. *Orphanet. J. Rare Dis.*, 2018, 13:130.

[35] Yüksel, A; Yalçınkaya, C; Işlak, C; Gündüz, E; Seven, M. Neuroimaging findings of four patients with Sandhoff disease. *Pediatr. Neurol.*, 1999, 21, 562-565.

[36] Sass, K; Wiebe, S; Lemire E. Infantile Sandhoff's disease. *SA. J. Radiol.*, 2009, 13, 66-70.

[37] Agamanolis, DP. Lysosomal Storage Diseases: Early Diagnosis and New Treatments, Rosella, Parini; Generoso, Andria. in: *Mariani Foundation Pediatric Neurology series*, 23, John Libbey Eurotext, Montrouge., 2010, 184.

[38] Ospina, LH; Lyons, CJ; McCormick, AQ. "Cherry-red spot" or "perifoveal white patch"?. *Can. J. Ophthalmol.*, 2005, 40, 609-610.

[39] Suvarna, J; Hajela, S. Cherry-red spot. *J. Postgrad. Med.*, 2008, 54, 54-57.

[40] Gahramanova, L; Galbinur, T; Mammadkhanova, A. Late-Onset lysosomal storage disorders with macular cherry-red spot. *Retin. cases Brief rep.*, 2019. doi:10.1097/ICB.0000000000000860.

[41] Kalbag, N; Roy, M. Sialidosis: Bilateral Cherry-Red Macular Spot. *EC. Ophthalmol.*, 2018, 95, 82-85.

[42] Hendriksz, C; Corry, P; Wraith, J; Besley, G; Cooper, A; Ferrie, C. Juvenile Sandhoff disease-nine new cases and a review of the literature. *J Inherit Metab Dis.*, 2004, 27, 241-249.

[43] Delnooz, C; Lefeber, D; Langemeijer, S; Hoffjan, S; Dekomien, G; Zwarts, M; et al. New cases of adult-onset Sandhoff disease with a cerebellar or lower motor neuron phenotype. *J Neurol. Neurosurg. Psychiatry.*, 2010, 81, 968-972.

[44] Sung, AR; Moretti, P; Shaibani, A. Case of late-onset Sandhoff disease due to a novel mutation in the HEXB gene. *Neurol. Genet.*, 2018, 4, e260.

[45] Ashrafi, MR; Amanat, M; Garshasbi, M; Kameli, R; Nilipour, Y; Heidari, M; Rezaei, Z; Tavasoli, AR. An update on clinical, pathological, diagnostic, and therapeutic perspectives of childhood leukodystrophies. *Expert Rev. Neurother.*, 2020, 20, 65-84.

[46] Vanderver, A; Prust, M; Tonduti, D; Mochel, F; Hussey, HM; Helman, G; Garbern, J; Eichler, F; Labauge, P; Aubourg, P; Rodriguez, D; Patterson, MC; Van Hove, JL; Schmidt, J; Wolf, NI;, Boespflug-Tanguy, O; Schiffmann, R; van der Knaap, MS; GLIA Consortium. Case definition and classification of leukodystrophies and leukoencephalopathies. *Mol. Genet. Metab.*, 2015, 114, 494-500.

[47] Çalis, M; Özmen, M; Beck, M; Apak, S. Thalamic hyperdensity—is it a diagnostic marker for Sandhoff disease?. *Brain Dev.*, 1993, 15, 387-388.

[48] Schiffmann, R; van der Knaap, MS. Invited article: an MRI-based approach to the diagnosis of white matter disorders. *Neurol.*, 2009, 72, 750-759.

[49] Autti, T; Joensuu, R; Åberg, L. Decreased T2 signal in the thalami may be a sign of lysosomal storage disease. *Neuroradiology.*, 2007, 49, 571-578.

[50] Van Der Knaap, MS; Valk, J. *Magnetic resonance of myelin, myelination and myelin disorders*: Springer. 1995, eBook ISBN: 978-3-662-03078-3.

[51] Brismar, J; Brisma, G; Coates, R; Gascon, G; Ozand, P. Increased density of the thalamus on CT scans in patients with GM2 gangliosidoses. *AJNR. AM. J. Neuroradiology*., 1990, 11, 125-130.

[52] Smith, NJ; Winstone, AM; Stellitano, L; Cox, TM; Verity, CM. GM2 gangliosidosis in a UK study of children with progressive neurodegeneration: 73 cases reviewed. *Dev. Med. Child Neurol.*, 2012, 54, 176-182.

[53] Chamoles, NA; Blanco, M; Gaggioli, D; Casentini, C. Tay-Sachs and Sandhoff diseases: enzymatic diagnosis in dried blood spots on filter paper: retrospective diagnoses in newborn-screening cards. *Clin. Chim. Acta*., 2002, 318, 133-137.

[54] McGinniss, MJ; McGinniss, MA. Carrier Screening and Heterozygote Testing. *Emery and Rimoin's Principles and Practice of Medical Genetics and Genomics*: Elsevier., 2019, 283-98.

[55] Lee, JS; Choi, J-M; Lee, M; Kim, SY; Lee, S; Lim, BC; Cheon, JE; Kim, IO; Kim, KJ; Choi, M; Seong, MW; Chae, JH. Diagnostic challenge for the rare lysosomal storage disease: late infantile GM1 gangliosidosis. *Brain Dev*., 2018, 40, 383-390.

[56] Ebrahimzadeh-Vesal, R; Hosseini, S; Moghaddassian, M; Abbaszadegan, MR. Identification of novel missense HEXB gene mutation in Iranian-child with juvenile Sandhoff disease. *Meta. Gene*., 2017, 12, 83-87.

[57] Clarke, JT; Mahuran, DJ; Sathe, S; Kolodny, EH; Rigat, BA; Raiman, JA; et al. An open-label Phase I/II clinical trial of pyrimethamine for the treatment of patients affected with chronic GM2 gangliosidosis (Tay–Sachs or Sandhoff variants). *Mol. Genet. Metab*., 2011, 102, 6-12.

[58] Tsuji, D; Akeboshi, H; Matsuoka, K; Yasuoka, H; Miyasaki, E; Kasahara, Y; Kawashima, I; Chiba, Y; Jigami, Y; Taki, T; Sakuraba, H; Itoh, K. Highly phosphomannosylated enzyme replacement therapy for GM2 gangliosidosis. *Ann. Neurol*., 2011, 69, 691-701.

[59] Woodley, EJ; Osmon, K; Thompson, P; Karumuthil-Melethil, S; Gray, S; Walia, J. Enhancement of Gene Therapy Treatment for Sandhoff Disease Through Complimentary Drug Therapy. *Mol Ther.*, 2016, 24, S221.

[60] Wang, D; Tai, PW; Gao, G. Adeno-associated virus vector as a platform for gene therapy delivery. *Nat Rev Drug Discov.*, 2019, 18, 358-378.

[61] McCurdy, V; Rockwell, H; Arthur, J; Bradbury, A; Johnson, A; Randle, A; Brunson, BL; Hwang, M; Gray-Edwards, HL; Morrison, NE; Johnson, JA; Baker, HJ; Cox, NR; Seyfried, TN; Sena-Esteves, M; Martin, DR. Widespread correction of central nervous system disease after intracranial gene therapy in a feline model of Sandhoff disease. *Gene Ther.*, 2015, 22, 181-189.

[62] Hosseini Bereshneh, A; Soltani, D; Roodbarani, R; Modarressi, MH. Stem cells: progressions and applications in clinical medicine. *Tehran Univ. Med. J.*, 2016, 74, 77-83.

[63] Allende, ML; Cook, EK; Larman, BC; Nugent, A; Brady, JM; Golebiowski, D; Sena-Esteves, M; Tifft, CJ; Proia, RL. Cerebral organoids derived from Sandhoff disease-induced pluripotent stem cells exhibit impaired neurodifferentiation. *J. Lipid Res.*, 2018, 59, 550-563.

[64] Arthur, J; Lee, J; Snyder, E; Seyfried, T. Therapeutic effects of stem cells and substrate reduction in juvenile Sandhoff mice. *Neurochem. Res.*, 2012, 37, 1335-1343.

[65] Ornaghi, F; Sala, D; Tedeschi, F; Maffia, MC; Bazzucchi, M; Morena, F; Valsecchi, M; Aureli, M; Martino, S; Gritti, A. Novel bicistronic lentiviral vectors correct β- Hexosaminidase deficiency in neural and hematopoietic stem cells and progeny: implications for *in vivo* and *ex vivo* gene therapy of GM2 gangliosidosis. *Neurobiol. Dis.*, 2020, 134, 104667.

[66] Jeyakumar, M; Lee, JP; Sibson, NR; Lowe, JP; Stuckey, DJ; Tester, K; Fu, G; Newlin, R; Smith, DA; Snyder, EY; Platt, FM. Neural stem cell transplantation benefits a monogenic neurometabolic disorder

during the symptomatic phase of disease. *Stem Cells.*, 2009, 27, 2362-2370.

[67] Maegawa, GH; Stockley, T; Tropak, M; Banwell, B; Blaser, S; Kok, F; Giugliani, R; Mahuran, D; Clarke, JT. The natural history of juvenile or subacute GM2 gangliosidosis: 21 new cases and literature review of 134 previously reported. *Pediatrics.*, 2006, 118, e1550-1562.

[68] Bley, AE; Giannikopoulos, OA; Hayden, D; Kubilus, K; Tifft, CJ; Eichler, FS. Natural history of infantile GM2 gangliosidosis. *Pediatrics.*, 2011, 128, e1233-1241.

[69] Kwon, JM. Neurodegenerative disorders of childhood. *Nelson Textbook of Pediatrics.*, 2016, 19, 2011.73-74.

[70] Ou, L; Kim, S; Whitley, CB; Jarnes-Utz, JR. Genotype-phenotype correlation of gangliosidosis mutations using in silico tools and homology modeling. *Mol. Genet. Metab. Rep.*, 2019, 20, 100495.

In: Neurochemistry of Metabolic Diseases ISBN: 978-1-53618-339-9
Editor: Sankar Surendran

Chapter 7

METACHROMATIC LEUKODYSTROPHY: MOLECULAR MECHANISM AND THERAPEUTIC EFFECT

Soumya Sundaram[1,*], Soumya V. Chandrasekharan[2] and Sruthi S. Nair[2]

[1]Department of Neurology, Comprehensive Care Centre for Neurodevelopmental Disorders, Sree Chitra Tirunal Institute for Medical Sciences and Technology, Trivandrum, India

[2]Department of Neurology, Sree Chitra Tirunal Institute for Medical Sciences and Technology, Trivandrum, India

ABSTRACT

Metachromatic leukodystrophy (MLD), a lysosomal storage disorder, is the most common autosomal recessive leukodystrophy. MLD occurs due to deficiency of the enzyme arylsulfatase-A (ASA), encoded by the

---

[*] Corresponding Author's Emails: drsoumya@sctimst.ac.in; ssdr.soumya@gmail.com.

gene ARSA on chromosome 22. ASA is the first enzyme in the degradation pathway of cerebroside sulfate, an important component of myelin. In the absence or reduction of functional activity of ASA, sulfatides accumulate in the central and peripheral nervous system, which leads to progressive demyelination of brain and peripheral nerves. MLD is classified into three subtypes based on the age of onset. The late infantile MLD typically manifests between 12 and 18 months of age, juvenile form between 4 and 16 years and adult form after 16 years of age. Cerebral involvement can manifest as gait disturbances, regression of developmental milestones, spasticity, ataxia, seizures, dementia and neuropsychiatric features depending on the age at presentation. Peripheral nervous system involvement causes hypotonia, areflexia and weakness. The progressive nature of motor and cognitive dysfunction engenders rapid decline of quality of life and mortality. Magnetic resonance imaging, electroneurography and nerve biopsy act as ancillary tests to support the clinical diagnosis before proceeding to more definitive and diagnostic biochemical and genetic tests. There is no curative therapy for MLD. Hematopoietic stem cell transplantation and gene therapy are the emerging specific therapies. Meanwhile, supportive therapy with symptomatic pharmacological management and rehabilitation should be provided for every patient. This chapter comprehensively reviews the clinical features, genetic and biochemical abnormalities and recent therapeutic advances in MLD.

1. Introduction

Metachromatic leukodystrophy [(MLD) (MIM 250100)] is one of the most frequently encountered lysosomal storage disorders (LSDs). MLD results from deficiency of the enzyme arylsulfatase-A (ASA) and has an autosomal recessive inheritance [1]. ASA plays a pivotal role in sulfatide metabolism by hydrolyzing the 3-O ester bond of 3-O-sulfogalacto-sylceramide and 3-O-sulfolactosylceramide [2]. Sulfatides are complex lipids and a major component of myelin. Deficiency of ASA leads to accumulation of sulfatides, predominantly in oligodendrocytes in the central nervous system (CNS) and Schwann cells in the peripheral nervous system (PNS) which result in central and peripheral demyelination respectively [3]. This is appreciated as periventricular white matter changes in brain imaging and demyelinating neuropathy in electroneurography [4, 5]. The metabolites also get accumulated in various visceral organs such as kidney, liver, gallbladder, adrenal cortex, pancreas, sweat glands, testes and rectal tissue [6, 7]. Saposin B is an activator protein of ASA and its deficiency is also reported to cause an MLD-like syndrome [8].

Metachromatic leukodystrophy can present in any age ranging from second year of life to late adulthood. Based on the age of onset, MLD is clinically classified into late infantile, juvenile onset, and adult onset forms. The classical infantile (late infantile) form of MLD presents with psychomotor regression, gait ataxia, dysarthria, seizures, cognitive decline and spastic quadriparesis, rapidly progressing to decerebrate state and death. In contrast, the adult forms are slowly progressive, usually manifesting with neuropsychiatric symptomatology and dementia. Juvenile onset form has a clinical presentation intermediate between infantile onset and adult onset forms [9]. The definitive confirmation of the diagnosis is by molecular genetic testing. However, pathological demonstration of metachromatic granules in the urine or from nerve or brain tissue is also diagnostic in MLD [4]. A diagnosis based on ASA enzymatic activity alone is not specific as partial deficiency of ASA can be found in asymptomatic individuals, a situation commonly referred to as pseudo-deficiency [10]. Despite significant advances in the management of LSDs, curative treatment for MLD still eludes us. Hematopoietic stem cell transplantation (HSCT) is the only specific therapy which is accessible outside research settings. Best results were seen in late juvenile and adult onset forms if done in sufficiently early or in the pre-symptomatic stages of the disease. HSCT was found to have little benefit in the late infantile form [4]. Gene therapy, enzyme replacement therapy (ERT) and substrate reduction therapy (SRT) are other promising strategies in the management of MLD [11]. Meanwhile, supportive therapy with pharmacological management and rehabilitation care needs to be provided for every patient. The genetics, molecular mechanisms, clinical features, diagnosis and therapeutic aspects of MLD will be dealt in detail in this chapter.

2. History of the Disease

In 1910, German neuropathologist, Lois Alzheimer, gave a brief description of an adult patient with dementia who had pathological evidence for myelin destruction and brightly stained metachromatic deposits in glial cells. Later, in 1921, Witte demonstrated the accumulation of metachromatic granules in various organs including liver and gall bladder. He proposed that the diagnosis of this condition might be possible by examining metachromatic materials excreted through urine [12]. This disorder was known as 'diffuse brain sclerosis' during this time and the term metachromatic leukodystrophy (metachromatischen leukodystrophien) was coined later by Peiffer in 1959 [4]. Infantile onset MLD was formerly known as Greenfield disease after Joseph Godwin Greenfield, a British neuropathologist, who gave a detailed illustration of this condition [13]. It was the work done by Austin and colleagues (1963) that identified ASA as the enzyme deficient in MLD, the first enzyme to be connected with any leukodystrophy [14]. Two decades later, *ARSA* gene was cloned and nucleotide sequence of the full-length complementary deoxyribonucleic acid (cDNA) was reported by Stein and his team [15]. One year later, the genomic organization of *ARSA* was described by Kreysing [16].

3. Epidemiology of the Disease

The prevalence of LSDs ranges from 7.5 to 23.5 per 100,000 live births [17]. General prevalence of MLD ranges from 1:40,000 to 1:100,000 [18]. MLD is pan-ethnic and is described in several populations including European, Japanese, Indians, Jewish, Arabs, Lebanese, South African, Algerian, Alaskan and Eskimos. In geographical areas where consanguinity is practiced, the prevalence is still higher, 1:75 in Habbani Jews in Israel, 1: 2,500 in Eskimos and 1:8,000 in Israeli Arabs [4]. There are no differences in the clinical profile and survival of MLD across various geographical regions or based on sex or race [11].

4. MOLECULAR GENETICS OF THE DISEASE

Metachromatic leukodystrophy arises from the deficiency of the enzyme ASA which is encoded by *ARSA* gene. ASA is a lysosomal enzyme which participates in the metabolism of complex lipids by hydrolyzing cerebroside 3-sulfate to cerebroside and sulfate [3]. This is the first enzyme in the degradation pathway of sulfatide and its absence or deficiency leads to substrate accumulation proximal to the blockade. Cerebroside sulfate is a major component of myelin and when in excess, causes damage to myelin in the central and peripheral nervous systems [9].

4.1. Structure of Arylsulfatase A Gene (ARSA)

The gene encoding the ASA enzyme, *ARSA*, is mapped to the long arm of chromosome 22q13.33. *ARSA* has a total length of 3.2 kilobases (kb) and consists of eight exons. *ARSA* gene spans 3.2 kilo-base pairs and consists of 8 exons (Figure 1A). The *ARSA* cDNA hybridizes to any one of the three mRNA species, 2.1, 3.7 and 4.8 kb. The three mRNA species are generated using different polyadenylation signals [16]. The 2.1kb mRNA is translated into a precursor polypeptide of molecular weight 62 kilodalton (kd). Further processing of this precursor by various biochemical pathways lead to the formation of the human ASA enzyme (cerebroside-3-sulfatase) of 100-120 kd [18].

4.2. Arylsulfatase A Gene Alleles

Over 200 mutations have been reported in *ARSA* gene, of which more than 70% are missense mutations as per the recent report available from the Human Gene Mutation Database (HGMD). Frame shift mutations, nonsense mutations and splice region variants contribute to the rest: http://www.hgmd.cf.ac.uk/ac/gene.php?gene=ARSA [19, 20]. Metachromatic leukodystrophy is an autosomal recessive disease and pathogenesis requires the presence of homozygous or compound heterozygous pathogenic mutations in both the *ARSA* alleles.

Three classes of *ARSA* alleles with low enzymatic activity are identified [4].

i. *ARSA*-MLD allele: The pathogenic variants causing MLD in their homozygous or compound heterozygous states are termed *ARSA* - MLD allele.
ii. *ARSA*-PD allele: The variants that result in pseudo-deficiency of ASA enzyme are termed *ARSA*-PD alleles. In pseudo-deficiency of ASA enzyme, the individual has no clinical manifestation of MLD in spite of a low functional enzymatic activity of 5-20% of the controls. They remain asymptomatic as a mere 5 -15% of ASA is adequate for the metabolism of cerebroside sulfate.
iii. Cis configuration: In cis configuration, two *ARSA* sequence variants are noted in the same chromosome. About 0.5 to 1% of ARSA-PD alleles carry an *ARSA*-MLD allele in 'cis configuration'.

4.3. Genotype-Phenotype Correlation

The type of *ARSA*-MLD allele determines the enzymatic activity in an affected individual. Mutations in the gene can produce 'I type' or 'null' alleles associated with no enzymatic activity or 'R' alleles with minimal residual enzymatic activity. *ARSA*-MLD with homozygous or compound heterozygous null alleles show no detectable functional enzymatic activity and commonly present earlier in life with severe manifestations. In contrast, individuals with one or two *ARSA*-MLD R alleles with residual functional enzyme activity of ≥1% tend to have a later age of disease onset [21]. Accordingly, if an individual has two I alleles, the presentation will be of late infantile type, with I and R alleles, juvenile-MLD and with two R alleles, adult onset MLD suggesting a genotype-phenotype correlation [22]. However, this genotype-phenotype correlation is not absolute and displays higher fidelity in late infantile forms [4].

4.4. Mutations in the ARSA Gene

The most common mutation in *ARSA* is the splice donor site mutation of the exon 2- intron 2 border, c.459+1G > A which accounts for 15%–43% of MLD alleles, and is associated with the late infantile form of MLD (Figure 1B). The second most common *ARSA* mutation is c.1277C > T due to change of proline at position 426 to leucine (p.P426L) usually referred to as 'the common adult mutation'. Together, they contribute to 50% of all *ARSA* mutant alleles in MLD patients [23]. The third most prevalent *ARSA* mutation is c.536T > G (p.I179S), which, when in heterozygosity with the c.1277C > T (p.P426L) mutation, is associated with adult onset form of the disease [22]. A detailed account of all the recognized *ARSA* mutations can be accessed from Human Gene Mutation Database (HGMD) and ClinVar (https://www.ncbi.nlm.nih.gov/clinvar/) [19].

Homozygosity for alleles that do not allow the synthesis of any functional enzyme [splice site mutations (c.459+1G > A and c.1204+1G > A) and deletions (1401_1411del] cause the most severe presentation, late infantile form of the disease [24]. The alleles which allow the synthesis of low amounts of functional enzyme (e.g., c.536T > G and c.1277C > T) are the common alleles in the juvenile and adult onset forms [23]. The c.1049A > G, c.1172C > G and c.1049A > G, c.896A > G are the commonest *ARSA*-PD alleles [4].

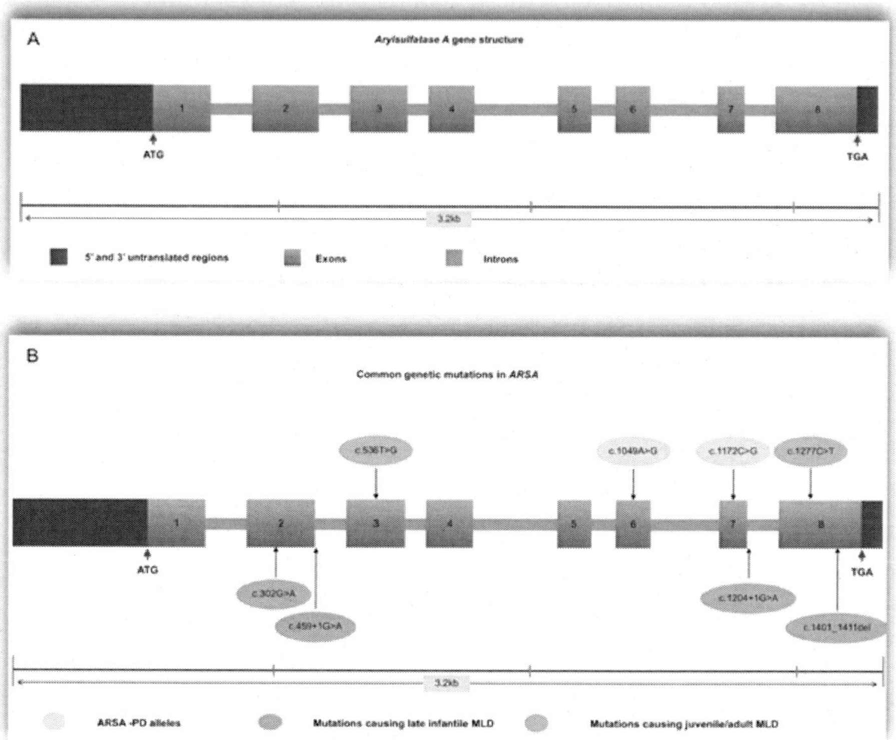

Figure 1. A) Structure of Arylsulfatase A gene: The light blue box indicate the exons. Grey lines are introns. Dark blue boxes are 3' or 5' untranslated regions. B) Common mutations in Arylsulfatase A gene: The mutations causing the late infantile form of MLD is given in green boxes, mutations causing juvenile and adult forms of MLD is depicted in pink boxes and the pseudo deficiency alleles are shown in yellow boxes.

4.5. Arylsulfatase-A Pseudo-Deficiency Alleles

Arylsulfatase-A pseudo-deficiency is caused by homozygosity for *ARSA* alleles with certain nucleotide variations, resulting in reduced amounts of functional enzyme. Pseudo-deficiency state is very prevalent and is reported in 5% and 20% of European and Australian population respectively. The *ARSA*-PD allele N350S causes loss of a potential N-glycosylation site leading to two oligosaccharide side chains instead of three as in wild type ASA [25]. A second mutation was discovered in the first polyadenylation signal downstream of the termination codon causing deficiency of 2.1kb ARSA mRNA species [26]. These result in reduction of ASA synthesis and enzymatic activity in spite of which pseudo-deficient individuals remain asymptomatic. Hence, biochemical demonstration of ASA deficiency should be accompanied by molecular genetic analysis to reveal whether the proband carries the pseudo-deficiency allele or pathogenic allele [4].

4.6. Saposin B Activator Deficiency (MIM 249900)

Rare reports have described individuals with MLD-like clinical presentation who had normal ASA enzyme levels and without any mutations in *ARSA*. Later, these patients were identified to have mutations in prosaposin gene (*PSAP*) on chromosome 10q22 [8, 27]. *PSAP* encodes prosaposin, a 524 amino acid glycoprotein with 4 homologous protein domains. Prosaposin is cleaved into four smaller proteins referred to as saposin A, B, C and D. Saposin B is the activator protein for enzyme ASA [27]. Saposin B solubilizes cerebroside sulfate so that ASA can initiate the hydrolysis of this compound. Saposin B is also required for the degradation of globotriaosylceramide. This lipid is also accumulated in saposin B deficiency which is not seen in ASA- deficient MLD [3].

5. Molecular Mechanism of the Disease

5.1. Synthesis of Arylsulfatase-A Enzyme

Arylsulfatase-A is a homo-octamer composed of a tetramer of dimers $(\alpha 2)_4$ and consists of 507 amino acids. The homodimers are synthesized in the rough endoplasmic reticulum (ER) and undergoes configurational change in interaction with the components of the ER folding system. Once the protein folding is completed, ASA is targeted to trans-Golgi network. Uridine diphosphate (UDP)-N-acetyl glucosamine-1 phosphotransferase and N-acetyl glucosamine-1-phosphodiester alpha-N-acetyl glycosaminidase act upon ASA and catalyze the binding and formation of mannose-6-phosphate (M6P) residue [28]. M6P is the recognition marker of lysosomal hydrolases [29]. M6P residues enable ASA to interact with M6P receptors and gain entry into the lysosomal compartment. ASA assumes its final homo-octameric conformation in the acidic pH of lysosomal compartment [11].

Different mutations in the *ARSA* gene affect the various steps in ASA synthesis resulting in the alteration of protein structure and folding and defective function. For example, the c.1277T > G (p.P426L) mutation prevents formation of homo-octamers. The P426 residue is located proximal to the E424 which is required for the octamerization process. Cleavage sites of the enzyme is protected by the octamerization in wild type ASA. In this abnormal protein, the cleavage sites are exposed and is recognized by lysosomal protease cathepsin-L, which degrades the enzyme [30]. Most of the missense mutations result in misfolded ASA which are diverted to the ER-associated degradation (ERAD) pathway and prematurely targeted to the ubiquitin-proteasome system [31].

5.2. Biochemical Role of ASA

Sphingosine, a long-chain amino alcohol combines with long chain fatty acid to form ceramides which are complex lipids [32]. UDP-galactose interacts with 2-hydroxylated or non-hydroxylated ceramide and galactose is transferred to 2-hydroxylated, or non-hydroxylated ceramide. This reaction is catalyzed by galactosyltransferase in the endoplasmic reticulum and galactocerebroside is formed. The galactocerebroside is then transported to the Golgi apparatus where it reacts with 3'-phosphoadenosine-5'-phosphosulfate (PAPS) to form cerebroside 3-sulfate (Figure 2). Sulfatide degradation occurs in the lysosomes.

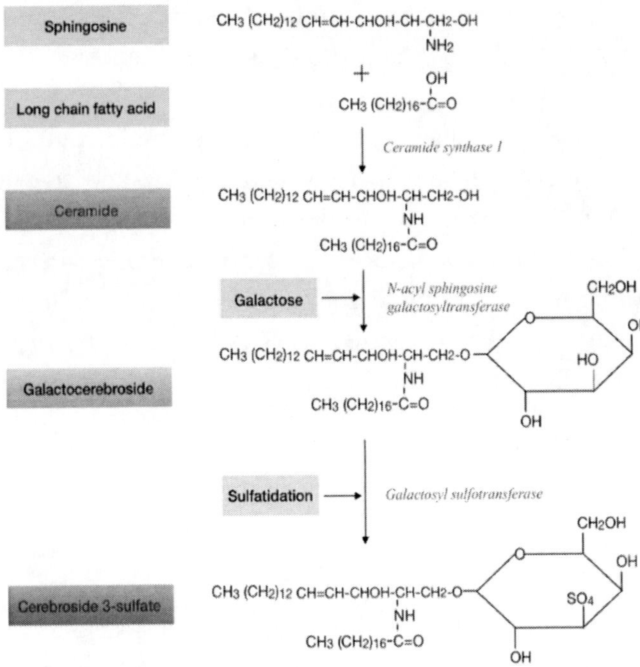

Figure 2. Biosynthetic pathway of sulfatide.

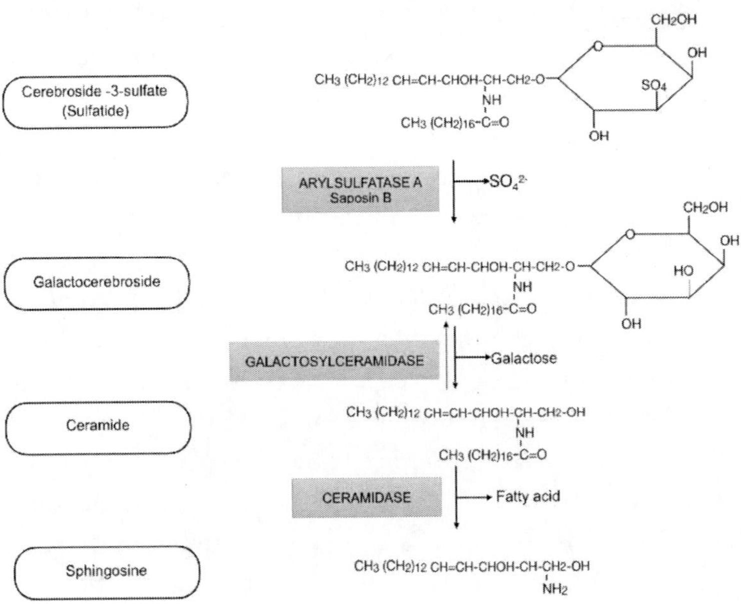

Figure 3. Degradation pathway of sulfatide.

Here, ASA hydrolyzes the sulfate group of cerebroside 3-sulfate in the presence of a sphingolipid activator protein, Saposin B to form galactocerebroside. Following desulfation, galactoceramidase cleaves the galactose moiety from galactocerebroside. Ceramide thus formed is cleaved by ceramidase enzyme to form sphingosine and free fatty acid. Functionally, ASA participates in desulfation of 3-O-sulfogalactosyl-bound sphingolipids (Figure 3). 3-O-galactosylceramides (cerebroside 3-sulfates) are the main sulfated sphingolipids in the myelin of both CNS and PNS. The sulfatides are synthesized by oligodendrocytes in CNS and Schwann cells in PNS which constitute around 3-4% of the myelin protein [4].

5.3. Pathogenesis

In MLD, deficiency of ASA enzyme adversely affects the degradation pathway of sulfated cerebroside. As a result, the excess sulfated cerebroside accumulates in the oligodendrocytes and Schwann cells predominantly and the neural and glial cells to a smaller extent. Myelin synthesis is unaffected in MLD, however, the degradation and recycling of myelin lipids is defective. The lysosomal storage of sulfatides cause destruction of myelin producing cells [33].

Sulfatides confer stability to the myelin structure by two mechanisms. First, the hydrophobic components of myelin repel the hydrophilic cytosol and extracellular fluids surrounding it. Secondly, the hydrophobic structures, mainly sulfatide and galactosyl ceramide, have strong attractive forces among them through formation of hydrogen bonds, making myelin a compact structure. In MLD, the excess of sulfatides and deficiency of cerebrosides lead to abnormal myelin composition that affect the formation of a stable lipid bilayer [34]. Further, galactosyl sphingosine metabolite causes cytotoxicity leading to death and dysfunction of neuronal cells. Sulfatides released from dying cells are picked up by histiocytes. The lysosomal-endosomal system becomes dysfunctional with progressive accumulation of sulfatides. This stimulates secondary pathogenic cascades involving alteration in calcium homeostasis, mitochondrial damage, altered lipid trafficking, generation of reactive oxygen species, and immune activation, ultimately resulting in cell death [35]. Eventually all these mechanisms lead to progressive demyelination in both CNS and PNS, which correlates with the broad range of clinical manifestations of MLD. 3-O-sulfate-lactosyl ceramide and lysosulfatide or psychosine sulfatide are other substrates for ASA. Hence, in ASA deficiency, the metabolism of these sulfated lipids is also interrupted. Myelin is required for the insulation of the axons and for the rapid conduction of electrical impulses and hence, nervous system is predominantly affected in ASA deficiency.

The sulfated complex lipids also accumulate in gall bladder, renal tubular epithelium, respiratory tract, gastric mucosa and uterine endometrium. Since sulfatide is mainly a constituent of myelin, the accumulation of sulfatide in extra neural tissues infrequently results in functional impairment [36-38]. Occasionally, gall bladder dysfunction can result in sludge, gallstones, haemobilia, cholecystitis, polyposis and papillomatosis [36, 37]. The sulfatides are excreted through the kidneys which forms the basis of measuring urinary sulfatides in patients with MLD [36]. ASA also catalyzes desulfation of 3-O-sulfagalactosyl sphingolipids (glycerol containing sulfated sphingolipids) which are present in the mammalian testes and sperm. They are known as seminolipids and their exact role is unknown [39].

6. Neuropathology of the Disease

6.1. Brain

Deficiency of ASA results in accumulation of myelin lipid sulfatide in oligodendrocytes and Schwann cells as described earlier, ultimately leading to demyelination of the brain. The telltale signs of MLD are diffuse demyelination and metachromasia. The white matter shows diffuse loss of myelin which spares the subcortical U fibers till late. The lamellar structure of myelin is altered and oligodendroglia cells are lost. The sulfatides accumulated in the cytoplasm display different color (metachromasia) when stained with certain aniline dyes [40]. With acid cresyl violet stain, these deposits appear brown in color (brown metachromasia), hence the term MLD [41].

The metachromatic granules are found within the glial cells, macrophages and neurons. They are also seen free in the tissues. Cell bodies of the neurons are distended due to these deposits [40]. They are also present in the various nuclei of brainstem, dentate nucleus and in the motor and sensory cells of the spinal cord. Earliest neuropathological studies in a case of adult MLD revealed morphological and histochemical differences in the sulfatide bodies found in the glial and nerve cells. The metachromatic material in the glial cells appear amorphous under light microscope, yellowish in unstained specimens, stains violet with toluidine blue, are periodic acid Schiff stain (PAS) positive and show variable staining with Sudan black. They do not stain with haematoxylin and eosin. On the contrary, metachromatic materials in nerve cells appear globular and are colourless in unstained specimens. They appear brownish red in toluidine blue stains and are PAS and Sudan black positive. Immune histochemical (IHC) studies showed microglial involvement early in the course of disease, prior to myelin breakdown [41]. Within the pre-lesional region, the phagocytes display an amoeboid morphology which increase continuously towards the centre of the lesion and subsequently lose microglia markers [42].

6.2. Peripheral Nerves

Nerve biopsy was used for the diagnosis of MLD before the advent of the biochemical and molecular genetic tests. The histopathological features of the peripheral nerves have advanced our knowledge of the pathogenesis of MLD. Metachromatic granules are seen in the peripheral nerves, the first account of which was given by Jacobi [43]. The sulfatides and lysosulfatides accumulate in the lysosomes of Schwann cells and endoneural macrophages due to deficient degradation of these complex lipids. Their accumulation disrupts the cellular homeostasis resulting in the death of Schwann cells and phagocytes. The Schwann cells and endoneural macrophages with lysosomal inclusions of sulfatides are metachromatic and are termed inclusion bodies [44]. Under electron microscope, they appear as zebra, tuffstone, prismatic, lamellar and granular bodies. Higher numbers of inclusion bodies and tuffstone bodies are noted in late infantile form, whereas, zebra bodies are more frequent in juvenile and adult forms [45, 46]. The death of Schwann cells and the myelin disruption by the accumulated sulfatides cause peripheral demyelination and subsequent clinical manifestations of demyelinating peripheral neuropathy [44].

The late infantile form has more severe demyelination of the peripheral nerves with little remyelination. However, in the later onset forms, remyelination of large demyelinated fibers can be observed as thinly myelinated nerve fibers [43]. Studies have shown no definite correlation between the severity of the peripheral nerve involvement and the cerebral white matter changes as assessed by gross motor functional classification scale and MRI brain [47]. There are reports of cranial nerves and cauda equina involvement in MLD [5, 48]. Onion bulb formation and hypertrophied nerves which are the hallmarks of acquired demyelinating neuropathies and some inherited neuropathies are rarely observed in MLD [43].

7. Clinical Features of the Disease

Three main clinical types of MLD have been described according to the age at onset, rate of progression of neurological symptoms and their severity, namely late infantile, juvenile and adult forms (Table 1). Late infantile form (classic) manifests at 1-2 years of life, early juvenile form between 4 and 6 years, late juvenile form between 7 and 16 years and adult form after 16 years of age [49]. This classification is not absolute as the clinical profile of MLD can be regarded as a spectrum. The severity of involvement of central and peripheral nervous systems and disease progression vary among the different forms. Late infantile and early juvenile types are the commonest forms of MLD. They have a very severe phenotype with rapid progression due to involvement of both brain and peripheral nerves. The common clinical presentation includes developmental delay or psychomotor regression, ataxia, progressive spastic quadriparesis, dysphagia, blindness, deafness, seizures, diffuse atrophy and weakness [4].

Table 1. Clinical features of MLD subtypes

MLD subtypes	Age of onset	Clinical features	Prognosis
Late infantile MLD	6 months – 2 years	Progressive loss of motor developmental milestones followed by speech and intellectual functions, hypotonia followed by spasticity, peripheral neuropathy	Death within 5 years of onset
Juvenile MLD	Early: 4-6 years Late: 6-15 years	Progressive deterioration in school performance followed by gait disturbances, seizures can occur, peripheral neuropathy is very common	Slower progression than late infantile form
Adult MLD	≥16 years	Predominant neuropsychiatric symptoms or dementia as initial manifestations, followed by gait disturbances, ataxia and spastic paraparesis, peripheral neuropathy may be seen	Very slow progression, mean survival is 12 years but can extend up to decades

7.1. Late Infantile Form

The late infantile form presents typically with difficulty in walking as the initial symptom. Later, there is progressive loss of previously attained motor developmental milestones followed by decline in speech and intellectual functions. Occasionally, patients can present with features of peripheral neuropathy such as muscular hypotonia and hyporeflexia/ areflexia, later on, followed by appearance of corticospinal tract involvement (spasticity, and hyperreflexia) [4]. Ataxia, spastic paresis, and optic atrophy are also common accompaniments of this form. Systematic review of literature has shown that nearly 61% patients present with motor or gait abnormalities and 39% with seizures [50]. Loss of both motor and cognitive functions is often rapid with neurological deficits in the form of pseudobulbar palsy resulting in impaired feeding and swallowing, seizures and severe psychomotor retardation and decerebrate state. Death typically occurs within 5 years of onset of clinical symptoms [3].

7.2. Juvenile Form

Juvenile form of MLD can be further subdivided into early and late juvenile forms which is based on the age of onset and clinical features. Early juvenile form usually presents with gradual deterioration in school performance as the first symptom in the majority. Progressive gait disturbances follow cognitive manifestations. In others, they can present with difficulty in walking and spasticity followed by intellectual decline. Seizures can occur. Clinical examination reveals ataxia, hyperreflexia followed by hyporeflexia, as the disease progress. Juvenile type progresses more slowly when compared to late infantile type. Gall bladder involvement can result in acute cholecystitis or pancreatitis in a few, however, visceral involvement is usually asymptomatic in MLD [3].

Late juvenile type progresses slower than early juvenile type and presents with behavioral disturbances or mental subnormality. Decline in school or work performance may be reported as the first complaint. Seizures may occur at any age and may be the only presenting symptom of this type of MLD. Death usually occurs within 10-15 years of diagnosis, mostly before 20 years of age. [4]. The various clinical presentations in decreasing frequency includes inattention and difficulties at school (66%), gait difficulties (26%), tremor or ataxia (18%), neuropathy (13%) and seizures (5%) [50].

7.3. Adult Type of MLD

Patients with the adult type may have an even slower progression than those with the late juvenile form. Hagemann et al. in 1995 gave an account of 25 patients with adult onset MLD. The mean age of onset was 23 years with the most common presentation being dementia in 40.5% of the cohort and behavioral disturbances in 32.4%. Other common presentations were ataxia (21.6%), paraparesis (10.8%), peripheral neuropathy (10.8%) and psychosis (2.7%). In contrast to the late infantile form, combination of mental and behavioral symptoms and ataxia predominate the clinical picture in adult MLD [51]. Seizures were also reported in 12% of the patients [50]. Frontal subcortical type of dementia characterized by personality and behavior changes, inattention, poor working memory and apathy predominate. The progression may range from years to decades. As the dementia advances, self-care skills are lost and patients require help for activities of daily living [4].

Genotype-phenotype correlations have been identified in late onset MLD. P426L homozygotes typically starts with gait disturbance due to spastic paraparesis or cerebellar ataxia. Those with heterozygous mutation of I179S presents with inappropriate or disorganized behavior and social dysfunction which is often misdiagnosed as schizophrenia or schizo-affective disorder [52].

7.4. Atypical Manifestations of MLD

Congenital form of MLD: The onset of MLD below one year of age is extremely rare. Occasional case reports of congenital MLD has been described. In one report, a newborn presented with abdominal distension and pronounced cyanosis and died within 24 hours of birth. Autopsy revealed multisystem involvement and extensive metachromatic deposits in cerebral white matter thus confirming the diagnosis of MLD. No genetic tests were done since this case was described prior to discovery of *ARSA* gene [53].

Cranial nerve involvement: Patients presenting with symptoms suggestive of cranial nerve involvement prior to the cerebral white matter involvement is seldom reported. There is a case report of a two and half year old girl who had manifested initially with right lateral palsy and bifacial weakness prior to the gait disturbances. MRI showed multiple cranial nerve enhancement along with other radiological features of MLD [54]. Cranial nerve involvement can also occur in Krabbe disease [48].

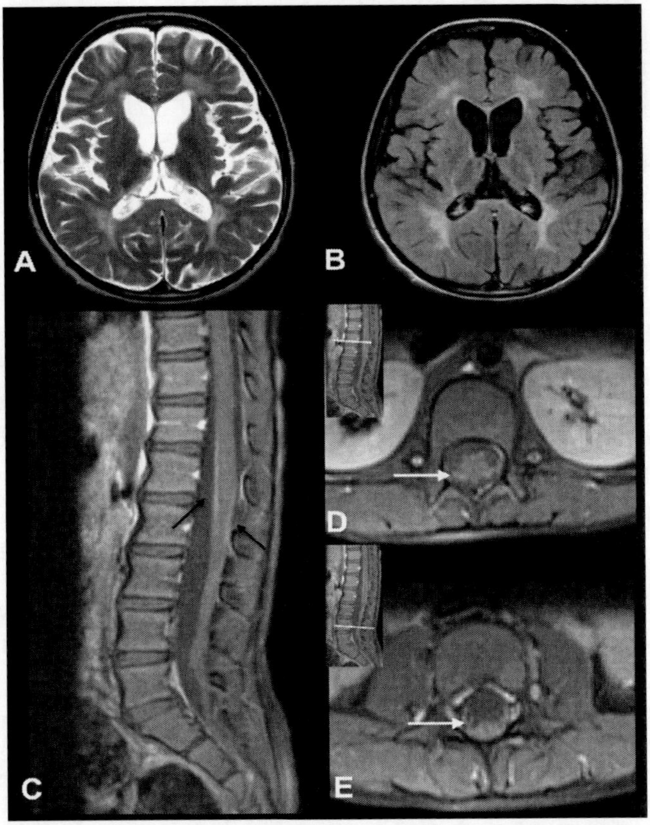

Figure 4. Cauda equina involvement in MLD: MRI brain A) axial T2W and B) FLAIR showing periventricular hyperintensity, lumbosacral spine C) sagittal sequence and D&E) axial showing clumping and enhancement of roots.

Cauda equina involvement: Cauda equina involvement has been reported previously in patients with MLD who had presented with peripheral neuropathy. MRI of lumbosacral spine revealed clumping and enhancement of caudal equina (Figure 4) [5]. Simultaneous involvement of cranial nerves and caudal equina have been observed in late infantile MLD and Krabbe disease. The exact pathogenesis of the contrast enhancement of roots and cranial nerves is unclear. A breakdown of blood nerve barrier due to sulfatide accumulation and inflammatory changes subsequent to this has been proposed as one plausible explanation [48].

8. Diagnosis of the Disease

In routine clinical practice, confirmation of a definitive diagnosis of MLD is made by molecular genetic testing. If the clinical features and the MRI of brain shows a classical pattern of MLD, apart from genetic analysis of *ARSA,* other diagnostic investigations are not generally warranted. However, if alternative differentials are under consideration during evaluation of the patient, then electroneurographic studies and ASA enzyme levels can serve as ancillary tests in narrowing the differential diagnosis. Biopsy of the nerve to demonstrate metachromatic granules are not required routinely in the current era of molecular genetics. Histopathological analysis of a nerve tissue was used in the past for the diagnosis before genetic testing became widely available and affordable. In a typical scenario, it is not recommended since it is an invasive test, but can be pursued according to the clinical picture and when the confirmatory tests are inconclusive. CSF study and electroneurography are no longer necessary in routine clinical settings, but can be used for monitoring the treatment response and also in research settings [4].

8.1. Magnetic Resonance Imaging (MRI) of the Brain

Damage to CNS myelin in MLD is visualized in MRI as bilateral symmetric confluent sheets of high signal intensity in T2 weighted (T2W) and fluid-attenuated inversion recovery (FLAIR) sequences predominantly in periventricular white matter. These lesions are hypointense in T1 weighted (T1W) sequences (Figure 5, A-D). These radiological features are suggestive of demyelinating pattern corroborating with the pathological evidence. The white matter of frontal, parieto-occipital and temporal regions are involved. Subsequently, the lesions extend to centrum semiovale but spares subcortical U fibers in the early stages suggestive of centripetal pattern [55]. The other structures classically affected include internal capsule, descending cortical spinal tracts, corpus callosum and cerebellar white matter (Figure 6). The sparing of perivascular white matter gives a distinctive 'tigroid' or 'leopard skin appearance', but this sign is not specific for MLD and is observed in other leukodystrophies as well. The lesions do not enhance on gadolinium administration. The subcortical U fibers can get involved when the disease process advances.

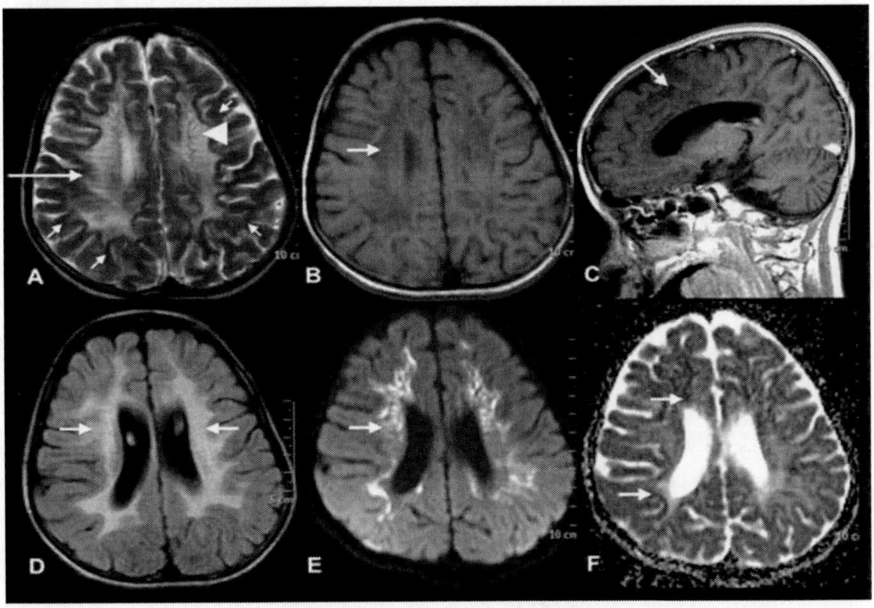

Figure 5. MRI brain T2W axial sections showing A) bilateral symmetric periventricular white matter hyperintensity (arrow head) along with typical tigroid pattern (long arrow), subcortical U fibers are spared (short arrows), B&C) The T2W hyperintensity signals appear hypointense in T1W axial and sagittal sequences and D) hyperintense in FLAIR sequence, E) The DWI axial sequence shows hyperintensity in periventricular white matter and the corresponding areas, F) ADC sequence are hypointense suggesting diffusion restriction.

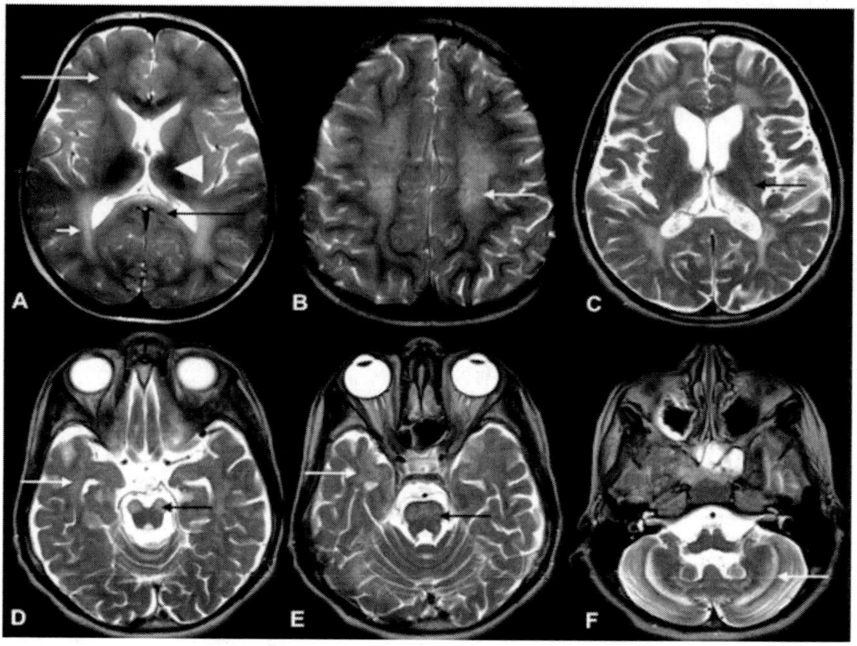

Figure 6. MRI of T2W axial sections showing affected regions of the brain in MLD. A) hyperintensity of the frontal and parieto-occipital white matter (white arrows), corpus callosum (black arrow) and bilateral symmetric hypo intensity of thalamus (arrowhead), B) leopard appearance, C) hyperintense posterior limb of internal capsule, D and E) hyperintensity of temporal white matter (white arrow) and corticospinal tract at the level of midbrain and pons (black arrow), F) hyperintensity of cerebellar white matter.

In the late stages, the cerebral and cerebellar atrophy ensues [56]. Although MLD is regarded as a predominant white matter disorder, T2 hypo intensity in the thalamus and atrophy of the thalamic and caudate nuclei points towards an additional gray matter pathology. Corpus callosal involvement shows a peculiar pattern of involvement, a diffuse high signal intensity of splenium in the early stages, later becoming curvilinear and progressing to atrophy [57].

A scoring system has been developed for MLD and it serves as a valuable tool for assessing disease severity and evaluating response to treatment. MRI-MLD scoring consists of maximum score of 34 points. This is analogous to the scoring system devised for adrenoleukodystrophy which has proven to be an efficient tool in guiding the treatment strategy

[58]. The major brain areas assessed in the scoring system are frontal white matter (periventricular, central and U fibers), parieto-occipital white matter (periventricular, central and U fibers), temporal white matter (periventricular, central and U fibers), corpus callosum (genu and splenium) and projection fibers (posterior and anterior limbs of internal capsule and midline pons). Each of the subareas is graded as 0, 1 or 2. The grade 0 indicates normal intensity, 1 faint hyperintensity and 2 dense hyperintensity. A global atrophy measure is also included to distinguish between ventricular enlargement or inner widening (1 point) and inner and outer CSF space widening (2 points). In addition to these categories, the basal ganglia and thalamus are also scored, but as 0 and 1 based on decreased signal intensities. Cerebellum (white matter and atrophy) is also given either 0 or 1 point. Three stages are defined based on the total score: mild disease, 1– 6, moderate disease, 7–15, and severe disease, 16 –34 [59].

8.2. Advanced MR Imaging of the Brain

Diffusion weighted (DWI) and apparent diffusion coefficient (ADC) images show linear pattern of diffusion restriction in the periventricular white matter and corpus callosum (Figure 5 E & F). The DWI shows hyperintensity whereas the corresponding ADC is hypointense suggestive of diffusion restriction. The diffusion restriction is related to the accumulation of sulfatides within the oligodendrocytes and myelin edema [60]. This finding is not specific for MLD as diffusion restriction is also observed in other leukodystrophies such as adrenoleukodystrophy, Canavan's disease and Krabbe disease [61]. In diffusion tensor imaging (DTI), the fractional anisotropy (FA) is decreased and the mean diffusivity (MD) and radial diffusivity (RD) are increased in patients when compared to controls. Changes are also noted in the normal appearing white matter which suggest alterations in brain microstructure. DTI can be a useful tool to monitor response to HSCT [62].

Magnetic resonance spectroscopy (MRS) in MLD shows a reduced N-acetylaspartate (NAA) in gray and white matter, elevated choline and myo-inositol (Figure 7). The MRS picture differs between the various clinical forms of MLD [63, 64]. Reduced NAA peak and elevated choline /creatinine (Cho/Cr) ratio are commonly found in late infantile form whereas elevated myo-inositol predominates in juvenile form [60]. Reduction in NAA peak reflects neuronal distress and increase in myo-inositol peak correspond to either galactosylceramide accumulation or secondary glial activation. NAA level is considered a sensitive disease marker, correlated to clinical motor and cognitive function performance, which can be used to assess treatment efficacy. An elevated lactate peak correlates with anaerobic metabolism from myelin destruction and elevated choline peaks with cell membrane degradation due to the accumulation of sulfatides [65].

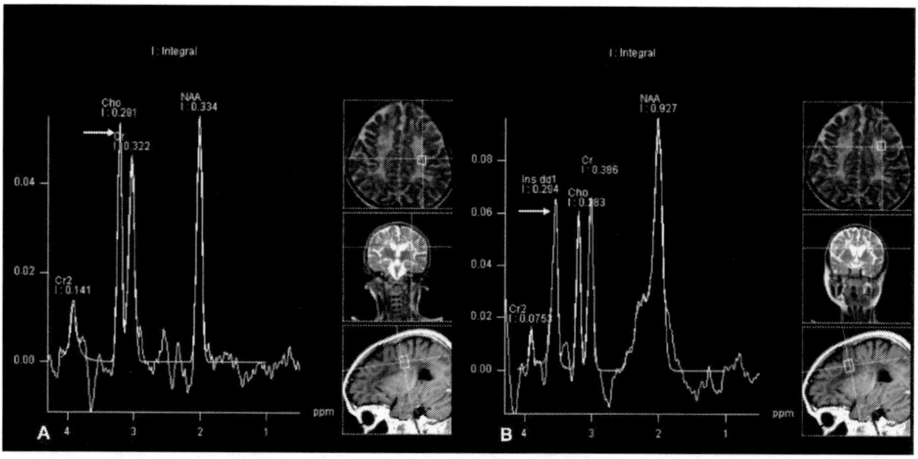

Figure 7. Magnetic resonance spectroscopy of MLD: A) images from left periventricular intermediate TE* (135ms) shows normal metabolic resonances with mild increase in choline peak at 3.2 ppm with preserved NAA peak, B) short TE (30ms) shows myoinositol peak at 3.5ppm.

8.3. Arylsulfatase-A Enzyme Analysis

Biochemical analysis in MLD refers to measurement of ASA activity in leukocytes or cultured fibroblasts. It provides an easy, fast, and non-invasive method for diagnosing MLD. ASA activity is also present in urine but the enzyme normally has low specific activity in urine. An activity of less than 10% of normal controls using the usual synthetic substrate-based assay is diagnostic of MLD. The assay is carried out using p-nitrocatechol sulfate (pNS) as the substrate. Since arylsufatase B also releases sulfate from pNS, conditions of the assay are adjusted and carried out at pH 4.9, rather than at pH 6, which favours arylsulfatase B activity. Further, the presence of chloride and pyrophosphate in the assay system inhibit arylsulfatase B more than arylsulfatase A. Hence, by this method, arylsulfatase B contributes only 2 percentage of activity [66]. There is considerable variability in enzyme activities among individuals. ASA activity in cultured fibroblasts varies with culture conditions and the presence of the pseudo-deficient allele, which accounts for 5–15% of residual enzyme activity, which could lead to an incorrect diagnosis of carrier status. Normal ASA activity is seen in patients with saposin B deficiency, which is another limitation. The artificial substrate used for the biochemical tests for ASA is water soluble and does not require the help from saposin B for hydrolysis of this substrate [3]. ASA activity in cultured amniotic cells or chorionic villus samples was used previously for prenatal diagnosis. The main hurdle of this approach is a 2-3-week delay in obtaining sufficient cell growth for the testing [67].

8.4. Urinary Sulfatide Levels in MLD

Urine sulfatide determinations are also a useful test for the diagnosis of MLD. All patients with MLD excrete large amounts of sulfatides in their urine. High performance liquid chromatography (HPLC), tandem mass spectrometry (TMS), and thin-layer chromatography (TLC) are the various methods which can be used to measure the urine sulfatide levels [68-70].

Because urine sulfatide excretion is highly variable, ideally it is measured in a 24-hour urine sample or normalized to the urinary excretion of creatinine. Urinary sulfatide excretion is increased in patients with MLD and is more than ten times the normal value. It is only elevated by less than ten times the normal value in patients with saposin B deficiency. Urinary sulfatide excretion is normal in patients with pseudo deficiency [4]. If ASA enzyme levels are found to be low, demonstration of urine metachromatic granules can differentiate pseudo deficiency state from MLD [27]. Multiple sulfatase deficiency can also have an elevated urine sulfatide excretion and low ASA enzyme activity. However, the presence of dysmorphic features, dysostosis multiplex and ichthyosis may favor a diagnosis of multiple sulfatase deficiency rather than MLD [71].

8.5. Electroneurography (Nerve Conduction Study)

Peripheral neuropathy is constantly present in early onset forms of MLD in whom it manifests as a demyelinating neuropathy. Electroneurography shows progressive and severe reduction of nerve conduction velocities [46]. In a review of 12 patients, it was found that infantile form was associated with a severe diffuse demyelinating sensorimotor peripheral neuropathy with conduction velocities in the range of 19–21 m/s in median nerve and 15–20 m/s in tibial nerve [5]. Conduction blocks in multiple nerves were also reported in MLD which can be confused with an acquired demyelinating polyradiculoneuropathy if the patient has a rapid progression [5, 46]. Conduction blocks are typically associated with acquired form of demyelinating neuropathies such as Guillain Barre syndrome and chronic inflammatory demyelinating polyneuropathy. But many exceptions to this rule have been reported in some hereditary neuropathies like Charcot Marie Tooth disease, MLD, and Krabbe disease which infrequently demonstrate conduction block [72].

8.6. Nerve Biopsy

The utility of nerve biopsy for diagnosis of MLD is currently limited with the wide availability of molecular genetic test. When an alternate diagnosis is to be ruled out, sural nerve is the preferred biopsy site. The pathognomonic finding is the presence of metachromatic granules with loss of large myelinated fibers and presence of thinly myelinated fibers (Figure 8).

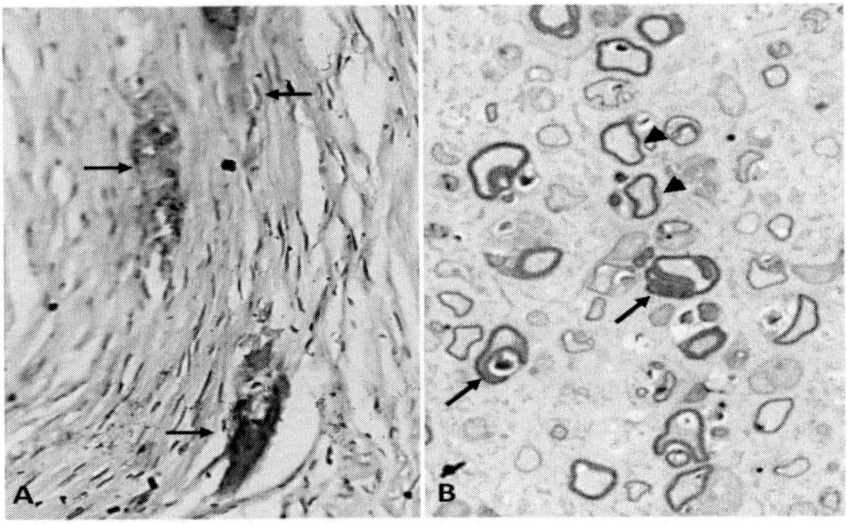

Figure 8. Histopathology of nerve in MLD: Cresyl violet stain A) showing perivascular brown metachromatic deposits (arrow) within the endoneurium. B) Semithin section stained with Toluidine blue showing myelin folds (arrows) along with several thinly myelinated fibers (arrow heads). (Courtesy: Dr. Anita Mahadevan and Dr. Radhika Mhare, Department of Neuropathology, National Institute of Mental Health and Neurosciences, India).

8.7. Other Tests

Cerebrospinal fluid analysis shows elevated protein levels especially in childhood forms, but this is not a uniform finding in adult forms. Routine hematological and biochemical parameters are usually normal and not helpful for the diagnosis in MLD [40]. Screening of patients for gall bladder pathology can detect gall bladder distension and polyps. In a study of 34 MLD patients, almost one fourth had gall bladder polyps and one-third underwent cholecystectomy. Normal gall bladder was seen only in 23% of patients. Histopathology revealed abnormal findings such as hyperplastic polyps, metaplasia and sulfatide storage [73].

8.8. Genetic Tests

ARSA gene analysis provides the most important diagnostic tool for MLD. As described previously, the four most common mutations (c.459+1G > A, c.1204+1G > A, p.Pro426Leu, and p.Ile179Ser) accounts for one half of the cases. Further sequencing of the entire coding region of *ARSA* has often led to identification of novel variants. During the interpretation of the tests results, it is necessary to differentiate the pathogenic variants (*ARSA*-MLD) from the pseudo-deficient alleles (*ARSA*-PD).

The molecular genetic testing approaches can include a targeted single-gene testing, i.e., sequence analysis of *ARSA* gene alone or a targeted multi-gene panel for leukodystrophy. If the clinician is definitive about the diagnosis of MLD after clinical and radiological concordance along with low residual enzymatic activity, single gene sequencing of *ARSA* is the test of choice. Since Sanger sequencing of a single gene is cost effective, in situations where clinical suspicion is high, this approach can be pursued. If only one or no pathogenic variant is found, gene-targeted deletion/ duplication analysis should be performed next. The multigene panel for leukodystrophy including *PSAP* sequencing is pursued later if broader diagnostic entities need to be excluded. If the above tests fail to yield results, a comprehensive genomic testing such as whole exome sequencing and genome sequencing can be considered in a clinical or research setting [4].

Table 2. Differential diagnosis for late infantile MLD

Disorder	Genetics	Protein deficient	Clinical Features	MRI	Diagnosis
Multiple Sulfatase deficiency	*SUMF1*	Formyl glycine-generating enzyme (FGE) deficiency	Gross motor and speech delay, coarse facial features, deafness, HSM, kyphoscoliosis, icthyosis	Progressive demyelination, prominence of the perivascular spaces, cerebral volume loss, hydrocephalus	Decreased activity of at least two sulfatase enzymes on lysosomal enzyme testing analysis, elevated urinary GAG levels, elevated urinary sulfatides
ALD (cerebral form)	*ABCD1*	Peroxisomal membrane protein ALDP (transmembrane transport of VLCFA)	Cognitive decline, apraxia, astereognosis, auditory impairment, decreased visual acuity, hemiparesis or spastic tetra paresis, cerebellar ataxia and seizures	Predominant parieto-occipital white matter and corpus callosal involvement, Schaumberg's zone and contrast enhancement	Genetic tests and elevated VLCFA levels
Infantile Krabbe disease	*GALC*	Galactocerebr-oside-β-galactosidase	Loss of motor milestones, spasticity, truncal hypotonia, OA esotropia, seizures, painful tonic spasms, demyelinating peripheral neuropathy	Demyelinating pattern with involvement of periventricular white matter and centrum semiovale, bilateral T2 hypo intensity of thalamus, optic nerve and chiasm involvement	Enzyme assay and genetic tests

The genetic testing needs to be done after providing detailed genetic counselling and obtaining a written informed consent from the patient or parents in case of minors. Genetic testing of the unaffected siblings, parents and other family members needs to be contemplated in consultation with clinical geneticist and considering the individual case scenario. Screening of the unaffected siblings is warranted, as HSCT has been proven to be more effective in pre-symptomatic and early stages of the disease process. Genetic testing is usually performed from samples from amniocentesis or chorionic villous biopsy for prenatal diagnosis [40]. Hence, optimal genetic diagnosis and prenatal counselling require a multidisciplinary consultation involving neurologist, geneticist and obstetrician.

Table 3. Selected differential diagnosis of late onset juvenile and adult forms of MLD

Conditions	Disorders
Lysosomal storage disorders	Adrenoleukodystrophy, Krabbe disease, Neuronal ceroid lipofuscinosis (Kuf's disease), Niemann-Pick disease type C, Gaucher's disease (type 2 and 3), GM2 gangliosidosis
Other metabolic disorders	Fahr's disease, MELAS, other mitochondriopathies, Cerebro-tendinous xanthomatosis, Wilson's disease, Methylenetetrahydrofolate reductase deficiency, Homocystinuria
Leukodystrophy	Alexander disease, Vanishing white matter disorder, Adult polyglucosan body disease, Hereditary diffuse leukoencephalopathy with axonal spheroids (HDLS)
Early onset forms of neurodegenerative dementia	Alzheimer dementia, Frontotemporal dementia, Lewy body dementia
Vascular dementia	Small vessel ischemic disease, CADASIL, cerebral amyloid angiopathy, CNS vasculitis
Heredodegenerative dementia	Huntington's disease, Spinocerebellar ataxia
Infections	Creutzfeldt Jakob disease, Subacute sclerosing pan encephalitis, HIV, Neurosyphilis, Whipple disease, PML
Inflammatory disorders	Multiple sclerosis, Sarcoidosis
Nutritional	Vitamin B12 deficiency, Pellagra, Thiamine deficiency
Endocrinological dysfunction	Hypothyroidism, hypo and hyperparathyroidism
Psychiatric disorders	Schizophrenia and other psychosis, bipolar disorders
Miscellaneous	Heavy metal poisoning like mercury, arsenic and lead

9. Differential Diagnosis

Several disorders need to be enlisted as alternate possibilities while dealing with a phenotype similar to MLD. Multiple sulfatase deficiency (Austin disease), Krabbe disease and adrenoleukodystrophy are a few differentials which need to be excluded in late infantile and early juvenile forms of MLD (Table 2) [27]. There is a broader differential diagnosis for late onset forms and these cases should be approached like any young onset dementia. Table 3 provides a concise list of the major differential diagnosis [74]. An optimal combination of clinical evaluation, MRI pattern recognition, biochemical analysis and molecular genetic tests can help in the accurate diagnosis of MLD.

10. Therapeutic Approaches in MLD

Therapies for MLD can be broadly classified into disease-specific therapies and general therapies.

10.1. Disease Specific Therapies

Specific therapies for MLD target the rectification of enzyme deficiency and/or sulfatide toxicity using cell-based or protein-based methods. None of the current therapies are curative, but many holds promise for the future. Allogenic HSCT, enzyme replacement therapy (ERT) and gene therapy are the three main avenues of therapy widely explored in animal models and human studies. Small molecule-based therapies for substrate reduction and enhancing enzyme levels also warrant more biochemical and therapeutic trials in MLD. (Figure 9). Among these, only HSCT is available for clinical use at present while others are still in the experimental phases [75].

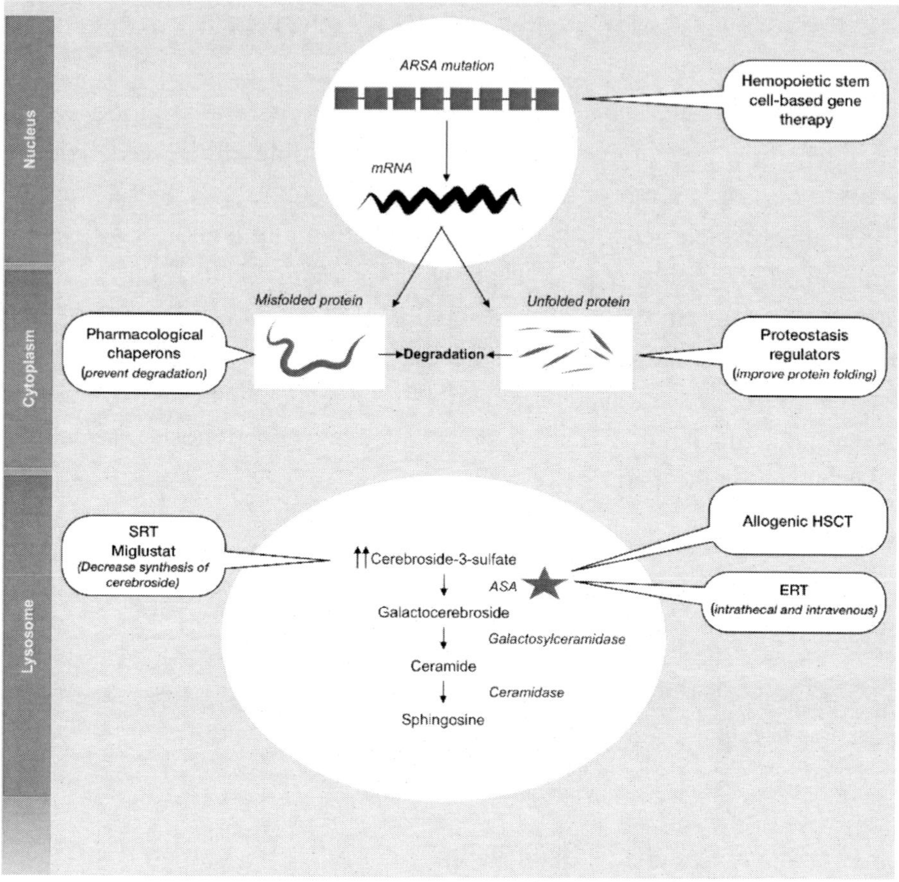

Figure 9. Pharmacological strategies in MLD. Mutations in the ARSA resulting misfolded or unfolded proteins, which are degraded by lysosomal hydrolases, endoplasmic reticulum associated degradation or ubiquitin proteosomal system.

10.2. Concept of Replacement Therapies in MLD

The most promising therapies in MLD attempt the normalization of ASA levels in brain and CSF by HSCT, gene therapy or ERT. In humans, about 10-15% of normal ASA activity is adequate to prevent manifestations of MLD, a principle employed in most of the replacement strategies [4]. The concept of HSCT (allogenic and gene-corrected autologous) arose from the principle of 'cross-correction' noted in the late

1960s and 1970s. When cells of patients with LSD, deficient in specific enzymes, were exposed to media containing cells with normal enzyme activity, the metabolic defect was corrected by enzyme transfer from the normal to the deficient cells [76]. In MLD, this is achieved by M6P residues in the ASA which are recognition markers for endocytosis of the enzyme. During biosynthesis of ASA, a considerable fraction of the enzyme escapes to the extracellular space which is reabsorbed into the cell through M6P receptors on the plasma membrane and transported back to the lysosomes. The same mechanism facilitates the cross-correction of enzyme deficient cells from the metabolically normal cells. Intravenous and intrathecal ERT also rely on the endocytosis of ASA by M6P or mannose receptors [77].

10.3. Hematopoietic Stem Cell Therapy

The reassuring success of HSCT in early Hurler syndrome paved the way for the similar trials in other inborn errors of metabolism (IEM). The principle of 'cross correction' is employed here with the premise that toxic substrate accumulation can be prevented by the presence of newly transplanted cells capable of supplementing the deficient enzyme [76]. The donor-derived hematopoietic cells secrete ASA into the blood, but the enzyme is incapable of crossing the blood brain barrier (BBB). However, the transplanted cells can migrate to the CNS compartment and differentiate into microglial cells which act as the source of the deficient enzyme in the brain (Figure 10) [78].

HSCT for IEM uses allogenic hematopoietic cells from the bone marrow, peripheral blood (mobilized by growth factors), and umbilical cord blood. The donor cells from a non-diseased volunteer are prepared in vitro and infused into the recipient who then undergoes an intensive immunosuppressive regimen to reduce likelihood of graft rejection and graft versus host disease. The donor-derived stem cells or progenitor cells cross the BBB, engraft within the CNS and differentiate into cells of myeloid lineage and microglial cells capable of secreting ASA [79]. In addition, the myeloid cells play an important role in limiting the pathogenic processes contributing to tissue damage including inflammation and oxidative stress.

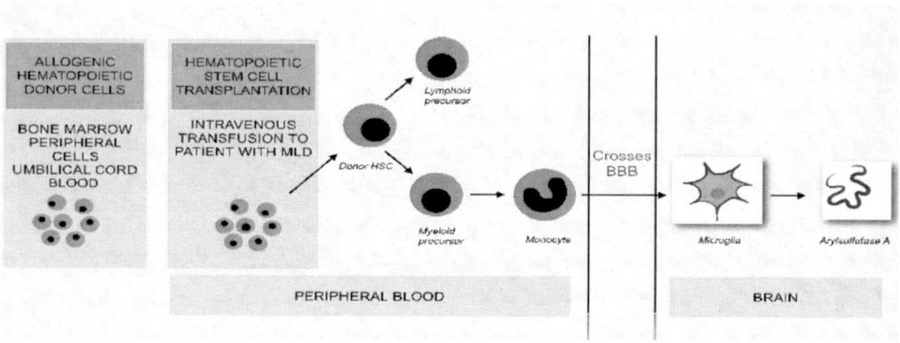

Figure 10. Hematopoietic stem cell transplantation: Allogenic hematopoietic cells from the bone marrow, peripheral blood and umbilical cord blood is used for hematopoietic stem cell transplantation (HSCT). The donor cells from a healthy volunteer was prepared in vitro and infused into patient. The donor-derived stem cells or progenitor cells differentiate into different blood cell lineages. Myeloid precursors differentiate into monocytes and cross the BBB. They finally differentiate into microglial cells and recreate arylsulfatase-A enzyme.

The expertise for allogenic HSCT is widely available and has been attempted in more than 100 subjects with MLD across different centers. The technique can potentially halt the progression of the disease, especially in the early and pre-symptomatic stages. The main limitation is the prolonged time to disease stabilization due to the slow repopulation of the cells, spanning a period of 12 to 24 months [80]. HSCT is generally ineffective in late infantile MLD and MLD with severe neurological symptoms where the speed of disease worsening overwhelms the correction of enzyme level. Hence, the outcome is better when HSCT is given early in the disease course (pre-symptomatic or mild symptoms) and when the symptom onset is later in life (adult onset MLD than late infantile or juvenile). In murine models, transplantation of hematopoietic stem cells within the cerebral lateral ventricles resulted in faster engraftment of microglia-like cells [81]. A second limitation is that the improvement is confined to the CNS compartment whereas no effect is noted for peripheral neuropathy. Significant gait deterioration with loss of ambulation can occur due to worsening peripheral neuropathy over time [82]. High risk of transplant related complications and mortality also dampen the desirability of the technique. Graft versus host disease, graft failure and infections contribute to mortality in 10 to 15% of subjects, although the incidence of these have markedly reduced over the decades due to improvement in procedures and immunosuppressive regimens [75].

In the largest single center experience with HSCT, among 40 transplanted patients with MLD, the estimated 5-year survival rate was 59%. Most of the deaths were related to transplant related complications. Juvenile and adult onset MLD had better long-term outcome with stabilization of MRI. The source of stem cells was associated with the outcome. Bone marrow from sibling and umbilical cord blood transplantation from unrelated donors showed better outcome compared to bone marrow from unrelated donors [83]. In comparison with non-transplanted patients, transplant recipients had better language and motor functions on long term follow up. Stabilization of motor functions occurred in 55 to 60% the transplanted subjects [84].

MRI stabilization is noted in transplant recipients pari passu with the clinical outcomes [75]. Favorable baseline MRI measures for a good outcome included low MRI-MLD severity score (especially temporal and parieto-occipital sub scores) and lack of U fibers involvement [83]. Case series and reports have shown increase in white matter lesions for 6 to 12 months after transplant indicating the delay in achievement of enzyme activity. A reversal of high choline - NAA ratio in MRS was reported after 12 months, indirectly indicating the time to correction [85-87].

The good prognostic categories for HSCT in MLD are therefore, those with mild disease (mild motor and cognitive dysfunction), later age of symptom onset and lower MRI severity scores. The worst prognostic categories include severe neurological symptoms and prolonged duration from symptom onset to institution of therapy. The current recommendation for HSCT in MLD is to offer this as a standard for adult MLD in the early or asymptomatic phases and as an option for late infantile and juvenile MLD [88].

10.4. Gene Therapy in MLD

Gene therapy involves the genetic modification of a vector or tissue to express the *ARSA* gene, usually in supraphysiological levels. The commonly practiced technique is the hemopoietic stem cell-based gene therapy (HSC-GT) which involves the genetic modification of autologous hematopoietic stem cells [77]. The greatest advantage over HSC-GT is the use of autologous stem cells which pose very low risk of graft versus host reaction [89]. The *ARSA* cDNA can be transferred to the cells using adeno virus, adeno associated virus (AAV), lentivirus and non-lentiviral retrovirus vectors [77, 90].

Among the different vectors, techniques using lentiviral vectors have met with the most success in human studies. Autologous stem cells are harvested from the bone marrow and transduced with a lentiviral vector encoding human *ARSA* cDNA. The cells are conditioned to secrete supraphysiological doses of ASA which effectively compensates for the enzyme deficiency. Patients are conditioned with busulfan in myeloablative doses for 4 days pre-transplantation to ensure engraftment [89, 91]

Preclinical trials using gene-corrected lentiviral vectors in murine models with deficient ASA activity resulted in correction of neurological deficits in affected mice and prevented disease onset in pre-symptomatic animals [92]. Open label phase I/II studies in limited human subjects with pre-symptomatic late-infantile/early juvenile MLD and early symptomatic early juvenile MLD resulted in stabilization of neurological parameters after 24 to 36 months [89, 91]. Peripheral conduction abnormalities showed improvement in 3 of 9 patients [91]. There was no immediate procedure related mortality in this cohort. Demonstration of tissue correction of metabolic defects and randomized control studies are essential to fully elucidate the clinical applicability of gene therapy [77].

In vivo gene therapy is an alternate method for correction of metabolic defects in LSDs. Vectors containing human cDNA for ASA are infused intravenously which transduce the host cells to produce the deficient enzyme. Here, the lack of BBB permeability of the enzyme is an important limiting factor. Proof of concept studies utilizing intrathecal and intracerebral delivery systems show promise with AAV and lentiviral vectors [93].

Though the potential of gene therapy is exciting, many hurdles exist in the clinical translation. The prime limitation of gene therapy is the uncertain risk of cancer associated with insertional mutagenesis [77, 89]. The supraphysiological expression of a particular sulfatase may also lead to complications. Lysosomal sulfatases undergo a rate-limiting post translational modification which is essential for their activation. An overexpression of one enzyme can potentially lead to deficiencies of other endogenous sulfatases [77].

10.5. Enzyme Replacement Therapy in MLD

Enzyme replacement therapy (ERT) involves the infusion of the deficient enzyme which is taken up by the cells and transported to the lysosomes. The enzyme supplementation is required life-long. Intravenous ERT was proven to be effective in LSDs without CNS involvement like Gaucher's disease, Pompe disease, Fabry disease, and mucopolysaccharidosis types I, II and VI. But in conditions like MLD where the brunt of the disease falls on the CNS, intravenous ERT is limited by the inability of the agents to cross the BBB [80]. An intrathecal/intracerebral route of delivery is needed to circumvent this limitation.

Preclinical studies in transgenic mice deficient in ASA could demonstrate a reduction in sulfatide storage in brain and spinal cord following intrathecal administration of the enzyme [94]. Phase I and II clinical trials of recombinant human arylsulfatase A (rhASA) in humans have been undertaken in centers in Europe and North America, some of which have completed the protocol. The final results of these studies will be important in understanding the role of ERT in MLD [95]. The need for repeated intrathecal administration to circumvent the BBB poses a serious challenge as this is labor-intensive and has the attendant risk of infections.

10.6. Small Molecule-Based Therapies

Small molecules (molecular weight < 500 Da) have shown promising results in Gaucher's disease and Nieman Pick disease. They can cross the BBB and can influence the synthetic and catabolic pathways at different levels [75, 11]. Small molecules can enhance activity of the deficient enzyme, reduce substrate accumulation, and modulate downstream pathogenic cascades [11].

Certain small molecules can interact with misfolded ASA enzyme and rescue them. Pharmacological chaperones enhance the level of misfolded mutant enzymes by preventing their degradation. Small molecules called proteostasis regulators improve the protein folding capacity of cells, thereby increasing the levels of folded mutant proteins. Pharmacological chaperones and proteostasis regulators can act synergistically to preserve the structural integrity of the enzyme and modify the downstream pathways [75].

Small molecules can also produce substrate (sulfatide) reduction. Vitamin K plays a decisive role in the sphingolipid synthesis pathway as a cofactor in the conversion of cerebrosides to sulfatides. The accumulation of sulfatide can be hypothetically reduced by a vitamin K antagonist like warfarin. A small clinical trial with 4 subjects using warfarin, however, failed to show therapeutic efficacy [96]. Molecules like miglustat which can inhibit ceramide synthetase enzyme can also potentially reduce sulfatide build-up [11].

At present, there are very few trials which have looked into the effectiveness of small molecules in MLD and more are expected in the future. The clinical trials related to HSCT and gene therapy are depicted in Table 4 [83-85, 89, 91, 97-105].

Table 4. Clinical studies on hematopoietic stem cell therapy and gene therapy in metachromatic leukodystrophy

Intervention	LI-MLD (n)	J-MLD (n)	A-MLD (n)	Median follow up (y)	Survival	Clinical outcome	MRI	NCS	Remarks	Reference
HSCT	1	0	0	2.75	1/1	Marked delay in disease progression, gaining milestones	N/A	Worsening	Gross motor skills achieved slower that fine skills	[97]
HSCT	2	2	0	4.5	4/4	Motor and cognitive regression persisted	Worsening	N/A		[98]
HSCT	0	1	3	11	4/4	Stabilization of neurological symptoms in 2/4, improvement in 2/4	Stable in 4/4	Stable in 2/4, improved in 2/4	Marked difference compared to siblings who continued to deteriorate, all patient > 15 years at disease onset	*[99], [100]
UCBT	0	3	0	5	3/3	2/3 stabilized after 2 years, 1/3 deteriorated	2/3 improved	2/3 stable	Good outcome for two presymptomatic patients	[85], * [101]
Autologous HSC-GT	3	0	0	1.5	3/3	1/3 mild developmental delay, 2/3 asymptomatic	Stable	Improved in 1 with severe neuropathy, stable in 2 with none to mild neuropathy		[89]
UCBT	10	17	0	5.1	20/27	Stabilization or improvement in 10/14 J-MLD, none of LI-MLD	16/19 showed improved Loes score	Worsened in 4/6 LI-MLD and 3/11 J-MLD	Presymptomatic patients benefitted the most, J-MLD showed better stabilization of cognitive than motor skills	[103]

Table 4. (Continued)

Intervention	LI-MLD (n)	J-MLD (n)	A-MLD (n)	Median follow up (y)	Survival	Clinical outcome	MRI	NCS	Remarks	Reference
HSCT, UCBT	4	27	9	12	21/40	Motor regression in 14/16, slower rate than published natural history	MRI demyelination stabilization in 12/23, worsening in 7/23	Worsened in 16/21	Improved survival with related BMT and unrelated UCBT	[83]
UCBT	0	3	0	6	3/3	Clinically stable	Stable	Stable	Marked deterioration noted in siblings	[104]
HSCT	0	24	0	7.5	18/24	Less motor and cognitive worsening for transplanted patients, 11/20 had stable disease, 9/20 progressed	No significant increase in MRI severity scores post-transplant, lower scores at last follow up compared to non-transplant group	N/A	Stable disease course more with no or mild motor deficits, age of onset > 4y, low MRI severity scores (≤17)	[84]
Autologous HSC-GT	6	2	0	3	9/9	8/9 slow or no worsening	7/9 normal	3/9 improved		[91] #
HSCT, UCBT	2	5	6	5	10/13	Deterioration of motor function in LI-MLD and J-MLD, stabilization in A-MLD, progressive neuropathy in LI-MLD and J-MLD	Improved in 5/10 survivors	N/A	No transplant related mortality, no benefit noted in severe motor (inability to walk unsupported) or cognitive (IQ 75) dysfunction	[105]

* Studies with shared patients are described together.

#1 patient had early onset disease that could not be classified.

Abbreviations: A-MLD adult metachromatic leukodystrophy, HSC- hematopoietic stem cell, HSCT- hematopoietic stem cell transplantation, HSC-GT hematopoietic stem cell gene therapy, J-MLD juvenile metachromatic leukodystrophy, LI-MLD late infantile metachromatic leukodystrophy, MRI magnetic resonance imaging, n- number, N/A not available, NCS- nerve conduction study, UCBT- umbilical cord blood transplantation, y –years.

10.7. General therapies for the Disease

The general symptomatic and supportive therapies are common for many leukodystrophies. Multidisciplinary symptomatic care, family support and genetic counselling are the core components of care. The multidisciplinary team should essentially include neurologist, physiotherapist, orthotist, occupational therapist, speech therapist, nutritionist, and psychologist with referrals to endocrinologist, orthopedician, gastroenterologist, geneticist, oral and dental surgeons, and pulmonologist as appropriate.

10.8. Symptomatic Therapy

All patients with MLD including those in advanced stages of the disease and those otherwise ineligible for a definitive therapy need close follow up to ensure the best possible quality of life. A consensus statement for the symptomatic care in leukodystrophies was revised in 2017 and the principal recommendations are summarized below [106].

The disorders of tone, spasticity and dystonia, are progressive and impact ambulation, mobility, hygiene, respiratory function, sleep and sexual function. Assessment tools for tone should be administered during each visit and should preferably be validated in the local setting. Mild spasticity can be managed with antispastic agents like baclofen and diazepam and physical therapy with daily stretching. Axial hypotonia is common in MLD and can be worsened by antispastic drugs. Severe spasticity and painful spasms may necessitate botulinum toxin chemo denervation, intramuscular neural lysis with phenol and/or intrathecal baclofen. Tendon surgeries or dorsal rhizotomy may be required in selected patients.

Dystonia can be symptomatically treated with anticholinergics (trihexyphenidyl), dopaminergic agents (L-dopa), dopamine depletors (tetrabenazine), and antispastic agents (baclofen, diazepam). Severe dystonia may benefit with deep brain stimulation.

In addition to CNS dysfunction, peripheral neuropathy is a major contributor to ambulatory dysfunction. Ambulation should be optimized with physical therapy and weight-bearing exercises. Assisted ambulation devices should be utilized to maintain functional independence. Fall prevention strategies are vital.

A high risk for low bone mineral density and fractures stem from immobility and poor nutrition. Bone health should be actively supervised with monitoring of serum parathormone and serum 25 hydroxy vitamin D. High risk patients should be monitored for osteoporosis with dual-energy X-ray absorptiometry (DEXA) scans. Referral for endocrinology care is essential when studies are abnormal. Bone health is adversely affected by many anticonvulsants and proton pump inhibitors which need to be modified as necessary. Scoliosis, hip dislocation and contractures are common and should be addressed by physical therapy and surgery.

Nutritional deficiencies result primarily from problems of upper gastrointestinal tract which include oropharyngeal dysphagia, hypersalivation, dental issues and gastroesophageal reflux. Assessment should be particularly directed to identify swallowing dysfunction and risk of aspiration. The diet should be nutritionally complete, and deficiencies should be corrected. When feeding is compromised, placement of gastrostomy tubes will alleviate the discomfort and maintain nutrition.

Bladder and bowel dysfunction are common, primarily, urinary incontinence, recurrent urinary tract infection and constipation. Acid-base abnormalities, especially, metabolic acidosis can occur in a quarter of MLD patients due to sulfatide accumulation [107]. Sleep disordered breathing and sleep disturbances are common and should be actively sought. Progressive respiratory dysfunction results from scoliosis, immobility, and respiratory muscle weakness and is worsened by aspiration pneumonia, community acquired pneumonia and obstructive sleep apnea. Infection prevention strategies include immunization, treatment of sialorrhea and dysphagia, positioning and physiotherapy. Mechanical ventilation is required in advanced disease. Seizures can occur in about half of MLD patients and occur in all stages of the disease [108]. Antiseizure medications are required after ruling out provoked seizures and seizure mimics. Other complications include autonomic dysfunction, pain, skin disease and ophthalmological dysfunction.

The entire family requires psychological support and counselling to cope with the diagnosis of this progressive and fatal disease. Genetic counselling is an integral component in the management of MLD. Opinion of a clinical geneticist should be sought, especially while planning pregnancy, for prenatal counselling and antenatal diagnosis.

11. GENETIC COUNSELLING

Genetic counselling sessions in MLD should elaborate on providing information to individuals and families regarding the nature and prognosis of the disease, the inheritance pattern and implications of genetic disorders so as to aid medical and personal decisions. Families should be made aware of the progression of the disease, current standard of care and the various research trials available in MLD. Sessions should focus on the mode of inheritance, risk of disease in siblings and planning for future pregnancy.

Since MLD has an autosomal recessive inheritance pattern, each sibling of an affected individual has 50% chance of being an asymptomatic carrier, 25% chance of having MLD and 25% chance that he/she is unaffected and not a carrier. The parents of an affected child are usually obligate heterozygotes and are carriers. The offspring of an individual with ASA deficiency are obligate heterozygotes. The determination of genetic risk, carrier status testing and exploring the availability of prenatal diagnosis should be done before pregnancy. The option for DNA banking and prenatal diagnosis by molecular or biochemical testing by amniocentesis or chorionic villus sampling should be offered [4].

CONCLUSION

MLD is a fatal and devastating disease. The last century witnessed many advancements that improved the understanding of the disease, its genetics and neuropathogenesis. Subsequently research has been intensified to identify a cure for this condition in the backdrop of promising treatments developed for some of the LSDs. Various clinical trials are ongoing in gene therapy, enzyme replacement therapy and strategies to stabilize the enzyme with pharmacological chaperons and proteostasis regulators [11]. Gene therapy has been proven successful in animal models and is believed to bear fruit in human trials in the near future. However, apart from HSCT in selected cases, other strategies require further clinical trials before they can be recommended in routine clinical practice. Till then, symptomatic management using pharmacological and rehabilitation strategies and genetic counselling remain the standard of care that can be offered.

ACKNOWLEDGMENTS

The authors express sincere gratitude to Dr. Anita Mahadevan and Dr. Radhika Mhare, Department of Neuropathology, National Institute of Mental Health and Neurosciences, India) for providing the images of histopathology of nerve. Authors also acknowledge the contribution by Mr. Krishnakumar, senior imaging technician, Department of Imaging Sciences and Interventional Radiology, SCTIMST for providing the MRI pictures.

REFERENCES

[1] Gieselmann, V, Zlotogora, J, Harris, A, Wenger, DA, Morris, CP. Molecular genetics of metachromatic leukodystrophy. *Hum. Mutat.* 1994, 4, 233-242.

[2] Gieselmann, V, Krageloh-Mann, I. Metachromatic leukodystrophy--an update. *Neuropediatrics.* 2010, 41, 1-6.

[3] Eckhardt, M. The role and metabolism of sulfatide in the nervous system. *Mol. Neurobiol.* 2008, 37, 93e103.

[4] Gomez-Ospina N. Arylsulfatase A Deficiency. In: Adam MP, Ardinger HH, Pagon RA, et al., editors. *GeneReviews®* [Internet]. Seattle (WA): University of Washington, Seattle, 1993-2020. 2006 May 30 [Updated 2017 Dec 14]. Available from: https://www.ncbi.nlm.nih.gov/books/NBK1130/

[5] Raina, A, Nair, SS, Nagesh, C, Thomas, B, Nair, M, Sundaram, S. Electroneurography and advanced neuroimaging profile in pediatric-onset metachromatic leukodystrophy. *J. Pediatr. Neurosci.* 2019, 14, 70-75.

[6] Malone, MJ, Stoffyn, PA. comparative study of brain and kidney glycolipids in metachromatic leucodystrophy. *J. Neurochem.* 1966, 13, 1037-1045.

[7] Takamatsu, K. Phytosphingosine-containing neutral glycosphingolipids and sulfatides in the human female genital tract: their association in the cervical epithelium and the uterine endometrium and their dissociation in the mucosa of fallopian tube with the menstrual cycle. *Keio. J. Med.* 1992, 41, 161-167.

[8] Hahn, AF, Gordon, BA, Feleki, V, Hinton, GG, Gilbert, JJ. A variant form of metachromatic leukodystrophy without arylsulfatase deficiency. *Ann. Neurol.* 1982, 12, 33-36.

[9] Gieselmann, V. Metachromatic leukodystrophy: genetics, pathogenesis and therapeutic options. *Acta Paediatrica.* 2008, 97, 15–21.

[10] Kudoh, T, Wenger, DA. Diagnosis of metachromatic leukodystrophy, Krabbe disease, and Farber disease after uptake of fatty acid-labeled cerebroside sulfate into cultured skin fibroblasts. *J. Clin. Invest.* 1982, 70, 89-97.

[11] Patil, SA, Maegawa, GH. Developing therapeutic approaches for metachromatic leukodystrophy. *Drug Des. Devel. Ther.* 2013, 7, 729-745.

[12] Friede, RL. Metachromatic Leukodystrophy (Sulfatase A Deficiency) and Multiple Sulfatase Deficiency. In: *Developmental Neuropathology*. Vienna: Springer, 1975 doi: https://doi.org/10.1007/978-3-7091-3338-5_38.

[13] Jervis, GA. Infantile metachromatic leukodystrophy. (Greenfield's disease). *J Neuropathol. Exp. Neurol.* 1960, 19, 323-41.

[14] Austin, J, McAfee, D, Armstrong, D, O'Rourke, M, Shearer, L, Bachhawat, B. Low sulfatase activities in metachromatic leukodystrophy (MLD). A controlled study of enzymes in 9 living and 4 autopsied patients with MLD. *Trans. Am. Neurol. Assoc.* 1964, 89, 147-150.

[15] Stein, C, Gieselmann, V, Kreysing, J, Schmidt, B, Pohlmann, R, Waheed, A, Meyer, HE, O'Brien, JS, von Figura, K. Cloning and expression of human arylsulfatase A. *J. Biol. Chem.* 1989, 264, 1252-1259.

[16] Kreysing, J, von Figura, K, Gieselmann, V. Structure of the arylsulfatase A gene. *Eur J Biochem.* 1990, 191, 627-631.

[17] Kingma, SD, Bodamer, OA, Wijburg, FA. Epidemiology and diagnosis of lysosomal storage disorders, challenges of screening. *Best Pract. Res. Clin. Endocrinol. Metab.* 2015, 29, 145-157.

[18] Lukatela, G, Krauss, N, Theis, K, Selmer, T, Gieselmann, V, von Figura, K, Saenger, W. Crystal structure of human arylsulfatase A: the aldehyde function and the metal ion at the active site suggest a novel mechanism for sulfate ester hydrolysis. *Biochemistry* 1998, 37, 3654–3664.

[19] HGMD® (The Human Gene Mutation Database) database at the Institute of Medical Genetics in Cardiff, UK. Website http://www.hgmd.cf.ac.uk/ac/gene.php?gene=ARSA Accessed March 1st, 2020.

[20] Stenson, PD, Ball, EV, Howells, K, Phillips, AD, Mort M, Cooper, DN. The Human Gene Mutation Database: providing a comprehensive central mutation database for molecular diagnostics and personalized genomics. *Hum. Genomics* 2009, 4, 69-72.

[21] Cesani, M, Capotondo, A, Plati, T, et al. Characterization of new arylsulfatase A gene mutations reinforce genotype-phenotype

correlation in metachromatic leukodystrophy. *Hum. Mutation* 2009, 30, E936–E945.

[22] Ługowska, A, Ponińska, J, Krajewski, P, Broda, G, Płoski, R. Population carrier rates of pathogenic ARSA gene mutations: is metachromatic leukodystrophy underdiagnosed? *PLoS. One*. 2011, 6, e20218.

[23] Polten, A, Fluharty, AL, Fluharty, CB, Kappler, J, von Figura, K, Gieselmann, V. Molecular basis of different forms of metachromatic leukodystrophy. *N. Engl. J. Med.* 1991, 324, 18-22.

[24] Narayanan, DL, Matta, D, Gupta, N. et al. Spectrum of ARSA variations in Asian Indian patients with Arylsulfatase A deficient metachromatic leukodystrophy. *J. Hum. Genet.* 2019, 64, 323–331.

[25] Gieselmann, V, Polten, A, Kreysing, J, von Figura, K. Arylsulfatase A pseudodeficiency: loss of a polyadenylylation signal and N-glycosylation site. *Proc. Natl. Acad. Sci. USA*. 1989, 86, 9436-9440.

[26] Ameen, M, Chang, PL. Pseudo arylsulfatase A deficiency. Biosynthesis of an abnormal arylsulfatase A. *FEBS. Lett.* 1987, 219, 130-134.

[27] Ferreira, CR, Gahl, WA. Lysosomal storage diseases. *Transl. Sci. Rare Dis.* 2017, 2, 1-71.

[28] Sommerlade, HJ, Hille-Rehfeld, A, von Figura, K, Gieselmann, V. Four monoclonal antibodies inhibit the recognition of arylsulphatase A by the lysosomal enzyme phosphotransase. *Biochem. J.* 1994, 297, 123-130.

[29] Ghosh, P, Dahms, NM, Kornfeld, S. Mannose 6-phosphate receptors: new twists in the tale. *Nat. Rev. Mol. Cell Biol.* 2003, 4, 202-212.

[30] von Bulow, R, Schmidt, B, Dierks, T, Schwabauer, N, Schilling, K, Weber, E, Usón, I, von Figura, K. Defective oligomerization of arylsulfatase a as a cause of its instability in lysosomes and metachromatic leukodystrophy. *J. Biol. Chem.* 2002, 277, 9455-9461.

[31] Qi, L, Tsai, B, Arvan, P. New insights into the physiological role of Endoplasmic Reticulum-Associated Degradation. *Trends Cell. Biol.* 2017, 27, 430–440.

[32] Carlos, FR, William, GA. *Lysosomal Storage Diseases*. ios press, 2017, 1 – 71.

[33] Zoller, I, Meixner, M, Hartmann, D, Bussow, H, Meyer, R, Gieselmann, V., Eckhardt, M. Absence of 2-hydroxylated sphingolipids is compatible with normal neural development but causes late-onset axon and myelin sheath degeneration. *J. Neurosci.* 2008, 28, 9741-9754.

[34] O'Brien, JS, Sampson, EL. Myelin Membrane: a molecular abnormality. *Science* 1965, 150, 1613-1614.

[35] Vitner, EB, Platt, FM, Futerman, AH. Common and uncommon pathogenic cascades in lysosomal storage diseases. *J. Biol. Chem.* 2010, 285, 20423-20427.

[36] Kim, TS, Kim, IO, Kim, WS, Choi, YS, Yeon, KM, Hwang, YS. Involvement of the gallbladder in childhood metachromatic leukodystrophy: ultrasonographic findings. *J. Ultrasound Med.* 1996, 15, 821-825.

[37] Sugano, K, Tai, T, Kawashima, I, Kotani, M, Natomi, H, Kamisago, S, Fukushima, Y, Yazaki, Y, Iwamori, M. Localization of sulfatides in the epithelial lining of gastric mucosa: studies with a monoclonal antibody to sulfatides. *J. Clin. Gastroenterol.* 1995, 21 Suppl 1, S98-103.

[38] Natowicz, MR, Prence, EM, Chaturvedi, P, Newburg, DS. Urine sulfatides and the diagnosis of metachromatic leukodystrophy. *Clin. Chem.* 1996, 42, 232-238.

[39] Honke, K, Zhang, Y, Cheng, X, Kotani, N, Taniguchi, N. Biological roles of sulfoglycolipids and pathophysiology of their deficiency. *Glycoconj J*, 2004, 21, 59–62.

[40] Kohlschütter, A. Lysosomal leukodystrophies: Krabbe disease and metachromatic leukodystrophy. *Handb. Clin. Neurol.* 2013, 113:1611-1618.

[41] Guseo, A, Deak, G, Szirmai, I. An adult case of metachromatic leukodystrophy. Light, polarization and electron microscopic study. *Acta. Neuropathol.* 1975, 32, 333-339.

[42] Bergner, CG, van der Meer, F, Winkler, A, Wrzos, C, Türkmen, M, Valizada, E, Fitzner, D, Hametner, S, Hartmann, C, Pfeifenbring, S, Stoltenburg-Didinger, G, Brück,W, Nessler, S, Stadelmann, C. Microglia damage precedes major myelin breakdown in X-linked adrenoleukodystrophy and metachromatic leukodystrophy. *Glia.* 2019, 67, 1196-1209.

[43] Beerepoot, S, Nierkens, S, Boelens, JJ, Lindemans, C, Bugiani, M, Wolf, NI. Peripheral neuropathy in metachromatic leukodystrophy: current status and future perspective. *Orphanet. J. Rare Dis.* 2019, 14, 240.

[44] Malone, MJ, Stoffyn, P. Peripheral nerve glycolipids in metachromatic leukodystrophy. *Neurology.* 1967, 17, 1033–1040.

[45] Meier, C, Bischoff, A. Sequence of morphological alterations in the nervous system of metachromatic leucodystrophy. Light- and electron microscopic observations in the central and peripheral nervous system in a prenatally diagnosed foetus of 22 weeks. *Acta. Neuropathol.* 1976, 36, 369–379.

[46] Bindu, P.S, Mahadevan, A, Taly, AB, Christopher, R, Gayathri N, Shankar, SK. Peripheral neuropathy in metachromatic leucodystrophy. A study of 40 cases from south India. *J. Neurol. Neurosurg. Psychiatry.* 2005, 76, 1698-1701.

[47] Cí, D, Barton, NW, Farah, MH, Moldovan, M, Månsson, JE, Nair, N, Dunø, M, Risom, L, Cao, H, Pan, L, Sellos-Moura, M, Corse, AM, Krarup, C. Sulfatide levels correlate with severity of neuropathy in metachromatic leukodystrophy. *Ann. Clin. Transl. Neurol.* 2015, 2, 518–533.

[48] Morana, G, Biancheri, R, Dirocco, M, Filocamo, M, Marazzi, MG, Pessagno, A, Rossi, A. Enhancing cranial nerves and cauda equina: an emerging magnetic resonance imaging pattern in metachromatic leukodystrophy and krabbe disease. *Neuropediatrics.* 2009, 40, 291-294.

[49] Von Figura, KGV, Jaeken, J. Metachromatic leukodystrophy. In: Scriver CR, William S, Editors. *Metabolic basis of inherited disease*. New York: McGraw-Hill, 2001, 3695–3724.

[50] Mahmood, A, Berry, J, Wenger, DA, Escolar, M, Sobeih, M, Raymond, G, Eichler, FS. Metachromatic leukodystrophy: a case of triplets with the late infantile variant and a systematic review of the literature. *J. Child Neurol.* 2010, 25, 572-580.

[51] Hageman, AT, Gabreëls, FJ, de Jong, JG, Gabreëls-Festen, AA, van den Berg, CJ, van Oost, BA, Wevers, RA. Clinical symptoms of adult metachromatic leukodystrophy and arylsulfatase A pseudodeficiency. *Arch. Neurol.* 1995, 52, 408-413.

[52] Rauschka, H, Colsch, B, Baumann, N, Wevers, R, Schmidbauer, M, Krammer, M, Turpin, JC, Lefevre, M, Olivier, C, Tardieu, S, Krivit, W, Moser, H, Moser, A, Gieselmann, V, Zalc, B, Cox, T, Reuner, U, Tylki-Szymanska, A, Aboul-Enein, F, LeGuern, E, Bernheimer, H, Berger, J. Late-onset metachromatic leukodystrophy: genotype strongly influences phenotype. *Neurology.* 2006, 67, 859-863.

[53] Bubis, JJ, Adlesberg, L. Congenital metachromatic leukodystrophy. *Acta. Neuropathol.* 1966, 6, 298–302.

[54] Singh, RK, Leshner, RT, Kadom, N, Vanderver, AL. Isolated cranial nerve enhancement in metachromatic leukodystrophy. *Pediatr. Neurol.* 2009, 40, 380–382.

[55] Resende, LL, de Paiva, ARB, Kok, F, da Costa Leite, C, Lucato, LT. Adult Leukodystrophies: A step-by-step diagnostic approach. *Radiographics.* 2019, 39, 153-168.

[56] Cheon, JE, Kim, IO, Hwang, YS, Kim, KJ, Wang, KC, Cho, BK, Chi, JG, Kim, CJ, Kim, WS, Yeon, KM. Leukodystrophy in children: a pictorial review of MR imaging features. *Radiographics.* 2002, 22:461–476.

[57] Martin, A, Sevin, C, Lazarus, C, Bellesme, C, Aubourg, P, Adamsbaum, C. Toward a better understanding of brain lesions during metachromatic leukodystrophy evolution. *AJNR. Am. J. Neuroradiol.* 2012, 33, 1731-1739.

[58] Loes, DJ, Hite, S, Moser, H, et al. Adrenoleukodystrophy:a scoring method for brain MR observations. *AJNR. Am. J. Neuroradiol.* 1994,15, 1761– 1766.

[59] Eichler, F, Grodd, W, Grant, E, Sessa, M, Biffi, A, Bley, A, et al. Metachromatic leukodystrophy: a scoring system for brain MR imaging observations. *AJNR. Am. J. Neuroradiol.* 2009, 30, 1893-1897.

[60] Oguz, KK, Anlar, B, Senbil, N, Cila, A. Diffusion-weighted imaging findings in juvenile metachromatic leukodystrophy. *Neuropediatrics.* 2004, 35, 279-282.

[61] Patay, Z. Diffusion-weighted MR imaging in leukodystrophies. *Eur. Radiol.* 2005, 15, 2284–2303.

[62] van Rappard, DF, Königs, M, Steenweg, ME, Boelens, JJ, Oosterlaan, J, van der Knaap, MS, Wolf, NI, Pouwels, PJ. Diffusion tensor imaging in metachromatic leukodystrophy. *J. Neurol.* 2018, 265, 659-668.

[63] Galanaud, D, Aubourg, P, Kalifa, G, Adamsbaum, C. What is your diagnosis? Metachromatic leukodystrophy. *J. Neuroradiol.* 2002, 29, 173-175.

[64] i Dali, C, Hanson, LG, Barton, NW, Fogh, J, Nair, N, Lund, AM. Brain N- acetylaspartate levels correlate with motor function in metachromatic leukodystrophy. *Neurology.* 2010, 75, 1896-1903.

[65] Assadi, M, Wang, DJ, Velazquez-Rodriquez, Y, Leone, P. Multi-Voxel 1H-MRS in metachromatic leukodystrophy. *J. Cent. Nerv. Syst. Dis.* 2013, 5:25-30.

[66] Dulaney, JT, Moser, HW. Metachromatic leukodystrophy. In: Glew, RH, Peters, S.P Editors. *Practical enzymology of the sphingolipidoses.* New York: Alan R. Liss, 1977, 283-287.

[67] Besley, GT, Young, EP, Fensom, AH, Cooper, A. First trimester diagnosis of inherited metabolic disease: Experience in the UK. *J. Inherit. Metab. Dis.* 1991, 14, 128–133.

[68] Strasberg, PM, Warren, I, Skomorowski, MA, Lowden, JA. HPLC analysis of urinary sulfatide: an aid in the diagnosis of metachromatic leukodystrophy. *Clin. Biochem.* 1985, 18, 92-97.

[69] Hsu, FF, Bohrer, A, Turk, J. Electrospray ionization tandem mass spectrometric analysis of sulfatide. Determination of fragmentation patterns and characterization of molecular species expressed in brain and in pancreatic islets. *Biochim. Biophys. Acta.* 1998, 1392, 202-216.

[70] Berna, L, Asfaw, B, Conzelmann, E, Cerny, B, Ledvinova, J. Determination of urinary sulfatides and other lipids by combination of reversed-phase and thin-layer chromatographies. *Anal. Biochem.* 1999, 269, 304-311.

[71] Schlotawa, L, Adang, L, De Castro, M, et al. Multiple Sulfatase Deficiency. In: Adam MP, Ardinger HH, Pagon RA, et al., editors. *GeneReviews®* [Internet]. Seattle (WA): University of Washington, Seattle, 1993-2020, 2019 Available from: https://www.ncbi.nlm.nih.gov/books/NBK538937/.

[72] Cameron, CL, Kang, PB, Burns, TM, Darras, BT, Jones, HR Jr. Multifocal slowing of nerve conduction in metachromatic leukodystrophy. *Muscle Nerve* 2004, 29, 531-536.

[73] van Rappard, DF, Bugiani, M, Boelens, JJ, van der Steeg, AF, Daams, F, de Meij, TG, van Doorn, MM, van Hasselt, PM, Gouma, DJ, Verbeke, JI, Hollak, CE, van Hecke, W, Salomons, GS, van der Knaap, MS, Wolf, NI. Gallbladder and the risk of polyps and carcinoma in metachromatic leukodystrophy. *Neurology.* 2016, 87, 103-111.

[74] Kuruppu, DK, Matthews, BR. Young-onset dementia. *Seminars in neurology.* 2013, 33, 365–385.

[75] van Rappard, DF, Boelens, JJ, Wolf, NI. Metachromatic leukodystrophy: Disease spectrum and approaches for treatment. *Best Pract. Res. Clin. Endocrinol. Metab.* 2015, 29, 261-273.

[76] Fratantoni, JC, Hall, CW, Neufeld, EF. Hurler and Hunter syndromes: Mutual correction of the defect in cultured fibroblasts. *Science.* 1968, 162, 570–572.

[77] Matzner, U, Gieselmann, V. Gene therapy of metachromatic leukodystrophy. *Expert. Opin. Biol. Ther.* 2005, 5, 55-65.

[78] Krall, WJ, Challita, PM, Perlmutter, LS, Skelton, DC, Kohn, DB. Cells expressing human glucocerebrosidase from a retroviral vector repopulate macrophages and central nervous system microglia after murine bone marrow transplantation. *Blood.* 1994, 83, 2737-2748.

[79] Peters, C, Steward, CG. Hematopoietic cell transplantation for inherited metabolic diseases: an overview of outcomes and practice guidelines. *Bone Marrow Transplant.* 2003, 31, 229–239.

[80] Biffi, A, Lucchini, G, Rovelli, A, Sessa, M. Metachromatic leukodystrophy: an overview of current and prospective treatments. *Bone Marrow Transplant.* 2008, 42, S2-6.

[81] Capotondo, A, Milazzo, R, Garcia-Manteiga, JM, Cavalca, E, Montepeloso, A,Garrison, BS,Peviani, M, Rossi, DJ, Biffi, A. Intracerebroventricular delivery of hematopoietic progenitors result in rapid and robust engraftment of microglia-like cells. *Sci. Adv.* 2017, 3, e1701211.

[82] Sevin, C, Aubourg, P, Cartier, N. Enzyme, cell and gene-based therapies for metachromatic leukodystrophy. *J. Inherit. Metab. Dis.* 2007, 30, 175e83.

[83] Boucher, AA, Miller, W, Shanley, R, et al. Long-term outcomes after allogeneic hematopoietic stem cell transplantation for metachromatic leukodystrophy: the largest single-institution cohort report. *Orphanet. J. Rare Dis.* 2015, 10, 94.

[84] Groeschel, S, Kühl, JS, Bley, AE, Kehrer, C, Weschke, B, Döring, M, Böhringer, J, Schrum, J, Santer, R, Kohlschütter, A, Krägeloh-Mann, I, Müller, I. Long-term outcome of allogeneic hematopoietic stem cell transplantation in patients with juvenile metachromatic leukodystrophy compared with nontransplanted control patients. *JAMA. Neurol.* 2016, 73, 1133-1140.

[85] Pierson, TM, Bonnemann, CG, Finkel, RS, Bunin, N, Tennekoon, GI. Umbilical cord blood transplantation for juvenile metachromatic leukodystrophy. *Ann. Neurol.* 2008, 64, 583-587.

[86] Krägeloh-Mann, I, Groeschel, S, Kehrer, C, Opherk, K, Nägele, T, Handgretinger, R, Müller, I. Juvenile metachromatic leukodystrophy

10 years post-transplant compared with a non-transplanted cohort. *Bone Marrow Transplant.* 2013, 48, 369-375.

[87] van Egmond, ME, Pouwels, PJ, Boelens, JJ, Lindemans, CA, Barkhof, F, Steenwijk, MD, van Hasselt, PM, van der Knaap, MS, Wolf, NI. Improvement of white matter changes on neuroimaging modalities after stem cell transplant in metachromatic leukodystrophy. *JAMA. Neurol.* 2013, 70, 779-782.

[88] Boelens, JJ, Orchard, PJ, Wynn, RF. Transplantation in inborn errors of metabolism: current considerations and future perspectives. *Br. J. Haematol.* 2014, 167, 293-303.

[89] Biffi, A, Montini, E, Lorioli, L, et al. Lentiviral hematopoietic stem cell gene therapy benefits metachromatic leukodystrophy. *Science.* 2013, 341, 1233158.

[90] Rosenberg, JB, Kaminsky, SM, Aubourg, P, Crystal, RG, Sondhi, D. Gene therapy for metachromatic leukodystrophy. *J. Neurosci. Res.* 2016, 94,1169-1179.

[91] Sessa, M, Lorioli, L, Fumagalli, F, Acquati, S, Redaelli, D, Baldoli, C, Canale, S, Lopez, ID, Morena, F, Calabria, A, Fiori, R, Silvani, P, Rancoita, PM, Gabaldo, M, Benedicenti, F,Antonioli, G, Assanelli, A, Cicalese, MP, Del Carro, U, Sora, MG, Martino, S,Quattrini, A, Montini, E, Di Serio, C, Ciceri, F, Roncarolo, MG,Aiuti, A, Naldini, L,Biffi, A. Lentiviral haemopoietic stem-cell gene therapy in early-onset metachromatic leukodystrophy: an ad-hoc analysis of a non-randomised, open-label, phase 1/2 trial. *Lancet.* 2016, 388, 476-487.

[92] Biffi, A, De Palma, M, Quattrini, A, Del Carro, U, Amadio, S, Visigalli, I, Sessa, M, Fasano, S, Brambilla, R, Marchesini, S, Bordignon, C, Naldini, L. Correction of metachromatic leukodystrophy in the mouse model by transplantation of genetically modified hematopoietic stem cells. *J. Clin. Invest.* 2004, 113, 1118–1129.

[93] Penati, R, Fumagalli, F, Calbi, V, Bernardo, ME, Aiuti, A. Gene therapy for lysosomal storage disorders: recent advances for metachromatic leukodystrophy and mucopolysaccaridosis I. *J. Inherit. Metab. Dis.* 2017, 40, 543-554.

[94] Matthes, F, Stroobants, S, Gerlach, D, Wohlenberg, C, Wessig, C, Fogh, J, Gieselmann, V, Eckhardt, M, D'Hooge, R, Matzner, U. Efficacy of enzyme replacement therapy in an aggravated mouse model of metachromatic leukodystrophy declines with age. *Hum. Mol. Genet.* 2012, 21, 2599e609.

[95] Troy, S, Wasilewski, M, Beusmans, J, Godfrey, CJ. Pharmacokinetic modelling of intrathecally administered recombinant human arylsulfatase A (TAK-611) in children with metachromatic leukodystrophy. *Clin. Pharmacol. Ther.* 2019, doi: 10.1002/ cpt.1752.

[96] Assadi, M, Wang, DJ, Anderson, K, Carran, M, Bilaniuk, L, Leone P. Vitamin k antagonist warfarin for palliative treatment of metachromatic leukodystrophy, a compassionate study of four subjects. *J. Cent. Nerv. Syst. Dis.* 2012, 4, 73–79.

[97] Bayever, E, Ladisch, S, Philippart, M, Brill, N, Nuwer, M, Sparkes, RS, Feig, SA. Bone-marrow transplantation for metachromatic leucodystrophy, *Lancet.* 1985, 2, 471– 473.

[98] Malm, G, Ringdén, O, Winiarski, J, et al. Clinical outcome in four children with metachromatic leukodystrophy treated by bone marrow transplantation. *Bone Marrow Transplant.* 1996, 17, 1003-1008.

[99] Solders, G, Celsing, G, Hagenfeldt, L, Ljungman, P, Isberg, B, Ringdén, O. Improved peripheral nerve conduction, EEG and verbal IQ after bone marrow transplantation for adult metachromatic leukodystrophy. *Bone Marrow Transplant.* 1998, 22, 1119-1122.

[100] Solders, M, Martin, DA, Andersson, C, Remberger, M, Andersson, T, Ringdén, O, Solders, G. Hematopoietic SCT: a useful treatment for late metachromatic leukodystrophy. *Bone Marrow Transplant.* 2014, 49, 1046-1051.

[101] Cable, C, Finkel, RS, Lehky, TJ, Biassou, NM, Wiggs, EA, Bunin, N, Pierson, TM. Unrelated umbilical cord blood transplant for juvenile metachromatic leukodystrophy: a 5-year follow-up in three affected siblings. *Mol. Genet. Metab.* 2011, 102, 207e9.

[102] de Hosson, LD, van de Warrenburg, BP, Preijers, FW, Blijlevens, NM, van der Reijden, BA, Kremer, HP, Lefeber, DJ, Allebes, WA, Al-Ali, H, Niederwieser, DW, Schaap, NP, Schattenberg, AV. Adult metachromatic leukodystrophy treated by allo- SCT and a review of the literature. *Bone Marrow Transpl.* 2011, 46, 1071e6.

[103] Martin, HR, Poe, MD, Provenzale, JM, Kurtzberg, J, Mendizabal, A, Escolar, ML. Neurodevelopmental outcomes of umbilical cord blood transplantation in metachromatic leukodystrophy. *Biol. Blood Marrow Transplant.* 2013, 19, 616-624.

[104] Chen, X, Gill, D, Shaw, P, Ouvrier, R, Troedson, C. Outcome of early juvenile onset metachromatic leukodystrophy after unrelated cord blood transplantation: a case series and review of the literature. *J. Child Neurol.* 2016, 31, 338-344.

[105] van Rappard, DF, Boelens, JJ, van Egmond, ME, Kuball, J, van Hasselt, PM, Oostrom, KJ, Pouwels, PJ, van der Knaap, MS, Hollak, CE, Wolf, NI. Efficacy of hematopoietic cell transplantation in metachromatic leukodystrophy: The Dutch experience. *Blood*, 2016, 127, 3098-101.

[106] Adanga, LA, Sherbinia, O, Ball, L, et al. Revised consensus statement on the preventive and symptomatic care of patients with leukodystrophies. *Mol. Genet. Metab*. 2017, 122, 18-32.

[107] Lorioli, L, Cicalese, MP, Silvani, P, et al. Abnormalities of acid-base balance and predisposition to metabolic acidosis in metachromatic leukodystrophy patients, *Mol. Genet. Metab.* 2015, 115, 48–52.

[108] Balslev, T, Cortez, MA, Blaser, SI, Haslam, RH. Recurrent seizures in metachromatic leukodystrophy. *Pediatr. Neurol.* 1997, 17, 150-154.

In: Neurochemistry of Metabolic Diseases
Editor: Sankar Surendran
ISBN: 978-1-53618-339-9

Chapter 8

PARKINSON'S DISEASE ASSOCIATION WITH GAUCHER DISEASE AND THERAPEUTIC EFFECT

Srinivasagam Rajasankar[1,*],
Veerappachetty Venkateshgobi[2] and Sankar Surendran[1]
[1]Velammal Medical College Hospital and Research Institute, Tamil Nadu, India
[2]Department of Anatomy, Sivaraj Medical Colleges, Tamil Nadu, India

ABSTRACT

Parkinson's disease (PD) is a neurodegenerative disorder with a progressive loss of dopaminergic neurons in the substantia nigra pars compacta. The motor and non-motor symptoms in the disease include movement disorder, depression, dementia, hypnotics and autonomic dysfunction. Elevated levels of NAA is reported in the brain of patients with PD. Glucocerebrosidase gene mutations lead to Gaucher disease, a

---

[*] Corresponding Author's Email: anatomysrs@yahoo.com.

lysosomal storage disorder. Mutations in the same gene also contribute to PD. Hence, lysosomal dysfunction is one of the events in the pathophysiology seen in PD. Autophagy is found to be affected in some subtypes of PD and therefore, regulating autophagy function is important to protect cells against toxicity of aggregate-prone proteins.

1. INTRODUCTION

Parkinson disease (PD) is a progressive neurodegenerative disease affecting one million people in the United States. After Alzheimer's disease, Parkinson disease is a major neurodegenerative disorder with approximately one percentage of the population above sixty years are affected by the disease [1]. The clinical symptoms seen in PD include gait disturbance, tremors, impaired handwriting, speech disturbance, rigidity, grip force, mild cognitive impairment and dementia. Fatigue, hallucinations, cognition, and urinary problems were symptoms seen in patients with PD with increasing disability and reducing quality of life [2-5]. Progressive supranuclear palsy is an atypical Parkinsonism resembling PD. Patient's pain increases when parkinsonian symptoms become severe [6]. Movement disorder mainly seen in the disease is associated with the accumulation of intracytoplasmic aggregate prone protein. Impairment of autophagy is one of the events seen in some subtypes of PD. Autophagy is a degradative pathway that delivers cytoplasmic content to lysosomes for degradation of aggregated cellular proteins and dysfunctional organelles.

2. FACTORS CAUSING PARKINSON'S DISEASE AND GAUCHER DISEASE

More than 25 genes have been ascribed with the cause of PD pathophysiology [7-9]. However, a common mutation found worldwide in the late-onset of PD is G2019S in the leucine-rich repeat kinase 2 gene. The Juvenile parkinsonism is caused by mutations in the Parkinson's disease genes of Parkin, protein deglycase DJ-1/Parkinson disease protein

7 or PTEN-induced kinase 1. Two cannabinoid receptors, cannabinoid receptor type 1 and cannabinoid receptor type 2 have major role in the basal ganglia involved in the pathogenesis of PD. Therefore, these two receptors have been proposed as a target in treating the disease [10].

N-acetyl aspartic acid (NAA) is the second abundant metabolite in the brain and is rich in neurons [11-14]. N-acetyl aspartic acid is vital for the maintenance of healthy neurons. While NAA is converted into aspartate and acetate in the central nervous system, kidney metabolizes NAA to carbon dioxide and mammary gland converts NAA to lipids [15]. The NAA is rich in food items including vegetables, soy beans, coffee, tea, cocoa, corn and meats. Increased levels of NAA also induce inflammation and contractility [13, 14, 15-18]. N-acetyl aspartic acid level is slightly elevated in the brain of Patients with PD. Elevated levels of NAA with sustained activity affects potential genes and proteins associated with oxidative stress to lead oxidative stress and thus contribute in the disease pathophysiology [15-19].

Gaucher disease (GD) is an autosomal recessive disorder, caused by deficiency of glucocerebrosidase activity, a lysosomal enzyme, resulting elevated levels of the substrate, glucosylceramide. The disease frequency is approximately one in fifty thousand births and the disease is most prevalence in Ashkenazi Jews. Infiltration of the bone marrow, spleen, and liver by Gaucher cells is ascribed with the splenomegaly, cytopenia, hepatomegaly and bone lesions seen in the disease. Glucocerebrosidase gene mutations not only causing Gaucher disease but also contribute in Parkinson's disease pathophysiology by affecting lysosomal functions. Fifty six percent of Parkinson's disease patients have at least one lysosomal storage disorder gene variant and twenty one percent carry multiple alleles [20]. Hence, lysosomal storage disorder is also one of the events in PD pathophysiology.

3. Biochemical Diagnosis of the Parkinson's Disease

Some biochemical assays used to determine PD are symptomatic. Measuring blood and cerebrospinal fluid levels of α-synuclein and protein deglycase DJ-1/Parkinson disease protein 7 is useful to determine PD or Parkinsonism. Nicotinamide phosphoribosyl transferase, an adipokine regulating lipid and glucose metabolism, is higher in early-stage and drug-naïve patients with PD [21]. Urate levels in the serum is correlated with PD [22-23]. Reduction in microRNA19b is associated with patients with rapid eye movement sleep behavior disorder [24].

Measuring dopamine transporter appears to be an accurate method to determine dopamine neuron loss seen in PD [25]. Manifestation of homovanillic acid level with xanthine is proposed to determine PD [26]. Lower level of plasma apolipoprotein A1 is related with a high risk of PD [27]. Measurement of α-synuclein oligomers in the cerebrospinal fluid of patients with PD by α-synuclein protein misfolding cyclic amplification is useful to determine PD [28].

4. Subtypes of Parkinsonism

Over eighty percentage of patients diagnosed with Parkinson's disease have primary parkinsonism/idiopathic Parkinson's disease. The word idiopathic means cause of the disease is not known. Idiopathic Parkinson disease worsens with increase in time. Patients with PD shows the symptoms of impairment of normal balance, gait and posture [29]. Diagnosing these symptoms is important to distinguish Parkinson's disease from vascular parkinsonism and atypical parkinsonism such as progressive supranuclear palsy, corticobasal syndrome and multiple system atrophy. Vascular parkinsonism is generally caused by strokes resulting clot in the brain. Vascular parkinsonism affects the lower body to lead gait abnormality rather than tremor. Atypical Parkinsonism shows some of the symptoms seen in Parkinson's disease, but that may not respond to levodopa drug treatment. Drugs containing benzamide derivatives have been ascribed as one of the major causes of drug induced parkinsonism. Patients who stopped eating these drugs could improve symptoms seen in drug induced parkinsonism. Drug induced parkinsonism shows symptoms such as postural instability, rigidity, and gait disturbance as seen in idiopathic Parkinson disease [30]. Approximately 300,000 people with idiopathic Parkinson's disease are living in Germany [31]. The patients with juvenile parkinsonism develop parkinsonian symptoms before twenty-one-year-old. The symptoms in Juvenile parkinsonism include cognitive decline, movement disorder and psychiatric disorder [32]. Dystonia is seen in atypical parkinsonian disorders such as progressive supranuclear palsy, multiple system atrophy, and corticobasal degeneration. The body distribution, severity, timing of appearance and relationship to dopaminergic and other medications may differ among atypical parkinsonian types [33]. Dopamine has a role on wake-promoting efficacy, as administration of dopaminergic analogues leads to increased activation of cortical electroencephalogram (EEG) and behavioral excitation.

5. Subtypes of Gaucher Disease

Gaucher disease (GD, OMIM #230800, ORPHA355) is an autosomal recessive disorder caused by mutations in the glucocerebrosidase 1 gene (GCase 1) resulting decreased levels of glucocerebrosidase (EC: 4.2.1.25) enzyme activity. The enzyme deficiency leads to the accumulation of the substrate, glucosylceramide. Elevated levels of the substrate forms fibrillar aggregates in macrophages and these cells are called as Gaucher cells. The disease is characterized by hepatosplenomegaly, cytopenia and severe bone involvement [34]. Type-1 Gaucher disease is mainly seen in patients from Europe and USA. The disease is characterized by the viscera effects such as splenomegaly [35-36], hepatomegaly [37], fatigue and delayed puberty [38], acute pain in the pelvis and lower limbs [39] with normal neurological function. Meanwhile, type 2 and type 3 Gaucher disease develop neurological impairment [40]. Type-2 Gaucher disease is characterized by severe neurological impairment starting at age 2–6 months old with hepatosplenomegaly, rigidity of the neck and trunk, oculomotor paralysis, bulbar signs and bilateral fixed strabismus [41]. Type-3 Gaucher disease phenotype differ among patients with less than twenty percentage patients showed progressive myoclonus epilepsy, less than sixty percentage patients had cerebellar ataxia or spasticity and dementia [42-44].

6. Biochemical Diagnosis of Gaucher Disease

Prenatal diagnosis of GD can be performed by determining glucocerebrosidase levels and gene mutation analysis of the cultured amniotic cells [45]. The reduced levels of the enzyme activity can be measured in leukocytes, mononuclear cells and cultured fibroblasts to determine GD. Elevated levels of Chitotriosidase was used as a biomarker of the disease [46]. However, the increased levels of chitotriosidase was also reported in other diseases such as Niemann–Pick disease [47], multiple sclerosis, β-thalassemia and visceral leishmaniasis. Therefore, measurement of chitotriosidase along with other phenotypes will help in determining GD. Measuring plasma C-C Motif Chemokine Ligand 18 [48-49] and glucosyl sphingosine levels are useful, as these levels are elevated in patients with GD [50]. These levels along with other phenotypes may be used in diagnosing GD.

7. Clinical Symptoms of Parkinson's Disease

The Fear of Falling Scale is a valid method to assess fear of falling in PD. Fear of falling score is associated with the presence of anxiety disorder, major depression, poor balance-related motor ability, more severe impairments in activities of daily living and increased motor fluctuations.

The generalized anxiety disorder is useful to predict number of falls during a 12-month period [51]. Floor patterns incorporating transverse oriented large rectangular visual cues may help patients with PD. Transverse floor stones are better than diagonal, whereas regular pattern stones were excellent to irregular in walking factors [52]. Thickening of rhomboid fossa is observed in patients with PD (Figure 1).

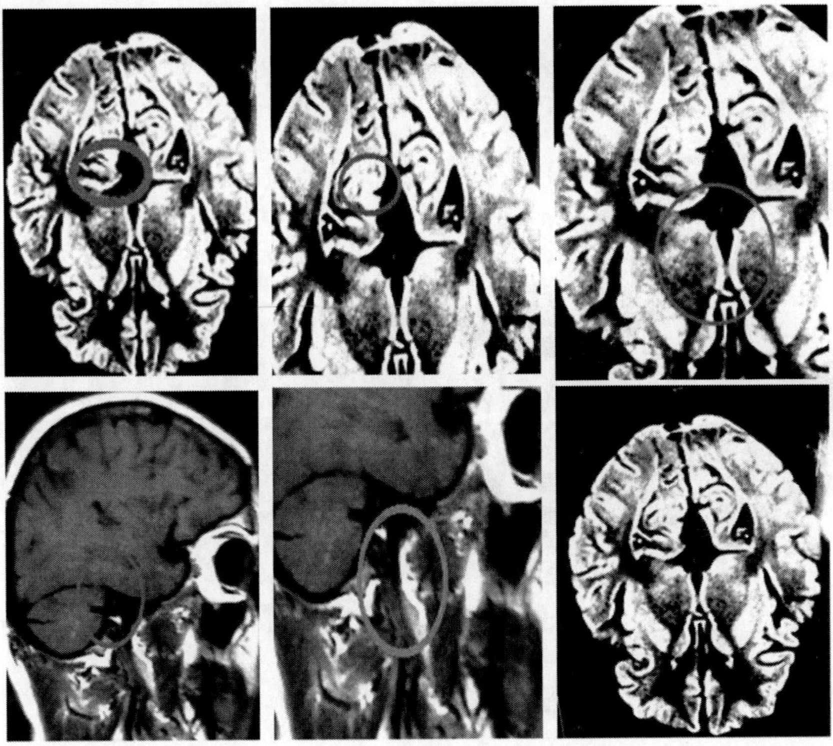

Figure 1. Parkinson disease patients brain showing thickening of rhomboid fossa.

Patients with PD show restless legs syndrome, leg motor restlessness and other leg restlessness related to sensorimotor symptoms. Late-onset leg restlessness when more than fifty-year old, including restless legs syndrome, leg motor restlessness and other leg restlessness, particularly if frequent and asymmetrical are early nonmotor manifestation of PD [53]. Pain and other non-motor symptom may severely affect normal life of

Patients with PD compared to the motor symptoms [54]. Pro-saccadic characteristics of duration, latency, peak and average velocity reduced in executive function, attention, global cognition and memory over fifty-four months in PD. Reduction in global cognition and attention were predicted by pro-saccadic metrics in adults. Saccadic characteristics are affected in early stage of the disease and therefore can be used to predict cognitive decline in PD [55]. Parkinson's disease patients show various abnormalities including spondylitis of cervical vertebra, posterior lateral thickening of rhomboid fossa and cuneus thickening of median occipital cortex (Figure 2). Patients with PD have stiffness of muscles in hand and fingers (Figure 3).

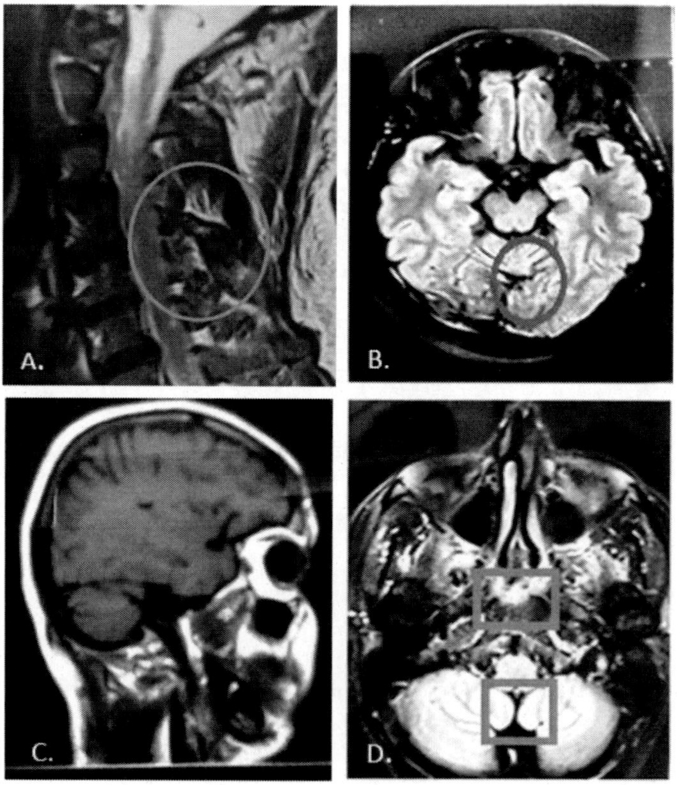

Figure 2. Parkinson disease patient showing abnormalities. A. spondylitis of cervical vertebra. B. Posterior lateral thickening of Rhomboid fossa. C-D. Cuneus thickening of median occipital cortex.

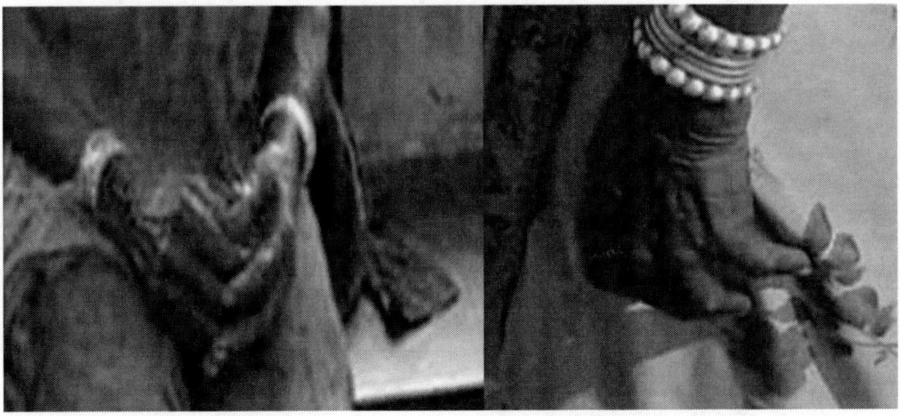

Figure 3. Patients with PD showing stiffness of muscles in the hand and fingers.

Table 1. Parkinson's disease patients showing clinical symptoms

Age	72	70
Sex	Female	Male
Onset of Symptoms	The patient started with pain in Left shoulder with numbness of fingers on left side	Watering of eyes right side irritation, deviation of angle of mouth, Stiffness of joints of both lower limbs
Tremor Rigidity	Tremor on left 4 digits	Tremor started in lips progressing to digits of fingers and toes
Bradykinesia	Movs slowly with trembling of both limbs	Moves slowly with trembling of digits
Posture & Gait	Mild stooping with slow stepping gait	Slow stepping gait
Unilateral or Bilateral	Initial trembling of limbs of right sided with slurring of speech	Initial trembling of limbs of right sided with slurring of speech
Initial presenting Symptoms	Bilateral, she had initial trembling of limbs of right sided with slurring of speech	Generalized stiffness of neck, hands and toes
Speech Difference	Yes	Initial symptoms of Aphonia
Gastro-intestinal	No	No
Disturbances	Initial grade with illusion	Initial grade with illusion
Dementia	conscious responds to	Responds to conversations
Psychomotor Abnormality	conversations	
Sensory Symptoms	ND	Irritable temperament

In one patient with PD, the rate of tremor increased progressively with 3-6 cycles per second by affecting distal part of the digits. Onset of the tremor was in one limb for months then affects the other limb. When the disease matures, tremor was observed in the tongue, eyelids and lips. Two cases of PD patients showing symptoms are given in the Table 1.

8. Clinical Symptoms of Gaucher Disease Subtypes

Patients with type 1 Gaucher disease show normal neurological functions. Less than forty percentage children with the disease showed growth retardation and delayed puberty. Splenomegaly, hepatomegaly, pain in the pelvis and lower limbs due to osteoporosis have been observed in patients with type 1 GD. Infiltration of Gaucher cells in the lungs leads to pulmonary fibrosis and pulmonary arterial hypertension [56-59].

Patients with type 2 Gaucher disease showed severe neurological impairment at 2– 6 months old, hepatosplenomegaly, rigidity of the neck and trunk, bulbar signs, oculomotor paralysis and hypertonia [41].

Adult patients with type 3 Gaucher disease showed cerebellar syndrome, mild splenomegaly, frontal myoclonic jerks, loss of intellectual abilities, slight ophthalmoplegia, mild hepatomegaly, mild thrombopenia and mental retardation [60]. While the normal subjects' hemoglobin levels range from 11-17 g%, GD patients hemoglobin levels are found to be reduced. Wintrobe tube method showed packed cell volume range in normal subjects' is between 35-52%, while GD patients packed cell volume is found to be reduced (Table 2).

Table 2. Analysis of blood in Gaucher disease patients

Age	73	65	60	58
Sex	F	M	M	F
Hemoglobin (g%)	9.6	32	9.6	10
Packed cell volume (%)	26	ND	28	28

9. Parkinson's Disease Association with Gaucher Disease

The GCase 1 gene is located on the long arm of chromosome 1q21 with 11 exons [61]. The enzyme deficiency leads to Gaucher disease, a lysosomal storage disorder. GTP-binding protein type A1 (GBA1) encodes GCase 1. Mutations in the GBA1 gene may degrade the protein, disrupting lysosomal targeting and decreased performance of the enzyme in the lysosome [62]. More than five hundred mutations have been identified in the GBA1 gene. The gene mutations N370S, L444P, IVS2 + 1G > A, V394L, and R496H [63-66] resulting enzyme deficiency also involved in the cause of pathophysiology seen in PD. The L444P and W378R mutations have been related with the cause of severe form of PD pathophysiology [67-69]. Both patients with Gaucher disease and heterozygous carriers are at increased risk of developing Parkinson disease and Dementia. Patients with sporadic Parkinson disease have decreased glucocerebrosidase activity. Deficiency of glucocerebrosidase activity resulting lysosomal dysfunction and mitochondrial disorder contributes to PD pathophysiology [70-71]. Motor, cognitive, olfactory and psychiatric symptoms [72] are more severe in glucocerebrosidase mutation resulting severe enzyme deficiency and Gaucher Disease-PD compared to mild glucocerebrosidase mutation resulting enzyme deficiency and idiopathic PD.

10. Effects and Side Effects of Parkinson's Disease Therapy

Invasive treatments such as application of chronic subthalamic nucleus stimulation in patients with PD improved musculoskeletal pain and dystonic pain with long-term pain relief [73]. In contrast, in patients with peripheral neuropathic pain they observed a worsening of the peripheral neuropathic pain. Subthalamic nucleus stimulation was effective in patients with dystonic pain [74]. Bilateral pallidotomy also improved pain [75-76]. To avoid invasive treatments in patients with PD, noninvasive drugs effects have been studied.

Music therapy improved depression seen in patients with PD. Patients with physical therapy showed decrease in Dynamic Gait Index percentage. The evaluation of patients by Romberg's test showed the positive results compared with patients above fifty percentage needed help to complete the task. After physical therapy classes the percentage decreased. Patients static balance improved significantly [77].

Botulinum neurotoxin blocks the release of acetylcholine at the neuromuscular junction to reduce pain and therefore used as a safe and effective treatment for spasticity in various diseases including stroke, and spinal cord injury, tremor, multiple sclerosis and dystonia [78]. It was prescribed in the treatment of both dystonic and central pain.

Dopamine replacement therapy (L-DOPA, dopamine agonists, monoamine oxidase B inhibitors and catechol-O-methyltransferase inhibitors) have been used to improve dyskinesias, motor and non-motor symptoms. Treatment of non-motor symptoms in PD includes antidepressants, hypnotics, analgesics, anxiolytics, antidementive agents and drugs for autonomic dysfunction [79]. Pimavanserin, quetiapine and clozapine were useful in treating PD psychosis [80]. Regulating autophagy pathway is one of the therapeutic options to protect cells against toxicity of aggregate-prone proteins in neurodegenerative diseases [81].

11. Effects and Side Effects of Gaucher Disease Therapy

Several enzymes are available such as Imiglucerase, alglucerase, Cerezyme (Genzyme), Vpriv (Shire) and Elelyso (Pfizer). Enzyme replacement therapy was found to be effective in treating patients with GD with a dose of 15–30 U/kg/month. Application of lower doses 2.3 U/Kg three times weekly or 30 U/Kg/month did not give much difference compared to higher doses 120 U/Kg/Month [82]. However, enzyme replacement therapy shows less effect on neurological abnormalities seen in GD [83].

To reduce the levels of glucocerebrosidase substrate, glucosyl-ceramide, substrate reduction therapy was attempted. Oral administration of Miglustat (Actelion) is effective in reversing clinical symptoms seen in mild to moderate disease type I Gaucher patients [84]. However, Miglustat causes diarrhea, flatulence and abdominal pain/discomfort [85]. Oral administration of Eliglustat (Genzyme), the substrate inhibitor, showed improvement on patients with type 1 Gaucher patients.

CONCLUSION

Parkinson's disease is a neurodegenerative disorder. Several factors have been reported in the cause of PD pathophysiology. N-acetyl-L-aspartic acid is found to be slightly elevated in the brain of patients with PD. Glucocerebrosidase gene mutations resulting enzyme deficiency seen in Gaucher disease, a lysosomal storage disorder, also contributes to PD pathophysiology. However, glucocerebrosidase enzyme deficiency may not be a common factor in treating PD.

REFERENCES

[1] Tysnes, OB, Storstein, A. Epidemiology of Parkinson's disease. *J. Neural. Transm. (Vienna)* 2017, 124, 901–905.

[2] Grosset, D, Antonini, A, Canesi, M, Pezzoli, G, Lees, A, Shaw, K, Cubo, E, Martinez- Martin, P, Rascol, O, Negre-Pages, L, Senard, A, Schwarz, J, Strecker, K, Reichmann, H, Storch, A, Löhle, M, Stocchi, F, Grosset, K. Adherence to antiparkinson medication in a multicenter European study. *Mov. Disord.* 2009, 24, 826–832.

[3] Skorvanek, M, Gdovinova, Z, Rosenberger, J, Saeedian, RG, Nagyova, I, Groothoff JW, van Dijk, JP. The associations between fatigue, apathy, and depression in Parkinson's disease. *Acta Neurol. Scand.* 2015, 131, 80–87.

[4] Valldeoriola, F, Coronell, C, Pont, C, Buongiorno, MT,Cámara, A,Gaig, C, Compta, Y, ADHESON Study Group. Socio-demographic and clinical factors influencing the adherence to treatment in Parkinson's disease: the ADHESON study: socio-demographic and clinical factors in treatment of Parkinson's disease. *Eur. J. Neurol.* 2011, 18, 980–987.

[5] Herlofson, K, Kluger, BM. Fatigue in Parkinson's disease. *J. Neurol. Sci*. 2017, 374, 38–41.

[6] Nègre-Pagès, L, Regragui, W, Bouhassira, D, Grandjean, H, Rascol, O, DoPaMiP Study Group. Chronic pain in Parkinson's disease: the cross-sectional French DoPaMiP survey. *Mov. Disord.* 2008, 23, 1361–1369.

[7] Singleton, AB, Farrer, MJ, Bonifati, V. The genetics of Parkinson's disease: progress and therapeutic implications. *Mov. Disord.* 2013, 28: 14–23.

[8] Bras, J, Guerreiro, R, Hardy, J. SnapShot: genetics of Parkinson's disease. *Cell.* 2015, 160, 570.e1.

[9] Verstraeten, A, Theuns, J, Van Broeckhoven, C. Progress in unraveling the genetic etiology of Parkinson disease in a genomic era. *Trends Genet.* 2015, 31: 140–149.

[10] Han, QW, Yuan, YH, Chen, NH. The therapeutic role of cannabinoid receptors and its agonists or antagonists in Parkinson's disease. *Prog. Neuropsychopharmacol. Biol. Psychiatry.* 2019, 20, 109745.

[11] Jacobson, HB. Studies on the role of N-acetylaspartic acid on mammalian brain. *J. Gen. Physiol.* 1957, 43, 323-333.

[12] Birken, DL, Olendorf, WH. N-acetyl aspartic acid: a literature review of a compound prominent in 1H-NMR spectroscopic studies of brain. *Neurosci. Biobehav. Rev*. 1989, 13, 23-31.

[13] Surendran, S, Kumaresan, G. Neurochemical changes and therapeutic approaches in Canavan disease. In: Surendran S, editor.

Neurochemistry of metabolic diseases: lysosomal storage diseases, phenylketonuria and canavan disease: Trivandrum, India: Transworld research network, 2007, pp 119-132.

[14] Surendran, S, Kaya, N, Ozand, P. Canavan disease: molecular pathology, phenotype and therapeutic approaches. In: Surendran S, editor. *Neurochemistry of metabolic diseases: lysosomal storage diseases, phenylketonuria and canavan disease*: New York, USA: NOVA science publishers, 2012, pp 241-263.

[15] D'Adamo, AF, Jr, Yatsu, FM. Acetate metabolism in the nervous system. N-acetyl-L- aspartic acid and the biosynthesis of brain lipids. *J. Neurochem.* 1966, 13, 961–965.

[16] Surendran, S, Bhatnagar, M. Upregulation of N-acetylaspartic acid induces oxidative stress to contribute in disease pathophysiology. *Int. J. Neurosci.* 2011, 121, 305-309.

[17] Surendran S. Upregulation of N-acetylaspartic acid resulting nitric oxide toxicity induces aspartoacylase mutations and protein interaction to cause pathophysiology seen in Canavan disease. *Med. Hypotheses.* 2010, 75, 533-534.

[18] Surendran, S. Upregulation of N-acetylaspartic acid alters inflammation, transcription and contractile associated protein levels in the stomach and smooth muscle contractility. *Mol. Biol. Rep.* 2009, 36, 201-206.

[19] Surendran, S, Kondapaka, SB. Altered expression of neuronal nitric oxide synthase in the duodenum longitudinal muscle-myenteric plexus of obesity induced diabetes mouse: implications on enteric neurodegeneration. *Biochem. Biophys. Res. Commun.* 2005, 338, 919-922.

[20] Robak, LA, Jansen, IE, van Rooij, J, Uitterlinden, AG, Kraaij, R, Jankovic, J, International Parkinson's Disease Genomics Consortium (IPDGC), Heutink P, Shulman JM. Excessive burden of lysosomal storage disorder gene variants in Parkinson's disease. *Brain.* 2017, 140, 3191-3203.

[21] Santiago, JA, Littlefield, AM, Potashkin, JA. Integrative transcriptomic meta-analysis of Parkinson's disease and depression

identifies NAMPT as a potential blood biomarker for de novo Parkinson's disease. *Sci. Rep.* 2016, 6, 34579.

[22] Noyce, AJ, Bestwick, JP, Silveira-Moriyama, L, Hawkes, CH, Giovannoni, G, Lees, AJ, Schrag, A. Meta-analysis of early nonmotor features and risk factors for Parkinson disease. *Ann. Neurol.* 2012, 72, 893–901.

[23] De Lau, LML, Koudstaal, PJ, Hofman, A, Breteler, MMB. Serum uric acid levels and the risk of Parkinson disease. *Ann. Neurol.* 2005, 58, 797–800.

[24] Fernández-Santiago, R, Iranzo, A, Gaig, C, Serradell, M, Fernández, M, Tolosa, E, Santamaría, J, Ezquerra, M. MicroRNA association with synucleinopathy conversion in rapid eye movement behavior disorder. *Ann. Neurol.* 2015, 77, 895–901.

[25] Suwijn, SR, van Boheemen, CJ, de Haan, RJ, Tissingh, G, Booij, J, de Bie, RM. The diagnostic accuracy of dopamine transporter SPECT imaging to detect nigrostriatal cell loss in patients with Parkinson's disease or clinically uncertain parkinsonism: a systematic review. *EJNMMI. Res.* 2015, 5, 12.

[26] LeWitt, P. Recent advances in CSF biomarkers for Parkinson's disease. *Parkinsonism Relat. Disord.* 2012, 18 Suppl 1, S49-51.

[27] Qiang, JK, Wong, YC, Siderowf, A, Hurtig, HI, Xie, SX, Lee, VM, Trojanowski, JQ, Yearout, D, Leverenz, J, Montine, TJ, Stern, M, Mendick, S, Jennings, D, Zabetian, C, Marek, K, Chen-Plotkin, AS. Plasma apolipoprotein A1 as a biomarker for Parkinson disease. *Ann. Neurol.* 2013, 74, 119–127.

[28] Shahnawaz, M, Tokuda, T, Waragai, M, Mendez, N, Ishii, R, Trenkwalder, C, Mollenhauer, B, Soto, C. Development of a Biochemical Diagnosis of Parkinson Disease by Detection of α-Synuclein Misfolded Aggregates in Cerebrospinal Fluid. *JAMA. Neurol.* 2017, 74, 163-172.

[29] Raccagni, C, Nonnekes, J, Bloem, BR, Peball, M, Boehme, C, Seppi, K, Wenning, GK. Gait and postural disorders in parkinsonism: a clinical approach. *J. Neurol.* 2019, doi: 10.1007/s00415-019-09382-1.

[30] Byun, JH, Cho, H, Kim, YJ, Kim, JS, Baik, JS, Jang, S, Ma, HI. Trends in the Prevalence of Drug-Induced Parkinsonism in Korea. *Yonsei. Med. J.* 2019, 60, 760-767.

[31] Waldthaler, J, Timmermann, L. Update on diagnostics and therapy of idiopathic Parkinson's disease. *Fortschr. Neurol. Psychiatr.* 2019, 87, 445-461.

[32] Niemann, N, Jankovic, J. Juvenile parkinsonism: Differential diagnosis, genetics, and treatment. *Parkinsonism Relat. Disord.* 2019, 67,74-89.

[33] Marsili, L, Bologna, M, Kojovic, M, Berardelli, A, Espay, AJ, Colosimo, C. Dystonia in atypical parkinsonian disorders. *Parkinsonism Relat. Disord.* 2019, 66, 25-33.

[34] Hruska, KS, LaMarca, ME, Scott, CR, Sidransky, E. Gaucher disease: Mutation and polymorphism spectrum in the glucocerebrosidase gene (GBA). *Hum. Mutat.* 2008, 29, 567–583.

[35] Hill, SC, Reinig, JW, Barranger, JA, Fink, J, Shawker, TH. Gaucher disease: sonographic appearance of the spleen. *Radiology.* 1986, 160, 631-634.

[36] Neudorfer, O, Hadas-Halpern, I, Elstein, D, Abrahamov, A, Zimran, A. Abdominal ultrasound findings mimicking hematological malignancies in a study of 218 Gaucher patients. *Am. J. Hematol.* 1997, 55, 28-34.

[37] Stirnemann, J, Vigan, M, Hamroun, D, Heraoui, D, Rossi-Semerano, L, Berger, MG, Rose, C, Camou, F, de Roux-Serratrice, C, Grosbois, B, Kaminsky, P, Robert, A, Caillaud, C, Froissart, R, Levade, T, Masseau, A, Mignot, C, Sedel, F, Dobbelaere, D, Vanier, MT, Valayanopoulos, V, Fain, O, Fantin, B, de Villemeur, TB, Mentré, F, Belmatoug, N. The French Gaucher's disease registry: clinical characteristics, complications and treatment of 562 patients. *Orphanet. J. Rare Dis.* 2012, 7, 77.

[38] Kaplan, P, Andersson, HC, Kacena, KA, Yee, JD. The clinical and demographic characteristics of nonneuronopathic Gaucher disease in 887 children at diagnosis. *Arch. Pediatr. Adolesc. Med.* 2006, 160, 603-608.

[39] Wenstrup, RJ, Roca-Espiau, M, Weinreb, NJ, Bembi, B. Skeletal aspects of Gaucher disease: a review. *Br. J. Radiol.* 2002, 75 Suppl 1, A2-12.

[40] Sidransky, E. Gaucher disease: Insights from a rare Mendelian disorder. *Discov. Med.* 2012, 14, 273–281.

[41] Mignot, C, Doummar, D, Maire, I, De Villemeur, TB. French Type 2 Gaucher Disease Study Group Type 2 Gaucher disease: 15 new cases and review of the literature. *Brain Dev.* 2006, 28, 39–48.

[42] Tylki-Szymańska, A, Vellodi, A, El-Beshlawy, A, Cole, JA, Kolodny, E. Neuronopathic Gaucher disease: demographic and clinical features of 131 patients enrolled in the International Collaborative Gaucher Group Neurological Outcomes Subregistry. *J. Inherit. Metab. Dis.* 2010, 33, 339-346.

[43] Kraoua, I, Sedel, F, Caillaud, C, Froissart, R, Stirnemann, J, Chaurand, G, Flodrops, H, Tari, S, Gourfinkel-An, I, Mathieu, S, Belmatoug, N, Billette de Villemeur, T, Mignot, C. A French experience of type 3 Gaucher disease: Phenotypic diversity and neurological outcome of 10 patients. *Brain Dev.* 2011, 33, 131-139.

[44] Mullin, S, Beavan, M, Bestwick, J, McNeill, A, Proukakis, C, Cox, T, Hughes, D, Mehta, A, Zetterberg, H, Schapira, AHV. Evolution and clustering of prodromal parkinsonian features in GBA1 carriers. *Mov. Disord.* 2019, 34, 1365-1373.

[45] Yoshida, S, Kido, J, Matsumoto, S, Momosaki, K, Mitsubuchi, H, Shimazu, T, Sugawara, K, Endo, F, Nakamura, K. Prenatal diagnosis of Gaucher disease using next-generation sequencing. *Pediatr. Int.* 2016, 58, 946-949.

[46] Hollak, CE, van Weely, S, van Oers, MH, Aerts, JM. Marked elevation of plasma chitotriosidase activity. A novel hallmark of Gaucher disease. *J. Clin. Invest.* 1994, 93, 1288-1292.

[47] Bargagli. E, Bennett, D, Maggiorelli, C, Di Sipiom P, Margolliccim M, Bianchim N, Rottolim P. Human chitotriosidase: a sensitive biomarker of sarcoidosis. *J. Clin. Immunol.* 2013, 33, 264-270

[48] Boot, RG, Verhoek, M, de Fost, M, Hollak, CE, Maas, M, Bleijlevens, B, van Breemen, MJ, van Meurs, M, Boven, LA, Laman,

JD, Moran, MT, Cox, TM, Aerts, JM. Marked elevation of the chemokine CCL18/PARC in Gaucher disease: a novel surrogate marker for assessing therapeutic intervention. *Blood.* 2004, 103, 33-39.

[49] Deegan, PB, Moran, MT, McFarlane, I, Schofield, JP, Boot, RG, Aerts, JM, Cox, TM. Clinical evaluation of chemokine and enzymatic biomarkers of Gaucher disease. *Blood Cells Mol. Dis.* 2005, 35, 259-267.

[50] Dekker, N, van Dussen, L, Hollak, CE, Overkleeft, H, Scheij, S, Ghauharali, K, van Breemen, MJ, Ferraz, MJ, Groener, JE, Maas, M, Wijburg, FA, Speijer, D, Tylki- Szymanska, A, Mistry, PK, Boot, RG, Aerts, JM. Elevated plasma glucosylsphingosine in Gaucher disease: relation to phenotype, storage cell markers, and therapeutic response. *Blood.* 2011, 118, e118-127.

[51] Terroba-Chambi, C, Bruno, V, Millar-Vernetti, P, Bruce, D, Brockman, S, Merello, M, Starkstein, S. Design and validation of a new instrument to assess fear of falling in Parkinson's disease. *Mov. Disord.* 2019, doi: 10.1002/mds.27820.

[52] Gál, O, Poláková, K, Hoskovcová, M, Tomandl, J, Čapek, V, Berka, R, Brožová, H, Šestáková, I, Růžička, E. Pavement patterns can be designed to improve gait in Parkinson's disease patients. *Mov. Disord.* 2019, 34, 1831-1838.

[53] Suzuki, K, Fujita, H, Watanabe, Y, Matsubara, T, Kadowaki, T, Sakuramoto, H, Hamaguchi, M, Nozawa, N, Hirata, K. Leg restlessness preceding the onset of motor symptoms of Parkinson disease: A case series of 5 patients. *Medicine (Baltimore).* 2019, 98, e16892.

[54] Barone, P, Antonini, A, Colosimo, C, Marconi, R, Morgante, L, Avarello, TP, Bottacchi, E, Cannas, A, Ceravolo, G, Ceravolo, R, Cicarelli, G, Gaglio, RM, Giglia, RM, Iemolo, F, Manfredi, M, Meco, G, Nicoletti, A, Pederzoli, M, Petrone, A, Pisani, A, Pontieri, FE, Quatrale, R, Ramat, S, Scala, R, Volpe, G, Zappulla, S, Bentivoglio, AR, Stocchi, F, Trianni, G, Dotto, PD, PRIAMO study group. The PRIAMO study: a multicenter assessment of nonmotor

symptoms and their impact on quality of life in Parkinson's disease. *Mov. Disord.* 2009, 24, 1641–1649.

[55] Stuart, S, Lawson, RA, Yarnall, AJ, Nell, J, Alcock, L, Duncan, GW, Khoo, TK, Barker, RA, Rochester, L, Burn DJ, ICICLE-PD study group. Pro-Saccades Predict Cognitive Decline in Parkinson's Disease: ICICLE-PD. *Mov. Disord.* 2019, 34, 1690-1698.

[56] Amir, G, Ron, N. Pulmonary pathology in Gaucher's disease. *Hum. Pathol.* 1999, 30, 666– 670.

[57] Mistry, PK, Sirrs, S, Chan, A, Pritzker, MR, Duffy, TP, Grace, ME, Meeker, DP, Goldman, ME. Pulmonary hypertension in type 1 Gaucher's disease: Genetic and epigenetic determinants of phenotype and response to therapy. *Mol. Genet. Metab.* 2002, 77, 91–98.

[58] Collins, LM, Williams-Gray, CH, Morris, E, Deegan, P, Cox, TM, Barker, RA. The motor and cognitive features of Parkinson's disease in patients with concurrent Gaucher disease over 2 years: a case series. *J. Neurol.* 2018, 265, 1789-1794.

[59] Ruskey, JA, Zhou, S, Santiago, R, Franche, LA, Alam, A, Roncière, L, Spiegelman, D, Fon, EA, Trempe, JF, Kalia, LV, Postuma, RB, Dupre, N, Rivard, GE, Assouline, S, Amato, D, Gan-Or, Z. The GBA p. Trp378Gly mutation is a probable French-Canadian founder mutation causing Gaucher disease and synucleinopathies. *Clin. Genet.* 2018, 94, 339- 345.

[60] Detollenaere, C, Benghergbia, M, Brassier, A, de Villemeur, TB, Amsallem, D, Berger, M, Stirnemann, J, Belmatoug, N, Rose, C. Type 3 Gaucher disease, diagnostic in adulthood. *Mol. Genet. Metab. Rep.* 2017, 13, 1-2.

[61] Horowitz, M, Wilder, S, Horowitz, Z, Reiner, O, Gelbart, T, Beutler, E. The human glucocerebrosidase gene and pseudogene: structure and evolution. *Genomics.* 1989, 4, 87- 96.

[62] Velez-Pardo, C, Lorenzo-Betancor, O, Jimenez-Del-Rio, M, Moreno, S, Lopera, F, Cornejo-Olivas, M, Torres, L, Inca-Martinez, M, Mazzetti, P, Cosentino, C, Yearout, D, Waldherr, SM, Zabetian, CP, Mata, IF. The distribution and risk effect of GBA variants in a large

cohort of PD patients from Colombia and Peru. *Parkinsonism Relat. Disord*. 2019, 63, 204-208.

[63] Aharon-Peretz, J, Badarny, S, Rosenbaum, H, Gershoni-Baruch, R. Mutations in the glucocerebrosidase gene and Parkinson disease: phenotype-genotype correlation. *Neurology*. 2005, 65, 1460-1461.

[64] Clark, LN, Ross, BM, Wang, Y, Mejia-Santana, H, Harris, J, Louis, ED, Cote, LJ, Andrews, H, Fahn, S, Waters, C, Ford, B, Frucht, S, Ottman, R, Marder, K. Mutations in the glucocerebrosidase gene are associated with early-onset Parkinson disease. *Neurology* 2007, 69, 1270-1277.

[65] Do, J, McKinney, C, Sharma, P, Sidransky, E. Glucocerebrosidase and its relevance to Parkinson disease. *Mol. Neurodegener*. 2019, 14, 36.

[66] Sato, C, Morgan, A, Lang, AE, Salehi-Rad, S, Kawarai, T, Meng, Y, Ray, PN, Farrer, LA, St George-Hyslop, P, Rogaeva, E. Analysis of the glucocerebrosidase gene in Parkinson's disease. *Mov. Disord*. 2005, 20, 367-370.

[67] Cilia, R, Tunesi, S, Marotta, G, Cereda, E, Siri, C, Tesei, S, Zecchinelli, AL, Canesi, M, Mariani, CB, Meucci, N, Sacilotto, G, Zini, M, Barichella, M, Magnani, C, Duga, S, Asselta, R, Soldà, G, Seresini, A, Seia, M, Pezzoli, G, Goldwurm, S. Survival and dementia in GBA-associated Parkinson's disease: The mutation matters. *Ann. Neurol.* 2016, 80, 662-673.

[68] Lubomski, M, Hayes, M, Kennerson, M, Ellis, M, Chu, S, Blackie, J, O'Sullivan, JD, Nicholson G. A novel Parkinson's disease risk variant, p. W378R, in the Gaucher's disease GBA gene. *Mov. Disord.* 2018, 33, 1662-1664.

[69] Mullin, S, Hughes, D, Mehta, A, Schapira, AHV. Neurological effects of glucocerebrosidase gene mutations. *Eur. J. Neurol.* 2019, 26, 388-e29.

[70] Li, H, Ham, A, Ma, TC, Kuo, SH, Kanter, E, Kim, D, Ko, HS, Quan, Y, Sardi, SP, Li, A, Arancio, O, Kang, UJ, Sulzer, D, Tang, G. Mitochondrial dysfunction and mitophagy defect triggered by heterozygous GBA mutations. *Autophagy* 2019, 15, 113-130.

[71] Pitcairn, C, Wani, WY, Mazzulli, JR. Dysregulation of the autophagic-lysosomal pathway in Gaucher and Parkinson's disease. *Neurobiol. Dis*. 2019, 122, 72-82.

[72] Thaler, A, Bregman, N, Gurevich, T, Shiner, T, Dror, Y, Zmira, O, Gan-Or, Z, Bar-Shira, A, Gana-Weisz, M, Orr-Urtreger, A, Giladi, N, Mirelman, A. Parkinson's disease phenotype is influenced by the severity of the mutations in the GBA gene. *Parkinsonism Relat. Disord.* 2018, 55, 45-49.

[73] Oshima, H, Katayama, Y, Morishita, T, Sumi, K, Otaka, T, Kobayashi, K, Suzuki, Y, Fukaya, C, Yamamoto, T. Subthalamic nucleus stimulation for attenuation of pain related to Parkinson disease. *J. Neurosurg*. 2012, 116, 99–106.

[74] Jung, YJ, Kim, HJ, Jeon, BS, Park, H, Lee, WW, Paek, SH. An 8-year follow-up on the effect of subthalamic nucleus deep brain stimulation on pain in parkinson disease. *JAMA. Neurol.* 2015, 72, 504–510.

[75] Honey, CR, Stoessl, AJ, Tsui, JK, Schulzer, M, Calne, DB. Unilateral pallidotomy for reduction of parkinsonian pain. *J. Neurosurg*. 1999, 91, 198–201.

[76] Loher, TJ, Burgunder, JM, Weber, S, Sommerhalder, R, Krauss, JK. Effect of chronic pallidal deep brain stimulation on off period dystonia and sensory symptoms in advanced Parkinson's disease. *J. Neurol. Neurosurg. Psychiatry*. 2002, 73, 395–399.

[77] Andrejeva, J, Kasradze, M, Misiukeviciute, L, Radziuviene, R. The effect of physical therapy with use of muscical elements in patients with Patients with Parkinson's disease. *Georgian Med. News*. 2019, 291, 82-85.

[78] Abrams, SB, Hallett, M. Clinical utility of different botulinum neurotoxin preparations. *Toxicon*. 2013, 67, 81–86.

[79] Foppa, AA, Chemello, C, Vargas-Peláez, CM, Farias, MR. Medication therapy management service for patients with Parkinson's disease: a before-and-after study. *Neurol. Ther*. 2016, 5, 85–99.

[80] Schneider, RB, Iourinets, J, Richard, IH. Parkinson's disease psychosis: presentation, diagnosis and management. *Neurodegener. Dis. Manag*. 2017, 7, 365-376.

[81] Karabiyik, C, Lee, MJ, Rubinsztein, DC. Autophagy impairment in Parkinson's disease. *Essays Biochem*. 2017, 61, 711-720.

[82] Beutler, E, Demina, A, Laubscher, K, Garver, P, Gelbart, T, Balicki, D, Vaughan, L. The clinical course of treated and untreated Gaucher disease. A study of 45 patients. *Blood Cells Mol. Dis.* 1995, 21, 86-108.

[83] Weiss, K, Gonzalez, AN, Lopez, G, Pedoeim, L, Groden, C, Sidransky, E. The clinical management of Type 2 Gaucher disease. *Mol. Genet. Metab*. 2015, 114, 110–122.

[84] Aerts, JM, Hollak, CE, Boot, RG, Groener, JE, Maas, M. Substrate reduction therapy of glycosphingolipid storage disorders. *J. Inher. Metab. Dis*. 2006, 29, 449–456.

[85] Belmatoug, N, Burlina, A, Giraldo, P, Hendriksz, CJ, Kuter, DJ, Mengelm E, Pastoresm GM. Gastrointestinal disturbances and their management in miglustat-treated patients. *J. Inherit. Metab. Dis.* 2011, 34, 991–1001.

In: Neurochemistry of Metabolic Diseases ISBN: 978-1-53618-339-9
Editor: Sankar Surendran

Chapter 9

PHENYLKETONURIA: DIAGNOSIS AND THERAPEUTICAL OPTIONS

Jaume Campistol[1,*] and Sankar Surendran[2]

[1]PKU Unit, Department of Neurology,
Hospital Sant Joan de Deu, Barcelona. Spain
[2]School of Medicine, Louisiana State University,
Health Sciences Center, New Orleans, LA, US

ABSTRACT

Phenylketonuria is a genetic disorder of autosomal recessive transmission, in which an alteration occurs in the metabolism of hydroxylation of phenylalanine (Phe) to tyrosine (Tyr), by the phenylalanine hydroxylase (PAH) activity. As a consequence, there is an increase in plasma Phe levels and a decrease in Tyr concentration. Although Phe is an essential amino acid, elevated levels of Phe concentrations in the plasma and tissue resulting toxicity affects the central nervous system. The PAH gene is located on chromosome 12q

* Corresponding Author's Email: campistol@hsjdbcn.es.

(q22-q24.1) and there are more than 700 different mutations. The tolerance to Phe intake depends on the residual activity of the enzyme. The most severe form of hyperphenylalaninemia (HPA) is classical phenylketonuria (PKU). Nutritional treatment in this disease aims to control the intake of Phe to achieve non-toxic levels, provide Tyr and to offer the correct amount of carbohydrates, lipids, proteins and trace elements to achieve a normal growth and development. Some patients respond to administration of BH4 which acts as a chaperone. Enzyme replacement therapy is now available for some PKU patients and other therapies are in course.

1. Introduction

Hyperphenylalaninemia (HPN) is a generic term for a biochemical phenotype in which there is a persistent increase in the plasma concentration of phenylalanine (Phe) caused by disorders of hepatic hydroxylation of this amino acid [1]. This system of hydroxylation of Phe to tyrosine essentially involves the enzyme phenylalanine hydroxylase (Phe 4-monooxygenase, PAH; EC 1.14.16.1) and the coenzyme tetrahydrobiopterin (BH4), which is reduced in the hydroxylation reaction and must be regenerated by another enzyme, dihydropterin reductase (DHPR; EC 1.6.99.7) [1]. Any defect that interferes with the hydroxylation system (deficiency of phenylalanine hydroxylase, dihydropterin reductase activity, or defects in tetrahydrobiopterin biosynthesis) will cause persistent HPN. This system is the main determinant of Phe homeostasis in human beings. The main cause of HPN is the defect in phenylalanine hydroxylase activity that causes PKU (OMIM 261600), which constitutes 98% of diagnosed cases [2].

2. History

In 1934, Fölling described the disease for the first time in two brothers with intellectual disability and a special body odor, by the observation of their acidified urine, turned into an intense green color, when added with ferric chloride. Fölling deduced that what determined the color and smell of urine was phenylpyruvic acid [3]. The study of other patients with intellectual disabilities admitted to special institutions showed that eight of them belonging to three families excreted urine, with the same odor and color, when added with ferric chloride [3]. Based on these data, he described the disease as a hereditary metabolic disorder, calling it "phenylpyruvic idiocy", and relating intellectual disability for the first time to a congenital error in metabolism.

In 1937 the disease was called phenylketonuria (PKU) by Penrose and Quastel [4]. In 1953, Jervis demonstrated a defect in the activity of the liver enzyme phenylalanine hydroxylase. In the same year, Bickel described the first possibility of therapy, by restricting the Phe of the diet, which is the basis of treatment for these patients [5, 6].

In 1963, Guthrie published a method of screening Phe in blood to be applied to the entire population in the neonatal period, which allowed the early treatment of PKU and avoided the intellectual disability of patients treated prematurely [7]. In 1980, Lenke and Levy described maternal PKU embryopathy and in 1983, Woo located the PAH gene on chromosome 12q24.1 [2, 8, 9]. More than 700 mutations have been identified in the PAH gene. Kure in 1999 described treatment with BH4 in some patients with PKU and that has opened a new therapeutic strategy [10].

3. Biochemical Diagnosis of the Disease

The Guthrie test is based on the fact that a high concentration of Phe in blood impregnated in a filter paper (Guthrie card) causes the cancellation of the inhibitory action of bacterial growth of a compound added to the culture medium, producing a growth halo around from the patient' s blood [2, 3, 7]. It was soon applied in numerous American states and spread throughout Europe. The first early detection programs appeared in the 1960s by semi-quantitative determination of Phe in blood samples impregnated on filter paper. Early detection procedures were based on the Guthrie method (still used in some countries) and later on chromatographic, fluorometric, immunoassay, and spectrophotometric methods, but they are gradually being displaced by the use of tandem mass spectrometry (MS/MS). This method allows the detection of a large number of aminoacidopathies, organic acidurias and beta-oxidation defects of fatty acids in the same dried blood sample, which is why it is currently being adopted in most neonatal screening centers [2, 7]. If the detected concentrations of Phe exceed 120-150 μmol/L, the patient is referred to the referral center for PKU, where they will proceed to check, differential diagnosis and start treatment, if necessary.

The biochemical tests necessary for differential diagnosis are initiated with verification of the result of early diagnosis in the patient' s blood, by rapid determination of plasma Phe concentrations (by HPLC or fluorimetry). This allows evaluating the variation of the Phe concentration in the period of time (10-15 days) required for the result of early diagnosis, at the same time that treatment is started if high plasma Phe concentrations are verified, while continuing with differential diagnosis.

Once hyperphenylalaninemia has been verified, the differential diagnosis continues basically focused on two aspects: 1) ruling out a defect in the metabolism (synthesis or recycling) of BH4, and 2) if there is no such defect, the patient' s response to BH4 treatment, to check whether it can be treated totally or partially with said cofactor or the restricted diet should be immediately introduced into Phe [2].

Tetrahydrobiopterin (BH4) is a cofactor, can increase residual PAH activity, has a major role in the conversion of Phe to tyrosine and in the production of neurotransmitters [10-14] (Figure 1). Tetrahydrobiopterin is synthesized from guanosine triphosphate in a three-step process. First, guanosine triphosphate is converted into dihydroneopterin triphosphate by GTP cyclohydrolase I. Subsequently, dihydroneopterin triphosphate is converted into 6-pyruvol tetrahydropterin by 6-pyruvoyl-tetrahydropterin synthase. Finally, 6-pyruvol tetrahydropterin is converted into tetrahydrobiopterin by sepiapterin reductase (Figure 2). Thus, reduced levels of BH4 in PKU affects normal conversion of Phe to tyrosine to contribute in PKU pathophysiology.

The determination of the dihydropterin reductase activity makes it possible to exclude the defect in the activity of this enzyme, that is, the recycling of BH4. The assessment of pterins in urine is essential to diagnose the different defects of tetrahydrobiopterin metabolism.

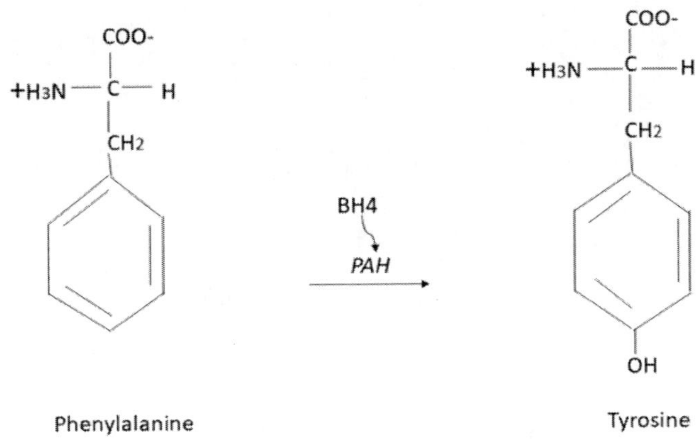

Figure 1. Phenylalanine hydroxylase catalyzes L-Phenylalanine to L-Tyrosine.

The BH4 oral overload test (20 mg/kg body weight) can be performed simultaneously with the differential diagnosis and allows the response to this cofactor to be checked. Complete and rapid normalization of HPN (before 8 hours post-overload) suggests a deficiency in metabolism to BH4, whereas gradual reduction of Phe or the absence of reduction of the amino acid is related to the response to BH4, and they allow choosing the appropriate treatment option [2, 5, 15].

In addition to PAH, BH4 also acts a co-factor for other agents. BH4 is a cofactor for tyrosine hydroxylase, an enzyme required for the conversion of L-tyrosine to L-DOPA. Thus, BH4 deficiency can lead to decline in the levels of dopamine, norepinephrine and epinephrine. BH4 is a cofactor for tryptophan hydroxylase, an enzyme required for the conversion of L-tryptophan to 5-hydroxytryptophan. Since normal levels of dopamine and serotonin are important for the brain regulatory function [11], tetrahydrobiopterin deficiency resulting reduced levels of dopamine and serotonin may lead to central nervous system disorders. BH4 is a cofactor for nitric oxide synthase, which catalyzes the conversion of guanidino nitrogen of L-arginine to nitric oxide. BH4 is also a cofactor for ether lipid oxidase, which catalyzes the conversion of 1-alkyl-sn-glycerol to 1-hydroxyalkyl-sn-glycerol. Thus, BH4 plays major role in the regulation of biochemical function in the human body. The structure of BH4 is shown in Figure 3.

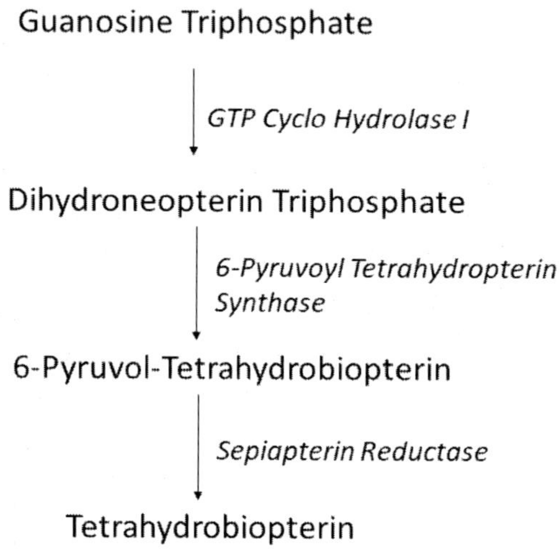

Figure 2. Synthesis of Tetrahydrobiopterin from guanosine triphosphate.

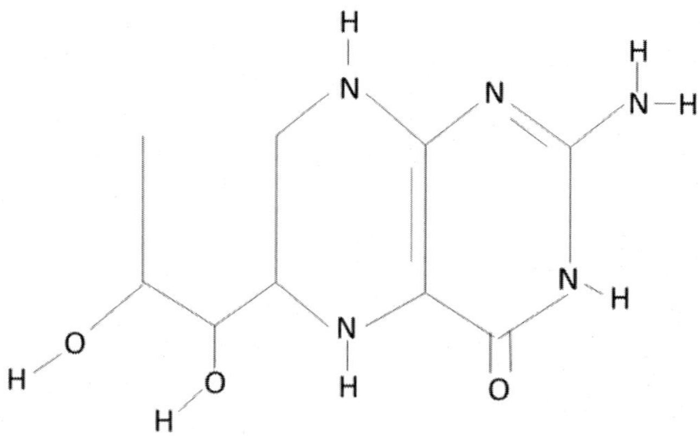

Figure 3. Structure of Tetrahydrobiopterin.

4. Gene Defect Causing the Disease

PKU/HPA shows an autosomal recessive inheritance, caused by mutations in the PAH gene. PKU has an overall incidence of 1 : 4,000/ 21,195 newborns depending on the geographical area [2, 5, 15]. In Europe it is generally 1 : 10,000 live births, but in Turkey and Northern Ireland it is 1 : 4,000, while in Finland it is 1 : 100,000 live births and in the United States it is 1 : 15,000 live births [2, 5, 15-23]. The incidence of carriers for the disease is 2% of the general population in our geographic area.

The PAH gene encoding the PAH enzyme is located on chromosome 12 (12q22-24. PKU is a very heterogeneous disease with more than 700 described mutations [15-22]. There are differences between the mutational spectra of the different populations and races [18-19, 21]. In general, even the most prevalent mutations occur at a very low frequency, so there are few recurring mutations and a large number of rare mutations in the same population. A greater heterogeneity is observed in the mediterranean area than in the rest of Europe [22].

Most of the mutations described in the PAH gene are punctual, affecting one or very few base pairs, many of them being located in exon 7. However, mutations have been described that involve nucleotide changes, a truncated enzyme protein, or a change in reading pattern. Deletions and insertions account for 12% compared to other types of mutations [15-23], as well as large deletions, which tend to be recurrent in specific population [19, 20, 22]. The most frequent mutation in southern Europe, Chile, Argentina and Mexico is IVS10, whose origin seems to come from the Itálica Peninsula [22]. In Spain, due to the different colonizations that have populated us and the abundant immigration, the mutational spectrum is wide. Most PKU/HPA patients are combined heterozygotes, making genotype-phenotype correlation difficult. In our experience cognitive and neurological are closely related to early diagnosis and treatment, and good control of the diet in the PKU, being independent of the mutation [22].

During the last decade and especially due to the introduction of BH4 therapy to which patients with certain mutations respond well (www.biopku.org), numerous expression studies have been carried out on the enzyme protein of mutated PAH alleles [17, 18].

5. Clinical Manifestations in Phenylketonuria

HPN could present itself in different clinical forms that must be known. Untreated classical phenylketonuria Untreated PKU become apparent from the first months of life and presents with psychomotor retardation, microcephaly, epilepsy, intellectual disability in the moderate-severe range, and psychotic behavior with marked hyperactivity, impulsiveness, destructive behavior, stereotyping and even autism [2, 5, 23, 24] (Figure 4). They usually have characteristic physical features such as hypopigmentation of the eyes, skin and hair, a special body odor and eczema (30% of cases). To all this are added pyramidal signs, tremor and even parkinsonism [23, 25, 26]. It should be noted that 1 to 2% of PKU patients with late diagnosis show an atypical evolution. They do not present cognitive impairment or only a slight decrease in their intellectual capacity despite never having received treatment [23]. In these patients, it has been described that despite having high concentrations of Phe in blood, Phe concentrations in the nervous system are practically within normal limits [23]. It is possible that allelic variations in the cerebral transporter of Phe and other amino acids, may be responsible for these observed interindividual differences [2, 15, 22]. Untreated PKU can present epilepsy in 25% of cases (generalized or West syndrome) and EEG abnormalities (70-95% of cases). In adults, epilepsy can be difficult to control.

Adults with untreated PKU, develop symptoms such as tremor, parkinsonism, leukoencephalopathy (Figure 5), spastic paraparesis, vision loss, brisk reflexes and psychiatric symptoms [25-26]. The early treated PKU patient who stopped diet 6 years before is shown in Figure 5. Elevated Phe levels affect normal dopamine and serotonin levels [27] to contribute in neurocognitive disorder seen in PKU [22, 25-29]. Reduced levels of serotonin lead to decline in social behavior, mood disorders [30-31] and abnormal executive function [32]. Although melatonin and serotonin are deficient in early-treated PKU patients, sleep disorder did not change from normal subjects [30].

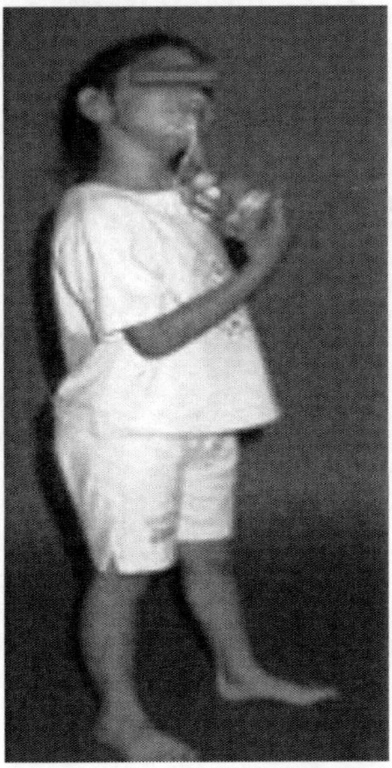

Figure 4. Untreated 8 yr old female PKU patient with autistic spectrum disorder and epilepsy.

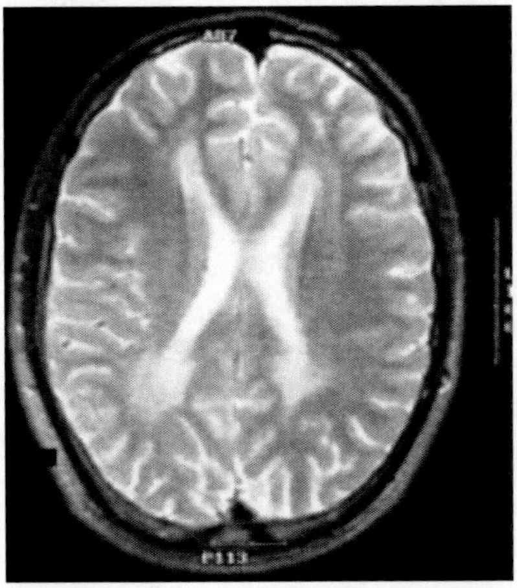

Figure 5. MRI T2 weighted showing signal alteration in the periventricular white matter of posterior dominance.

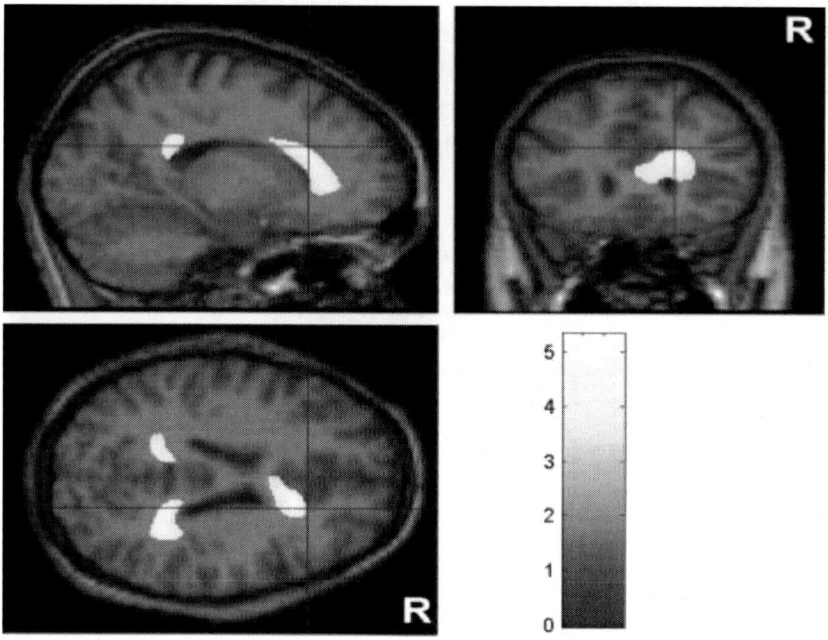

Figure 6. MRI volumetric study in PKU patients.

MRI demonstrated abnormalities in white matter that disappear some months after treatment [2, 23, 32-33]. We have detected volumetric changes in brain parenchyma in PKU patients. Relative decrease of volume in the white matter (Figure 6).

5.1. Early Treated Phenylketonuria

Due to the body's protein requirements, complete elimination of Phe from the diet is not desirable, and therefore even early treated children maintain mild elevation of Phe in the plasma (values 3-5 times higher than normal) and also in the brain. These children follow an excellent evolution, although they can present slight alterations in some cognitive functions. Their IQ is normal but lower than that of their healthy siblings or control groups, and they show deficits mainly in executive functions (attention control, strategic planning, response inhibition, working memory, cognitive flexibility, and processing) [2, 5, 23, 34-38]. Alterations in other cognitive functions have also been described, such as problems with fine motor skills, and visuospatial and visuoconstructive difficulties [34-36]. All these alterations are likely related to the higher incidence of school difficulties compared to the control groups presented by these patients [38-39]. In older patients it is common to find emotional problems such as depression and anxiety. In this aspect, not only a neurobiological alteration (less serotonin synthesis), but also the emotional stress associated with any chronic disorder could be involved [27-29].

Two hypotheses are currently being considered as the cause of the cognitive disorders described in early treated PKU patients. The first lies in a dysfunction of the prefrontal cortex (PFC) due to a decrease in the synthesis of dopamine [26-28, 40-42]. The second hypothesis is based on the fact that the primary lesion in the brain of treated PKU patients is the loss of myelin that secondarily affects the production of neurotransmitters and the ability to conduct action potential through the axon [43] (Figure 7). The presence of tremor in PKU patients is probably due to CNS dysfunction and may be an indicator of brain damage [44].

The interruption or relaxation of the diet from adolescence is followed by complications, especially if Phe values above 1200 μmol/L. The majority of patients often present difficulties of concentration and emotional instability, as well as a slower reaction time [34, 41]. The resumption of diet of the diet improves symptoms, and that is why the recommendations in recent years are to maintain dietary treatment throughout life [45, 46]. Early and strict treatment during childhood is of great importance in the development of IQ. The SB abnormalities identified in PKU individuals can also compromise brain functions due to impaired conduction velocity or disruptions in interconnectivity between different brain regions. Recently [43], a decrease in connectivity within the CPF itself and between the CPF and other brain areas has been demonstrated by functional MRI in patients treated early, even without evident structural abnormalities in PKU patients (Figure 7).

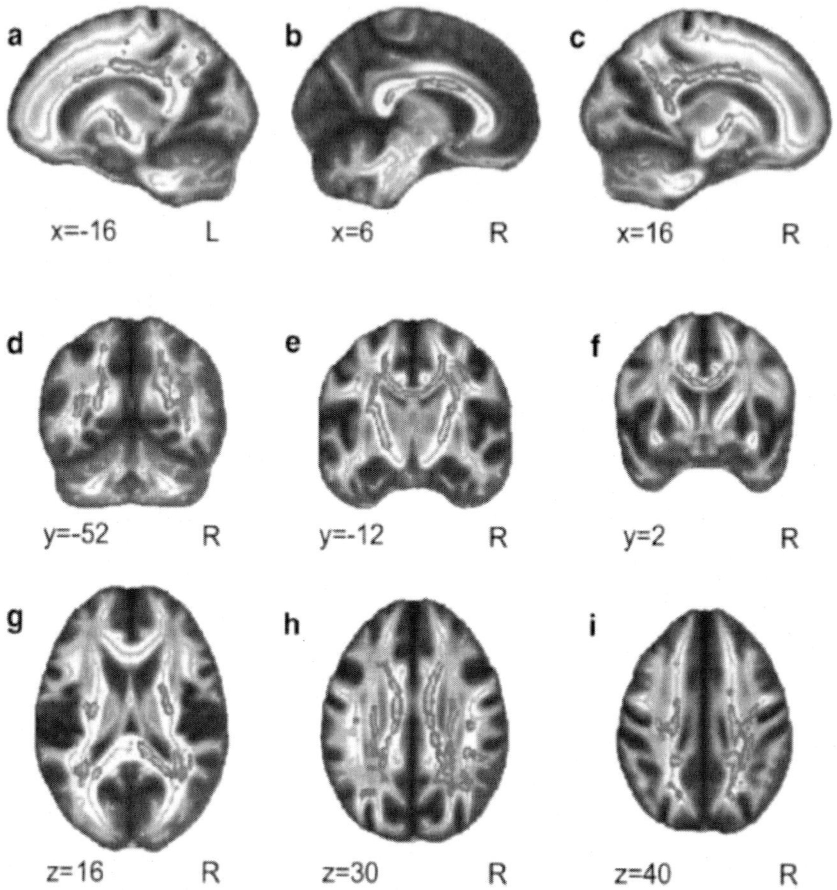

Figure 7. Decreased Mean Diffusivity values of white matter tracts across the whole brain in patients with early treated PKU.

5.2. Mild Hyperphenylalaninemia

Mild HPA is a benign form of the disease, caused by a partial enzyme defect, which determines that this condition does not require dietary treatment. The evolution of patients with mild HPA is favorable. They do not show significant alterations in the evaluations of cognitive functions, although the performance on the tests is usually intermediate between that of PKU children in dietary treatment and control groups. Follow-up of these patients in the first years of life is important since in some cases a progressive increase in Phe levels has been observed, which has required starting treatment [2, 6, 45, 46]. In women from fertile age, it is recommended to maintain controls due to the possibility of elevated plasma Phe concentrations during pregnancy with the risk of embryopathy.

5.3. Malignant Hyperphenylalaninemia

There are variants of hyperphenylalaninemia, which do not respond to restrictive treatment with Phe. These are disorders of the metabolism of BH4. Affected patients show, despite adequate treatment, symptoms of neurological deterioration due to deficits in neurotransmitters (catecholamines and serotonin). Clinical signs may begin in the first months of life with microcephaly, developmental delay, and progressive neurologic decline with respiratory distress, parkinsonism, myoclonus, chorea, dystonia, pyramidal signs, refractory epilepsy (infantile spasms, or generalized epilepsy), and hyperthermia [47].

5.4. Maternal Phenylketonuria Embryopathy

Maternal phenylketonuria syndrome (mPKU) is an embryopathy observed in offprings of PKU mothers who have elevated plasma Phe concentrations during the previous months and/or during pregnancy [2, 8, 23, 48]. Maternal Phe levels during pregnancy are directly related to the incidence of abnormalities in the future child, since the fetus is unable to properly metabolize the transplacental flow of Phe due to the immaturity of the liver hydroxylation system and its carrier status. The embriopathy can lead intellectual disability in 92% of cases, microcephaly in 73%, intrauterine growth retardation in 40%, cardiac malformations of various types in 12%, and less frequently esophageal atresia and facial dysmorphias [48].

6. Therapeutical Options

There are many therapeutic options in PKU. However, classic dietary phenylalanine restriction therapy can be applied to all PKU patients. The early detection of the disease and the immediate start of the diet offer to PKU patients a normal development and good quality of life [23, 45, 46].

The treatment of PKU is for life and is well based on the reduction of the foods containing Phe, combined with the administration of a special formula Phe free, supplemented with Tyr, micronutrients and with a content of the rest of amino acids similar to that of milk [45, 49]. To consider optimal management of these patients treatment requires: early diagnosis, within the first month of life, treatment and periodic monitoring during childhood, adolescence and adult life, and especially maintaining blood Phe concentrations in a safe range: less than 360 μmol/L up to adolescence and 600 μmol/L in adults [23, 45].

All foods with high biological value proteins : meat, fish, eggs, milk and derivatives (except butter) contains the highest amount of Phe and are highly restricted. Cereals, legumes and their derivatives contain less Phe amount, and they must be controlled foods in their intake and, finally, garden fruits, vegetables and fruits are foods with a lower content of Phe and their consumption may be higher.

The diet of these patients suffers from a restriction in natural proteins, which is solved by special formulas that are used to provide all amino acids except Phe and with supplements of Tyr and micronutrients. There are also a number of special low-protein foods that are used in the preparation of daily menus [45, 49].

New supplements have recently been proposed based on the finding of a natural protein the glycomacropeptide [50, 51], which is generated in cheese production and is Phe free. As an intact protein, the glycomacropeptide is more physiological and improves the feeling full sensation.

The diet is monitored by clinical, biochemical and nutritional status controls, especially observing signs of protein malnutrition. Periodic analyzes must be carried out to assess Phe levels, the state of the trace elements, since deficiencies have been observed in relation to the antioxidant system, minerals, especially selenium, carnitine [52], fatty acids polyunsaturated [53], etc. As for polyunsaturated fatty acids, low levels of docosahexaenoic acid in plasma phospholipids have been demonstrated not only in PKU patients but even in children with mild HPA without dietary treatment [53]. The risk of osteopenia that patients with PKU can present should be carefully assessed, using biochemical markers and bone densitometry [54]. Additional problems may arise in PKU patients with low-income families, with psychosocial, cultural, economic, educational difficulties that influence adherence to treatment [23, 55].

The optimization of the growth and development of the patients [45, 46, 49], as well as the good adherence to the diet, has given rise to numerous recommendations based on retrospective studies of patient groups from different countries [23]. Diet previous and during pregnancy should be strict to avoid maternal PKU embryopathy.

6.1. BH4 Treatment

Treatment with BH4 (sapropterin dihydrochloride) is applicable only to patients with mutations that respond to the cofactor, which increases tolerance to Phe, allowing the diet restricted in this amino acid to be liberalized and sometimes even making the special formula unnecessary [10, 11, 56]. The selection of patients with a good response to the cofactor is performed using a BH4 overload test (20 mg/kg weight), which can last 48 hours [57]. Patients in whom the maximum concentration of Phe decreases by 30% at 8 hours or by 50% 48 hours after the overload are considered to have a good response. The BH4 doses used in long-term treatment range from 5-20 mg/kg body weight/day, so the initial doses applied should be modified according to metabolic control, suggesting the need to apply individualized therapeutic protocols [57, 58]. Treatment with BH4 is an effective therapy in many patients with moderate or mild PKU, which allows responding patients to keep practically with free diet, abandoning the special formula, with good clinical and nutritional control and without side effects and improving quality of life [58]. The normalization of concentrations of trace elements and vitamins, but also of polyunsaturated fatty acids, has been demonstrated in children treated with BH4 [59, 60]. It has also been shown that the higher protein intake in these patients allows a better bone mass [58, 59, 60]. Currently its use is recommended as early as the neonatal period [61].

Another option is large neutral amino acid supplements that compete with the same system of transport of the Phe through the blood-brain barrier [62]. Supplementation with large neutral amino acids (tyrosine, tryptophan, threonine, isoleucine, leucine, valine, methionine and histidine) would thus have a competitive effect on the transport of Phe to the brain through the blood-brain barrier [22, 62, 63].

6.2. Therapeutic Options for the Future

Substitution therapy is based on the use of an alternative enzyme, phenylalanine ammonium lyase (PAL, EC 4.3.1.5), a recombinant enzyme derived from Rhodosporium toruloides that transforms Phe into transcinamic acid (which is excreted in the form of hippurate) and traces of ammonia [50, 64, 65, 66]. It has the advantage over PAH that it does not require a cofactor, even if it does require Tyr supplementation, since this amino acid is not the product of the reaction and therefore, it continues to be an essential amino acid, just as in dietary treatment [50, 65-67]. This treatment is currently used in PKU patients over the age of 16, but it has some side effects, especially at the level of immune adverse reactions against the enzyme, requires a daily subcutaneous dose and for the moment is an expensive treatment.

Gene therapy is based on the introduction of a functional PAH gene into somatic cells from PKU patients and the first therapeutic trials are in advanced stages [23, 50].

The use of pharmacological chaperones to stabilize or promote the correct folding of the mutated PAH protein represents a promising therapy for the future, especially considering that many PKU patients have mutations that cause folding disorders [23, 50]. Another of the primary goals of treatment, apart from reducing Phe levels, is to achieve an improvement in the quality of life of all patients with PKU [68-70]. More and more work is being done for these purposes and the improvements are truly remarkable with the scientific advances, the PKU monitoring units and the role of associations.

CONCLUSION

Phenylketonuria (PKU; OMIM 261600) is an inborn error of metabolism caused by mutations in the phenylalanine hydroxylase (PAH) gene (EC 1.14.16.1). These mutations lead to a total or partial decrease of PAH activity, which catalyzes the hydroxylation of Phe into tyrosine (Tyr), using tetrahydrobiopterin (BH4) as a cofactor. The biochemical consequences are Phe accumulation in biological tissues and fluids, as well as a deficit in the availability of Tyr. It is well-known that untreated PKU causes severe neurological disorders such as intellectual disability, epilepsy, progressive motor disorder, and severe behavioral disorders. Treatment of PKU should begin in the first weeks of life as early as possible and consists of a Phe restricted diet combined with the administration of a special formula, or alternatively with BH4 and total or partial diet liberalization in patients who respond to it. Phenylketonuria is known for several decades. Several treatments have been applied to cure the disease. BH4 effect in treating PKU patients is limited to the type of mutation. Although BH4 reduces blood Phe levels, the drug is effective only in some PKU patients with the improvement in quality of life. Long term application of BH4 affects micronutrients intake and therefore, patients under chronic BH4 therapy needed to be advised with micronutrients supplementation. Work is being done to improve the quality of life of PKU patients. The prognosis of PKU has improved dramatically with the introduction of screening, diet, clinical-biochemical -nutritional controls, neuropsychological follow-up, and the consolidation of PKU diagnostic, treatment, and follow-up units.

REFERENCES

[1] Güttler, F; Woo, SL. Molecular genetics of PKU. *J. Inherit. Metab. Dis.*, 1986, 9(Suppl1), 58–68.

[2] Scriver, CR. The PAH gene, phenylketonuria, and a paradigm shift. *Hum. Mutat.*, 2007, 28, 831–845.

[3] Følling, A. Über Ausscheidung von Phenylbrenztraubensäure in den Harn als Stoffwechselanomalie in Verbindung mit Imbezillität [Excretion of phenylpyruvic acid in the urine as a metabolic abnormality in connection with incontinence]. *Hoppe-Seyler's Zeitschrift für Physiologische Chemie.*, 1934, 227, 169–181.

[4] Penrose, LS; Quastel, JH. Metabolic studies in phenylketonuria. *Biochem, J.*, 1937, 31, 266– 271.

[5] Bickel, H; Gerrard, J; Hickmans, EM. Influence of phenylalanine intake on phenylketonuria. *Lancet*, 1953, 11, 812–813.

[6] Bickel, H; Gerrard, J; Hickmans, EM. The influence of phenylalanine intake on the chemistry and behaviour of a phenyl-ketonuric child. *Acta. Paediatr.*, 1954, 43, 64-77.

[7] Guthrie, R; Susi, A. A Simple Phenylalanine Method for Detecting Phenylketonuria in Large Populations of Newborn Infants. *Pediatrics.*, (1963), 32, 338–343.

[8] Lenke, RR; Levy, HL. Maternal phenylketonuria and hyperphenylalaninemia. An international survey of the outcome of untreated and treated pregnancies. *N. Engl. J. Med.* 1980, 20, 1202-1208.

[9] Woo, SL; Lidsky, AS; Güttler, F; Chandra, T; Robson, KJ. Cloned human phenylalanine hydroxylase gene allows prenatal diagnosis and carrier detection of classical phenylketonuria. *Nature*, 1083, 306, 151-155.

[10] Kure, S; Hou, DC; Ohura, T; Iwamoto, H; Suzuki, S; Sugiyama, N; Sakamoto, O; Fujii, K; Matsubara, Y; Narisawa, K. Tetrahydrobiopterin-responsive phenylalanine hydroxylase deficiency. *J. Pediatr.*, 1999, 135, 375-378.

[11] Thöny, B; Auerbach, G; Blau, N. Tetrahydrobiopterin biosynthesis, regeneration and functions. *Biochem. J.*, 2000, 347, 1–16.

[12] Wang, L; Surendran, S; Michals-Matalon, K; Bhatia, G; Tanskley, S; Koch, R; Grady, J; Tyring, SK; Stevens, RC; Guttler, F; Matalon, R. Mutations in the regulatory domain of phenylalanine hydroxylase and response to tetrahydrobiopterin. *Genet. Test.*, 2007, 11, 174-178.

[13] Opladen, T; Abu Seda, B; Rassi, A; Thöny, B; Hoffmann, GF; Blau, N. Diagnosis of tetrahydrobiopterin deficiency using filter paper blood spots: further development of the method and 5 years experience. *J. Inherit. Metab. Dis.*, 2011, 34, 819-826.

[14] Erlandsen, H; Pey, AL; Gámez, A; Pérez, B; Desviat, LR; Aguado, C; Koch, R; Surendran, S; Tyring, S; Matalon, R; Scriver, CR; Ugarte, M; Martínez, A; Stevens, RC. Correction of kinetic and stability defects by tetrahydrobiopterin in phenylketonuria patients with certain phenylalanine hydroxylase mutations. *Proc. Natl. Acad. Sci. USA.*, 2004, 101, 16903-16908.

[15] Blau, N. Genetics of Phenylketonuria: Then and Now. *Hum. Mutat.*, 2016, 37, 508-515.

[16] Lidsky, AS; Law, ML; Morse, HG; Kao, FT; Rabin, M; Ruddle, FH; Woo, SL. Regional mapping of the phenylalanine hydroxylase gene and the phenylketonuria locus in the human genome. *Proc. Natl. Acad. Sci. USA.*, 1985, 82, 6221–6225.

[17] Hofman, KJ; Steel, G; Kazazian, HH; Valle, D. Phenylketonuria in U.S. blacks: Molecular analysis of the phenylalanine hydroxylase gene. *Am. J. Hum. Genet.*, 1991, 48, 791-798.

[18] Camp, KM; Parisi, MA; Acosta, PB; Berry, GT; Bilder, DA; Blau, N; Bodamer, OA; Brosco, JP; Brown, CS; Burlina, AB; Burton, BK; Chang, CS; Coates, PM; Cunningham, AC; Dobrowolski, SF; Ferguson, JH; Franklin, TD; Frazier, DM; Grange, DK; Greene, CL; Groft, SC; Harding, CO; Howell, RR; Huntington, KL; Hyatt-Knorr, HD; Jevaji, IP; Levy, HL; Lichter-Konecki, U; Lindegren, ML; Lloyd-Puryear, MA; Matalon, K; MacDonald, A; McPheeters, ML; Mitchell, JJ; Mofidi, S; Moseley, KD; Mueller, CM; Mulberg, AE; Nerurkar, LS; Ogata, BN; Pariser, AR; Prasad, S; Pridjian, G;

Rasmussen, SA; Reddy, UM; Rohr, FJ; Singh, RH; Sirrs, SM; Stremer, SE; Tagle, DA; Thompson, SM; Urv, TK; Utz, JR; van Spronsen, F; Vockley, J; Waisbren, SE; Weglicki, LS; White, DA; Whitley, CB; Wilfond, BS; Yannicelli, S; Young, JM. Phenylketonuria Scientific Review Conference: state of the science and future research needs. *Mol. Genet. Metab.*, 2014, 112, 87-122.

[19] Zhang, Z; Gao, JJ; Feng, Y; Zhu, LL; Yan, H; Shi, XF; Chang, AM; Shi, Y; Wang, P. Mutational spectrum of the phenylalanine hydroxylase gene in patients with phenylketonuria in the central region of China. *Scand. J. Clin. Lab. Invest.*, 2018, 78, 211- 218.

[20] Avigad, S; Cohen, BE; Bauer, S; Schwartz, G; Frydman, M; Woo, SL; Niny, Y; Shiloh, YA. single origin of phenylketonuria in Yemenite Jews. *Nature*, 1990, 344, 168-170.

[21] Konecki, DS; Schlotter, M; Trefz, FK; Lichter-Konecki, U. The identification of two mis-sense mutations at the PAH gene locus in a Turkish patient with phenylketonuria. *Hum. Genet.*, 1991, 87, 389–393.

[22] Eisensmith, RC; Okano, Y; Dasovich, M; Wang, T; Güttler, F; Lou, H; Guldberg, P; Lichter-Konecki, U; Konecki, DS; Svensson, E; Hagenfeldt, L; Rey, F; Munnich, A; Lyonnet, S; Cockburn, F; Connor, JM; Pembrey, ME; Smith, I; Gitzelmann, R; Steinmann, B; Apold, J; Eiken, HG; Giovannini, M; Riva, E; Longhi, R; Romano, C; Cerone, R; Naughten, ER; Mullins, C; Cahalane, S; Özalp, I; Fekete, G; Schuler, D; Berencsi, GY; Nász, I; Brdicka, R; Kamaryt, J; Pijackova, A; Cabalska, B; Boszkowa, K; Schwartz, E; Kalinin, VN; Jin, L; Chakraborty, R; Woo, SLC. Multiple origins for phenylketonuria in Europe. *Am. J. Hum. Genet.*, 1992, 51, 1355–1365.

[23] van Spronsen, FJ; van Wegberg, AM; Ahring, K; Bélanger-Quintana, A; Blau, N; Bosch, AM; Burlina, A; Campistol, J; Feillet, F; Giżewska, M; Huijbregts, SC; Kearney, S; Leuzzi, V; Maillot, F; Muntau, AC; Trefz, FK; van Rijn, M; Walter, JH; MacDonald, A. Key European guidelines for the diagnosis and management of

patients with phenylketonuria. *Lancet Diabetes Endocrinol.*, 2017, 5, 743-756.

[24] Joshua, GE; Chandy, S; Radhakrishnan, AN; Mammen, D; Mathai, KV. Phenylketonuria in Indian children. *J. Inherit. Metab. Dis.*, 1978, 1, 67-70.

[25] Daelman, L; Sedel, F; Tourbah, A. Progressive neuropsychiatric manifestations of phenylketonuria in adulthood. *Rev. Neurol. (Paris).*, 2014, 170, 280-287.

[26] Anwar, MS; Waddell, B; O' Riordan, J. Neurological improvement following reinstitution of a low phenylalanine diet after 20 years in established phenylketonuria. *BMJ. Case Rep.*, 2013, 2013.

[27] Trefz, F; Maillot, F; Motzfeldt, K; Schwarz, M. Adult phenylketonuria outcome and management. *Mol. Genet. Metab.*, 2011, 104, S26-30.

[28] Yano, S; Moseley, K; Azen, C. Large neutral amino acid supplementation increases melatonin synthesis in phenylketonuria: a new biomarker. *J. Pediatr.*, 2013, 162, 999-1003.

[29] Gassió, R; González, MJ; Sans, O; Artuch, R; Sierra, C; Ormazabal, A; Cuadras, D; Campistol, J. Prevalence of sleep disorders in early-treated phenylketonuric children and adolescents. Correlation with dopamine and serotonin status. *Eur. J. Paediatr. Neurol.*, 2019, 23, 685-691.

[30] Brumm, VL; Bilder, D; Waisbren, SE. Psychiatric symptoms and disorders in phenylketonuria. *Mol. Genet. Metab.*, 2010, 99, S59-63.

[31] Gentile, JK; Ten Hoedt, AE; Bosch, AM. Psychosocial aspects of PKU: hidden disabilities a review. *Mol. Genet. Metab.*, 2010, 99, S64-67.

[32] Anderson, JP; Leuzzi, V. White matter pathology in phenylketonuria. *Mol. Genet. Metab.*, 2010, 99, S3–9.

[33] Pérez-Dueñas, B; Pujol, J; Soriano-Mas, C; Ortiz, H; Artuch, R; Vilaseca, MA; Campistol, J. Global and regional volume changes in the brains of patients with phenylketonuria. *Neurology*, 2006, 66, 1074-1078.

[34] Gassió, R; Artuch, R; Vilaseca, MA; Fusté, E; Boix, C; Sans, A; Campistol, J. Cognitive functions in classic phenylketonuria and mild hyperphenylalaninaemia: experience in a paediatric population. *Dev. Med. Child Neurol.*, 2005, 47, 443-448.

[35] De Roche, K; Welsh, M. Twenty-five years of research on neurocognitive outcomes in early-treated phenylketonuria: intelligence and executive functions. *Dev. Neuropsychol.*, 2008, 33, 474-504.

[36] Jahja, R; Huijbregts, SCJ; de Sonneville, LMJ; van der Meere, JJ; Legemaat, AM; Bosch, AM; Hollak, CEM; Rubio-Gozalbo, ME; Brouwers, MCGJ; Hofstede, FC; de Vries, MC; Janssen, MCH; van der Ploeg, AT; Langendonk, JG; van Spronsen, FJ. Cognitive profile and mental health in adult phenylketonuria: A PKU-COBESO study. *Neuropsychology*, 2017, 31, 437-447.

[37] Burlina, AP; Lachmann, RH; Manara, R; Cazzorla, C; Celato, A; van Spronsen, FJ; Burlina A. The neurological and psychological phenotype of adult patients with early-treated phenylketonuria: A systematic review. *J. Inherit. Metab. Dis.*, 2019, 42, 209-219.

[38] Antshel, KM. ADHD, learning, and academic performance in phenylketonuria. *Mol. Genet. Metab.*, 2010, 99, S52-58.

[39] Pietz, J; Fätkenheuer, B; Burgard, P; Armbruster, M; Esser, G; Schmidt, H. Psychiatric disorders in adult patients with early-treated phenylketonuria. *Pediatrics.*, 1997, 99, 345-350.

[40] Smith, I; Knowles, J. Behavior in early treated phenylketonuria: a systematic review. *Eur. J. Pediatr.*, 2000, 159, S89-93.

[41] Gassió, R; Fusté, E; López-Sala, A; Artuch, R; Vilaseca, MA; Campistol, J. School performance in early and continuously treated phenylketonuria. *Pediatr. Neurol.*, 2005, 33, 267-271.

[42] Campistol, J; Gassió, R; Artuch, R; Vilaseca, MA. Neurocognitive function in mild hyperphenylalaninemia. *Dev. Med. Child. Neurol.*, 2011, 53, 405–408.

[43] González, MJ; Rebollo, M; Ripollés, P; Gassió, R; Ormazabal, A; Sierra, C; Roura, RC; Artuch, R; Campistol, J. White matter

microstructural damage in early treated phenylketonuric patients. *Orphanet. J. Rare Dis.*, 2018, 13, 188.

[44] Pérez-Dueñas, B; Valls-Solé, J; Fernández-Álvarez, E; Conill, J; Vilaseca, MA; Artuch, R; Campistol, J. Characterization of tremor in phenylketonuric patients. *J. Neurol.*, 2005, 252, 1328-1334.

[45] MacDonald, A; Gokmen-Ozel, H; van Rijn, M; Burgard, P. The reality of dietary compliance in the management of phenylketonuria. *J. Inherit. Metab. Dis.*, 2010, 33, 665-670.

[46] de Baulny, HO; Abadie, V; Feillet, F; de Parscau, L. Management of phenylketonuria and hyperphenylalaninemia. *J. Nutr.*, 2007, 137, (6 Suppl 1), 1561S-1563S.

[47] Williams, RA; Mamotte, CD; Burnett, JR. Phenylketonuria: An inborn error of phenylalanine metabolism. *Clin. Biochem. Rev.*, 2008, 29, 31-41

[48] Campistol, J; Arellano, M; Poo, P; Escofet, C; Pérez, P; Vilaseca, MA. Embriopatía por fenilcetonuria materna. Una causa de retardo mental poco diagnosticada. Revisión de 8 observaciones. *An. Esp. Ped.*, 1999, 51, 139-142.

[49] Manta-Vogli, PD; Dotsikas, Y; Loukas, YL; Schulpis, KH. The phenylketonuria patient: A recent dietetic therapeutic approach. *Nutr. Neurosci.*, 2018, 1-12.

[50] van Spronsen, FJ; Enns, GM. Future treatment strategies in phenylketonuria. *Mol. Genet. Metab.*, 2010, 99, S90-95.

[51] Solverson, P; Murali, SG; Litscher, SJ; Blank, RD; Ney, DM. Low bone strength is a manifestation of phenylketonuria in mice and is attenuated by a glycomacropeptide diet. *PLoS One*, 2012, 7, e45165.

[52] González, MJ; Gassió, R; Artuch, R; Campistol, J. Impaired Neurotransmission in Early-treated Phenylketonuria Patients. *Semin. Pediatr. Neurol.*, 2016, 23, 332-340.

[53] Gutiérrez, AP; Vilaseca, MA; Capdevila, A; Vidal, M; Alaonso, I; Colomé, R; López-Sala, A; Lambruschini-Ferri, N; Gutiérrez, A; Gassió, R; Artuch, R; Campistol, J. Evolución neurológica, neuropsicológica y oftalmológica tras un año de suplementación con

ácido docosahexaenoico en pacientes fenilcetonúricos. *Rev, Neurol.*, 2012, 55, 200-206.

[54] Pérez-Dueñas, B; Cambra, FJ; Vilaseca, MA; Lambruschini, N; Campistol, J; Camacho, JA. New approach to osteopenia in phenylketonuric patients. *Acta Paediatr.*, 2002, 91, 899-904.

[55] Gentile, JK; Ten Hoedt, AE; Bosch, AM. Psychosocial aspects of PKU: hidden disabilities--a review. *Mol. Genet. Metab.*, 2010, 99 Suppl 1, S64-67.

[56] Matalon, R; Koch, R; Michals-Matalon, K; Moseley, K; Surendran, S; Tyring, S; Erlandsen, H; Gamez, A; Stevens, RC; Romstad, A; Møller, LB; Guttler, F. Biopterin responsive phenylalanine hydroxylase deficiency. *Genet. Med.*, 2004, 6, 27-32.

[57] Doyle, S; O' Regan, M; Stenson, C; Bracken, J; Hendroff, U; Agasarova, A; Deverell, D; Treacy, EP. Extended Experience of Lower Dose Sapropterin in Irish Adults with Mild Phenylketonuria. *JIMD. Rep.*, 2018, 40, 71-76.

[58] Vieira Neto, E; Laranjeira, F; Quelhas, D; Ribeiro, I; Seabra, A; Mineiro, N; Carvalho, LM; Laerda, L; Ribeiro, MG. Genotype-phenotype correlations and BH4 estimated responsiveness in patients with phenylketonuria from Rio de Janeiro, Southeast Brazil. *Mol. Genet. Genomic Med.*, 2019, 7, e610.

[59] Vilaseca, MA; Lambruschini, N; Gómez-López, L; Gutiérrez, A; Moreno, J; Tondo, M; Artuch, R; Campistol, J. Long-chain polyunsaturated fatty acid status in phenylketonuric Patients treated with tetrahydrobiopterin. *Clin. Biochem.*, 2010, 43, 411-415.

[60] Keil, S; Anjema, K; van Spronsen, FJ; Lambruschini, N; Burlina, A; Bélanger-Quintana, A; Couce, ML; Feillet, F; Cerone, R; Lotz-Havla, AS; Muntau, AC; Bosch, AM; Meli, CA; Billette de Villemeur, T; Kern, I; Riva, E; Giovannini, M; Damaj, L; Leuzzi, V; Blau, N. Long-term follow-up and outcome of phenylketonuria patients on sapropterin: a retrospective study. *Pediatrics.*, 2013, 131, e1881–1888.

[61] Longo, N; Arnold, GL; Pridjian, G; Enns, GM; Ficicioglu, C; Parker, S; Cohen-Pfeffer, JL. Phenylketonuria demographics, outcomes and

safety registry. Long-term safety and efficacy of sapropterin: the PKUDOS registry experience. *Mol. Genet. Metab.*, 2015, 114, 557–563.

[62] Leuret, O; Barth, M; Kuster, A; Eyer, D; de Parscau, L; Odent, S; Gilbert-Dussardier, B; Feillet, F; Labarthe, F. Efficacy and safety of BH4 before the age of 4 years in patients with mild phenylketonuria. *J. Inherit. Metab. Dis.*, 2012, 35, 975-981.

[63] Matalon, R; Surendran, S; Matalon, KM; Tyring, S; Quast, M; Jinga, W; Ezell, E; Szucs, S. Future role of large neutral amino acids in transport of phenylalanine into the brain. *Pediatrics*, 2003, 112, 1570-1574.

[64] Kim, W; Erlandsen, H; Surendran, S; Stevens, RC; Gamez, A; Michols-Matalon, K; Tyring, SK; Matalon, R. Trends in enzyme therapy for phenylketonuria. *Mol. Ther.*, 2004, 10, 220-224.

[65] Zori, R; Ahring, K; Burton, B; Pastores, GM; Rutsch, F; Jha, A; Jurecki, E; Rowell, R; Harding, C. Long-term comparative effectiveness of pegvaliase versus standard of care comparators in adults with phenylketonuria. *Mol. Genet. Metab.*, 2019, S1096-7192, 30363-30364.

[66] Longo, N; Harding, CO; Burton, BK; Grange, DK; Vockley, J; Wasserstein, M; Rice, GM; Dorenbaum, A; Neuenburg, JK; Musson, DG; Gu, Z; Sile, S. Single-dose, subcutaneous recombinant phenylalanine ammonia lyase conjugated with polyethylene glycol in adult patients with phenylketonuria: an open-label, multicentre, phase 1 dose-escalation trial. *Lancet*, 2014, 384, 37-44.

[67] Cazzoria, C; Cegolon, L; Burlina, AP; Celato, A; Massa, P; Giordano, L; Polo, G; Daniele, A; Salvatore, F; Burlina, AB. Quality of Life (QoL) assessment in a cohort of patients with phenylketonuria. *BMC. Public Health*, 2014, 14, 1243.

[68] Demirdas, S; Maurice-Stam, H; Boelen, CC; Hofstede, FC; Janssen, MC; Langendonk, JG; Mulder, MF; Rubio-Gozalbo, ME; van Spronsen, FJ; de Vries, M; Grootenhuis, MA; Bosch, AM. Evaluation of quality of life in PKU before and after introducing

tetrahydrobiopterin (BH4); a prospective multi-center cohort study. *Mol. Genet. Metab.*, 2013, 110, S49–S56.

[69] Feldmann, R; Wolfgart, E; Weglage, J; Rutsch, F. Sapropterin treatment does not enhance the health-related quality of life of patients with phenylketonuria and their parents. *Acta. Paediatr.*, 2017, 106, 953–958.

In: Neurochemistry of Metabolic Diseases
Editor: Sankar Surendran
ISBN: 978-1-53618-339-9

Chapter 10

CURRENT TRENDS IN CANAVAN DISEASE RESEARCH AND THERAPEUTIC EFFECT

Sankar Surendran[1,*] and Vykuntaraju K. Gowda[2,3]

[1]School of medicine, Louisiana State University Health Sciences Center, New Orleans, LA, US

[2]Department of Pediatric Neurology, Indira Gandhi Institute of Child Health, Bangalore, India

[3]Child Neurology and Rehabilitation Center, Bangalore, India

ABSTRACT

Canavan disease (CD) is an autosomal recessive neurodegenerative disorder with degeneration in the white matter and gray matter degeneration of the brain leading to early death. Aspartoacylase (ASPA) deficiency, elevated levels of N-acetyl aspartic acid (NAA), N-acetylaspartylglutamate, and L-aspartate N-acetyltransferase activity defect have been observed in patients with CD. The brain regions affected in CD include caudate putamen, globus pallidus, corpus callosum,

* Corresponding Author's Email: sankar_surendran@yahoo.com.

periaqueductal gray matter, pons and thalamus. Although, macrocephaly was considered as one of the main features in CD, a recent study showing a CD patient with ASPA gene mutation developed microcephaly. Therefore, macrocephaly cannot be a common feature in CD. More than ninety-five mutations in the ASPA gene have been reported in CD. However, ASPA gene therapy alone could not improve all the pathophysiological abnormalities seen in CD. N-acetyl aspartic acid inducing oxidative stress contribute to the disease pathophysiology. Therefore, current studies have been focused to normalize the NAA level by regulating its upstream pathway. Inhibition of NAA synthesizing enzyme, L-aspartate N-acetyltransferase in a dose dependent manner may improve pathophysiology seen in CD.

1. Introduction

Canavan disease (CD) (OMIM 271900) is a rare inherited neurodegenerative disease found in multiethnic population. Although until past decade studies had been describing the presence of CD mainly on Ashkenazi Jewish population, recent studies from around the globe suggests that the disease is prevalent from east coast to west coast. The presence of patients with CD have been reported from several countries including United States of America, Saudi Arabia, Turkey, Egypt, Yemen, Kuwait, Tunisia, Canada, India and Pakistan. The disease was first reported as spongiform degeneration of the brain by Myrtelle M. Canavan in 1931 [1] and subsequently by van Bogaert and Bertrand in 1949 [2]. Patients with CD have reduced levels of aspartoacylase/aminoacylase 2/N-acetylaspartate acid amidohydrolase (ASPA/ACY2, EC# 3.5.1.15) activity in fibroblasts and elevated levels of N-acetylaspartic acid (NAA/NA-Asp) in urine [3-5]. The enzyme deficiency is found in various organs including brain, kidney and liver [6]. Elevated levels of NAA was also observed in the cerebrospinal fluid, plasma [3] and brain of patients with CD.

Patients with CD show various symptoms including hypotonia, mental retardation, ataxia, brisk reflexes, convergent strabismus, hypotonia, motor delay and difficulty to stand or walk. Macrocephaly was considered as one of the major phenotypes in CD. However, a recent study showed CD patient with ASPA gene mutation developed microcephaly [7]. Therefore, macrocephaly may not be considered as an important feature during diagnosis. Magnetic resonance imaging of the patient brain showed increased intensity in both white matter and gray matter of the brain including thalami, putamen, caudate nucleus, gray-white matter junctions and pons.

Over ninety-five mutations have been identified in the *ASPA* gene of patients with CD.

Aspartoacylase is a zinc containing carboxypeptidase metalloprotease family [8]. Although ASPA deficiency is seen in CD, ASPA gene transfer alone could improve some abnormalities seen in CD, however, it could not improve all the pathophysiological abnormalities seen in CD. Patients with CD have elevated levels of NAA. Altered levels of NAA resulting oxidative stress contribute to the disease pathophysiology. Therefore, recent studies have been focused to normalize NAA levels seen in CD by inhibiting NAA regulating pathways.

2. Aspartoacylase Gene Mutations in Patients with Canavan Disease

The human *ASPA* gene contains 5 introns and 6 exons with 313 amino acids. The mouse ASPA contains 312 amino acids and rat ASPA contains 312 amino acids (GI: 50926810) to 314 amino acids (GI: 5689082). The human ASPA protein has a molecular weight approximately 37 kDa. More than ninety-five mutations in the *ASPA* gene with CD have been identified from multiethnic population and these mutations are shown in Figure 1. A 13-year-old male patient from Canada had ASPA gene mutations Y288C and a deletion -2A, -3C at the acceptor site of exon 3 [6, 9]. Two CD patients from Saudi Arabia had a deletion of 3346 bp in the *ASPA* gene that started at intron 2 (chr17: 3,332,550 position) and ended at intron 3 (chr17: 3,335,897 position) [10]. A 10-month-old Turkish patient with CD had homozygous mutation (C432+1G>A) in the ASPA gene without macrocephaly [11]. Aspartoacylase gene mutations G274R and 527del108 have been identified in Turkish patients, and a C218X mutation was found in Gypsy patients [12].

Recent studies on patients with CD from around the globe showed deletion of several exons and introns. Some patients with CD had deletion of all six exons of the ASPA gene [10, 12]. A patient with compound heterozygosity had a deletion in all exons except exon 1 of the ASPA gene. Another patient with compound heterozygosity had 12.13 kb deletion which was involved by the deletion of the ASPA gene from intron 3 to intron 5 including exons 4 and 5 [12]. A child of consanguineous Turkish parents with CD showed deletion of complete ASPA gene. A 13-year old boy had p. Gly274Arg (c.820A>G) missense mutation [13]. These studies suggest that ASPA gene mutations contribute to CD by a single base pair change or deletion of several introns and exons in the ASPA gene. Two Egyptian patients were diagnosed with CD, the first patient had five missense mutations (c.427 A > G; p. I143V, c.502C > T; p. R168C, c.530 T > C; p. I177T, c.557 T > C; p. V186D c.548C > T; p. P183L) and a silent mutation (c.693 C > T; p. Y231Y). The second patient was homozygous for two missense mutations (c.427 A > G; p. I143V and c.557 T > A; p. V186D) [14]. An Iranian patient had homozygous C.202G>A mutation in the exon 1 of the ASPA gene [15].

A 2-year-old Egyptian child with CD had a novel homozygous missense variant c.91G > T, p.V31F in the ASPA gene [16]. A patient had p.A305E and p. A7Vdel8_69 mutations in the ASPA gene [17]. Two Egyptian patients had a novel missense mutation Ile177Thr in the exon 4 of the ASPA gene [18]. Two patients from India had ASPA gene mutations c.162 C > A (p. Asn54Lys) and c.859 G > A (p. Ala287Thr). Third patient had compound heterozygous for two novel mutations c.728 T > G, p. Ile243Ser; c.902 T > C, p. Leu301Pro [19]. A 9 months old Turkish girl with Canavan Disease had a homozygous mutation c.79G>A in the ASPA gene [20]. A child born to a consanguineous parent had a novel mutation Y88X in the ASPA gene [21]. A patient with CD from Pakistan had missense substitution 740A→G (p.G274R) in exon 6 of the ASPA gene [22]. A female infant at age 6 months had the mutation c.432G>A in exon 2 of the ASPA gene [23].

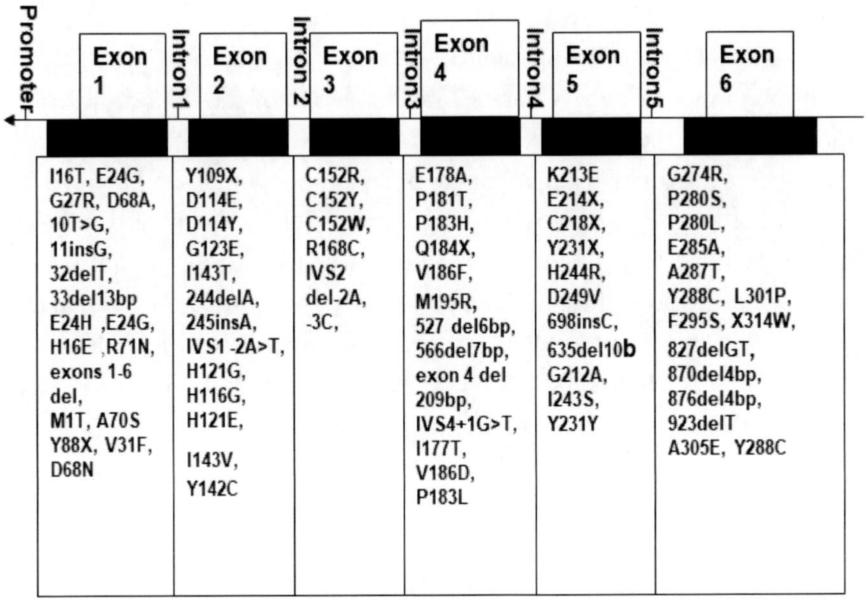

Figure 1. Aspartoacylase gene mutations in patients with CD.

3. Symptoms of the Disease

Patients with CD generally show clinical symptoms after four months of age. The clinical symptoms in CD include megalencephaly/ macrocephaly or microcephaly, developmental delay, loss of muscle tone (hypotonia) and psychomotor retardation (mental retardation) [2], poor visual function or partial blindness, loss of fibers in the optic nerve (optic atrophy) and axial hypotonia. Motor defect was severe in some patients with spastic quadriplegia or spastic diplegia, difficult to sit, walk or talk and also have feeding problem. Later stage, patients develop convulsions/seizures and may die within ten-year old if the disease is severe form of CD. Patients with mild form of CD show symptoms including partial cortical blindness, nystagmus, retinitis pigmentosa, mild developmental delay (reading skills delayed more than verbal skills) and signal intensity in the basal ganglia. In mild form of CD, urine NAA level is slightly elevated (99.90 ± 4.00 μg/mg creatinine) compared to normal subjects (< 83 μg/mg creatinine) [6, 9]. Some patients have poor sleep spindles and absence of visual acuity.

Although macrocephaly has been used as one of the important features to diagnose CD, recent study showed a child with ASPA gene mutation c.859 G>A (p. Ala287Thr) in exon 6 developed microcephaly. At ten-month old, the child showed developmental delay, visual difficulty and difficulty in head control. At ten-months of age, head circumference was 41 cm, which is less than 3 SD [7]. At three-year old, the patient head circumference was 43 cm, which is less than 3 SD (Figure 2). This study suggests that CD phenotype can be either macrocephaly or microcephaly. Parents of the child with microcephaly were normal suggesting parents were carrier of the disease.

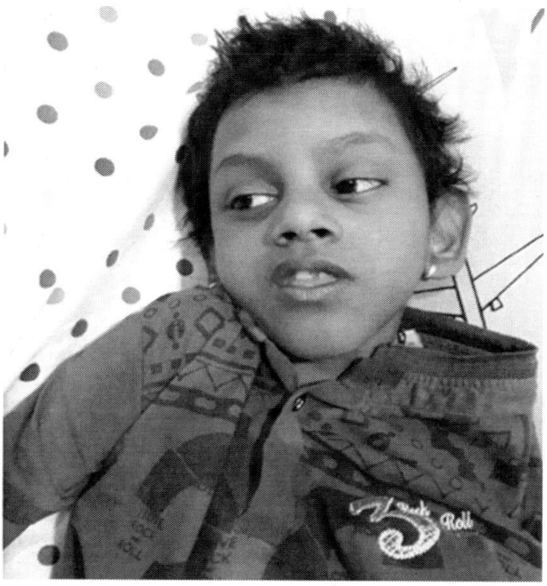

Figure 2. A four-year-old child with ASPA gene mutation showing microcephaly.

The symptoms seen in patients with CD reported from around the globe vary among patients. Patients with CD develop phenotype including mild ataxia, brisk reflexes, convergent strabismus [6, 9], hypotonia, motor delay, difficulty to stand or walk, spasticity and intractable seizures [24], spastic quadriparesis, oropharyngeal dysplasia, macrocephaly or microcephaly, mild seizures, oral phase dysphagia, severe upper pharyngeal dysphagia and spasticity, progressive neuroregression, difficulty in swallowing, spastic quadriparesis [10], axial hypotonia, lower limb symmetric hypertonia accompanied by brisk deep tendon reflexes, developmental delay without macrocephaly, mild defect in fine motor skills, strabismus, intentional tremor, poor eye contact and impaired fixing, sluggish response to sound, poor feeding and blindness. Electroencephalographic study showed an active right temporal spike-wave focus and epilepsy.

4. Brain Regions Affected in Patients with Canavan Disease

The brain regions affected in patients with CD reported from around the globe include putamen, caudate nucleus, thalamus, U-fibers of the occipital and temporal lobes, cerebellar white matter, pons, medulla [25], subcortical white matter at the gray-white matter junctions bilaterally, the tegmentum of the pons, white matter around the 4th ventricle [26], posterior fossa, supratentorial CSF spaces of the brain, cerebral white matter sparing the internal capsules, corpus callosum, globus pallidus, posterior part of sub-cortical deep white matter, posterior limb of the internal capsule, dentate nuclei of the cerebellum [27], lentiform nucleus, posterior periventricular white matter, periaqueductal gray matter, anterior limbs of internal capsules, external capsules, subcortical white matter, cerebellar white matter, dentate nuclei, cerebellum [15], optic radiations, substantia nigra [16] and brainstem. Magnetic resonance imaging of the brain of a patient with microcephaly is shown in Figure 3.

Brain US showed alteration of echogenicity of both gray and white matter with increasing of echogenicity of white matter, characterized by a homogenous fine texture with high echogenicity of the pial demarcation of the low echogenic cortex, mild ventricular dilatation and enlargement of sinocortical space [28].

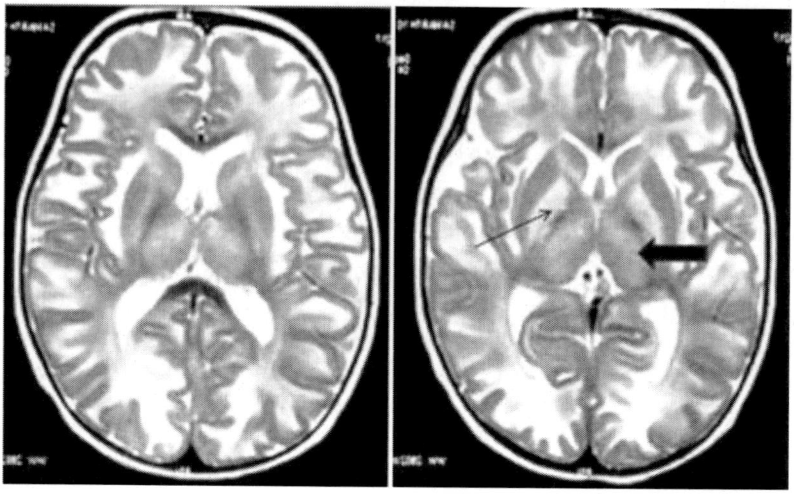

Figure 3. Magnetic resonance imaging of the brain of a CD patient with microcephaly. Thin arrow shows globus pallidus and thick arrow shows thalamus of the brain.

5. N-Acetylaspartylglutamate and N-Acetylaspartic Acid Levels in Canavan Disease

The neuropeptide, N-acetylaspartylglutamate (NAAG/NA-Asp-Glu) is localized in neurons with high affinity for metabotropic glutamate receptors, mGluR3, which is an antagonist at NMDA receptors. The mGlu3 expression is high in neurons of the thalamic reticular nucleus. While NAA and glutamate are ligases into NAAG by N-acetylaspartate-L-glutamate ligase in neurons [29], NAAG is hydrolyzed by glutamate carboxypeptidase II/ N-Acetylated-Alpha-Linked-Acidic-Dipeptidase (GCPII/NAALADase, EC# 3.4.17.21) into NAA and glutamate [30-31] (Figure 4). The GCPII is a zinc metalloenzyme expressed on astrocyte membranes. N-acetylaspartylglutamate level is approximately 20-fold higher in the urine of patients with CD [32-33].

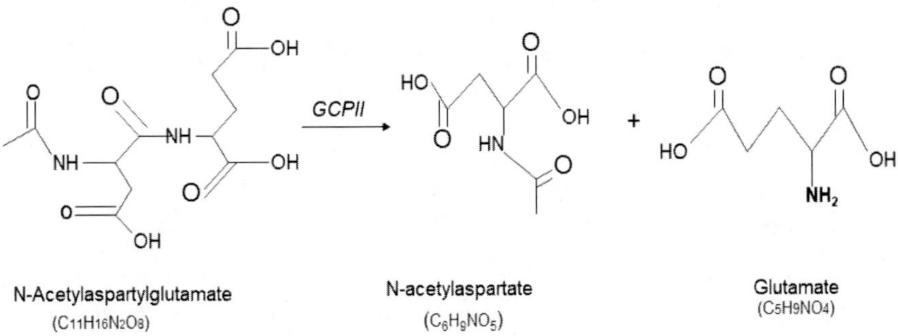

Figure 4. N-acetylaspartylglutamate is converted into N-Acetylaspartate and glutamate.

N-acetylaspartate ($C_6H_9NO_5$) is synthesized from acetyl-coenzyme A and aspartate by L-aspartate N-acetyltransferase [34]. N-acetylaspartic acid has a molecular mass of 175 Da and has a negative charge at physiological pH that enables transport across membranes. An up regulation by L-aspartate N-acetyltransferase would result in an increased NAA level, one of the possible ways of elevated NAA seen in CD. N-acetylaspartate is deacetylated into aspartate and acetate by ASPA [35]. Urine NAA in patients with severe form of CD is 1.18 mmol/mmol creatinine, while in control subjects the level is 3.41 ± 1.99 μmol/mmol creatinine. The level of NAA in CD patient serum is increased (18.0 μmol/L), while in normal human serum the level was not detectable [36]. The levels of NAA in control subjects are 6.6–35.4 μmol/mmol creatinine in urine; 0.17–0.81 μM in plasma; and 0.25–2.83 μM in cerebrospinal fluid. Prenatal diagnosis showed amniotic fluid NAA level was 8.68 μM in one of the pregnancies with CD, while control amniotic fluid levels were 0.30–2.55 μM [37]. The level of urine NAA in patients with severe form of CD is elevated over 50-80-fold. In brain interstitial space, the concentration of NAA is 80–100 mM [38]. The carrier transports at the prevalent interstitial NAA concentration was 100 mmol/l or 10 pmol/mg of protein/min [39]. In extracellular fluid, NAA level is elevated [40]. Elevated levels of NAA alter expression of genes associated with inflammation, contractility, and calcium channel. Contractility of circular smooth muscle cells was also affected by altered levels of NAA [41]. Elevated levels of NAA induce nitric oxide toxicity [41, 42] to affect healthy neurons.

Although white matter degeneration in CD brain was considered as major contributing factor in CD, recent studies suggests involvement of gray matter degeneration also plays major role in CD pathology [43]. N-acetyl aspartic acid is synthesized from acetyl coenzyme A and aspartate by a mitochondrial enzyme, L-aspartate N-acetyltransferase [44]. Therefore, recent studies have been focused to inhibit the enzyme, L-aspartate N-acetyltransferase to reduce NAA synthesis [45]. N-acetyl aspartic acid is mainly found in the gray matter of the brain [46] and also present at lower levels in the astroglia, white matter, superior cervical ganglion, splenic nerve, peripheral nervous tissue of spleen, lung, liver, kidney, muscle, ovary, thymus, stomach, heart, adrenal medulla and retina of fishes to mammals [47-48]. Human fetal brain NAA concentration in utero is approximately 2.5 μmol/g [49]. The normal adult human brain NAA concentration is 8-10 μmol/g [50-51]. Altered levels of NAA affects genes involved in inflammation, contractility and calcium channel to affect normal cell migration and normal myelination [41, 43]. The mitochondria are affected and astrocytes are swollen in the brain of patients with CD [52].

6. DIAGNOSIS OF THE DISEASE

Patients with CD have elevated levels of NAA in the urine [3-4] and therefore urinary NAA is used to diagnose CD. The fibroblasts of patients with CD show reduced levels of ASPA activity [3-5] and therefore fibroblasts enzyme activity is used to predict CD. To determine function of the mutations, expression analysis of the mutation is useful [6]. The levels of NAA in control subjects varies between 6.6-35.4 μmol/mmol creatinine in urine; 0.17-0.81 μmol/L in plasma; 0.25-2.83 μmol/L in cerebrospinal fluid and 0.30-2.55 μmol/L in amniotic fluid. The level of NAA in patients with CD is elevated from 50-fold [4] to 80-fold in urine and 20-fold in plasma compared to the control subjects [53]. Therefore, NAA is used as one of the markers of determining CD. LC-MS/MS method for determination of NAA in amniotic fluid is useful to determine NAA in a small volume of amniotic fluid for the prenatal diagnosis of CD. Quantification of NAA in the amniotic fluid can be performed using various methods including LC MS/MS, single-ion monitoring gas chromatography–mass spectrometry (SIM-GC–MS) [53-56] or liquid chromatography electrospray ionization tandem mass spectrometry (LC–ESIMS/MS) [57]. Preimplantation genetic diagnosis may be performed, if parents are known as the carrier of the disease. Embryos can be determined by genotype and unaffected embryos may be transferred for pregnancy [58]. Proton magnetic resonance spectroscopic analysis of NAA in the frontal white matter at TE 144 ms in a CD patient with microcephaly showed NAA:Cr. ratio 2.6:1 while normal subjects have 2.09 ± 0.45 (Figure 5).

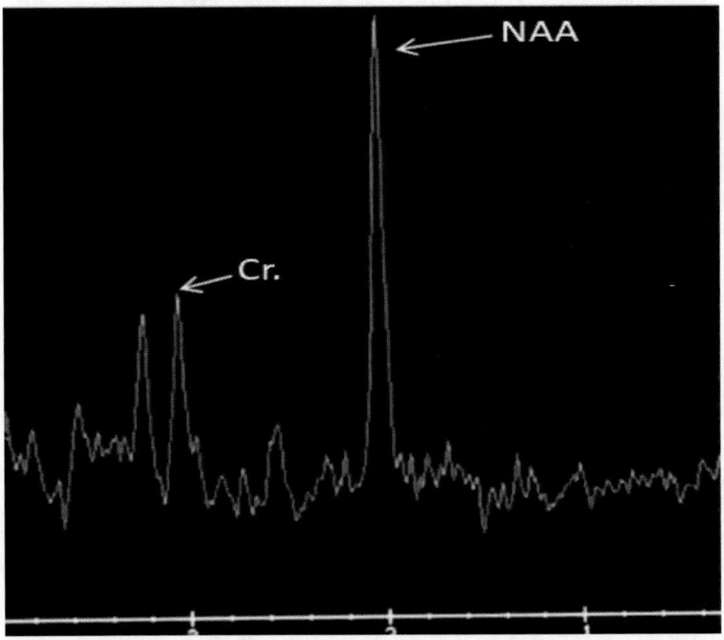

Figure 5. Magnetic resonance spectroscopy showing NAA peak and creatinine peak.

7. Therapeutic Approaches in Canavan Disease

Glyceryltriacetate (GTA) is a short-chain triglyceride has been used as an acetate precursor. Administration of GTA to infants with CD at a low dose (up to 0.25 g/kg/d) showed no clinical improvement. Treatment of two CD patients with GTA 4.5 g/kg/d at ages 8 months and 1 year for 4.5 and 6 months respectively showed no motor improvement [59]. Oral treatment of infants with CD aged 8 and 13 months with acetate precursor, glyceryl triacetate for up to 4.5 and 6 months, starting at 25 mg/kg twice daily, doubling the dose weekly until a maximum of 250 mg/kg [60] does not seem to prevent NAA accumulation in the brain or urine, as normal subjects' urine NAA level ranges between 6.6–35.4 μmol/mmol creatinine. Elevated levels of NAA is a pathological marker in CD.

Increased levels of NAA is one of the important contributing factor of CD pathophysiology. Therefore, normalizing NAA levels have been studied. A preliminary report showing inhibition of NAA synthesis by intracisternal administration of a locked nucleic acid antisense oligonucleotide to ASPA deficient mice reportedly reduced cerebellar and thalamic vacuolation, Purkinje cell dendritic atrophy and ataxia [61]. However, more study needs to be performed to understand whether the treatment cures all the symptoms seen in CD.

Lithium chloride 300 mg/kg/day for 4 days treated tremor rat showed 13% reduction of NAA [62]. Patients with CD develop seizure and this may be reduced with Rivotril treatment [10].

Adeno-associated virus mediated intracerebroventricular/intracisternal administration a short hairpin Nat8l inhibitory RNA to ASPA deficient mice reportedly reduced spongiform degeneration [63] suggesting Nat8l knockdown at a specific level improve spongiform degeneration. Although previous studies showed that ASPA gene transfer to ASPA deficient mice improved spongiform degeneration and recovered some of the functional abnormalities seen in CD, the treatment could not improve all the pathophysiological abnormalities seen in the CD mice. A recent study showing adeno-associated virus mediated ASPA gene transfer resulting super-mouse phenotype [64] suggests that ASPA gene transfer needs to be carefully performed to obtain better performance in treating CD.

L-aspartate N-acetyltransferase is a NAA synthesizing enzyme. Therefore, efficacy of L-aspartate N-acetyltransferase inhibitors have been studied in reducing NAA levels seen in CD [45].

Mice with ASPA deficiency (ASPA(nur7/nur7)) and N-acetyltransferase-8 like (Nat8L) deficiency (Nat8L(-/-)/Aspa(nur7/nur7)) could inhibit NAA production and showed normal levels of myelin, myelin sphingolipid composition and full reversal of spongiform myelin and axonal degeneration and the survival time of the mice was short. Meanwhile, ASPA (nur7/nur7) mice with only one intact Nat8L allele had reduced NAA level, decreased pathology with normal survival time [65] suggesting that partial inhibition of NAA synthase will be useful in reducing NAA levels and pathophysiology seen in CD.

To understand function of the elevated levels of NAA seen in CD, studies have been conducted by oral gavage administration of NAA in animals [66]. Mucosal barrier is important to contain the gastric acid required for digestion. If the mucosal barrier is damaged by the elevated levels of ingested acid, it can cause damage to the gastrointestinal system. Hence, oral gavage of NAA would lead to gastrointestinal damage and pain resulting functional changes in the animal.

CONCLUSION

Canavan disease is a neurodegenerative disorder. Macrocephaly was considered as one of the important phenotypes in diagnosing CD. However, a recent study showing microcephaly in a patient with CD suggests that CD phenotype can be either microcephaly or macrocephaly. Elevated levels of NAA resulting oxidative stress contribute to the disease pathophysiology. Therefore, current studies have been focused to reduce the NAA levels seen in CD by inhibiting NAA synthesizing enzyme, L-aspartate N-acetyltransferase.

References

[1] Canavan, MM. Schilder's encephalitis periaxialis diffusa. Report of a case in a child aged sixteen and one-half months. *Arch. Neurol. Psychiatr.* 1931, 25, 299–308.

[2] Van Bogaert, L; Bertrand, I. Sur une idiotie familiale avec degerescence sponglieuse de neuraxe (note preliminaire). *Acta Neurol.* 1949, 49, 572–587.

[3] Hagenfeldt, L; Bollgren, I; Venizelos, N. N-acetylaspartic aciduria due to aspartoacylase deficiency--a new aetiology of childhood leukodystrophy. *J. Inherit. Metab. Dis.* 1987, 10, 135-141.

[4] Matalon, R; Michals, K; Sebesta, D; Deanching, M; Gashkoff, P; Casanova, J. Aspartoacylase deficiency and N-acetylaspartic aciduria in patients with Canavan disease. *Am. J. Med. Genet.* 1988, 29, 463-471.

[5] Divry, P; Mathieu, M. Aspartoacylase deficiency and N-acetylaspartic aciduria in patients with Canavan disease. *Am. J. Med. Genet.* 1989, 32, 550-551.

[6] Surendran, S; Kumaresan, G. Neurochemical changes and therapeutic approaches in Canavan disease. In: Surendran S (Ed.): *Neurochemistry of metabolic diseases, lysosomal storage diseases, phenylketonuria and Canavan disease*: Trivandrum, India; Transworld research network; 2007; pp 119-132.

[7] Gowda, VK; Bhat, MD; Srinivasan, VM; Prasad, C; Benakappa, A; Faruq, M. A case of Canavan disease with microcephaly. *Brain Dev.* 2016, 38, 759-762.

[8] Hagenfeldt, L; Bollgren, I; Venizelos, N. N-acetylaspartic aciduria due to aspartoacylase deficiency--a new aetiology of childhood leukodystrophy. *J. Inherit. Metab. Dis.* 1987, 10, 135-141.

[9] Matalon, R; Michals, K; Sebesta, D; Deanching, M; Gashkoff, P; Casanova, J. Aspartoacylase deficiency and N-acetylaspartic aciduria in patients with Canavan disease. *Am. J. Med. Genet.* 1988, 29, 463-471.

[10] Surendran, S; Bamforth, FJ; Chan, A; Tyring, SK; Goodman, SI; Matalon, R. Mild elevation of N-acetylaspartic acid and macrocephaly: diagnostic problem. *J. Child Neurol.* 2003, 18, 809-812.

[11] Unalp, A; Altiok, E; Uran, N; Oztürk, A; Yüksel, S. Novel mutation of aspartoacylase gene in a Turkish patient with Canavan disease. *J. Trop. Pediatr.* 2008, 54, 208-210.

[12] Zeng, BJ; Wang, ZH; Torres, PA; Pastores, GM; Leone, P; Raghavan, SS; Kolodny, EH. Rapid detection of three large novel deletions of the aspartoacylase gene in non-Jewish patients with Canavan disease. *Mol. Genet. Metab.* 2006, 89, 156-163.

[13] Çakar, NE; Aksu Uzunhan, T. A case of juvenile Canavan disease with distinct pons involvement. *Brain Dev.* 2020, 42, 222-225.

[14] Zaki, OK; Krishnamoorthy, N; El Abd, HS; Harche, SA; Mattar, RA; Al Disi, RS; Nofal, MY; El Bekay, R; Ahmed, KA; George Priya Doss, C; Zayed, H. Two patients with Canavan disease and structural modeling of a novel mutation. *Metab. Brain Dis.* 2017, 32, 171-177.

[15] Ashrafi, M; Tavasoli, A; Katibeh, P; Aryani, O; Vafaee-Shahi, M. A Novel Mutation in Aspartoacylase Gene; Canavan Disease. *Iran J. Child. Neurol.* 2015, 9, 54-57.

[16] Zaki, OK; El Abd, HS; Mohamed, SA; Zayed, H. Novel mutation in an Egyptian patient with infantile Canavan disease. *Metab. Brain Dis.* 2016, 31, 573-577.

[17] De Bernardo, G; Giordano, M; Sordino, D; Buono, S. Early diagnosis of Canavan syndrome: how can we get there? *BMJ. Case Rep.* 2015, 2015, bcr2014208755.

[18] Di Pietro, V; Cavallari, U; Amorini, AM; Lazzarino, G; Longo, S; Poggiani, C; Cavalli, P; Tavazzi, B. New T530C mutation in the aspartoacylase gene caused Canavan disease with no correlation between severity and N-acetylaspartate excretion. *Clin. Biochem.* 2013, 46, 1902-1904.

[19] Bijarnia, S; Kohli, S; Puri, RD; Jacob, RJ; Saxena, R; Jalan, A; Sistermans, EA; Mahmood, S; Verma, IC. Molecular characterisation and prenatal diagnosis of Asparto-acylase deficiency (Canavan

disease)-report of two novel and two known mutations from the Indian subcontinent. *Indian J. Pediatr.* 2013, 80, 26-31.

[20] Eke, GH; Iscan, A; Cece, H; Calik, M. A mutation of aspartoacylase gene in a Turkish patient with Canavan disease. *Genet. Couns.* 2012, 23, 9-12.

[21] Durmaz, AA; Akin, H; Onay, H; Vahabi, A; Ozkinay, F. A novel aspartoacylase (ASPA) gene mutation in Canavan disease. *Fetal Pediatr. Pathol.* 2012, 31, 236-239.

[22] Hussain, R; Daud, S; Kakar, N; Ahmad, A; Baloch, AH; Tareen, AM; Kakar, MA; Ahmad, J. A missense mutation (p. G274R) in gene ASPA causes Canavan disease in a Pakistani family. *Mol. Biol. Rep.* 2012, 39, 6197-6201.

[23] Schober, H; Luetschg, J; Hoeliner, I; Kalb, S; Simma, B. Canavan disease: a novel mutation. *Pediatr. Neurol.* 2011, 45, 256-258.

[24] Caliebe, A; Vater, I; Plendl, H; Gesk, S; Siebert, R; Cremer, FW; Klein-Hitpass, L. A 439kb-sized homozygous deletion in 17p13.3 leading to biallelic loss of the ASPA as cause of Canavan disease detected by SNP-array analysis. *Mol. Genet. Metab.* 2010, 99, 184-185.

[25] Yalcinkaya, C; Benbir, G; Salomons, GS; Karaarslan, E; Rolland, MO; Jakobs, C; van der Knaap, MS. Atypical MRI findings in Canavan disease: a patient with a mild course. *Neuropediatrics.* 2005, 36, 336-339.

[26] Tacke, U; Olbrich, H; Sass, JO; Fekete, A; Horvath, J; Ziyeh, S; Kleijer, WJ; Rolland, MO; Fisher, S; Payne, S; Vargiami, E; Zafeiriou, DI; Omran, H. Possible Genotype-Phenotype correlations in Children with Mild Clinical Course of Canavan Disease. *Neuropediatrics.* 2005, 36, 252-255.

[27] Zhang, H; Liu, X; Gu, X. Two novel missense mutations in the aspartoacylase gene in a Chinese patient with congenital Canavan disease. *Brain Dev.* 2010, 32, 879-882.

[28] Drera, B; Poggiani, C. Brain ultrasound in Canavan disease. *J. Ultrasound.* 2014, 17, 215–217.

[29] Tyson, RL; Sutherland, GR. Labeling of N-acetylaspartate and N-acetylaspartylglutamate in rat neocortex, hippocampus and cerebellum from [1-13C] glucose. *Neurosci. Lett.* 1998, 251, 181-184.

[30] Robinson, MB; Blakely, RD; Couto, R; Coyle, JT. Hydrolysis of the brain dipeptide N-acetyl-L-glutamate. Identification of and characterization of a novel N-acetylated alpha linked acidic dipetidase activity from rat brain. *J. Biol. Chem.* 1987, 262, 14498-14506.

[31] Stauch, BL; Robinson, MB; Forloni, G; Tsai, G; Coyle, JT. The effects of N-acetylated alpha-linked acidic dipeptidase (NAALADase) inhibitors on [3H] NAAG catabolism in vivo. *Neurosci. Lett.* 1989, 100, 295-300.

[32] Burlina, AP; Ferrari, V; Divry, P; Gradowska, W; Jakobs, C; Bennett, MJ; Sewell, AC; Dionisi-Vici, C; Burlina, AB. N-acetylaspartylglutamate in Canavan disease: an adverse effector? *Eur. J. Pediatr.* 1999, 158, 406-409.

[33] Krawczyk, H; Gradowska, W. Characterisation of the 1H and 13C NMR spectra of N-acetylaspartylglutamate and its detection in urine from patients with Canavan disease. *J. Pharm. Biomed. Anal.* 2003, 31, 455-463.

[34] Goldstein, FB. The enzymatic synthesis of N-acetyl-L-aspartic acid by subcellular preparations of the rat brain. *J. Biol. Chem.* 1969, 244, 4257-4260.

[35] Birnbaum, SM; Levintow, L; Kingsley, RB; Greenstein, JP. Specificity of amino acid acylases. *J. Biol. Chem.* 1952, 194, 455–470.

[36] Bennet, MJ; Gibson, KM; Sherwood, WG; Divry, P; Rolland, MO; Elpeleg, ON; Rinaldo, P; Jakobs, C. Reliable prenatal diagnosis of Canavan disease (aspartoacylase deficiency): comparison of enzymatic and metabolite analysis. *J. Inherit. Metab. Dis.* 1993, 16, 831–836.

[37] Bennet, MJ; Gibson, KM; Sherwood, WG; Divry, P; Rolland, MO; Elpeleg, ON; Rinaldo, P; Jakobs, C. Reliable prenatal diagnosis of

Canavan disease (aspartoacylase deficiency): comparison of enzymatic and metabolite analysis. *J. Inherit. Metab. Dis*. 1993, 16, 831–836.

[38] Taylor, DL; Davies, SEC; Obrenovitch, TP; Urenjak, J; Richards, DA; Clark, JB; Symon, L. Extracellular N-acetylaspartate in the rat brain: in vivo determination of basal levels and changes evoked by high K+. *J. Neurochem*. 1994, 62, 2349–2355.

[39] Baslow, MH. Functions of N-Acetyl-L-aspartate and N-acetyl-L-aspartylglutamate in the vertebrate Brain. *J. Neurochem*. 2000, 75, 453–459.

[40] Sager, TN; Thomsen, C; Valsborg, JS; Laursen, H; Hansen, AJ. Astroglia contain a specific transport mechanism for N-Acetyl-L-Aspartate. *J. Neurochem*. 1999, 73, 807–811.

[41] Surendran, S. Upregulation of N-acetylaspartic acid alters inflammation, transcription and contractile associated protein levels in the stomach and smooth muscle contractility. *Mol. Biol. Rep*. 2009, 36, 201-206.

[42] Surendran, S. N-acetyl aspartate induces nitric oxide to result neurodegeneration in Canavan disease. *Biosci. Hypotheses*. 2008, 1, 228-229.

[43] Surendran, S; Kaya, N; Ozand, P. Canavan disease: molecular pathology, phenotype and therapeutic approaches. In: Surendran S (Ed.): *Neurochemistry of metabolic diseases, lysosomal storage diseases, phenylketonuria and Canavan disease. New York,* USA; NOVA science Publishers, 2013, pp 241-263.

[44] Goldstein, FB. The enzymatic synthesis of N-acetyl-L-aspartic acid by subcellular preparations of rat brain. *J. Biol. Chem*. 1969, 244, 4257–4260.

[45] Thangavelu, B; Mutthamsetty, V; Wang, Q; Viola, RE. Design and optimization of aspartate N-acetyltransferase inhibitors for the potential treatment of Canavan disease. *Bioorg. Med. Chem*. 2017, 25, 870-885.

[46] Tallan, HH; Moore, S; Stein, WH. N-acetyl-L-aspartic acid in brain. *J. Biol. Chem*. 1956, 219, 257-264.

[47] Miyake, M; Kakimoto, Y; Sorimachi, M. A gas chromatographic method for the determination of N-acetyl-L-aspartic acid, N-acetyl-α--acetylglutamic acid and β-citryl-L-glutamic acid and their distributions in the brain and other organs of various species of animals. *J. Neurochem*. 1981, 36, 804-810.

[48] Nadler, JV; Cooper, JR. N-acetyl L-aspartic acid content of human neural tumors and bovine peripheral nervous tissues. *J. Neurochem*. 1972, 19, 313-319.

[49] Kato, T; Nishina, M; Matsushita, K; Hori, E; Mito, T; Takashima, S. Neuronal maturation and N-acetyl L-aspartic acid development in human fetal and child brains. *Brain Dev*. 1997, 19,131-133.

[50] Frahm, J; Bruhn, H; Gyngell, ML; Merboldt, KD; Hanicke, W; Sauter, R. Stable isotope dilution analysis of N-acetylaspartic acid in CSF, blood, urine and amniotic fluid: accurate postnatal diagnosis and the potential for prenatal diagnosis of Canavan disease. *J. Inherit Metab. Dis*. 1991, 14, 653-660.

[51] Kreis, R; Ernst, T; Ross, BD. Absolute quantitation of water and metabolites in the human brain. Part II: Metabolite concentrations. *J. Magn. Reson*. 1993, 102, 9-19.

[52] Adachi, M; Torii, J; Schneck, L; Volk, BW. Electron microscopic and enzyme histochemical studies of the cerebellum in spongy degeneration (van Bogaert and Bertrand type). *Acta Neuropathol*. (Berl) 1972, 20, 22-31.

[53] Fares, F; Badarneh, K; Abosaleh, M; Harari-Shaham, A; Diukman, R; David, M. Carrier frequency of autosomal-recessive disorders in the Ashkenazi Jewish population: should the rationale formutation choice for screening be reevaluated? *Prenat. Diagn*. 2008, 28, 236–241.

[54] Jakobs, C; ten Brink, HJ; Langelaar, SA; Zee T, Stellaard, F; Macek, M; Srsnova, K; Srsen, S; Kleijer, WJ. Stable isotope dilution analysis of N-acetylaspartic acid in CSF, blood, urine and amniotic fluid: accurate postnatal diagnosis and the potential for prenatal diagnosis of Canavan disease. *J. Inherit. Metab. Dis*. 1991, 14, 653–660.

[55] Bennet, MJ; Gibson, KM; Sherwood, WG; Divry, P; Rolland, MO; Elpeleg, ON; Rinaldo, P; Jakobs, C. Reliable prenatal diagnosis of Canavan disease (aspartoacylase deficiency): comparison of enzymatic and metabolite analysis. *J. Inherit. Metab. Dis*. 1993, 16, 831–836.

[56] Kelley, RI. Prenatal detection of canavan disease by measurement of N-acetyl-L-aspartate in amniotic fluid. *J. Inherit. Metab. Dis*. 1993, 16, 918–919.

[57] Al-Dirbashi, OY; Kurdi, W; Imtiaz, F; Ahmad, AM; Al-Sayed, M; Tulbah, M; Al-Nemer, M; Rashed, MS. Reliable prenatal diagnosis of Canavan disease by measuring N-acetylaspartate in amniotic fluid using liquid chromatography tandem mass spectrometry. *Prenat. Diagn*. 2009, 29, 477–480.

[58] Yaron, Y; Schwartz, T; Mey-Raz, N; Amit, A; Lessing, JB; Malcov, M. Preimplantation genetic diagnosis of Canavan disease. *Fetal. Diagn. Ther*. 2005, 20, 465-468.

[59] Segel, R; Anikster, Y; Zevin, S; Steinberg, A; Gahl, WA; Fisher, D; Staretz-Chacham, O; Zimran, A; Altarescu, G. A safety trial of high dose glyceryl triacetate for Canavan disease. *Mol. Genet. Metab*. 2011,103, 203-206.

[60] Madhavarao, CN; Arun, P; Anikster, Y; Mog, SR; Staretz-Chacham, O; Moffett, JR; Grunberg, NE; Gahl, WA, Namboodiri, AMA. Glyceryl triacetate for Canavan disease: A low-dose trial in infants and evaluation of a higher dose for toxicity in the tremor rat model. *J. Inherit. Metab. Dis*. 2009, 32, 640-650.

[61] Hull, V; Wang, Y; Burns, T; Zhang, S; Sternbach, SJ; Guo, F; Pleasure, D. Antisense oligonucleotide reverses leukodystrophy in Canavan disease mice. *Ann. Neurol*. 2020, 87, 480-485.

[62] Baslow, M; Kitada, K; Suckow, RF; Hungund, BL; Serikawa, T. The effects of lithium chloride and other substances on levels of brain NAA in Canavan disease-like rats. *Neurochem. Res*. 2002, 27, 403–406.

[63] Bannerman, P; Guo, F; Chechneva, O; Burns, T; Zhu, X; Wang, Y; Kim, B; Singhal, NK; McDonough, JA; Pleasure, D. Brain Nat 8l

knockdown suppresses spongiform leukodystrophy in an aspartoacylase-deficient Canavan Disease mouse model. *Mol. Ther.* 2018, 26, 793-800.

[64] Gessler, DJ; Li, D; Xu, H; Su, Q; Sanmiguel, J; Tuncer, S; Moore, C; King, J; Matalon, R; Gao, G. Redirecting *N*-acetylaspartate metabolism in the central nervous system normalizes myelination and rescues Canavan disease. *JCI. Insight.* 2017, 2, e90807.

[65] Maier, H; Wang-Eckhardt, L; Hartmann, D; Gieselmann, V; Eckhardt, M. N-Acetylaspartate synthase deficiency corrects the myelin phenotype in a Canavan Disease mouse model but does not affect survival time. *J. Neurosci.* 2015, 35, 14501-14516.

[66] Appu AP; Moffett, JR; Arun, P; Moran, S; Nambiar, V; Krishnan, JKS; Puthillathu, P; Namboodiri AMA. Increasing N-acetylaspartate in the Brain during Postnatal Myelination Does Not Cause the CNS Pathologies of Canavan Disease. *Front. Mol. Neurosci.* 2017, 10, 161.

About the Editor

Sankar Surendran
College Station, Texas 77845, USA
Email: ssanka12@gmail.com

Education: MS, PhD
Awards and Honors: 6
Membership in Professional Societies: 13
Publications: https://www.researchgate.net/profile/Sankar_Surendran
Original Articles: 44
Abstracts: 12
Review Articles: 18
Book Chapters: 8
Books:

1) *Neurochemistry of metabolic Diseases: lysosomal storage diseases, phenylketonuria and Canavan disease* (2007) (Editor: Sankar Surendran) Transworld research network, INDIA
2) *Neurochemistry of metabolic Diseases: lysosomal storage diseases, phenylketonuria and Canavan disease* (ebook-2011) (hard copy-2013) (Editor: Sankar Surendran) NOVA publishers Inc, USA

Presentation of Work in National/International Meetings: 14
Attending Seminars, Symposia, Courses and Workshops: 21
International Examiner PhD Thesis: 8

List of Contributors

Dr. Fatma Al-Jasmi, MBBS
Department of Genetics & Genomics and Department of Paediatrics, College of Medicine and Health Sciences, United Arab Emirates University, Al Ain, United Arab Emirates; Department of Paediatrics, Tawam Hospital, Al Ain, United Arab Emirates

Aisha Al-Shamsi, MBBS
Department of Paediatrics, Tawam Hospital, Al Ain, United Arab Emirates

Dr. Amal Al Tenaiji, MBBS
Department of Paediatrics, Sheikh Khalifa Medical Centre Hospital, Abu Dhabi, United Arab Emirates

Dr. Fatma Al-Yahyai, MBBS
Department of Paediatrics, Tawam Hospital, Al Ain, United Arab Emirates

Dr. Bassam R. Ali, PhD
Department of Genetics & Genomics, Department of Pathology, College of Medicine and Health Sciences, United Arab Emirates University, Al Ain, United Arab Emirates

Dr. Mahmoud R. Ashrafi, MD
Myelin Disorders Clinic, Pediatric Neurology Division,
Children's Medical Center, Pediatrics Center of Excellence,
Tehran University of Medical Sciences, Tehran, Iran

Joanna Brokowska, MS
Department of Molecular Biology, University of Gdansk,
Wita Stwosza 59, 80-308 Gdansk, Poland

Dr. Jaume Campistol, MD, PhD
PKU Unit, Department of Pediatric Neurology, Hospital Sant Joan de Deu,
Barcelona. Spain

Dr. Soumya V. Chandrasekharan, MD
Department of Neurology, Sree Chitra Tirunal Institute for
Medical Sciences and Technology, Trivandrum, India

Zuzanna Cyske, MS
Department of Molecular Biology, University of Gdansk,
Wita Stwosza 59, 80-308 Gdansk, Poland

Lidia Gaffke, MS
Department of Molecular Biology, University of Gdansk,
Wita Stwosza 59, 80-308 Gdansk, Poland

Dr. Masoud Garshasbi, PhD
Department of Medical Genetics, Faculty of Medical Sciences,
Tarbiat Modares University, Tehran, Iran

Dr. Vykuntaraju K. Gowda, DCH, DNB, DM
Department of Pediatric Neurology, Indira Gandhi Institute
of Child Health, Bangalore, India and Child Neurology and
Rehabilitation Center, Bangalore, India

Dr. Morteza Heidari, MD
Myelin Disorders Clinic, Pediatric Neurology Division,
Children's Medical Center, Pediatrics Center of Excellence,
Tehran University of Medical Sciences, Tehran, Iran

Dr. Jozef Hertecant, MD
Department of Paediatrics, College of Medicine and Health Sciences,
United Arab Emirates University, Al Ain, United Arab Emirates;
Department of Paediatrics, Tawam Hospital, Al Ain, United Arab Emirates

Dr. Ali Hosseini, PhD
Prenatal Diagnosis and Genetic Research Center, Dastgheib Hospital,
Shiraz University of Medical Sciences, Shiraz, Iran

Dr. Fedah E. Mohamed, PhD
Department of Genetics & Genomics and Department of Pathology,
College of Medicine and Health Sciences,
United Arab Emirates University, Al Ain, United Arab Emirates

Dr. Adriana M. Montano, PhD
Department of Pediatrics and Department of Biochemistry and
Molecular Biology, School of Medicine, Saint Louis University,
St. Louis, Missouri, USA

Aadhira Nair, MS
Foundation for Research in Genetics and Endocrinology,
Institute of Human Genetics, Ahmedabad, Gujarat, India

Dr. Sruthi S. Nair, DM
Department of Neurology, Sree Chitra Tirunal Institute for
Medical Sciences and Technology, Trivandrum, India

Dr. Karolina Pierzynowska, PhD
Department of Molecular Biology, University of Gdansk,
Wita Stwosza 59, 80-308 Gdansk, Poland

Dr. Magdalena Podlacha, PhD
Department of Molecular Biology, University of Gdansk,
Wita Stwosza 59, 80-308 Gdansk, Poland

Dr. Srinivasagam Rajasankar MS, PhD
Velammal Medical College Hospital & Research Institute,
Tamil Nadu, India

Estera Rintz, MS
Department of Molecular Biology, University of Gdansk,
Wita Stwosza 59, 80-308 Gdansk, Poland

Dr. Parastoo Rostami, MD
Growth and Development Research Center,
Division of Endocrinology and Metabolism, Children's Medical Center,
Tehran University of Medical Sciences, Tehran, Iran

Dr. Consolato Sergi MD, PhD, MPH, FRCPC, FCAP, FACSc,
Department of Laboratory Medicine and Pathology, University of Alberta,
Edmonton, AB, Canada

Dr. Jayesh Sheth, PhD, FICMCH
Foundation for Research in Genetics and Endocrinology,
Institute of Human Genetics, Ahmedabad, Gujarat, India

Dr. Soumya Sundaram, DM
Department of Neurology, Sree Chitra Tirunal Institute for
Medical Sciences and Technology, Trivandrum, Kerala, India

Dr. Ali R. Tavasoli, MD
Myelin Disorders Clinic, Pediatric Neurology Division,
Children's Medical Center; Pediatrics Center of Excellence,
Tehran University of Medical Sciences, Tehran, Iran

Dr. Veerappachetty Venkateshgobi, BHMS, MS, PhD
Department of Anatomy, Sivaraj Medical Colleges, Tamil Nadu, India

Dr. Grzegorz Wegrzyn, MS, PhD, DSc
Department of Molecular Biology, University of Gdańsk,
Wita Stwosza 59, 80-308, Gdansk, Poland

INDEX

B

C

D

E

F

G

H

I

K

L

M

N

O

P

Q

R

S

T

U

V

W